GROUP WORK WITH ADOLESCENTS

Social Work Practice with Children and Families
Nancy Boyd Webb, Series Editor

SOCIAL WORK PRACTICE WITH CHILDREN
Nancy Boyd Webb

GROUP WORK WITH ADOLESCENTS:
PRINCIPLES AND PRACTICE
Andrew Malekoff

Group Work
with Adolescents

PRINCIPLES AND PRACTICE

Andrew Malekoff

The Guilford Press
NEW YORK   LONDON

© 1997 Andrew Malekoff

Published by The Guilford Press
A Division of Guilford Publications, Inc.
72 Spring Street, New York, NY 10012

Portions of the following works are reprinted by permission:

Carlos Castaneda, *A Separate Reality.* Copyright 1971 by Carlos Castaneda. Reprinted by permission of the author, c/o Toltec Artists, Inc., 11901 Santa Monica Blvd., Suite 596, Los Angeles, CA 90025; and reprinted by permission of Pocket Books, a Division of Simon & Schuster.

Developmental Research and Programs, Inc. Reprinted by permission from Developmental Research and Programs, Inc., Seattle, WA, developers of *Communities That Care,* a community risk-focused prevention training system. Information on *Communities That Care* training and materials is available from Developmental Research and Programs, Inc., 130 Nickerson, Suite 107, Seattle, WA 98109. Phone (800) 736-2630, fax (206) 286-1462.

T. S. Eliot, "Little Gidding" in *Four Quartets.* Copyright 1943 by T. S. Eliot and renewed 1971 by Esme Valerie Eliot. Reprinted by permission of Harcourt Brace & Company.

Robert Frost, "The Road Not Taken" from *The Poetry of Robert Frost,* edited by Edward Connery Lathem. Copyright 1916, 1969 by Henry Holt & Co., copyright 1944 by Robert Frost. Reprinted by permission of Henry Holt & Co., Inc.

Lao-Tze, quoted in the book *The Medium Is the Massage,* by Marshall McLuhan and Quentin Fiore, produced by Jerome Agel. Copyright 1967 by Jerome Agel. Republished 1996 by HardWired Publishing, of San Francisco, Calif. Reprinted by permission.

Edna St. Vincent Millay, "Upon this age, that never speaks its mind" from *Collected Poems,* HarperCollins. Copyright 1939, 1967 by Edna St. Vincent Millay and Norma Millay Ellis. Reprinted by permission of Elizabeth Barnett, literary executor.

Calvin Tomkins, *Eric Hoffer: An American Odyssey.* Copyright 1968 by Calvin Tomkins, text; copyright 1968 by George Knight, photographs. Reprinted by permission of Dutton Signet, a division of Penguin Books USA Inc.

Eiji Yoshikawa, *Musashi.* English translation copyright 1981 by Kodansha International Ltd. Reprinted by permission.

Printed in the United States of America

This book is printed on acid-free paper.

Last digit is print number: 9 8 7 6 5 4 3 2 1

Library of Congress Cataloging-in-Publication Data

Malekoff, Andrew.
    Group work with adolescents / Andrew Malekoff.
        p.   cm.—(Social work practice with children and families)
    Includes bibliographical references and index.
    ISBN 1-57230-209-7
    1. Social work with teenagers. 2. Social group work.   I. Title. II. Series.
HV1421.M35 1997
362.7'083—dc21   96–47770
                                                                                    CIP

This book is dedicated to what all young people need:

> *safe places to go,*
> *worthwhile things to do,*
> *a sense of belonging,*
> *a sense of competence,*
> *a feeling of hope,*
>
> *and*
>
> *relationships with people who can help*
> *to make a difference*
> *in their lives*

Preface

In my experience, group work with adolescents is like a roller coaster ride, but in a new configuration each time around; harrowing yet fun, with unexpected twists and turns, ascents and declines; you experience anxious anticipation and vertigo-inducing surround-sound; you wish it would end, and you hope it never does. Sometimes, however, it's not so exciting—more like a crawling commute in rush hour traffic, enervating, meandering, puzzling, endless.

It has always been my wish, as someone who works with young people in groups, to capture the moments and madness of the work through the written word in a style that would be fun to read, encouraging, practical, supportive, reflective, full of life, and deeply embedded in the tradition of social work with groups. What my experience advises me is that group work with adolescents is not for the faint hearted, but rather for the young at heart.

Group Work with Adolescents is organized into three parts and 14 chapters. Part I focuses on the normative issues that face adolescents in the multiple contexts of their lives. Part II is method oriented, highlighting time-honored group work traditions and themes. Part III is organized thematically, with guidelines for practice and extensive illustrations addressing critical needs and salient issues facing adolescents and group workers at the turn of the 21st century.

Group Work with Adolescents is structured to include a combination of brief illustrations, longer vignettes, original poetry, and verbatim transcripts of group work practice with young people. The illustrations include many examples from my own direct practice in a variety of settings (school, community center, home, street corner, mental health clinic, chemical dependency program) over almost a quarter century of group work with adolescents. It is my hope that by including analyses of my own work, I will help the reader see that group workers can be reflective *and* active—can think *and* do at the same time. With a growing emphasis on briefer interventions in the current era of cost containment, there is the risk that the work will become so programmed for brevity that self-reflection will be lost.

I believe strongly that practitioners and group members must be problem focused, clear about goals, and active in the pursuit of their aims—hardly a new idea for social work with groups. However, group workers must also be prepared for emergent problems that occur in the life of the group, to expect the unexpected, to be ready for group work on the go.

It is my sincerest wish that *Group Work with Adolescents* will encourage readers to work with young people in groups, provide conceptual clarity to sharpen practice, encourage practitioners to be active and reflective, stimulate debate, and inspire aspiring and practicing group workers to be innovative and share their work publicly so that social work with groups may again, one day soon, find its rightful place among the movements and methods for change.

Acknowledgments

Many friends and colleagues have contributed to this book, including those who critiqued the evolving work, provided technical support, shared practice illustrations, and offered encouragement.

First, I would like to thank the staff and board of directors, past and present, of North Shore Child and Family Guidance Center for developing a stable, caring, and progressive environment to be creative and practice *real* social work with groups, especially Marion Levine, Executive Director, for leading the way for more than two decades.

My gratitude goes to the members, past and present, of the Association for the Advancement of Social Work with Groups, a special organization to which I belong that serves as a steady source of inspiration and a constant reminder of what it means to be a social worker.

Thanks to Nancy Boyd Webb, Series Editor, who invited me to write this book, and Rochelle Serwator, Anna Brackett, and Sharon Panulla, editors at The Guilford Press, for their ongoing support, encouragement, and suggestions.

I am indebted to my friend Ralph Kolodny, who has always been most generous with his time, experience, intellectual acumen, encouragement, and endless stream of stories, anecdotes, wisdom, and humor. And to my friend Ted Kawa who introduced me to group work, many thanks.

Fortunately I had the wisdom to know, from the start of this project, that I would first have to get lost in order to find my way. How lost might I get? That I could not predict. Many thanks to my wonderfully generous and honest guides—friends and colleagues—who graciously gave of themselves in reviewing portions of this book and who helped me to find my way and my voice: Marty Birnbaum, Margo Breton, Maeda Galinsky, Bruce Kaufstein, Ralph Kolodny, Roselle Kurland, Irving Levine, Ruth Middleman, Bob Salmon, Peter Scales, Sandy Wolkoff, and Jane Yazdpour.

I am very grateful to those who shared their work by contributing wonderful practice illustrations to supplement the descriptions of my own practice and to help bring the concepts in this book to life: Regina Barros, Trudy Duffy, Ariel Greenidge, Nellie Taylor-Walthrust, Bruce Kaufstein, Karen Patykewich, Andrew Peters, Julio Reategui, Ronda Fein, Robin Stockton, Sondra Josel, Betty Iannotti, and Petty Figueroa.

My sincere appreciation goes to those who provided technical assistance: Toby Kass, Miriam Martinez, Jane Yazdpour, and Sabrina Yazdpour.

Thank you, Dad—my father, Isadore Malekoff, who taught me the value of kindness and respect for children.

Thank you, Mom—my mother, Evelyn Malekoff, who taught me the value of generosity, devotion, and tenacity.

And to Dale, my wife, for listening to my ideas, helping to develop a concept for the book cover, reading everything I write (including incomprehensible first drafts), and for telling me honestly whether or not what I write makes any sense at all, my utmost gratitude.

Thanks to Jamie and Darren, my sons, who are a never-ending source of humility for this "expert on working with kids." As Darren (age 8) might say, "Yeah, right!" And, I predict, one day soon Jamie (age 12) will discover what the product of all this time I've been spending on the computer is and will announce, "How could you write anything about teenagers when you don't even understand me!" Thanks also boys, for interrupting my writing over the years and reminding me of what is really important by asking, "Dad, can I sit on your lap?"

And my appreciation to those family and friends who cheer me in any venture.

Finally, to all of the children, teenagers, parents, colleagues, and others who have been members of groups that I have been a part of over the past 20-plus years, thank you for all that you have taught me.

Contents

PART I

The Adolescent in Context

| # Adolescent Development, Risk, and Opportunity

A BRIEF REFLECTION ON WORKING WITH ADOLESCENTS

In my almost 25 years of working with adolescents, I have noticed a trend in my conversations with people who are not involved with adolescents in groups and who inquire about what kind of work I do. When they discover that much of my life has been devoted to working with adolescents, often in groups, there is a typical reaction that I've come to expect. The discussion usually goes something like this:

COLLEAGUE: You work with adolescents? [Translation: Omigosh!]

ANDY: Yeah, mostly.

> (*A moment of silence follows, perhaps an unconscious offering of condolence.*)

COLLEAGUE: (*nervous laughter*) You must have a lot of patience. [Translation: I'm glad that it's you and not me.]

ANDY: (*in a feeble attempt to cut through the tension*) Yeah, well, actually I've been doing this for close to 25 years. Before that, I was an adolescent myself so I guess I never quite escaped; probably never will.

COLLEAGUE: (*chuckling*) What kind of work do you do with them?

ANDY: Some individual, some family, some outreach, a little of this and a little of that, but mostly I like to work with kids in groups. (*and then, in my best advocacy voice*) Kids really need to have good experiences in groups, ya know?

> (*There is no concealing the combined expression of shock and amazement staring me in the face.*)

COLLEAGUE: You work with them in groups? I don't know how you do it! (*smiling, head shaking*) I tried it just once or twice. That was enough. What a disaster. I couldn't get them to do anything. They wouldn't talk. They were, like, totally out of control, did whatever they wanted, and didn't listen to a thing I said, a real waste of time—mine and theirs. You work with them in groups? Really? [Translation: What a *jerk*.]

THE DEVELOPMENTAL CONTEXT

The composite picture of the behavior of
this age is contradictory and confused.
—H. S. Sullivan (1953, p. 93)

Adolescence . . . roughly the second decade of life is well known as a period of accelerated physical, psychological, and social growth. Individual variation in the rate of maturation makes it impossible to assign a specific chronological age to the onset of adolescence (Bloch, 1995). In my view, elasticity and overlap are invaluable allies in observing human development through the lens of theory. Evolving stages of psychosocial development can be viewed as having permeable boundaries through which the growing individual moves almost imperceptibly from one phase to the next and, during periods of regression, slips back from time to time for self-protection and refueling. The age range of the young people who populate the pages of *Group Work with Adolescents* includes individuals from 9 to 21 years old, a span covering what will be referred to throughout this book as young/early (9–14), middle (14–16), and older/later adolescence (16–21).

The Journey Begins

The upper and lower age limits of adolescence have expanded over the years with, according to some estimates, physical/pubertal growth occurring up to 4 years earlier than it did a century ago. The dramatic change in the onset of puberty, which is principally determined by genetic predisposition and environmental factors (e.g., climate), has been attributed to industrialization and improvements in health, sanitation, and nutrition (Bloch, 1995; Steinberg, 1986). Pubertal growth is most easily observable by change in the physical size of the child and the transformation from a generally undifferentiated body shape to a gender-distinctive shape. Boys get taller, are able to produce sperm, have a deeper voice, and develop pubic hair. Along with a slightly earlier growth spurt, changes in girls include breast development, menstrual period, and pubic hair. In females, changes in height, weight, and general body characteristics begin any-where between 9½ and 14 years of age. In males, these changes occur, on average, about a year later (Newton, 1995).

The accelerated physical growth during adolescence has profound social and psychological implications for the individual, transcending the mere fact that one's appearance and physique have changed. Sensitivity about one's appearance and its relationship to peer-group affiliation are potential sources of emotional stress for adolescents. This may be espe-cially so for individuals who experience precocious or delayed physical growth and who experience social estrangement as a result.

Aside from and/or alongside the physical changes of puberty, there is an observable trend in which many 9-, 10-, and 11-year-olds are assuming the bearing of older teenagers. Their clothing, hair styles, jewelry, make-up, swagger, posturing, language, and overall relational style create the illusion of individuals more than slightly beyond their years. Beyond style, increasing numbers of preteenagers are exhibiting behaviors traditionally associated with teenagers including: opposition to adult authority and influence; disrespect for others rights and property (e.g., stealing, vandal-ism); experimentation with drugs, alcohol, smoking, and sex (Bloch, 1995).

Some of this behavior can be explained by the normative process of children emulating behaviors of their parents or members of a social group or gang that has assumed certain family-like functions (Bloch, 1995). Another influence is the increased access to media and various forms of information technology (i.e., personal computers, on-line services). As a consequence, younger children are gaining an uncanny familiarity with the intricacies and accoutrements of the older world without the accom-panying emotional and cognitive equipment necessary to manage this information.

Television seems to exist primarily "to deliver an audience with just the right demographic composition to a corresponding advertiser" (Stras-burger, 1995, p. 17). This marketing strategy impacts heavily on children and adolescents in the critical health-related areas affecting their lives (e.g., violence, sexuality, drugs, and nutrition). For example, various clothing advertisers (e.g., for blue jeans, underwear) leave the consumer with photographically rendered illusions of sensuality and physical maturity that, in all likelihood, extend beyond the maturity of the individual who is used to project the image.

How is this kaleidoscope of ideas and images metabolized by young people who are lacking the psychic tools to sort it out and put it into some perspective? Without external support to fill the gap and make some sense of this whirlwind of information and values, what the young person does with it is either left to chance or the misfortunes of ill-informed choice. *Group work is one avenue for promoting the reflection and critical thinking necessary to clarify values and make healthy decisions.*

The Developmental Tasks of Adolescence

Regardless of any argument concerning the chronological onset of adolescence or social influences impacting on developing children, there is universal agreement that "developmental tasks" necessary for adolescents in our culture to become healthy, functioning adults require great effort and time to achieve. They can be summed up as follows:

- *Separating from family:* testing and experimentation in relationships with peers and authority figures leading to the achievement of emotional independence from parents and other adults; increasing autonomous functioning; developing a capacity for greater intimacy with peers.
- *Forging a healthy sexual identity:* accepting one's body/physique and learning to use it effectively; achieving a masculine or feminine social role.
- *Preparing for the future:* skill development and selection of an economic career; preparing for relational aspirations, for example, marriage and family life.
- *Developing a moral value system:* developing a set of values and an ethical system to guide one's behavior; desiring and achieving socially responsible behavior.

Adolescence today is an age of particular vulnerability, a time in which young people are experiencing the sexual awakenings of puberty, facing increasing social and educational demands, and experimenting with more freedom, autonomy, and choice than ever before. *Group work is an indispensable method for helping children to meet the developmental tasks and navigate the changing currents of adolescence.*

Quantum Leap

In the cartoon "Calvin and Hobbes," Calvin is a precocious child and his friend Hobbes is a stuffed toy tiger brought to life by Calvin's vivid imagination. Their "conversations" often belie Calvin's years. For example:

> CALVIN: We all want meaningful lives. We look for meaning in everything we do. But suppose there is no meaning! Suppose life is fundamentally

absurd! Suppose there's no reason, or truth, or rightness in anything! What if nothing means anything? What if nothing really matters?

HOBBES: I guess there's no harm in a little wishful thinking.

CALVIN: Or suppose *everything* matters. Which would be worse??

—B. Watterson (1995)

As the child moves from the "earthbound" quality of concrete thinking to more "intergalactic," formal operational thinking, the young adolescent becomes capable of constructing contrary-to fact-hypotheses, of leaping "with the mind into untracked cognitive terrain, cognitive terra incognito, to travel in inner space, and out, to everywhere and anywhere, flying with the mind" (Dulit, 1972, p. 28). Herein lies the source of the adolescent's growing ability and fervor for challenging others' ideas, beliefs, and values and for engaging in furious debate, often to the dismay of parents, teachers, and other adults.

Accompanying the transition from concrete thinking to the more abstract world of formal operations is the growing capacity for cognitive flexibility. Reasoned arguments gradually replace simple reliance on authoritative pronouncements by grown-ups. Opposites such as good and bad, or black and white, or yes and no can be held in one's mind simultaneously, enabling the individual to examine the subtle shadings of disparate ideas and to tolerate the ambiguities that are generated by thoughtful debate. This "quantum leap" in thinking enables the child to consider many viewpoints at once, use inductive and deductive thinking to reason, and test reality by challenging contradictions and inconsistencies. Young adolescents can begin to argue for argument's sake—for the fun of it. And all of this enables youth to become future-oriented by expanding their grasp of what is real and what is possible—"what 'could be' and not merely what 'is' or 'was' " (Dulit, 1972, p. 284).

Piaget (1950) believes that formal operations are initiated through cooperation with others. It is not enough to accept the imposed truths of others, no matter how rational in content. To learn to reason logically, one needs to engage in relationships that allow for an exchange and coordination of viewpoints. *Group work and the dialectical processes it promotes to advance mutual aid provide an ideal context for accommodating and fostering this quantum leap in cognitive development during adolescence.*

Building Bridges across the Generations

It is no surprise that there are grown-ups who are reticent about becoming involved with adolescents. However if adults can avoid becoming defensive or intimidated and can adopt a selective "devil's-advocate-may-care" attitude, they might be pleased to discover that from the same source of cognitive combativeness and intellectual intransigence spring seeds of inspiration and idealism. Adolescents enjoy a good "fight" with adults who don't feel a need to dominate or win and who are willing to really listen.

Anna Freud (1985) provides the quintessential description of the puzzling contradictions and paradoxes inherent in adolescence.

> Adolescents are excessively egoistic, regarding themselves as the center of the universe and the sole object of interest, and yet at no time in later life are they capable of so much self-sacrifice and devotion. . . . On the one hand, they throw themselves enthusiastically into the life of the community, and on the other, they have an overpowering longing for solitude. They oscillate between blind submission to some self-chosen leader and defiant rebellion against any and every authority. They are selfish and materially minded and at the same time full of lofty idealism. . . . At times their behavior to other people is rough and inconsiderate, yet they themselves are extremely touchy. Their moods veer between light-hearted optimism and the blackest pessimism. Sometimes they will work with indefatigable enthusiasm and at other times they are sluggish and apathetic. (p. 138)

Blos (1979) emphasizes that "the formation of a conflict between generations and its subsequent resolution is a normative task of adolescence" (p. 11). Coupled with access to an endless flow of technologically generated information and images, the cognitive leap of adolescence leads many a young person to believe that he/she can know more than his/her parents and to realize that some adults are not very bright (Schave & Schave, 1989). Taken to the extreme, such "cognitive conceit" can be very unsettling to the adults in their lives, particularly when expressed with a more sophisticated arsenal of thoughts and ideas. As Aristotle (1927) pointed out, in a reflection on adolescence, "They think they know everything, and are always quite sure about it. . . . They are fond of fun and therefore witty, wit being well-bred insolence" (pp. 323–325).

An interesting brew of revolt and conformity during this phase paints many unsuspecting parents with a broad brush, as if they represent some monolithic adult value system. During the protest-laden 1960s there was the familiar refrain by young people "You can't trust anyone over 30." Ironically, today it is many of the free-spirited, baby-boomer parents of adolescents who are struggling to convince their own adolescent children that they should "Do as we say, not as we did," in a world of ever-increasing risk.

In her diary, 13-year-old Anne Frank (1995), under unimaginable stress in hiding from the Nazis, expressed many of the normal developmental experiences of a young adolescent girl attempting, in close quarters, to separate from her family. One recurrent theme in her entries reflects her emerging differentiation from her mother, which she expressed with a not-so-subtle edge: "I understand my girlfriends better than my own mother, isn't that a shame?" She then takes the argument a step further, indicting the whole family: "I don't fit in with them. . . . They're so sentimental together, but I'd rather be sentimental on my own. They're always saying how . . . we get along so well, without giving a moment's thought to the fact that I don't feel that way" (p. 42).

Still another former teenager (and group-work pioneer-in-the-making) shares a page from her diary, illustrating the danger of adults dismissing all adolescent angst as a sign of self-absorption. Confusion about physical development, sexuality, and a lack of access to information led to her growing disillusionment with the adults in her life and her growing commitment to change the world for future adolescents.

> I had started to menstruate. . . . I was very happy about that, because now I was a woman!. . . . Now, in East Prussia, especially around the wedding time, I saw young men and women in tight embrace in the bushes. . . . I really didn't know how a child was conceived. I suddenly thought that I might be pregnant. It was a terrifying experience. . . . How had I become pregnant? I thought it may have happened because I was swimming with boys, and possibly one could be impregnated in the water. There simply was no other explanation. I did know that menstruation would cease when one became pregnant, and I did not menstruate at the time that I expected it, so I assumed I was pregnant. I became very unhappy and anxious. There was nobody to whom to turn. . . . Mother sensed that there was something very wrong with me, and she asked gently, "What is it child?" But I could not tell her. You cannot tell your mother! I asked mother how children were born, and she told me; but she could not tell me how they were conceived, that was impossible to her. So I suffered until the period returned. I kept a diary at that time, which I do not have anymore. But I know that I wrote into the diary that never, ever would I allow young people to grow up without knowledge of their own sexuality and or sexual functions. (Konopka, 1988, pp. 36–37)

More recently in a coed group, 16-year-old Marisa tried to downplay the risks involved in her method of birth control and protection from sexually transmitted diseases—"pulling out." Another member, Alex, supported the myth by instructing, "As long as you pull out in time, there is no risk—the worst that could happen is that a drop [of semen] is left behind." Finally, another typically shy and quiet member, Krista, revealed that she had become pregnant using the same method.

An upsurge of high-risk behaviors among young people led one author to reflect on the life-long consequences of a lack of information, misinformation, and poorly informed decisions.

I've often wondered what it would be like if we taught young people swimming in the same way we teach sexuality. If we told them that swimming was an important adult activity, one they will all have to be skilled at when they grow up, but we never talked to them about it. . . . Suddenly, when they would turn 18, we would fling open the doors to the swimming pool, and they would jump in. Miraculously, some might learn to tread water, but many would drown. (Roberts, 1983, p. 10)

Without adequate information and support, an adolescent's belief in her personal uniqueness can become a conviction that belies reality and invites risk. "This complex of beliefs in the uniqueness of her/his feelings and of her/his immortality and or indestructibility might be called a *personal fable,* a story which she/he tells herself and which is not true" (Elkind, 1974, p. 93). Risky behavior (drug use, carrying weapons, engaging in unprotected sex) can be carried out without any expectation of serious consequence.

Despite the common belief to the contrary, adolescents have not cornered the market on a sense of invincibility (Scales, 1996). Researchers have shown that adults also feel invincible, only in different circumstances relative to their life-stage experiences (Quadrel, Fischoff, & Davis, 1993). Scales (1996) dispels the myth that all risk is bad by pointing out that trying new experiences, pushing boundaries, and testing limits are part of normal adolescent development. "If risk = developmental exploration + environmental danger, then our job as caring adults is to reduce the environmental danger part of the equation. This can be accomplished by ensuring that youth have the external and internal assets they need to navigate normal risky development with a high degree of safety" (p. 7). *Group work can provide young people, in collaboration with adults, with a range of experiences to stretch their physical, emotional, intellectual, and social limits in many challenging and healthy ways.*

One Path May Lead to Divergent Routes

The rites of passage to adult status are not as clear as they once were. At the older end of adolescence the changing job market and economy are forcing many young people in their early 20s to remain or return home, prolonging the period of time in which they move on to adulthood. The terms "slackers" and "Generation X" have been used to describe some of these young people in their early 20s who have yet to find a traditional niche and who are "facing a world of diminished expectations with fewer opportunities" (Gozzi, 1995). High school graduation, college and/or military service, and marriage once constituted a relatively certain, if not uncomplicated, path from preparation to achievement of adulthood. The path appears considerably more ambiguous and obstacle-laden at the dawn of the 21st century.

In the later adolescent years, roughly ages 17 through 21, more serious decision making regarding one's future begins as career choice and life trajectory move into consciousness. A passage from Robert Frost's poem "The Road Not Taken" (1971) helps to illustrate the theme of choice at this stage of development.

> Two roads diverged in a yellow wood,
> And sorry I could not travel both
> And be one traveler, long I stood
> And looked down one as far as I could
> To where it bent in the undergrowth;
>
> Then took the other as just as fair,
> And having perhaps the better claim.
>
> I shall be telling this with a sigh
> Somewhere ages and ages hence:
> Two roads diverged in a wood, and I—
> I took the one less traveled by,
> And that has made all the difference.

Another intriguingly mystical variation on the same theme describes a young man's journey through the teachings of his spiritual guide.

> Anything is one of a million paths (*un camino entre cantidades de caminos*). Therefore you must always keep in mind that a path is only a path; if you feel you should not follow it, you must not stay with it under any conditions. . . . I warn you. Look at every path closely and deliberately. Try it as many times as you think necessary. Then ask yourself, and yourself alone, one question: Does this path have a heart?. . . . If it does, the path is good; if it doesn't, it is of no use. Both paths lead nowhere; but one has a heart, the other doesn't. One makes for a joyful journey; as long as you follow it, you are one with it. The other will make you curse your life. One makes you strong; the other weakens you. (Castaneda, 1974, p. 106)

Both literary pieces emphasize the interrelated themes of choice and commitment to life-guiding values that will chart the course for one's future work and relational life. It is with the emancipation of later adolescence that choices of vocation, career, politics, spiritual affiliation, intimate relationships, and friendships start to take hold. This is a time for making "ultimate commitments," publicly and privately and with increasing discrimination (Blos, 1979; Erikson, 1968).

In a qualitative study of Latino youth from different regions of Puerto

Rico, the narrative voices of several adolescents revealed that many of them discovered their "genius" at a very early age, somewhere between 3 and 12 years old. This contradicts the traditional belief that serious consideration and planning for the future—college, vocation, work—begins during the high-school years. The narratives underscored that children's notions of "What you want to be when you grow up" is a "deeply rooted vision that they grasp tightly, albeit with small hands" (Munoz, 1995, p. 176).

The narratives of these young people cry out for a recognition, validation, and nurturance of the "genius" in all children. In this paradigm, adolescence is not the beginning of career development, rather it is one point on a continuum. The challenge for all those involved with young people is how to tap into the *genius* of children at an early age and to then nurture it in adolescence, encouraging and supporting the attainment of long-held goals and dreams. *Group work, with its traditional emphasis on program and the use of activity, is an ideal place to nourish childhood genius in youth—to help adolescents to reach back and then move forward with their genius well in tow.*

Despite the drive and effort to become emancipated—emotionally, morally, physically and spiritually—adolescents continue to need the committed involvement in their lives of healthy, caring and competent adults—family members, friends, or relevant others from schools, health systems, and/or community-based agencies. Paradoxically, the path to independence and self-hood, while traveled alone, cannot be an empty path. Rather than abandoning the path in frustration, parents and others must simply reposition themselves along the way in order to help the uneasy traveler on his/her way. *Group work is one path for joining the generations and enabling them to reach out to one another and discover common ground.*

What are the risks and opportunities facing adolescents at the turn of the 21st century? What must group workers know and do in order to contribute to a protective environment to help mitigate against the multiple risks faced by youth in today's world? Much work has begun in assessing the need. The next step is action. And any action must involve how young people's needs are addressed through the group experience.

RISK AND OPPORTUNITY AT THE TURN OF THE 21ST CENTURY

The first comprehensive study of community organizations serving adolescents found that millions of young people spend at least 5 hours daily unsupervised and exposed to significant risks. These organizations are failing to reach these teens who "need safe places to go, a sense of belonging to a valued group, and activities that enable them to develop personal and work skills and a sense of social responsibility" (Hamburg, 1986).

It is ironic that the bulk of early group work attention was on children with normal developmental needs, while today "the 'market' for group work appears to have shifted from an emphasis on normal children and activities to adults with problems and talk" (Middleman & Wood, 1990b). Perhaps this explains, to some extent, the ever-widening legion of unsupervised and understimulated youngsters (Kurland & Malekoff, 1993a).

Risk Factors in Adolescence

What differentiates people with negative outcomes from those who grow up in similar circumstances and bounce back from great adversity? This question has stimulated much speculation and a dramatic growth of literature on risk, vulnerability, and resiliency (Garmezy, 1991; Garmezy & Rutter, 1983; Werner, 1990, 1989; Werner & Smith, 1992; Dryfoos, 1990; Schorr, 1989; Rutter, 1979; Sameroff, 1988; Anthony, Koupernik, & Chiland, 1978). What differentiates youth who are troubled, in trouble, and or causing trouble from their contemporaries with similar backgrounds who are not? These questions illustrate the special interest of those who are committed to understanding the relationship between risk-reduction strategies and the promotion of positive mental health.

Understanding risk is unlikely to lead to reliable predictions about individual outcomes, but it does help to make accurate assessments of probabilities. The relationship between nature (constitution) and nurture (environment) guides us in assessing risk. It is believed that the double hazard of deficits in both of these realms accounts for the increased risk of a poor outcome. Extensive studies (Werner, 1990; Sameroff, 1988; Rutter, 1979) found that stimulating and supportive environments are a significant counterforce to constitutional vulnerabilities in children and that risk factors potentiate one another. Single vulnerabilities alone are less likely than "multiple and interacting risk factors to produce damaging outcomes" (Schorr, 1989, p. 28).

Risks factors include deficiencies in individual constitution (i.e., physiological, neurological) and life context (i.e., the impact of the physical, cultural, social, political, and economic environment). Examples of risk factors for adolescents are illustrated in Table 1.1.

A societal response is necessary to address the needs of children and adolescents bearing the following risks, as identified by Schorr (1989).

- Children growing up with parents who are not only poor but isolated, impaired, undermined by their surroundings, and stressed beyond their ability to endure.
- Children who have been accumulating burdens both from before birth,

TABLE 1.1. Risk Factors and Their Association with Behavior Problems in Adolescents

Risk factors	Adolescent problem behaviors				
	Substance abuse	Delinquency	Teen pregnancy	School dropout	Violence
Community					
Availability of drugs	×				
Availability of firearms		×			×
Community laws and norms favorable toward drug use, firearms, and crime	×	×			×
Media portrayals of violence					×
Transitions and mobility	×	×		×	
Low neighborhood attachment and community disorganization	×	×			×
Extreme economic deprivation	×	×	×	×	×
Family					
Family history of the problem behavior	×	×	×	×	
Family management problems	×	×	×	×	×
Family conflict	×	×	×	×	×
Favorable parental attitudes and involvement in the problem behavior	×	×			×
School					
Early and persistent antisocial behavior	×	×	×	×	×
Academic failure beginning in elementary school	×	×	×	×	×
Lack of commitment to school	×	×	×	×	
Individual/peer					
Alienation and rebelliousness	×	×		×	
Friends who engage in a problem behavior	×	×	×	×	×
Favorable attitudes toward the problem behavior	×	×	×	×	
Early initiation of the problem behavior	×	×	×	×	×
Constitutional factors	×	×			×

Note. Copyright 1995 Developmental Research and Programs, Inc. Adapted by permission.

when their mothers' health was not well cared for, and neither was their own neonatal health as infants and small children cared for.

- Children growing up in families whose lives are out of control, with parents too drained to provide the consistent nurturance, structure, and stimulation that prepares other children for school and for life.
- Children whose experience of failure is compounded and reinforced by not learning the skills that schools are meant to teach, who soon become aware that the future holds little promise for them, and who enter adolescence with no reason to believe that anything worthwhile will be lost by dropping out of school, committing crimes, or having babies as unmarried teenagers.
- Children, such as those indicated above, who lack the hope, dreams, and stake in the future that is the basis for coping successfully with adversity and the ability to sacrifice immediate rewards for long-term gains. (p. 31)

Protective Factors for Adolescents

Despite their exposure to multiple risk factors, there are young people who do not succumb to serious health and behavior problems (e.g., substance abuse, violence, teen pregnancy, school dropout, and delinquency). "Protective factors are conditions that buffer young people from the negative consequences of exposure to risk by either reducing the impact of the risk or changing the way a person responds to the risk" (Hawkins, 1995, p. 14). Three general categories of protective factors for adolescents are identified.

- *Individual characteristics:* A resilient temperament, intelligence, and positive social orientation (all considered innate and difficult to change).
- *Bonding:* Positive relationships with a parent, caregiver, other significant adult, or attachment to a social group including the opportunity for an active involvement in these relationships; having the skills needed to succeed once involvement gets underway; and a consistent system of recognition and reinforcement.
- *Healthy beliefs and clear standards:* Developing prosocial affiliations and clear values and beliefs regarding what is ethical and healthy behavior; and beliefs in children's competence to succeed in school and avoid drugs and antisocial behavior, coupled with ability to accept clearly established expectations and rules governing their behavior (Hawkins, 1995).

Practitioners working with adolescents in groups must have a knowledge of risk factors to know where to begin to reduce health and behavior problems. However, they must also have group work knowledge and skill in order to take the necessary steps to reduce risk through the group experience.

Opportunity: Group Work as a Protective Factor

For adolescents to become healthy and constructive adults they must find ways to reach the following goals: find a valued place in a constructive group; learn how to form close, durable human relationships; feel a sense of worth as a person; achieve a reliable basis for making informed choices; know how to use support systems available to them; express constructive curiosity and exploratory behavior; find ways of being useful to others; and believe in a promising future with real opportunities (Carnegie Council on Adolescent Development,1995).

It is imperative that group work be a major influence in supporting and working towards these goals.

CONCLUSION

Group work has been, for the past century, a significant protective factor for youth. It has helped to guide many young people through normative life transitions, supporting mastery of the developmental tasks that confront them. Group work has also been instrumental in preparing adolescents for democratic participation in community life. For those young people at risk, group work has always been there to address specific needs and enable members to find ways to better mediate the various systems impacting on their lives, reducing the probability of a poor outcome in one's life. In order for the goals identified above to be reached, young people need safe places to go to, worthwhile things to do, a sense of belonging, a sense of competence, a feeling of hope, and support from adults who understand how to help to make all this happen.

Understanding how to make all this happen means understanding adolescents and how to work with them in groups. Increasing this understanding and the accompanying skills necessary to engage and maintain involvement with adolescents, is the purpose of *Group Work with Adolescents*.

CHAPTER 2 | # Between Adolescent and Group Worker

Uncertainty, Fluidity, and Learning from the Inside Out

Upon this gifted age, in its dark hour,
Rains from the sky a meteoric shower
Of facts . . . they lie unquestioned, uncombined.
Wisdom enough to leech us of our ill
Is daily spun; but there exists no loom
To weave it into fabric. . . .
—*E. St. Vincent Millay (from "Upon this Age That Never Speaks Its Mind")*

INTRODUCTION: ASSUMING A STANCE OF UNCERTAINTY

Adolescents demand to be taken as whole people. Group workers may find it especially difficult to work with adolescents if they begin by assuming a position of certainty, relying upon scientifically sanctioned knowledge as the supreme truth. One cannot gain access to what another person is experiencing without also reaching for other legitimate sources of knowledge, not the least of which is the reality expressed through the narrative voice of the young person him/herself. This requires that the group worker "assume a stance of uncertainty" (Pozatek, 1994), a commitment to developing relationships with adolescents that transcends the traditional paradigm of practitioner as *knowledgeable expert* and client as *naive initiate,* relationships that capture the joys of human collaboration.

LABELING, DEVIANCE, AND CONTROL

Practitioners need to take the whole child into account in any assessment. Classification systems such as the *Diagnostic and Statistical Manual of*

Mental Disorders (DSM; American Psychiatric Association, 1994) should not be used without considering risk and protective factors impacting on the young person's life. Too often adolescents are defined by their deficits rather than their capacities. "The system may define all sorts of things, and may attach all sorts of names, but what it is concerned about is acceptable behavior: The issue is not a child's silent agony but these things about him which tend, either now or later to make him a nuisance or menace" (Schrag & Divocky, 1975, p. 240).

As group workers involved with adolescents, we must tune in to the relationship between labeling and control. Being able to label or categorize adolescents may give group workers an elevated sense of expertise in their own eyes as well as others. However, the group worker must be much more than a fixer of broken objects (Schwartz, 1994a). So often the sound and movement of the adolescent group makes colleagues, parents, and relevant others within earshot so uncomfortable as to compel them to question the efficacy of our efforts. They may derisively refer to the action as "fun and games," suggesting that nonverbal activity itself cannot be a legitimate avenue for growth and change. This is not in fact the case. As one colleague reminisced: "These 'unimportant' and 'superficial' kinds of group efforts that people like me [sic] engaged in made it possible for us to be around to capitalize on the frequently random and unintentionally therapeutic approaches troubled kids make toward one another, so that, often to their surprise, they felt free to *like* someone else, and *to be liked by them*" (Ralph Kolodny, personal communication, July 1995).

How might young people themselves respond to classification systems if they were invited to participate in the debate, as well they should be? Margaret Mead once advised that any meeting in which adults gather to address the plight of children ought to have at least one young person present as a living reminder of the subject of their deliberations. One teenager, who was confined to an extended stay in residential care, describes her experience as a labeled person through poetry (Dalrymple & Burke, 1995)[1]:

> What happened to my opinion and viewpoints?
> Why do they assess me this way?
> What happened to my freedom I must say?
> Why do they label me this way? (p. 7)

and

> Why do they label me—
> When I am only being me? (p. 114)
> —*Chrissie Elms Bennet*

---

[1]These lines are excerpts from two longer poems.

Some of the same issues, and especially the arrival of the managed mental health care era inspired me to write the following lines in a poem:

> measurable outcomes to help us cope
> and claim that they can quantify hope;
>
> but tell me why we get a label
> when you all know it's just a fable;
> —*A. Malekoff (1994g)*

Adolescents may be sensitive to being labeled and may easily feel misunderstood. Advocacy, however, must transcend denigrating conventional classification systems. The challenge is to discover innovative ways to strengthen the process of ongoing assessment. This might be done, for example, by using an inventory of risk and protective factors to supplement more traditional evaluation tools (Malekoff, 1997b; North Shore Child and Family Guidance Center, 1995).[2]

TRADITIONAL DIAGNOSIS AND ADOLESCENT CULTURE

I was surprised to discover, via a young group member, that a variation of traditional diagnosis has found a home within the protocols of an adolescent fantasy game (Wujcik, 1985). A 14-year-old aficionado of these games brought his guide books into a group meeting and shared them with the others who were new to the genre. The game's instructions explain that there are a variety of heroes, principled and unprincipled. They are described as "mentally and emotionally sound" unless beset by trauma. "Insanity tables" are organized into several categories including: affective disorder, neurosis, phobia, psychosis, alcoholism, and drug addiction. These are followed by "Cures for insanity," which include: therapy, counseling, hypnosis, drugs, and "prolonged repeated exposure to the object of fear" for phobias (pp. 16–17).

Controversy about such fantasy games usually revolves around questions of whether they promote violence, aggression, alienation, paranoid perceptions, and poor reality testing and judgment in adolescents (Ascherman, 1993). How ironic it is that the same nomenclature created to classify and hierarchize human emotional frailty (Saleeby, 1994; Goldstein, 1990) has mutated and been transported into a corridor of adolescent culture via the often-reviled fantasy game itself.

---

[2]See Appendix 2.1 for an example of a risk- and protective-factor inventory.

LOOKING WITH PLANNED EMPTINESS

Tuning in to context and encouraging narrative expression can serve as counterforces to deficit-model thinking and practice. A skill to assist one to assume a stance of uncertainty is to "look with planned emptiness" (Middleman & Wood, 1990a). The skill is described by Middleman and Wood as follows: "To look with planned emptiness is deliberately to cultivate an area in one's mind that is reserved for the unknown, that is ready to accommodate the new, perhaps alien idea and experience it, rather than rationalize it away or avoid it" (p. 24).

Perhaps this is what is meant by the expression, "Lose your mind and come to your senses!" When one adds context (social, familial, temporal, relational) and voice (personal narratives, stories) to an understanding of normal adolescent development (physical, cognitive, emotional, psychosocial) to tune in to the troubled teen, the picture becomes all that more complex, complete, and exhilarating. Looking with planned emptiness may appear a bit esoteric for some, yet it is an especially valuable tool for practitioners new to group work or most accustomed to the one-on-one interview. As some of those practitioners making the transition to the group have reported, "They often feel overwhelmed; like a young infant they possess neither the stimulus barrier to control inputs, the selective perceptions to enable differential response to them, nor the organizing apparatus to manage, give meaning to, or synthesize them" (Garland & Kolodny, 1981, p. 150). To look with planned emptiness is to hold to a position of uncertainty, to be willing to learn from the inside-out, and to enable oneself to weather the sometimes disorienting qualities of a group in motion.

ON BEING FLUID AND GROUNDED

The oscillating cycles of equilibrium and disequilibrium (i.e., conflicts, fights, playful hilarity, periods of calm, constructive activity) in adolescent groups point to the relationship among acting out, tension regulation, attending to task, and affectionate feelings (Blos, 1979; Offer, Marohn, & Ostrov, 1975; Aichorn, 1925). The alternating cycle of work and resistance has been described as the "central mechanism of tension regulation in adolescent groups" (Hurley, 1984). Worker flexibility, an ability to be fluid and grounded, is necessary to adjust sensitively and thoughtfully to the changing tides in adolescent groups. Lifton's concept of the "protean self" (1995), characterized by fluidity and many-sidedness, is one that seems ideally suited for group work with adolescents.

Assuming a position of uncertainty, looking with planned emptiness, and being both fluid and grounded are interrelated concepts that are indispensable for working with adolescents in groups.

STRUCTURING THE GROUP TO INVITE THE WHOLE PERSON

One of the problems of any youth-serving culture grounded in "deficit model thinking" is its "virtual abandonment of all 'normal' children and youth, or more precisely of the 'normal' in all children and youth" (Breton, 1990, p. 27). All practitioners working with children and adolescents in groups might ask themselves this question: Do I structure my groups so that the whole person is invited to participate, or only the troubled, or broken, or hurt parts?

Adolescents demand to be taken as whole people. They resent being categorized, diagnosed, and placed in "special" classes or groups. They want to deal not only with the personal troubles that have been highlighted by adults but also with normative issues that they find troubling, challenging, or simply interesting. And they want to have fun. It is critical for the group worker to hear the music behind seemingly unstructured activity such as spontaneous singing, rapping, dancing, and aimless horsing around. It is imperative for the group worker to be responsive to their curiosity and reflections about the world, and national and local scenes as well. The impression that the group is being unproductive during periods of nonverbal activity or discursive detours, for example, is an unfortunate view that robs the members of their humanity and discredits their natural ability to connect without words or the practitioner's direction.

It is a sad reality that there remain practitioners who believe that insight-oriented discussion is the only activity of value in group work and that worker competence is based upon an ability to "get them to talk." It is through play, recreation, competition, literature, music, art, dance, the acquisition of concrete skills, and shared learning and growing that group members "move to healing, a renewed quality of life, personal development and satisfaction, and fulfilling social relationships" (Bandler & Roman, 1991, p. 127). It is through the creative blend of discussion and activity (Malekoff, 1987) that doing, thinking, and feeling combine to support the emergence of the whole person.

A SENSE OF HUMOR AND A PLAYFUL SPIRIT

Having a sense of humor in working with adolescents doesn't necessarily refer to the practitioner's ability to be funny in the comedic sense, although that might prove to be an asset if exercised with good judgment and timing. The reference here is twofold: the ability to see the humor and/or absurdity in a situation or exchange and the capacity not to take oneself too seriously, or, to check one's ego at the door.

"Checking one's ego at the door" refers to the colloquial, as opposed to analytic, ego (as in "he has a big ego"). It is advisable, if one is planning to work with adolescents, especially in groups, not to do so solely for ego gratification. In fact, a group worker can expect his/her self-esteem to take quite a beating. Beyond obsessive internal questioning about one's efficacy and the puzzled expressions on the faces of uninitiated colleagues are the disorienting tactics of the young group members themselves. Many adolescents sadly discover that too many adults take their antics with a sort of deadly seriousness, which may damage the possibility of a decent relationship from ever developing.

On a number of occasions in one middle-adolescent boys' group I was leading, the topic of discussion turned to my wardrobe and grooming: "Andy, why is it that you always wear brown? Your shirt is brown, your pants are tan, your shoes are brown. What's up with that?"; and another aspect of my appearance, "Andy, did you ever hear about 'Hair Club for Men'?"; or my sex life, "Andy probably has the sex life of the rock." Then in the same discussion, after one member attempted to "defend my sex life," by stating that I have two children, another responded with this "witty rejoinder": "What happened, Andy, did the condom break twice?"

Group workers cannot afford to fall into the trap of replicating the negativity and rejection that youth may experience with many of the adults in their lives. As much as they love to dish it out, teens appreciate an adult who, if momentarily rattled, can take it in stride and in good humor (with ego intact—outside the door, of course).

For the purposes of this book, I seek to integrate what we think we know (based on theories we subscribe to and experiences we've had) with what we cannot know until we come to know it (based on individual and circumstantial uniqueness, the ever-changing experience and context of one's life). Working with adolescents, particularly in groups, provides the practitioner with a unique opportunity to increase one's comfort level with uncertainty, a threshold for tolerating ambiguity, an appreciation for paradox, and an ability to differentiate between the often contradictory "words" and "music" of the adolescent song. Nevertheless, group work with adolescents can be a lonely experience as well, especially when one is surrounded by the uninitiated.

> Although one frequently hears or reads that "group work is the modality of choice for adolescents," in practice few programs offer comprehensive group work services to teenagers. . . . adolescents are not the easiest population to

work with. Few of them come up to you and say, "thanks, that was a really great group, I got a lot out of it." One learns to receive nourishment from many small, often nonverbal rewards. (Bilides, 1992, pp. 142–143)

Practitioners working with adolescents in groups best not depend on their young group members for the narcissistic supplies necessary to sustain them. A light-hearted approach is a great asset, as I can attest by the following ringing endorsement of my well-honed skills(!): In a recent group meeting I had just finished stating my opinion in the midst of a heated debate. The group fell silent, no doubt in thoughtful consideration of my powerful and profound words. Or so I thought. A 15-year-old girl, the group's natural leader, who was sitting directly to my left turned to me and said softly but clearly enough for all to hear, "Andy, why is it that whenever you talk everyone falls asleep?" This above illustration demonstrates the absurdity of the moment. A contribution to the discussion deemed worthy of *reverence* by the worker is met by the *irreverence* of a group member.

The answer is not to try and manipulate the young to behave as little adults in the group, nor is it for practitioners to abandon the youthful spirit within themselves. There is a need to tap into and honor the natural forces of youth rather than attempt to exorcise them for the sake of professional image as recognized by Maier.

One of the major dilemmas and challenges of our times seems to be to let children be *children,* youth to be *youthful,* and adults achieving permission to be *joyfully playful,* each in their respective way. . . . Major trends in contemporary thinking, including in our own professional ambitions, have difficulties in granting the *young* to be young and older ones to be still young at heart. . . . Workers sometimes feel inhibited to encourage exuberant play, especially if these activities promise or threaten to lead to loud noise, or momentary breakdown of expendable controls. (Maier, 1994, p. 9; italics in original)

ACCESS TO ONE'S OWN CHILDHOOD MEMORIES

While it might be difficult for adolescents to believe that any adult, or any person for that matter, has ever experienced what they have, one of the worker's greatest allies is access to his/her own childhood memories. "Access" here refers to a conscious process of reaching back to reexperience all of the painful, pleasurable, and banal moments of one's own adolescence.

Access to my own early memories helped me, in the following illustration (Malekoff & Kolodny, 1991), tune in to a group member who found himself in a curious yet typically adolescent predicament.

Ian at 13½ was a warm and thoughtful boy with some mild neuro-logical deficits affecting his learning and speech. An avid science fiction reader, Ian's imagination and curiosity seemed to know no bounds. Ian was a tall, awkward-looking boy who appeared, physi-cally, to be older than his age. Described as a loner by school personnel, he was referred after making physical contact with a female teacher who became anxious that the touching, an awkward plea for a nurturant response, was a sexual overture.

After about a year in a boys' group, the typically gregarious and talkative Ian appeared one day to be in a low or down mood. The obviousness of his hanging head and uncharacteristic silence led to a volley of queries from the others. After a half-hearted attempt to deflect attention, he finally revealed that something had happened in school that day that had made him feel "physically sick to my stomach." After a barrage of requests ("Tell us," "C'mon, what happened?", and so on) and with some gentle encouragement, this articulate young man with a creative mind went on to describe, in a hushed tone, what had happened during his third-period social studies class.

According to Ian, the blackboard had contained a message that made everyone entering the classroom ecstatic: There would be a substitute teacher. Spontaneous cheering soon gave way to a few moments of anxious anticipation. While most of the students chattered and waited to see who they'd be terrorizing, Ian opened his paperback book and departed for some unknown galaxy. In a short time, the volume in the classroom lowered, and although Ian had been "lost in space," he beamed himself back, closed the book on his thumb expecting a quick return flight, and lifted his head to see *his mother* standing at the head of the class.

As Ian replayed the experience, he expressed thanks that no one had known the sub was his mother and that she hadn't let on by kissing him on the forehead or telling him that he had forgotten to clean his room or remove the trash. The "numbness" and sick feeling that had come with the disbelief of seeing her in that context had carried throughout the school day and into the group.

It was a feeling that I knew very well: When I was 13, my own parents had found it difficult to understand what it felt like to be seen in public with them. "What's wrong?" Mom would ask. "Are you ashamed of us?" This question always served as a marvelous tool for cutting me to the quick and revealing a lovely combination of anger, guilt, and shame to add to my already growing embarrassment. I wondered at the time, "Did others feel this way?" In order to answer this question, I began to make scientific observations of parent–teen interactions in local clothing stores. I chose clothing stores for my field research since there seemed to be nothing more humiliating, in my experience, than being subject to a middle-aged bald man with a piece of chalk playing with the crotch of one's pants, all the while under the watchful eye of dear old Mom and, to make things worse, with a group of friends doubled over in laughter on the sidewalk just beyond the store window. My careful observations revealed that most of the others were just as squirmy and impatient as I had been. Were they ashamed of their own parents?

Drawing from my recollection of this experience helped me to tune in to what Ian might have been feeling. Mundane moments like this seem to reveal new truths, shattering old perceptions and ideas. At my suggestion, they tried to put themselves in his shoes and thereby increase their abilities to resonate with him as they pictured their own moms or dads standing at the head of the class or in other "compromising positions." Since I had met all of the boys' parents, I was able to provide impersonations within a variety of embarrassing contexts as imagined by the boys. Through the use of role play, there was much good humor and kidding, but underlying it all was the confrontation with the mourning of childhood identity, the gradual departure from the family cocoon, and the realization of the lonely odyssey of youth.

Memories serve as a rich source of understanding and empathy for what adolescence feels like—not only troubled adolescence but normal adolescence as well. "We do not see through pristine eyes. The lenses of our eyes are smudged with history, spotted with personal and cultural experience" (Wood & Middleman, 1995). Access to one's own early memories can provide the worker with a unique tool for tuning in on many levels at once.

By listening to oneself, tuning in to feelings and memories evoked by encounters with adolescents in groups, the worker can achieve a greater sense of balance in potentially disorienting circumstances. With greater balance come greater clarity, differentiation, and empathy. Or they may not. And if not, tuning in at this level may at least help the worker to hang in for the remainder of the therapeutic ride until the road evens out. Adolescents need adults who can hang in there and not abandon hope.

COLLEGIAL SUPPORT

Practicing group work with adolescents requires collegial support. This can be sought from a variety of sources including literature, supervision, peer support from fellow workers, professional conferences, and membership in various professional organizations. Writing down, videotaping, and presenting one's work at various forums are also helpful. Sharing one's work through any of these means connotes a reciprocal process, a give and take, an invitation for a critical look, and, in return, the gift of an experience preserved.

It is within the collegial spirit that the contents of *Group Work with Adolescents* are offered. It is my sincerest wish that this volume will be supportive and useful; that it will ring true in both its most moving and more mundane moments; that it will illustrate practice in a way that will cause readers to smile, laugh, cry, yawn, throw their hands up in disbelief, scratch their heads in befuddlement, experience anxiety, and feel frustrated and satisfied; that it will open the door for agreement and disagreement, for discussion and debate; and that it will lead others to share their experiences through writing, speaking, videotaping, or through other means.

CONCLUSION

Maintaining a sense of balance amidst the rhythmic interplay of chaos, confusion, uncertainty, and clarity is characteristic of the practitioner's plight in working with adolescents in groups. Some of the concepts introduced above and developed further in the ensuing chapters include maintaining a sense of humor and playful spirit, structuring the group to invite the whole person, differentiating between the adolescent's words and music, and having access to one's childhood memories. The practitioner working with adolescents in groups is encouraged to assume a stance of uncertainty, be both fluid and grounded, check his/her ego at the door, and rely on collegial support to better navigate the "moments" and "madness."

> Thirty spokes are made one by holes in a hub,
> By vacancies joining them for a wheel's use;
> The use of clay in molding pitchers
> Comes from the hollow of its absence;
> Doors, windows, in a house,
> Are used for their emptiness;
> Thus we are helped by what is not,
> To use what is.
> —*Lao-Tze (in McLuhan & Fiore, 1967)*

APPENDIX 2.1. RISK- AND PROTECTIVE-FACTOR INVENTORY

Therapist name: _____

Admission Data (to be completed by intake worker)

Name: _____ Case number_____

I. **Risk factors**

Check if applicable

1. Child or sibling of a substance abuser (i.e., someone with contin- _____
   ued use despite recurrent work, family, or community problems—
   e.g., arrests, DWI, etc.). Please check 1A. Child_____   or 1B.
   Sibling _____
2. Child or sibling of a substance abuser in recovery (i.e., currently in _____
   a recovery program and/or following recovery principles). Please
   check 2A. Child_____   or 2B. Sibling_____
3. School dropout or long history of failure (i.e., years of academi- _____
   cally unacceptable failing grades in at least half of his/her major,
   academic areas).
4. Severe emotional problems (GAF of 50 or less) _____
5. Recent discharge (within the last 12 months) from hospitalization _____
   for substance abuse and/or psychiatric problems
6. Members of a family where severe emotional turmoil exists (e.g., _____
   depression, schizophrenia, suicide, etc.)
7. Severe medical problems (e.g., cancer, Huntington's, etc.) _____
8. Member of a family where severe medical problems exist in an- _____
   other member (e.g., cancer, Huntington's, etc.)
9. Has suffered physical or sexual abuse. Please check _____
   9A. Physical_____   or 9B. Sexual_____
10. Has suffered emotional maltreatment (i.e., systematic repeated be- _____
    littling and/or cold and rejecting attitude)
11. Has suffered neglect of physical, medical, and/or educational _____
    needs.
12. Lives in concentrated poverty (or has in past—indicate with aster- _____
    isk*)
13. Has manifested self-destructive impulses and has made suicidal _____
    gestures in recent months
14. Criminal justice involvement due to having committed a violent or _____
    delinquent act
15. History of violent, destructive behavior _____
16. Multiple home placements and inconsistent care _____

Note. Copyright 1995 North Shore Child and Family Guidance Association. Reprinted by permission

17. Poor birth and development history (i.e., severe medical complications prenatally and perinatally, and persistent delayed development) _____

18. Children whose parent(s) have died (indicate with asterisk*) or are separated or divorced _____

19. Special education placement (LD, ED) _____

20. Socially isolated (i.e., no friends and significantly limited social involvement with peers in school or community activities)

II. Protective factors (Indicate appropriate rating on the following scale):
1. Significant weakness; 2. Moderate weakness; 3. About average; 4. Moderate strength; 5. Significant strength; NA–not applicable

A. Constitutional
21. Sociability _____
22. Intelligence _____
23. Expressive language skills _____
24. Internal locus of control (individual perception of behavior: internally regulated vs. externally regulated) _____
25. Mother: biological____ adopted____ step-____ foster____

B. Affectional/emotional ties
26. Father: biological____ adopted____ step-____ foster____
27. Siblings: biological____ adopted____ step-____ foster____
28. Spouse/mate _____
29. Kin (specify _____) _____

C. External supports
30. School _____
31. Work _____
32. Organized religious or spiritual affiliation _____
33. Club _____
34. Other _____

III. Psychosocial stressors (identify one to three significant current/recent stressors)

_____

_____

_____

IV. Axis V rating _____

V. Abuse of alcohol or other drugs: Yes ____ No ____; if yes, indicate all substances used: _____

_____

PART II

Guidelines for Group Building

| CHAPTER 3 | # What's So Special about Group Work?
An Introduction to Tradition and Theory |

INTRODUCTION: THE PRICE OF NEGLECT

What's so special about group work?

What appeared as a noble attempt to enhance social work's identity through the development of an integrated method curriculum in the late 1960s and early 1970s and beyond ultimately left group work out in the cold (Birnbaum & Auerbach, 1992). Although some schools did integrate group work into the core curriculum together with individual and family work, this was not universal. Moreover, the offering of specialized group courses has declined. This shift in graduate social work education over the past three decades has seriously impacted on group work as a method of study. In many schools and agencies, social work educators and field instructors lack the knowledge base and skills that inform group work practice. As a result, students are graduating without any grounding or practice experience in group work. This book intends to remedy that deficit.

Practicing group work begins with some understanding of what makes it so special.

As times change, new approaches, or newly packaged old approaches, compete in the marketplace of ideas and influence. Many years ago there was acknowledgment of a strong drumbeat that told us that the road to change is to be found deep within oneself, as far as one dares go, for as long as the journey might take. Some time later, another group's drumbeat told us that an individual's symptoms signal distress within one's family and that the road to change begins in family relationships beyond oneself. Now we are beginning to hear another drumbeat that tells us that the path to change requires a swift alleviation of one's symptoms by modifying thinking, emotions, and behavior. For more than a century, amidst these ascending and receding "drumbeats" and despite the recent neglect of academia (Birnbaum & Auerbach, 1992), the strong and steady cadence of group work could be heard by those who cared to listen. It told us always to pay attention to both the near things and the far things.

Listen.

One of the earliest group work researchers, Wilbur Newstetter, composed what has been referred to as the first real definition of group work (1935). He highlighted a dual vision, later referred to by William Schwartz (1986) as a focus on both the *"near things* of individual need and the *far things* of social reform," an emphasis that is as relevant today as it was then.

> Group work may be defined as an educational process emphasizing (1) the development and social adjustment of an individual through voluntary group association; and (2) the use of this association as a means of furthering other socially desirable ends. It is concerned therefore with both individual growth and social results. Moreover, it is the combined and consistent pursuit of both these objectives, not merely one of them, that distinguishes group work as a process. (Newstetter, 1935, p. 291)

THE SETTLEMENT MOVEMENT

The history that preceded the formulation of Newstetter's definition coincided with group work's origins, dating back to the mid-1800s. Among the more salient developments were the Industrial Revolution and dramatic population shifts (i.e., large numbers of people moving from rural to urban communities and a wave of immigrants moving from Europe to large cities in the United States). Poverty, overcrowding, disease, illiteracy, and unhealthful living and working conditions plagued many of the people who lived in ever-deteriorating neighborhoods, for the most part located in large urban centers.

Responses to these conditions included the development of various organizations (e.g., settlements houses, YMCA, YWCA, national scouting groups, boys' clubs[1]) to address the spiritual, leisure time, and social needs

---

[1]For a fascinating study on the evolution of a boys' club refer to Sorin (1990). Several of the members of this club went on to become prominent group workers.

of their members. For example, the camping movement enabled young-sters to experience the natural world and to discover interesting ways to relate to the broader environment. Certainly in the early years of the 20th century, many children and young adolescents needed respite from the grueling hours and harsh conditions of factory work. In 1903 Jane Addams, founder of Hull House settlement in Chicago, said of these children, "The boys and girls have a particular hue, a color so distinctive that anyone meeting them on the street even on Sunday in their best clothes and mixed up with other children who go to school and play out of doors, can distinguish almost in an instant the children who work in the factory" (cited in Fatout, 1992, p. 7).

If she were with us today, what might Jane Addams say of the young people living in the streets, a century and an Industrial Revolution later? The settlement movement brought together people of all cultural and socioccomonic backgrounds to work together toward the goals of per-sonal, community, and social change (e.g., against poor working condi-tions, child labor, slum housing, inadequate health facilities, and political corruption). The settlement workers joined with those who were affected by unjust conditions to work collaboratively towards social change. Thus, groups were central to settlement house activity even though there was little recognition of group work as method at the time.

The settlement movement became a major force in addressing the health and educational needs of children and adolescents through the establishment of English classes, health clinics, and recreation programs, among others. Sadly today, almost 100 years later, the health and educa-tional needs of millions of young children and adolescents are not being adequately met in the most prosperous country on earth, not to mention in the rest of the world. "The last decade of the twentieth century will be a hazardous time for many children and their families in the United States," concluded Dryfoos (1994), a prominent investigator of adolescents' needs. Dryfoos invokes the names of the early child advocates—Jane Addams, Florence Kelly, Lillian Wald—and makes a plea for settlement houses in the schools—a "seamless institution, a community-oriented school with a joint governance structure that allows maximum responsiveness to the community, as well as accessibility and continuity for those in most need of services" (p. 12).

THE RECREATION MOVEMENT

The recreation movement represented a celebration of the whole person, tapping into the young person's capacity rather than his/her deficits, and supporting the individual's right to experience the "deep delight" of par-ticipation in a creative and democratic group (Coyle, 1955; Breton, 1990).

Access to recreation was universal. The accent was on what we might today refer to as promoting "wellness" or supporting normal development. Presently, confesses one scholar, "I am troubled by our virtual abandonment of 'normal' children and youth, or more precisely, of the 'normal' in all children and youth; I wonder if unwittingly we are contributing to the societal negligence of this segment of our population, a negligence that is a sad characteristic of our greedy age" (Breton, 1990, p. 27).

In group work, activity may emerge spontaneously, sparking the creative potential of individuals and the group and leading to a range of imaginative pursuits; or, activity may be planned, promoting critical thinking, rationality, decision making and problem solving in the group; or it may comprise some integration of the two (Papell & Rothman, 1980).[2] In any case, the essence of recreation as it relates to group work is best captured by Grace Coyle, who wrote in 1948, in *Group Work with American Youth*, "Success from the group worker's point of view is seen not in terms of games won, ceramics produced or information learned, but in terms of what the experience means to the participants" (p. 28). Good leadership in recreation requires nothing less. Group work emerged as a method out of this realization (see Chapter 8 on the use of "program"). We can only speculate how Grace Coyle, if she were with us today, might react to the following bit of latter 20th-century American folk wisdom: "Winning isn't everything; it's the only thing."

THE PROGRESSIVE EDUCATION MOVEMENT

John Dewey, the leading figure in the progressive education movement, advocated for children through educational reform. As with the settlement and recreation movements, the small group was viewed as the vehicle for growth and change in progressive education. The essence of this movement was to help students to learn skills for living and to prepare to become active participants in community affairs. Dewey saw an opportunity in the educational institution to move students from routine drill to meaningful activity. He envisioned students engaged in interaction and social aims that extended beyond the school walls (Dewey, 1916).[3]

The progressive education movement, in its efforts to reform the

---

[2]See Wilson and Ryland (1949) for the most comprehensive early text on the use of program content. Its contents include an interdisciplinary view, outside of social work, of various professions' (psychiatry, psychology, education, and recreation) thinking about the "underlying values of nonverbal content" in group work (Middleman, 1968, p. 38).

[3]S. R. Slavson, considered by many to be the father of group psychotherapy (Rachman & Raubolt, 1984), began as group worker whose roots were working with adolescents in progressive education and who wrote two early books on the subject (1937, 1939).

school system, contributed to group work's theoretical orientation. Some of the concepts from the movement that influenced the development of group work as a method are: the emphasis on the group rather than the individual child in the classroom; importance of interaction between children, rather than only with the teacher, as a source of learning; development of mutual aid through peer learning; role of the teacher as facilitator rather than rigid autocrat; and learning by doing through problem solving (see Chapter 7). If he were with us today, what might John Dewey say about violence and the need for metal detectors in schools, high school graduates who cannot read, open drug dealing on school grounds, teenage pregnancy, and the ongoing debate over condom distribution?

PROGRAMMING FOR EGO SUPPORT

In the late 1930s and early 1940s, Gisela Konopka (1949) in Pittsburgh and Fritz Redl and David Wineman (1951, 1952) in Detroit developed approaches, rooted in settlement house and community center practice with "normal youngsters," for helping emotionally disturbed children and adolescents. The core of their orientation was programming for ego support, approaches in which "activities normal to childhood (i.e., crafts, games, planned discussion, field trips) were deliberately and planfully employed in such ways as to bring each member's difficulties in relationships to the fore and afford him the possibility of altering his feelings and behavior toward others and to himself" (Garland & Kolodny, 1981, p. 84). This process has been referred to as the "clinical exploitation of life events" (Redl & Wineman, 1952).

Programming for ego support has relevance to working with youth groups in a broad range of settings and across disciplines of practice. Regardless of the practitioner's orientation, he/she must be attuned to what the adolescent "brings to the group" and "lives out in the group" by way of outside experiences. Over the years Redl extended his knowledge and experience by consistently applying his understanding of group work to the practical day-to-day concerns of the classroom, residential camp, residential treatment facility, and settlement house (Rachman & Raubolt, 1984). Although written almost half a century ago, Redl and Wineman's *Controls from Within: Techniques for the Treatment of the Aggressive Child* (1952) and *Children Who Hate* (1951) are essential reading for anyone working with young people today.[4] If he were with us today, what

---

[4]Another invaluable resource, akin to Redl and Wineman's classics and similarly developed from work with emotionally disturbed children in a therapeutic milieu, is Trieschman, Whittaker, and Brendtro (1969).

might Fritz Redl say of the social worker, psychologist, teacher, or counselor faced with a group of boisterous young adolescents who balks at the assignment saying, "I didn't go to graduate school to become a baby sitter."?

SOCIAL WORK WITH GROUPS: A FOUNDATION FOR ECLECTIC PRACTICE WITH ADOLESCENTS

Social work with groups has been described as a movement before was a formalized method (Papell, 1983). The method of practice described and illustrated in this volume has been forged from a rich tradition of social reform, practice innovation, and scholarship. This book does not espouse a particular theoretical model of practice, rather it represents an eclectic approach within which the practitioner may integrate his/her own theoretical base. The practitioner's orientation should, first and foremost, be influenced by the needs of the group members and the purpose and goals of the group (see Chapter 4). What in my view qualifies as social work practice with adolescents in groups? The following are questions that the practitioner might consider in determining goodness of fit between a preferred theoretical orientation[5] and the group work practice method described herein (adapted from Middleman & Wood, 1990b; Breton, 1990).

- Is the group structured to invite the whole person or only the broken, troubled and hurt parts?
- Are the group members valued as helpers or is there but one central helping person?
- Are members encouraged to interact and provide mutual aid or do communication and control flow principally through the practitioner?
- Does the practitioner understand, value, and respect group process as an important change dynamic throughout the life of the group, and within individual group meetings?
- Does the practitioner think about working him/herself out of a job, enabling the group to increase its autonomy within and outside of the group?
- Are group members helped to gain a sense of each other and their "groupness" at the beginning, throughout the course of the group's life, and at the point of separation—providing members with a real

[5]See Roberts and Northen (1976), Garland and Kolodny (1981), and Fatout (1992) for descriptions of various theoretical orientations in group work. These discourses provide reviews of historical and behavioral science foundations of group work models, philosophical and ethical considerations, group dynamic and developmental issues, and principles and methods of intervention, among other variables.

sense of connection to one another, why they've come together, where they are headed, and what their time together has meant?
- Does the practitioner value and actively encourage the development of program activities that are both planful and spontaneous, rational and imaginative, to address the needs of the members and the purposes of the group?
- Does the practitioner lend a vision that enables the group to reach both within and beyond themselves, helping young people to recognize and deal fully with the multiple contexts of their lives?

In summary, eclectic practice with adolescents epitomizes the following principles:

- Structuring the group to invite the "whole" person.
- Helping the members to develop a mutual aid system.
- Encouraging group and individual autonomy.
- Understanding group process as an important change dynamic.
- Emphasizing the "groupness" of the group throughout its developmental cycle.
- Using program activities (verbal and nonverbal) to promote belonging, competence, rationality and spontaneity.
- Focusing on the multiple contexts impacting on the members' lives.

The knowledge, values, skills, and processes suggested by these principles and described below and in the ensuing chapters are presented to the reader as critical components for competent group work practice with adolescents regardless of the practitioner's theoretical or ideological orientation. To begin exploration of the process, and to round out this chapter, a summary of curative and dynamic forces in group work with adolescents, a note on the ascendance of the cognitive–behavioral approach in group work, a review of two significant developmental models for social work practice with groups, and poetry on the stages of group development are provided.

DYNAMIC AND CURATIVE FORCES OF GROUP WORK

> We may either smother the divine fire
> of youth or we may feed it.
> —J. *Addams (1912, p. 161)*

This section is offered to reveal some of the potential benefits of group work for adolescents. To serve as a guide, Northen (1988) and Yalom (1985) have identified some of the curative and dynamic factors in group work and group psychotherapy, respectively. These include *mutual support, universalization, instillation of hope, altruism, acquisition of knowledge and skills, group control, catharsis, corrective emotional experiences,* and *reality testing.* The following is a summary of these forces as they apply to work with adolescents.

Mutual Support

As young people redefine their relationship within the family, they need to learn about and experience the capacity for mutuality outside the family (Coyle, 1947). In group work, attention to becoming a mutual aid system requires "valuation of the members as helpers—many and not just one central helping person" (Middleman & Wood, 1990b). Adolescents can learn what they have to offer, and how to offer it, in a cohesive group. This is a steppingstone to greater intimacy.

Universalization

Gaining a collective sense of common ground, that is, "we're all in the same boat," can serve as a counterforce to the isolation and frustration of feeling unheard and misunderstood. For adolescents who are moving away from the family and taking tentative steps toward the peer group, there is a susceptibility to periods of intense isolation that one may experience as being unique to oneself. The group experience helps to universalize this and other normative, transitional experiences, providing the young person with a sense of community and affinity with others who are encountering many of the same feelings.

Instillation of Hope

Lending a vision is a core group work skill that, along with universalization, can help the young person who feels "stuck" in predicaments and crises, real and existential, to emerge from the morass with a sense of hope that things can get better. "The practitioner communicates feelings of passion and commitment about the future to help members gain faith in their abilities" (Glassman & Kates, 1990, p. 198).

Altruism

Too many adults view adolescents as selfish and self-centered. As with many of the paradoxes of adolescence, selfishness is but one side of a coin. In fact, a greater percentage of adolescents volunteer in communities than

3. What's So Special about Group Work?   /   39

do adults (Scales, 1996). The opportunity to give as well as to receive is crucial for the young person who is looking to loosen ties of dependency, but not completely. Giving to others, receiving from others, giving to others, receiving from others . . . This is the essence of mutual aid—a process that enables the young person to make the transition from dependence to independence to interdependence (see Chapter 7).

Acquisition of Knowledge and Skills

Group work can provide members with opportunities to address openly both tame and taboo subjects. Misinformation and myths can be challenged. Issues of sexuality, alcohol and other drug use, cultural diversity, and other interrelated problems and needs can be confronted in a safe environment in group work. Skills for living can be developed by youth by learning from one another, gaining knowledge about how to access resources, and rehearsing new skills through activities such as role playing, problem solving and conflict resolution. Acquiring and practicing new skills can help to equip adolescents with the tools necessary for a physically and emotionally healthy life.

Group Control

Adolescents must adhere to certain norms and expectations that help the group as a whole to reach its goals. Group members must endure frustration, accept fair guidelines and limits, moderate their resistance to authority, and contain their inappropriate behavior. For example, after the New York Yankees won the 1996 World Series of baseball in dramatic fashion, observers marveled at some of the intangible features of team success. Prominently mentioned among these was the willingness of star players who were performing below par to sit in the dugout for a game or two and give a teammate a chance, all for the good of the team. Waiting to take turns, sharing center stage, and allowing others to contribute is the mark of a good team, and thus of a good group.

Catharsis

Giving expression to one's ideas, feelings, experiences, hopes, and dreams in an accepting environment can reduce anxiety and energize group members to work together to reach valued goals. One group of adolescents shared their frustration about violence after a widely publicized murder rocked the community. Rather than assume a position of helplessness they joined the March for Unity and organized its largest youth contingent, transforming feelings of despair and resignation into hope and possibility.

Corrective Emotional Experiences

The group can offer the individual(s) an opportunity to reexperience dysfunctional patterns and relationships and to work through these dynamics in a safe and supportive environment. For instance, for the young person(s) growing up in a capricious home and/or community environment characterized by unpredictability, the caring structure and consistency of a good group can lead to a corrective experience. For the individual(s) who has developed a behavioral pattern that invites rejection, the group becomes an arena in which the same behavior is repeated and addressed with the goal of behavioral and affective change. It is the enactment of dysfunctional and then corrective behaviors in the group—the doing and the positive reinforcement of the doing—that is a most powerful contributor to a corrective emotional experience and consequent behavioral–cognitive–affective change.

Reality Testing

Distortions in perception can be safely presented and challenged in the group. An adolescent group member might find it difficult to hear an adult; however the voice of a contemporary, especially a group of them, may be hard to escape. For example, a valued method in the treatment of chemical dependency is group work. The combination of confrontation and support provided by a group of peers "in the same boat" helps to challenge denial, minimization, and distortions of reality. In an era when adolescents are exposed to and involved with risky behaviors that can be life threatening (i.e., carrying weapons, unprotected sex, drug abuse), good reality testing can make a significant difference in the trajectory of one's life.

THE ASCENDANCE OF THE COGNITIVE–BEHAVIORAL APPROACHES AND THE ROLE OF GROUP WORK

At the outset of the 21st century, decreasing dollars for human services, the privatization of mental health, and the advent of managed care have contributed to a clamor for short-term "solution-focused" interventions for troubled youth. As a result, the cognitive–behavioral approaches for change have moved into the foreground. The central organizing principle of this orientation is that behavior, emotions, and cognitions are learned and therefore can be changed by new learning. The emphasis is on addressing problematic behavior as a target for modification, rather than as a symptom of an underlying condition or situation.

The leading proponent of the sociobehavioral approach in the field of group work is Sheldon Rose, who developed the multimethod approach of behavioral group therapy (Rose & Edelson, 1987; Rose, 1972, 1977). In this model, the small group is the context for social reinforcement of prosocial behavior, a concept most germane to working with adolescents. As the child begins to step beyond the family circle in adolescence, there is growing affinity for the peer group. Included among the various behavioral methods of teaching children and adolescents coping skills are problem solving and sociorecreational methods, both derivatives of the progressive education and recreation movements.[6]

In changing times, different theoretical approaches gain favor as an accommodation to the social, political, and economic realities of the day. Group workers who decide to adapt approaches that are rising in popularity, whatever these approaches might be, must not lose sight of the core principles of group work. For example, using a cognitive–behavioral approach in group work with adolescents doesn't preclude valuing the group members as helpers, fostering mutual aid, structuring the group to invite the whole person, using the group to promote competence and autonomy, enabling the members to experience their "groupness," mediating with outside systems, or understanding the role of group process as a powerful change dynamic.

Group workers have much to gain from acquiring knowledge about short-term group approaches. However, practitioners working with groups of adolescents in settings that may discourage longer-term groups for youth must actively work to connect their young group members to alternative group experiences in order to provide them with ongoing avenues for belonging and mastery.

The challenge for group workers is to create avenues for integration across disciplines and models, bringing what group work has to offer to the table. For example, almost any approach focused on working with adolescents in groups will be enhanced by a working knowledge of group developmental theory. There is a growing body of literature on exercises, techniques, and activities for working with adolescents in groups (e.g., conflict resolution, anger management, socialization, and so on). What is so often missing is a theoretical framework within which this content may be introduced and implemented. Instead there are recipes, as in a cookbook. There is a real danger in implementing any group-oriented approach or activity without a good foundation in group development, that is, knowing what groups tend to look like as they move through space and time and what the role of the group worker is along the way (starting with planning the group and ending with separation from the group).

[6]It is recommended that practitioners using this approach familiarize themselves with the work of Vinter (1974) and Garvin (1997) for direction in the implementation and analysis of program activities.

MODELS OF GROUP DEVELOPMENT

A vital tenet of group work practice is that "the worker must actively understand, value and respect the group process itself as the powerful change dynamic that it is" over time and in each meeting (Middleman & Wood, 1990a). This demands that the practitioner have a good knowledge base, reinforced by practice experience, of group developmental theory. Two distinguished developmental models, the interactional model (Schwartz, 1994a, 1994b; see Berman-Rossi, 1994) and the Boston model (Garland et al., 1973; Garland & Kolodny, 1981), are summarized below.

The Interactional Model

William Schwartz elevated earlier formulations of mutual aid by emphasizing the reciprocal relationship between the individual and group and the group and social environment (i.e., the significance of interacting systems with a stake in one another, seeking common ground and reaching out to one another for their mutual benefit and the common good).[7] The model stresses the functions of identifying and challenging obstacles in interacting systems; sharing information, ideas, facts, and values for problem resolution; identifying the requirements (and limitations) of all parties involved in order to effect change; and lending a vision to maintain commitment and inspire hope. Schwartz charged the social work profession with the function of mediating between the competing interests and demands of various interacting systems. He defined group work as follows:

> The group is an enterprise in mutual aid, an alliance of individuals who need each other, in varying degrees, to work on certain common problems. The important fact is that this is a helping system in which the clients need each other as well as the worker. This need to use each other, to create not one but many helping relationships, is a vital ingredient of the group process and constitutes a common need over and above the specific tasks for which the group was formed. (Schwartz, 1961, p. 19)

Schwartz's interactional model (alternately referred to as the mutual aid model, reciprocal model, and mediating model) is organized developmentally along a continuum of four phases, which are to be followed over the life of the group and within each meeting. They are: *tuning in* (preparation), *beginnings* (contracting), *middles* (work), and *endings* (transitional). In each of the phases, three major questions, also applicable

---

[7]Alex Gitterman and Lawrence Shulman are two of the leading educator/scholars who have carried forth the legacy of William Schwartz. See, for example, "The Legacy of William Schwartz: Group Practice as Shared Interaction" (special issue of *Social Work with Groups*, Volume 8, No. 4, 1986).

to other models of group development, are considered. These are (Schwartz, 1976):

- What is to be anticipated about what members might experience in each successive phase of development?
- What are the valued outcomes for the phase of development?
- What are the implementing acts and worker skills necessary at this phase of development?

These questions reflect the importance of preparation, what Schwartz referred to as "tuning-in" (see Chapter 4). In a description of a high-school program based on the interactional model to prevent adolescent substance abuse, Shields (1986) describes the surface affect of the group members—toughness, mistrust, and hostility, which serve to keep others at a distance. She then tunes in to the underlying feelings that reflect the reality—feeling frightened, vulnerable, and overwhelmed, and at a loss of how to cope with oneself and the world.

Another among Schwartz's considerable contributions is the importance of "contracting"—establishing a simple and straightforward statement of purpose that connects "the group members' *needs,* the agency's *assignment,* and the worker's *function*" (Schwartz, 1971, p. 15). An introductory guideline for contracting in group work includes the following components:

- To make a clear statement of why the service was being offered.
- To describe the worker's role in the agency and group.
- To encourage reaction to the statement and how it fits in with their own understanding and wishes.
- To come to agreement on the terms and frame of reference for working together.

(For further discussion on purpose and contracting see Chapters 4, 5, and 6.) A master at placing things in perspective, Schwartz left us with this sobering piece of advice about our role and the value of promoting autonomy by essentially working oneself out of a job: "The worker is an incident in the lives of his clients." The life processes into which the worker "enters and makes his limited impact have been going on for a long time before he arrived and will continue for a long time after he is gone" (Schwartz in Middleman and Wood, 1990b, p. 11).[8]

---

[8]Refer to Berman-Rossi (1994) for a comprehensive view of Schwartz's legacy to the theory and practice of group work. Other models of group development include Hartford (1971), Klein (1972), Trecker (1973), Sarri and Galinsky (1974), Tropp (1976), Levine (1979),
(continued)

The Boston model was first presented in an article entitled "A Model for Stages of Development in Social Work Groups," the seminal work of three practitioners/scholars—Garland et al. (1973). The method was formulated through observation in clinical practice settings and review of records of young-adolescent groups. The model consists of five stages of group development—*preaffiliation, power and control, intimacy, differentiation, and separation.* The authors postulate that *closeness* is the central theme running through all five stages:

> From the moment that a number of individuals consent to be together in one spot, through the period during which they make their first tentative efforts to acquaint themselves with and find satisfaction in one another, on through the time when they share the intense feelings they have toward one another, until the dissolution of their common bond, they must struggle with how near they will come to one another emotionally. (Garland et al., 1973, pp. 28–29)

The following is a summary, with illustrations, of the five stages of the Boston model organized into three more general phases—*beginnings, middles,* and *endings.* As with most theories of human development, the stages are overlapping, interrelated, and subject to regressive pulls. Different types of groups might have more difficulty with different stages, and some may not progress beyond a certain stage. It should be noted that issues of group development are covered in greater depth in the forthcoming chapters and that the following summary is intended as an introduction on the subject.[9]

The Boston Model

Beginning Phase

Preaffiliation Stage

Establishing trust is a predominant feature of this early stage. Members relate to one another, to the worker and to the situation at "arms length" (characteristically referred to as approach–avoidance behavior). The worker provides structure, thereby reinforcing a sense of physical and emotional safety and invites trust gently in this, the early life of the group. The beginning of the group may be particularly difficult for adolescents

---

(continued) Balgopal and Vassil (1983), Anderson (1984), Garvin (1997), Northen (1988), Henry (1992), and Toseland and Rivas (1995).

[9] Detailed appendices at the end of Chapters 5, 7, and 9 (complements of Roselle Kurland's generous notes and class handouts), provide a more generic guideline of beginnings, middles, and endings along three dimensions: *where the members are, what needs to happen,* and *the role of the worker.*

who have come from unstable family environments, characterized by inconsistent handling and unpredictable comings and goings. When a lack of trust pervades one's life experience, one can expect that experience to be carried into the group. Practitioners must tune in to this reality, as well to the natural tendency for some (not all) adolescents to mistrust adults in positions of authority. The members gradually move toward making a preliminary commitment to the group (see Chapter 5).

When a group consists of adolescent members for whom a lack of trust is a major theme in their lives, the work in the earliest stage of the group may be particularly intense and subject to reworking with every shifting tide and transition that the group experiences. For example, growing up in a family with active alcoholism, untreated mental illness, or ongoing domestic violence, suggests an atmosphere of chronic unpredictability, chaos (quiet or otherwise), and fear. Physically abused adolescents generally grow up in two kinds of families: authoritarian (inflexible) and overindulgent (inconsistent) (Strauss, 1994). If this is your life, establishing instantaneous trust in a new situation is highly unlikely. Young people living in families that are seriously dysfunctional may be hypervigilant, endlessly surveying the scene for land mines. Structure, predictability, flexible handling, clarity, and consistency in the group over time, are all necessary precursors to developing a feeling of trust. Any appearance of trust with any less care is likely to be no more than a pleasant illusion.

The group's developmental progress is not dependent upon a complete resolution of each prior stage for each member. If a core issue in an adolescent's life is establishing a sense of trust, he/she may make some preliminary gains enabling him/her to move ahead and then find the need to "regress in the service of the ego" as new challenges present themselves. The worker must be tuned in to each member and to the group-as-a-whole in order to help the group along.

Middle Phase

Power and Control Stage

Group members, readying themselves to lock horns with the reality of the group may experience a normative crisis. This is the result of discovering that few of the conventions that they are accustomed to seem to apply in the new group. This stage is usually where the greatest number of group "dropouts" occur, leading to a membership crisis among the remaining members. The worker must project a sense of hope, lending a vision of success, and encouraging the others to "hang in there." Testing limits and experimenting with risky behavior is a normal aspect of adolescence. It is during this stage, just beyond establishing a reasonable degree of trust, that the members are likely to begin testing the limits of the group.

If the group is composed of members who have a history of acting-out behavior, poor internal controls, and little in the way of environmental support, the group worker should not expect to be afforded any special dispensation such because he/she is a "nice person."

> In a young-adolescent boys' group in a child guidance center located in what was once a mansion, one of the members led the others to the top of the winding staircase at meeting's end. He reached his long arms over the railing and grabbed hold of a chain connected to a crystal chandelier, one of the few artifacts left intact when the building changed hands. "Look," Armand said, as he gently shook it above the heads of people seated below in the reception area, "Wanna bet I can rip this out of the ceiling and drop it?" The others looked on with amused curiosity, eagerly anticipating what he might do next and how the worker might respond. No one said "Stop that," or "Someone might get hurt," or "Property might be destroyed," or anything like that. As the worker approached, he commented to Armand on "What a great grip you have" and calmly asked him to leave hold of the chandelier. This incident, at the worker's urging, became the topic of early discussion in the following meeting. The group discussed the incident and rules and expectations. After that, whenever he passed by the chandelier Armand would reach out and touch it, smiling all the while, but never taking it further than that.

"Hanging in there" in the midst of often trying behavior is something that workers must do with young people and in particular with those who have experienced too many adults' "bailing out" on them.

This is a transitional stage for the group. The members move from known to unknown territory, sensing the possibility of greater closeness yet ambivalent about what intimacy might mean for them. One or more sets of norms and values is gradually replaced by another. For example, in an adolescent group, the idea of calling an adult by his/her first name might seem foreign and uncomfortable. On the one hand it's too familiar (too close for comfort), and on the other hand, it is an inviting departure from the convention of referring to teachers and others in positions of authority by more formal titles. The use of certain language that is unacceptable in the classroom might be allowed in the new situation. The discussion of taboo subjects (i.e., explicit sexuality, race/ethnicity) becomes possible in the group, in contrast with outside experiences where such discussions may be forbidden. The power and control stage has also been referred to as "preintimacy," or another step toward closeness.

Intimacy Stage

The intimacy stage is characterized by mutual revelation and continued testing of the norms. As the members draw closer to one another and to the situation, it is not uncommon for them to associate to one another as if in a family-like gathering. Comparisons to siblings are made, and sensitivity about who seems to be getting the worker's attention—positive or negative—is evident. This may be a tenuous stage for members whose family lives are so chaotic and unpredictable that they will do almost anything—most often unconsciously intended—to gum up the works so that familiar family dynamics are replicated. The worker's focus is to clarify positive and negative feelings and to continue to give in the face of turmoil. The following example illustrates this tactic.

> In a young-adolescent group for boys with learning disabilities, a party was planned by the members. They carefully assigned roles to each member (i.e., who brings the food, paper plates and napkins, music, etc.). The main course was to be pepperoni pizza. When the boy who was responsible for delivering the pizza came in late and empty handed, he was ripe to receive the wrath of the group—"How could you forget?" "What an asshole." "Now you can't have any of the other stuff we brought." The plan had been to have a party. The worker, who felt disappointed as well, refocused the group on how to salvage the party. They decided to order pizza from a local place. One of them would accompany the worker in his car, and they'd have their pizza in 20 minutes. The spirit of the party wasn't doused, but the feelings of disappointment carried over to subsequent meetings where the group grappled with the problem. The planning of the group's next party revealed the group's integration of what had happened: their ownership of the problem as a group issue and their well-reasoned—reminder phone calls to ensure that no one would forget.

Differentiation Stage

As the group moves into the differentiation stage, an outsider might observe the members working together more easily and supporting one another. In this stage, members tend to express themselves more freely and have to contend with fewer power problems. There is a growing ability to problem solve, resolve conflicts, and make decisions. The worker's focus is to help the group to "run itself" and to evaluate its work as it tackles new problems or issues. By this time, the group has developed a clear identity of its own. Casual observers will know immediately when they see a group at this stage of development that *they are a group*. The group described above serves to illustrate this dynamic movement.

> In this group, the boys eventually moved from pizza to more elaborate spreads of Chinese food that required more skill in planning and execution. They asked to move the parties from their meeting room into the larger agency conference room so that they could eat at a table rather than on their laps, pump up the volume of their music, and play games that a smaller office setting would not accommodate. At the conclusion of these parties, it was the comments of the receptionist and other staff members, a validating audience, that provided the group with an objective and unsolicited impression of how far they had come together in their ability to plan, organize, and work together—as a group.

Ending Phase

Separation Stage

Leavetaking in the group may involve denial that the group is really ending, regression to earlier forms of negative behavior that have long been mastered, flight from the situation ("I'll leave you before you leave me"), and direct pleas for continuation based on arguments that the group is still needed. The worker's focus at this stage is tuning-in to the resistance and helping the members to separate by recapitulating and evaluating the experience.

Recapitulation may be a conscious process of reminiscing and or a reenactment of past behaviors, a remembering without awareness. Regressive behavior need not be viewed as unwanted. In fact, the practitioner might encourage controlled regression in the service of the group ego during the separation stage. For example, in one group that met in a room that contained a number of percussion instruments, the members created a spontaneous symphony of drum beats in their final meeting. The drums had been, for the most part covered-up and off limits prior to this. However, the worker loosened the rules, realizing that this shared activity was a fitting ending to the group. The worker can also help the members to establish or reinforce connections with resources outside of the group, to ease the transition, and to encourage alternative pursuits for participation and belonging. In the end the worker must be tuned in to a reawakening of feelings from past losses. Members have an opportunity for a further "working through" of such feelings as they are experienced in the context of the group's separation (see Chapter 9).

Workers using the above models (or other stage theories) as a frame of reference for their work should be aware that members tend to experience a degree of ambivalence in the transition from one stage to another, with each new stage representing an increased demand and level of maturity.[10]

CONCLUSION

This chapter has reviewed some of the historical roots, curative and dynamic forces, and developmental models of social work practice with groups. The ensuing chapters have been designed to provide an eclectic framework for group work practice with adolescents that is thoughtful, practical, innovative, and creative. Included are specific steps in preparing, starting, and conducting groups; examples of democratic, reciprocal, self-help transactions among group members and with the worker; illustrations of the use of social–recreational activity as well as reflection; and demonstrations of practice that pays attention to young people as citizens getting ready to participate as socially responsible young adults.

APPENDIX 3.1. A NOTE ON INTEGRATING THE BOSTON MODEL

Since it was first published in the mid-1960s, "A Model for Stages of Development in Social Work Groups," has been widely cited in the literature, often becoming the framework for articles published in professional journals. In my personal experience, anything that takes a while to develop, takes a while to integrate. And so it was over the years, working with countless groups of children, adolescents, and adults in various settings and with a variety of purposes that I came to gradually integrate this model into my practice.

I always felt a need to share the model with others and particularly with those who questioned the concept of group process and the value of group work with children and adolescents. I have crossed paths with many who seemed unable to get beyond the noise and the movement of the "kids' group." In one way or another, they always seemed to be asking me "What is going on in there?" Whether by direct query or dubiously raised eyebrow, the message always seemed the same: suspicion that anything worthwhile was really happening. Some years later, inspired by the noise and movement of a group of young adolescents at a roller skating rink, I wrote the following poem (Malekoff, 1994d) about the stages of group development à la the Boston model. I wrote it for myself to enhance further

---

[10]See Appendix 3.1 for "A Note on Integrating the Boston Model."

integration; for others, to help them understand, respect, and trust group process; and as a tribute to the scholars who developed this and other models of group development to guide practitioners like us.

WHAT IS GOING ON IN THERE? QUESTION AND RESPONSE

What Is Going On in There? (The Question)

We bring our kids to you,
To see what you can do;

They meet a bunch of others,
See, we are all their mothers;

We hear a lot of noise,
And, yes, boys will be boys;

But what is going on in there?
Nothing much we fear.

Our rooms are side by side,
And it's not my style to chide;

But your group's a bit too crazy,
And what you're doing's kind of hazy;

After all they're here to talk,
Yet all they do is squeal and squawk;

What it going on in there?
Nothing much we fear.

Hi I'm from the school,
And it's not my style to duel;

But Johnny's in your group,
And I know that you're no dupe;

But his dad has called on me,
to gain some clarity;

So what is going on in there?
Nothing much, I fear.

Now here we are alas,
Facing you en masse;

We haven't got all day,
So what have you to say;

About this thing called group,
This strange and foggy soup;

Just what is going on in there?
Nothing much, we fear.

What Is Going On in There? (The Response)

If you
really
wish to
know,
have a
seat,
don't plan
to go.

It will
take
awhile
to get,
but you

will
get it,
so
don't you
fret.

A group
begins
by building
trust,
chipping away
at the
surface crust.

Once
the uneasy
feeling is
lost,
a battle rages
for who's
the boss;
Kings and
Queens/ of what's
okay
and who
shall
have the
final say.

Once that's
clear
a moment
of calm,
is quickly
followed
by the
slapping of
palms.

A clan-
like feeling
fills
the air,
the
sharing
of
joy,
hope,
and
despair.

Family
dramas
are replayed,
so new
directions
can be
made.

Then in
a while
each
one
stands out,
confident

of his
own
special
clout.

By then
the group
has
discovered
its
pace,
a secret gathering
in a
special place.

Nothing
like it
has occurred
before,
a bond
that exists
beyond
the door.

And
finally
it's time
to say
good-bye,
a giggle,
a
tear,
a
hug,
a
sigh.

Hard to
accept,
easy to
deny,
the
group
is
gone
yet
forever
alive.

So you've
asked me

"What is
going
on in
there?"
I hope
that my
story has
helped
make it
clear.

Maybe
now

it is
easier
to see,
that a
group
has a
life,
just
like
you
and
like
me.

| Planning in Group Work
Where We Begin

Planning has been described as the "neglected component" of group development (Kurland, 1978, p. 173) . There is a high price to pay for poor planning in group work with adolescents. Among the consequences are excessive dropouts, frequent absences, chronic lateness, poor motivation, an absence of parental support, low cohesiveness, and a lack of successful outcomes (Northen, 1988).

In group work, planning is where we begin.

The planning model developed by Kurland (1978, 1982) consists of seven interrelated components, a practical framework to guide the practitioner's thinking and decision making as he/she prepares to provide a group service. The components are need, purpose, composition, structure, content, pregroup contact, and social/agency context. The purpose of this chapter is to present the planning model as it applies to group work with adolescents.[1]

FAILED GROUPS: MISINFORMATION OR POOR PLANNING?

Failed groups may be blamed on unmotivated and resistant adolescents or uncooperative and sabotaging parents when, all too often, the real culprit is poor planning. One example of a creative rationale for several failed groups came from a beleaguered practitioner in a mental health clinic. He

---

[1]My thanks to Roselle Kurland for her generosity in sharing her insights and teaching materials on the planning model. See Appendix 4.1 for guidelines and cautionary notes for the use of the model.

asserted that "the literature states that groups don't work for ADD kids" (Kurland & Malekoff, 1996). (ADD or ADHD is a short hand label for people diagnosed with Attention-Deficit/Hyperactivity Disorder.) The statement that "The literature states that groups don't work for ADD kids" is reminiscent of the evaluation studies of the mid-1960s to mid-1970s that portrayed both group work and case work as ineffective (Meyer, Borgatta, & Jones, 1973; Fischer, 1973a) and that sounded a death knell for the profession (Briar, 1967; Fischer, 1973b). But . . . as responses to those studies (Wood, 1978; Geismar, 1972) aptly pointed out, sweeping generalizations and global statements are not at all helpful. Without agreement among group members and between the worker and members about what *needs* a group will attempt to meet, without clarity in regard to group *purpose* and individual goals, the effectiveness of a group cannot begin to be measured or evaluated.

NEED

Need refers to individual desires, drives, problems, issues, and areas of concern that are both *unique* to individuals in the target population (i.e., symptoms, presenting problems, risk factors, life circumstances) and *universal* to individuals in the target population (i.e., normative adolescent issues, developmental tasks, the need to negotiate difficult environments). Understanding need is a prerequisite to establishing group purpose and setting individual goals and objectives.

Normative, Specific, and Contextual Needs

The needs of adolescents may be assessed within three principal and overlapping dimensions—normative needs, specific needs, and contextual needs—to ensure that the whole person is taken into consideration.

Normative Needs

Normative needs are those needs that are universal to a target population and that include the developmental tasks of its constituents. For example, most adolescents share the following needs: the need for information to make healthy decisions about sexuality and alcohol and drug use; the need to develop life skills to prepare oneself for the challenge of increased mobility and access to the social world (i.e., socialization, problem solving, conflict resolution); the need for opportunities to increase competence in the social, intellectual, physical, emotional, moral, and spiritual realms of the person; the need to discover healthy and nondestructive ways to separate from the family; the need to learn how to live peaceably and cooperatively with diverse populations; and the need, in an increasingly violent world, to learn how to be safe and to settle differences without destructive and/or fatal consequences.

Specific Needs

Specific needs are those needs that fit into a more narrow frame, reflecting the problems of particular individuals in their own unique life circumstances (e.g., situational crises and transitions such as separation, dislocation, illness, death; placement in an alternative educational setting or foster home; chemical dependency in the family; victim of child abuse; witness to domestic violence; living in poverty; etc.). Specific needs may be gleaned from certain broad categories including gender, race, age, ethnicity, language, socioeconomic status, sexual orientation, and handicapping condition to name a few. For example, many gay, lesbian, and bisexual youth share the unique problem of how to acknowledge one's homosexuality, the "coming out" process, in potentially hostile environments (i.e., family, school, community) (see Chapter 12).

Contextual Needs

Along with the normative and specific needs of the adolescent, is the concurrent *need to negotiate difficult environments.* The social environment and cultural context of the group member's life must always be considered when one is making a determination of need. For example, do prospective members have a close bond with a parent or other adults in their lives? Are they receiving needed support from the school system when they experience trouble achieving academic or social success? Are there adequate supervision, enriching activities, and growth-related experiences available to sustain them during the after-school hours, weekends, and during the summer? Are health services available for the prevention and treatment of disease? Is the community environment safe? Is the family safe?

Hanging Out

Need may be determined through a variety of means, ranging from such formal procedures as interviewing and testing (i.e.. medical, psychological, vocational) to more informal means such as *hanging out.* A worker doesn't just ask young people, "What do you need?" They can't answer that question. Rather he/she assumes a "participant–observer" role by hanging out and listening to what they talk about and do among themselves. The worker looks for what interests the adolescents, what concerns them, how they spend their time, and so on. A diagnostic picture alone, based solely on a personality assessment of what a potential group member is and ought to be is an inadequate measure of need and a poor predictor of behavior. As Schwartz (1971) reminds us, "People tend to do different things in different situations [and to be] different under different conditions" (p. 14). For example:

> An outreach worker in a community center noticed that one of the most popular after-school activities was playing cards. There was always a lot of laughter, kidding, and good spirits around the card table. Once gaining permission to join them at the table, he was able to learn a great deal in a relatively short time. For example, he discovered that their weekend social activities usually involved excessive alcohol use. The informality of the card games and the accompanying free-flowing conversation helped the worker to identify a variety of needs, many of which related to the area of alcohol/drug prevention (i.e., need for accurate information, need for strategies to resist negative peer pressure, need for and access to fun experiences that don't include alcohol during weekends). All of this information, gained through hanging out at the card table, helped the worker in his role of developing needed programs for the center's youth.

Hanging Out in the Clinic

In a more formal setting such as a clinic, opportunities for hanging out in the informal manner described above may not exist. Under such circumstances, it is through the worker's use of self in the pregroup interview, that an atmosphere of informality is created. This may be accomplished by adopting an interviewing style that is conversational in nature and relaxed in tone. Hanging out in the clinic refers less to physical setting than to psychological space. The attitude and style that the worker brings to the interview can either expand or constrict psychological space and thereby influence the degree of openness in the encounter. Contrary to what some might believe, a casual approach does not imply a lack of professionalism, rather a cultural accommodation to a group's comfort zone. For example, exploring an adolescent's interests is a natural approach to learning about adolescent problems and concerns.

> In a pregroup interview in a mental health clinic, an initially reticent 17-year-old girl eagerly talked about her favorite music. Leanne said that her favorite musicians were Nirvana, a rock group whose lead singer, Kurt Cobain, had killed himself with a shotgun blast while he was strung out on heroin. This topic naturally opened the door to a

discussion of drug and alcohol use, depression, and suicide. All of this contributed to identifying some of Leanne's problems and concerns in a nonintrusive manner.

Hanging Out in the School

In some settings the hanging out must occur after the group has already been composed. For example, on occasion schools will assign whole classes for group sessions. When the group has been predetermined, mutual exploration of need begins in the group itself. Some practitioners have described such groups (i.e., a special education class or a detention group) as being "destined to fail" because of their mandated status. In one instance a worker, a member of a peer supervision group, described her early experience in a predetermined group as follows:

> I was assigned to work with this group—no, actually, it's a class. Not quite a special ed class, but one with kids who are constantly in trouble. They just put them all together. When I come into the room, they basically ignore me. I try to find out what they want to do in the group, but mostly they just talk among themselves. It's like I'm interrupting them or something. One week I got so frustrated that I just "up and left" and told them that it didn't seem to me like they even wanted a group. I was really surprised later, when one of them sought me out and asked if I was going to come back. They wanted me to come back? I don't get it.

In exploring the problem in some depth in the supervision group, what became clear was that the students in this group were engaged in lively conversation the whole time that they were meeting, however in smaller subgroups of their own. There was a culture that the class was already accustomed to. The worker was attempting to break into their culture instead of first trying to join with it. It was recommended to the worker, that, rather than being intrusive by trying to engage the whole class on her terms, she simply sit with different subgroups each week, to hang out with them during the meeting, in order to begin to understand what their interests were and to begin to formulate what some of their concerns might be. This informal approach provides a way in which the worker can join the resistance and begin where the client group is.

Hanging Out in the Community

As a young VISTA volunteer placed in a low-income Mexican American community in Grand Island, Nebraska, I (a Jewish American whose roots are in Newark, New Jersey) learned about the community and some of the needs of its young people by hanging out in a variety of places.

In particular, I was invited to attend the weekend dances at the local Latin Club where I became familiar with traditional and contemporary Mexican music and dance. I integrated myself into the community by sharing meals in a variety of homes and participating in dinner conversation about children's likes and dislikes; their academic, social, recreational, and health needs; and parenting concerns. I attended marathon social gatherings (many of which were around the clock) and learned about the "inside scoop" on the politics of the community, the dreams of the young people and their parents, and the obstacles that obscured their vision. I talked informally with various indigenous community leaders (learning about the various factions in the community—the more conservative group who identified themselves as Mexican American and the progressive group who referred to themselves as Chicano), I visited with a leading Mexican American professor at the University of Nebraska in Lincoln who told me about a then recent study about unfulfilled aspirations among Mexican American high school students; and I read anything and everything I could get my hands on regarding Mexican history, culture, and migration to the United States.

I also learned from the landscape, the geography of this place. There were unpaved roads situated literally on the other side of the tracks; screaming whistles and the disquieting commotion of the passing freight trains that shook the foundations of the homes day and night; the all-too-frequent summertime tornado alerts; and the cadence of the auctioneers transacting business at the nearby cattle auctions. This was the furthest society imaginable from my own experience growing up in the urban and then suburban northeast. To many in my new community, at least in the beginning, I was seen simply as an Anglo, or so it seemed to me at the time.

There were no community centers or facilities for youth in this part of town. But there was an old church no longer in use. The VISTA volunteers, in collaboration with local community members, would later renovate the old church into a community center. This place became the setting in which I had the privilege of forming my first group—six teenagers, three boys and three girls, who called themselves *Los Seis*.

The goals of *Los Seis* included preventing alcohol abuse and strengthening the cultural identity of its members. The group's activities, in addition to alcohol education, were culturally oriented. The content included classes in Mexican history, literature, music, and dance taught by local people. The *Los Seis* mark of distinction came through the integration of traditional Mexican dance and alcohol prevention. As the group developed, the teens performed for groups across the state of Nebraska, spreading the message of strengthening one's cultural identity as a protective factor against the risk of alcohol abuse. *Los Seis* and the many people in the community who supported them, under the auspices of the then newly renovated community center, illustrate a group whose needs were first gleaned by a worker *hanging out*.

The Consequence of Failing to Assess Need

A study of failed groups concluded that groups prematurely dissolved when the practitioner attempted to promote purposes that members had not agreed to (Levinson, 1973). For example:

> A number of families living in a low-income housing project were being asked to leave because they had teenagers who were in trouble with the law. To prevent this problem from being repeated in the future, an outreach worker decided to develop a group of mothers of preteen children who were experiencing difficulty in school. The idea was a good one, however, after great effort on the worker's part, no one attended the meetings. (Roselle Kurland, personal communication, February 1994)

In the above example, had the worker polled the potential members about belonging to a group with her intended purpose, she would have discovered that they feared being identified by the Housing Authority as parents of "troublesome" children who might, as a result, face eviction. Had the worker tuned in to their fears, the outcome might have been different. *A worker cannot begin to formulate group purpose without first assessing need.*

PURPOSE

Purpose refers to the ends toward which the group is formed, the group's destination. It encompasses both the goals and objectives that the group will pursue collectively (i.e., group purpose) and the hopes, expectations, goals, and objectives that each group member holds for what he/she will gain from participating in the group. Purpose and goals are derived from need.

Clarity versus Confusion

Purpose refers to a group's destination—where we are headed. Problems arise when the purpose of the group is not clearly stated or if it is different for the members than it is for the worker or the agency. For example, a social work intern placed with an inner-city housing authority provides an illustration of the confusion generated by an obscure purpose.

> My supervisor somehow knew that I knew how to cook, and my assignment was to formulate a cooking group drawing the participants from a preexisting teen organization located in the project. After the third session, the group fell apart.
>
> I suppose I was never exactly sure of what the purpose of the group was supposed to be. My supervisor kept stressing how I was supposed to use the group as a vehicle for expression to verbalize conflicts that came up and issues that occurred in the girls' daily experiences. I never quite knew how to use the group for this purpose, and it was clear to me the girls saw it as nothing more than a cooking group. Was that what it was supposed to be, or wasn't it? (Roselle Kurland, personal communication, February 1994).

In contrast, in a violence prevention group composed of middle school students, the coworkers' clear understanding of purpose and what was contracted for with the members enabled them to set limits and provide containment and safety when personal sharing threatened to overwhelm the group.

> The group was halfway through a unit on child sexual abuse when one sixth grade girl began to tell about an incident that happened to her when she was three, involving a man who exposed himself to her. The group members were silent after her story. The leaders handled the situation by calling the incident an example of one type of sexual abuse, generalizing the situation, thanking the girl for her contribution, and moving ahead with the lesson. The group responded well to this intervention but the leaders did not consider the incident closed. After the group meeting, they talked with the girl and offered her an opportunity to discuss her experience in individual counseling. (Bilides, 1992, p. 137)

Simplicity versus Obfuscation

The group purpose must be stated *simply, clearly, and overtly.* Too often the worker and/or agency have an agenda that has not been shared with the members. In one adolescent chemical dependency day treatment program (which I will not name here, so as to spare any embarrassment), the "program manual" reportedly stated the following purpose for its day care groups:

> Provide a safe place for members to talk freely and to get to know one another. In the process, old defensive structures are examined; some are discarded;

others are altered and personality maturation and growth occurs. Thoughts regarding any evaluation of their acts, past, present, or future, are discussed. Awareness of linkage of past and present behavior are [sic] brought out in the open for correction. Group members provide additional input, support, criticism, and identification for each other. The group leader's task is to work in the direction of progressive verbal communication so that members experience the ability to talk about uncomfortable feelings rather than acting them out.

Is this clear or confusing?

In a class assignment[2] aimed at critically assessing the planning process of this agency's group program, the social work intern who cited the passage from the manual interviewed several practitioners who worked in the program. He discovered many variations and deviations from the "official purpose" stated in the program manual. Responses to the intern's question "What is the purpose of your group?" ranged from "To alleviate family problems" to "Release energy, get feedback from peers, and gain confidence" to "I'm not sure."

The same practitioners were then asked to evaluate how their groups were functioning. They described their groups as doing poorly, citing the number one reason as "poorly motivated group members." Aside from voluntary membership in clubs or teams, the truth is that most "troubled" or "in trouble" adolescents are mandated to group services not by the court system but, most often, by parents. When groups like this fail to thrive, practitioners often point to the mandated status of the members— "They're forced to be here, what do you expect?" In such cases, it is the members who are blamed for the group's failure, when it is they who are the victims of poor planning.

It is helpful to first organize one's thoughts about group purpose into the three dimensions of need—normative, specific, contextual—presented earlier and then to translate need into purpose/goals. For example, several adolescent boys were referred to a mental health center for their impulsive and destructive behavior. The purposes agreed to were (1) to learn to put some space, a reflective pause, between impulse and action; (2) to gain knowledge and improve problem solving related to normal teenage concerns including sexuality, alcohol, and drug use/abuse; and (3) to learn skills to better negotiate with parents, school personnel, and others. These purposes were specific enough to address the behavior that led to the referral (the presenting problem), broad enough to address normative needs of the members, and sensitive enough to the context of their lives to

---

[2]See Appendix 4.2 for a description of the assignment, a useful exercise in critically assessing an agency's or program's planning process.

address the need to negotiate difficult environments. Whereas the first goal is specific to the target population, the latter two goals can be applied to almost any adolescent group's statement of purpose.

Clarity of purpose exists when, according to Kurland (personal communication, February 1994),

1. The purpose of the group can be stated clearly and concisely by both the worker *and* group member.
2. The stated purpose is the *same* for both group member and worker.
3. The purpose is specific enough that both client and worker will know when it has been achieved.
4. The purpose is specific enough to provide directed implications for the group content.

It is expected that adolescents, particularly younger ones, will use different language than the practitioner in describing purpose. That's okay. Members need not parrot the group purpose as well-programmed robots but, rather, express their understanding through their own style and vernacular. In the above example, the first stated purpose was "To learn put some space, a reflective pause, between impulse and action." A group member might describe the same purpose in a variety of ways, for example, "Stopping to think before acting"; "Learning to keep my cool before going off"; or "Learning to chill."

Both practitioner and members need to be aware of the group's changing goals as it "zigs and zags through its life space" (Henry, 1992, p. 6). Purpose and goals may change over time depending upon the group's progress, capacity, urgency, changing circumstances, duration, and level of interest. In short-term groups, goals that are achievable in a limited time frame should be set. What is important to remember about shifting purposes is that they should continue to be mutually determined and generated by the felt needs of the group members. For example, a support group of parents of sexually abused younger adolescents modified their purpose after deciding that they wanted to engage in social action in order to change the legal system's handling of abuse victims and their families. Having helped one another, they shared a felt need to extend their help to others and make the "system" more humane for future victims and their families—attending to the near things and the far things.

Evaluation of Purpose and Goals

Establishing a group purpose/goals includes consideration of how goals and objectives will be measured.[3] Evaluation of outcomes is an ongoing process that can be done in a variety of ways including through pre- and posttest measures, gathering anecdotal data from various sources (parents, school officials), observation of individual functioning in the group, and by the self-reporting of members themselves through formal and/or informal means. For example, in the group of impulsive and destructive boys described above, one of the purposes was to address impulsive behavior and frustration tolerance—to put some space, a reflective pause, between impulse and action. The members would, from time to time, share the details of a fight that was avoided or property that was spared destruction, or wasn't. Changing behavior in the group itself was another source of data regarding progress. Videotaping was used to provide members with an opportunity to review and track their feelings and responses to stressful situations inside the group. Collateral contact with parents and involved others (i.e., school personnel) enabled the worker to determine whether any reported behavioral changes had been generalized or whether any problem behavior had escalated.

In a short-term group of high school students identified as being at risk for drug and alcohol abuse, a multimedia and discussion approach was used to teach about the impact of chemical dependency on the family and to familiarize the students with how and where to access resources for help in the community. Pregroup and postgroup questionnaires were used to evaluate what knowledge had been gained through the group experience. The effectiveness of the program was also evaluated by the number of students who followed up by asking for help with personal/family problems related to substance abuse or who referred their friends to the program.

Finally, the following five questions are offered to help practitioners tune in to areas that might be included in a critical evaluation of one's work after a group's termination.

1. Did this group serve the purpose for which it was designed?
2. Were there special problems in any phase of the group process?
3. To what degree was the mediating function of linking the members to the environment achieved?
4. What did the members say during termination that would lead the worker to modify his/her approach in the future?
5. What specific behavioral changes in group members give evidence of change? (Phillips & Markowitz, 1989, p. 89)[4]

---

[3]There is sometimes confusion as to the difference between goals and objectives. Goals may be thought of as ends or aims. Objectives are intermediate steps taken to reach goals.

[4]See Coyle (1937, pp. 208–209) for discussion on practitioner self-evaluation.

COMPOSITION

Composition refers to the number and characteristics of both members and workers who will participate in the group. An understanding of need and a tentative formulation of purpose are key determinants of group composition.

Homogeneous or Heterogeneous?

It is insufficient to design the composition of a group solely on criteria of homogeneity or heterogeneity. Practitioners forming groups must ask themselves: Homogeneous along what dimensions? Heterogeneous along what dimensions? Redl's (1951) law of optimum distance is a useful concept in making decisions about group composition. It states that "the group should be homogeneous in enough ways to ensure their stability and heterogeneous enough in ways to ensure their vitality" (Northen, 1988, pp. 122–123). Variables to consider in the mix include age range, race and ethnicity, gender, cognitive capacity, health and physique, toughness–shyness range, socioeconomic background, known group sensitivities (based on past group experiences), and intensity of problem behavior.

The size of a group should be a function of the interaction necessary to meet the aims of the group. For example, on a basketball team only five players can be on the court at a time. There is room for additional players to substitute throughout the game and to contribute to the team's development during practice. If there are more players than are needed to fill the roles of the team, then discontent is likely to follow. If there are too few players to adequately prepare during practice or to ensure that everyone is well rested during games, then the team's energy will be depleted. In contrast, in a chorus or orchestra, there is room for many more participants. Too few might dilute the quality of the performance.

The conventional wisdom about group size in group work is best summed up by Hartford: "The group must be small enough for each person to be heard and to contribute, and also to feel the impact of the group upon his beliefs and behaviors. However, groups should not be so small as to over-expose members or to provide too little stimulation" (1971, p. 162).

In my experience, adolescent groups of five to nine members are usually ideal. However, *groups of more or less can work just as well*. The illustrations throughout this book include groups that vary in size, from two to 20 or more. When the "ideal" cannot be achieved, whatever the variables, the group can still be a success. Workers should not abandon hope when the desired group of seven members turns out to be three, for example. When all of the ingredients for a recipe aren't available, the worker has a choice: Abandon hope and give up, or accept the challenge and be creative. Concoct your own recipe.

Regarding "recipes" for group composition, Henry (1992) warns that "much of the literature is inconclusive and contradictory when it comes to guiding the worker's behavior." Workers should be cautioned that the principles gleaned from experience and the literature may be useful for deciding on the initial composition of the group, but "they cannot reliably predict how persons will behave later in the life of the group" (pp. 4–5).[5] In determining group composition, the practitioner might consider two fundamental questions posed by Northen (1988, p. 123):

- Will a person benefit from the group?
- Will a person be able to participate in a way that his [or her] presence will not interfere seriously with the realization of the purpose of the group for other members?

A Case of Faulty Group Composition

The following vignette illustrates an example of faulty group composition with a group of patients, including several adolescents, who had cystic fibrosis.

> All patients in the medical center were seen as needing a support group and were invited by their physicians to attend the group. The age range was from 12 to 29. There was a clash of interest between the eight members who were in junior or senior high school and the adults. The younger members needed help with their feelings about the diagnosis, the effects of the illness on their peer relationships, and responses to the knowledge that most patients die at an early age. The adults were concerned with broader issues, such as discrimination in employment, education of the public about the illness, and lack of community resources for patients. Different needs led to conflict [that was] resolved by the young people dropping out of the group. When a social worker consulted with the leader in charge of the group, the decision was made to divide the members into two groups, based primarily on age. The young people returned, and each group then pursued its particular goals. (Northen, 1988, p. 123)

As this illustration demonstrates, it is inadvisable to compose a group based on diagnosis alone. People who are assigned similar diagnoses may have vastly divergent needs. Groups are formed to meet needs not arbitrarily to herd people together who share identical conditions or labels.

---

[5]See Chapter 14 for an illustration of an adolescent boy diagnosed with schizophrenia who, against the conventional wisdom of the literature and advice of colleagues, was place in group composed of higher-functioning boys.

Practitioner Composition and the Use of Coworkers: Is More Better?

Contrary to popular belief, more is not necessarily better when is comes to practitioner composition in groups. Coleadership of groups requires regular pregroup preparation and postgroup debriefing, especially for new partners, teams of workers who are not yet accustomed to one another, and partnerships in which the coworkers' experience, authority, and/or orientation are significantly different. One consequence of poorly conceived coworkership in adolescent groups is the fallout from unexpressed differences about the rules, structure, composition, content, or goals of the group.

Disagreement among Coleaders

Adolescent group members need practitioners who are able to communicate effectively with one another as they ride the shifting tides of the group. Feelings of confusion, anger, and fear are likely to be evoked in group members who reexperience dysfunctional family dynamics in the group itself (i.e., adult partners who don't know how to communicate effectively and address differences). The following case illustrates such a situation.

> In an after-school group for young-adolescent children of alcoholics, the staff became locked in a battle over the rules and activities of the group. Some were comfortable with the nonverbal activities that required greater physical movement and generated more noise. Others advocated for more verbal activities such as structured group discussion. The problem was not that there were differences of opinion. This is to be expected. The problem was that the adults were not addressing their concerns directly or effectively with one another. A "cold war" had commenced. This was, in effect, a repetition of the dysfunctional dynamics that many of the group members experienced at home, reinforcing their belief that even so-called "experts" cannot communicate and work together in a healthy and effective manner. Fortunately, the program administrator had her "ear to the ground" and picked up a rumble of discontent among the staff. She observed lots of whispering. What unfolded was a subtle process in which staff members secretly lined up allies, rather than address the problem directly and openly. The problem had gone underground. In a special meeting of the program staff, the problem was surfaced and openly confronted, helping to raise consciousness among staff and establishing more open and direct lines of communication about workers' concerns regarding the group. Although there were a few anxious

moments at first, staff were relieved to have the "secret" out in the open. The result was improved communication leading to a more consistent structure, more democratic decision making, and decreased power and control problems among staff and with members.

If individual work with difficult populations evokes strong, often unconscious, feelings in the worker, then imagine what a group with two or more workers is likely to stir up. Coleadership of groups with adolescents requires great care and attention to building a strong partnership.[6]

A Thoughtful Approach to Determining Group Composition

The following is an example of the process of determining group composition in an extensive group work program in an inner-city middle school.

> Teachers, school staff, and parents referred students. However, the most fruitful source of referrals was the students themselves. Various group services were presented by program staff in homeroom meetings throughout the school. A wide range of group choices were displayed for students' consideration (activity groups, discussion groups, groups on serious topics and on fun topics, boys' groups, girls' groups, co-ed groups, and so on). The idea was to attract all students and not to further marginalize or pathologize those who have been labeled as "bad" or "defective." All students receive a form in which they prioritize their choices. (Bilides, 1992, p. 133)

A careful review process followed the homeroom meetings, including pregroup interviews with all prospective group members.

> Selection of group members is based on historical and clinical information gleaned from the interview and on the list of priorities. The group work coordinator tries to balance membership with regard to race or ethnicity, age, and, for co-ed groups, gender. An assessment is also made of each student's readiness for the group, based on past group experience, family situation, and school adjustment. (p. 133)

This thoughtful and painstaking process of mutually determining group composition, emphasizes the value of respecting young people's dignity and right to self-determination.

---

[6]Partnership, in this context, also refers to staff who "share" cases (i.e., one worker sees the child, and another sees the parents) and collaborators from different systems. When service responsibilities are shared, it is the responsibility of the collaborating workers/systems to join in the best interest of the client(s). This requires the development of an effective way of addressing differences.

STRUCTURE

Structure refers to both the concrete arrangements the worker makes to facilitate the actual conduct of the group (i.e., space, time, resources, finances) and initial steps the worker takes toward constructing parameters for the emotional security of group members (i.e., privacy, confidentiality, guidelines for contact with parents and relevant others, and other ground rules for ensuring safety—physical and emotional—in the group).

The Logistics of Caring

Structure refers to the concrete arrangements that contribute a sense of order, stability, and consistency in the group. This is vital for all youth, and particularly for those who grow up in unstable environments. The elements of structure include: the physical facility (space, equipment, room design and set-up, handicapped accessibility, assurance of privacy); time (when the group meets, how long each meeting lasts, and over what period of time); security (rules for emotional and physical safety and confidentiality); collateral involvement (clarity regarding the nature of involvement with parents and other systems with a stake in the members and the group service); availability of support services (such as child care for teen parents); transportation needs; and agency procedures and policies to which group members are expected to adhere.

Redl and Wineman (1952) suggest basic ingredients for a sound youth-care environment. Drawn from their considerable experience in residential settings for troubled youth, these descriptions read as a useful structural guideline for practitioners working in a myriad of settings with any population of young people:

> A house (or meeting place) that smiles; props which invite; space which allows; routines which relax; a program which satisfies; adults who protect; symptom tolerance guaranteed; old satisfaction channels respected; rich flow of tax-free love and gratification grants; leeway for regression and escape; freedom from traumatic handling; ample flexibility and emergency help; and cultivation of group emotional securities. (Redl & Wineman, 1952)

Some may view this thoughtful description and feel that they lack the support and or resources to bring it to life. First, one must value the depth of feeling and insight into young people's needs that such a guideline represents. Second, one must creatively apply this guideline in order to give it life, even in the absence of an ideal facility and scant resources. Expanding psychological and relational space in limited physical spaces is possible. A flexible approach and relaxed attitude by the worker is a good beginning. Most of us have known someone (maybe yourself) who grew up in a tight space with little in the way of material advantage. But those were places that "smiled," with props that "invited," and space that "allowed." And then too we have known someone (maybe yourself) who had all measure of advantage yet felt confined, stifled.

Advocacy is the worker's duty. Where needed resources and support are lacking, it is the responsibility of the worker to study the situation, develop a plan of action (perhaps with the group), and implement the plan. Enabling an adolescent group to empower itself to meet its own needs by gaining access to needed resources can be a pivotal aspect to the experience of the group as a whole.

Rule Setting: What, When, and by Whom?

Whose Rules?

Some rules must be established from the start, such as guidelines for confidentiality and safety. How specific one gets depends on the group, the worker, and the agency. Rules and norms for behavior will continue to be negotiated throughout the life of the group. To the surprise of some, adolescents are generally thoughtful (sometimes rigid) in determining rules once given the chance to contribute. In an early-adolescent group composed of boys who were referred to a mental health center after exhibiting poor social judgment and impulse control, the members developed the following guidelines for themselves after several months together:

Wednesday Evening Boys' Group—Guidelines

- Find something to talk about and stay on it.
- Contribute to the conversation and group.
- Think of something important to say.
- Keep eye contact with all members.
- Talk nicely, be friendly, don't act like an imbecile.
- Make facial expressions when you speak to make conversation more interesting.
- Express yourself, make yourself clear.
- Give other group members a chance to contribute.
- Try to find out the main idea of the discussion.
- One person speaks at a time.

I _____ agree to follow these rules as best as I can.
Signature _____ Date _____

Had such guidelines been provided for this group at the outset, perhaps as a *framework for improved social functioning,* they would have missed the opportunity to draw these ideas from their own experiences (including with one another in the group) and consequently, the opportunity to own them as opposed to rebelling against them. In another group, a coed community service club in a low-income community, the following ground rules that the group developed were posted on the wall in their meeting place:

Project Synergy Ground Rules

1 Everyone be quiet when someone is talking.
2. Respect each other.
3. Listen attentively.
4. Get everyone to talk.
5. Treat others the way you want to be treated.
6. Support others' ideas even if you disagree.
7. No dissing when someone is talking.
8. No cursing.

As the above examples suggest, the development of ground rules for the group provides members with a great opportunity to clarify values as well as provides structure and order. When a group formulates its own set of rules, as above, they become a policy statement of sorts, reflecting the wishes of the group and providing the members with the challenge of living up to and enforcing these rules.

The Sound and Fury of Adolescent Groups: Setting Limits

A common concern of group workers is where to set limits on behavior and language. It is not uncommon for adolescent groups (with some variation between groups and within groups) to be noisy, in motion, boisterous, raw, and uncensored. In my experience, this behavior, in general, is less a consequence of power and control and more a result of the worker's having established a sense of trust and intimacy in the group. The power and control problems are often a consequence of the worker not understanding this. As the group members become closer to one another and become more invested in the experience, the group begins to exude the feel and style of a natural group of adolescents—that is, they start to feel "at home" in the group, free to "kick their feet up," and "let it all hang out."

Practitioners need to make a distinction between what Redl and Wineman (1952) refer to as "reasonably controlled wildness" and "total destruction or panic producing breakdown of behavioral controls" (p. 91). Regarding language "swearing does not [necessarily] denote hostility, insult, or the like, but [can be] a cultural pattern for vehement or emphatic expression of positive feeling, sheer good spirits, or pleasure" (p. 95).

An almost-anything-goes policy is unwise, as is the arbitrary use of authority. Reasonable limits are important. Practitioners must carefully consider what limits are nonnegotiable from the start and what limits can be developed collaboratively with members.[7] One's own values and personal code of behavior, the policies of the agency, the sensibilities (and experience with adolescents) of colleagues who will be within earshot of the group, the needs of the group members, and the values and expectations of their parents and other adult stakeholders are just a few of the variables that should go into one's decision making regarding limits.

When Rules are Broken

In an adolescent boys' group in a mental health clinic there were clear rules about no physical fighting in the group and no destruction of property. At the end of one meeting, a conflict between two members spilled over, outside of the group, to the front of the building. The two adversaries taunted and threatened one another in a menacing fashion, using a creative combination of four-letter words to punctuate their points. All of this erupted as younger children and families tried to make their way into the building. The conflict was eventually defused with the intervention of the worker, the other members, and the combatants' parents. As the next meeting commenced, the members, suffering from a case of selective and collective amnesia, swore that they couldn't remember anything of any significance happening the week before. Nevertheless, and to the dismay of all of the boys, the bulk of the time was spent reviewing the incident, clarifying rules, and renegotiating them to include behavior outside of the group meeting room. A document was drafted outlining the rules and consequences for breaking them. It was signed by all members who wished to continue in the group. All members signed.

If the worker is discerning in his/her decisions about what behavior to confront and what to ignore, the group members have a greater chance of internalizing standards of behavior and regulating themselves. Adolescent group members are usually able to recognize the difference between

---

[7]See Setterberg (1991) and Cerda, Nemiroff, and Richmond (1991) for discussions on the importance of clear boundaries and consistent rules, explicit and enforced, in inpatient therapy groups with adolescents.

workers who exercise their authority fairly and those who do capriciously or dictatorially. By the way, practitioners working with adolescents should welcome rather than dread situations in which standards and values are challenged by group members.

Confidentiality and Context

Confidentiality in groups is not static but rather a dynamic process in which the group, in fact, exercises its own regulatory powers. For example:

> A worker with a group of boys in foster care found himself repeatedly charged with messages to take back to the caseworkers to be sure they understood what had happened in the group. Another found it impossible to prevent communication between her girls and their parents about what was happening in both the daughter and the parent groups. Furthermore, the sharing of information, far from creating the problems she expected, actually seemed to contribute greatly to the process in both groups. (Schwartz, 1971, p. 20)

In adolescent groups, the setting may contribute to how confidentiality is handled. For instance, in a residential setting, groups consist of members who are in close proximity to one another day and night. In a school setting, in addition to familiarity, group members are likely to come into contact with one another outside of the group in a variety of situations throughout the week. The risks associated with disclosure in these instances are greater than in settings and circumstances where the members come together as strangers and have no contact with one another outside of the group. One setting is not superior to another; however different situations require different emphases and approaches to negotiating privacy and confidentiality.

Laying out all of the rules in a neat package from the start deprives the group of a valuable experience in problem solving, decision making, negotiating with authority, and clarifying values. The worker's role in fostering a democratic group experience is to cultivate a group environment that values the expression of difference, dissent, and mutual respect.

CONTENT

Content refers to the means that will be used to achieve the purpose for which the group is formed. It encompasses what is done in the group, how it is done, and why it is done. Content is not to be confused with purpose. Purpose is where the group and its members are headed. Content is the means or activities the group uses to get there—what the group does.

What Are We Going to Do in This Group?

Ask someone who is working with a group: "What is the purpose of your group?" The answer will be revealing. He/she may respond by saying, "Socialization," "Recreation," "Rap," "Therapy," "Education," "Community service," or "Support." All of these responses represent what a group does—the content of the group. These descriptions, however, do not adequately define the purpose for which the group is formed: rap about what, to what end?; socialize in what way for what purpose?; what kind of therapy with what goals?; support through what means for what aim?; psychoeducation taught through what means for what ends?; and so on. Content may also include field trips, outside speakers, discussion, art, dance, role playing, psychodrama, wilderness trips, parties, arts and crafts projects, cooking, structured exercises, to name just a few (see Chapter 8).

Content is often confused with purpose. Purpose refers to what the group aims to achieve, its goals, where the group is headed. Content refers to *what the group does* to reach its goals. Too often what the group does has nothing to do with where it's headed. Instead, what it does is to keep the group busy and the practitioner free of anxiety. It is essential that content and purpose are integrally connected. The following is an example of *Los Seis,* a group that was introduced earlier in the chapter, to illustrate the interrelationship between purpose and content:

In *Los Seis,* the coed group of six Mexican American teenagers, the group purposes included to reduce their risk of alcohol abuse and alcoholism, to strengthen the members' cultural identity, and to have fun. The activities in the group included informal rap sessions about alcohol and alcoholism, guest speakers, field trips to rehabilitation centers, videotapes, developing their own photographic slides on alcohol and advertising, and a variety of culturally oriented activities (e.g., dancing, music, poetry, art, drama). One of the major objectives of the group was to organize a community presentation to include a homemade slide show on alcoholism, Mexican dance and clothing, and culturally oriented poetry readings. The presentation was conceived as a community service intended to raise consciousness about the growing problem of alcoholism in the local community and the importance of cultural identity, competence, and involvement as a counterforce. It was well attended by community members of all ages. Most importantly, many adults in the community contributed to the effort (e.g., teaching dance and history, helping with rehearsals, sewing traditional outfits). After the event, one of the group members, a 15-year-old boy whose father had allowed him to use his cherished sombrero for the program, recalled, "When I got home my father told me he was proud of me. I don't think he ever told me that before." A nice ending—or beginning—and a sad reality.

In my experience working with troubled youth for more than 20 years, one of the greatest barriers is convincing parents and colleagues across the allied professions that the content of the group, if it happens not to be exclusively a serious and earnest discussion about profound intrapsychic and interpersonal matters of the direst nature, is still valid. The laughter, commotion, and lively give-and-take of groups of adolescents are often followed by an inquisition of sorts: "Just what is going on in there anyway?" "Nothing serious, I'm sure." "It seems like he's having a good time, but he needs more than a socialization group." The sad reality is that this refrain is heard almost as often from uninitiated professionals as parents. A well-timed raised eyebrow speaks volumes to the group worker working with a group of noisy adolescents in a professionally unsupportive environment. (See poem "What Is Going On in There?" in Appendix 3.1.)

PREGROUP CONTACT

Pregroup contact refers to the securing of appropriate members for the group that is being planned and the preparation for their participation in the group. In groups with children and adolescents, pregroup contact most often requires some preliminary work with parents. Failure to adequately address this aspect of pregroup contact can thwart an otherwise excellent plan (see Chapter 6).

Pregroup contact involves *recruitment* (i.e., identifying and reaching out) of appropriate members for the group that is being planned and *pregroup interviewing* to prepare them for their participation in the group. Whenever possible, potential group members should be interviewed individually, by the worker, prior to the start of the group to begin to establish a relationship and preliminary commitment. The pregroup interview should include the following functions:

- *Assessment:* evaluating needs, problems, concerns, life situation, and strengths.
- *Screening:* determining potential group member's suitability for the group.
- *Engagement:* developing a beginning working alliance with the prospective members and parents.
- *Education:* providing information about the value of groups and how they function to meet needs.

- *Orientation:* briefing about the specific group service being offered, including the workers ideas about the tentative purpose of the group.
- *Contracting:* laying the groundwork for a working agreement by identifying individual, worker, and agency purposes/goals; clarifying procedures and methods to be used in the group; and reviewing expectations of the worker and member.

The following is an account of pregroup interviewing with potential members of a sexuality group for adolescent girls (Henry, 1992).

> The main purpose of the group, as I perceived it, would be to enhance the girls' search for identity and striving for personal growth through helping them to understand new dimensions of themselves. My first task . . . involved the recruitment of members. I contacted the nurse at the school, spelled out the purpose I had in mind, and asked for her help in identifying potential members who could use such a group. She agreed to provide me with the names of 10 girls between the ages of 12 and 14 who she felt would benefit from the group experience.
>
> The next step in the process involved my meeting individually with each of the girls. These individual sessions served a fourfold purpose: (1) to make known my intended purposes for the group in order to determine the girls' interest in becoming involved in the group experience; (2) to involve the girls in making decisions concerning the day and time for the group meeting; (3) to establish a verbal contract with each of the girls in order to reach an agreement about our goals and expectations; and (4) to make use of relationship to begin engaging each of the girls in the group experience. At the conclusion of the individual sessions, all the girls had expressed an interest in taking part in the group and all appeared to be suitable for group membership. (p. 50)

Tuning In to Feelings about Joining a New Group

Pregroup interviewing begins with the practitioner using the skill of anticipatory empathy to tune in to the potential group member's expectations, hopes, and fears in anticipation of beginning the group.[8] For example, some adolescents may experience feelings of self-doubt, rejection, and distrust that are reawakened by memories of unsatisfying group experiences in other contexts. By tuning in to the individual's "group sensitivities," the worker takes an important step toward allaying fears

---

[8]See Schwartz (1976) for details on the "tuning in" phase of group work. He organizes his thinking about this preparatory phase along three interrelated dimensions: (1) what you, the worker, are anticipating, (2) what you expect to happen, and (3) what skills are necessary.

and creating a vision about how the new situation can be different from the old.

Adolescents respect adults who don't "beat around the bush" or play "head games" with them. During pregroup interviewing, in addition to tuning in, the worker should be straightforward about the aims and means of the group, inviting open discussion and dissent—an important step towards the development of a democratic experience in the group.

A common area of concern for adolescents is whether they will be able (or willing) to meet the demands and expectations of the new situation—that is, "Will I have to talk in the group?" or "What will I have to do in the group?" The concepts of "mutual aid" and "use of activity" can be introduced to demystify and normalize the group experience. Many youth are surprised and relieved to discover that, in a group, what one has to *offer* is as important as what one might receive. In addition, prospective members' imaginative potential, creative energy, and investment in the enterprise can be stimulated by discovering that "talking about problems" is but one activity available to the group.

Pregroup Interviewing on the Road

Following is an account of a worker's extensive pregroup contact with a 12-year-old boy with a chronic medical illness (polio), emphasizing the skill, sensitivity, and patience that the practitioner brings to the situation (Kolodny, 1976).

> The worker made several home visits in which he would begin by chatting with Eric and his Mom and then take a drive with Eric, stopping for a burger and shake along the way. Eric was socially isolated since his return from the hospital and faced the challenge of adjusting to everyday life in the neighborhood. He had to get around on crutches and braces, unable to participate in the usual activities of an early-adolescent youngster. Eric was reticent about the group that was to be composed of him and other boys from the neighborhood. He would have to agree to allow the social worker to approach school personnel to get the ball rolling. Eric was anxious and ambivalent about the worker's plans to meet with the principal. He uneasily revealed feeling ashamed and embarrassed that others might discover that he doesn't have any friends. A very painful subject for Eric, he was only able to discuss it haltingly and for just a few moments at a time. The worker patiently did his best to reassure him that there was no rush to form the club, that they could take their time.

There may be concern that extensive contact prior to joining the group will inhibit the prospective member's use of the group and cause him/her to become overly dependent on the worker. However there are situations in which a series of pregroup interviews are necessary for the youngster to even consider becoming involved in a group. By the next home visit, Eric's ambivalence had shifted slightly in favor of moving forward with the group.

> We talked of how hard it was for some people to make friends and related this to his many years of hospitalization and real lack of opportunity. After about five or ten minutes there was a lull in the conversation during which time he wanted to listen to the radio . . . then suddenly he blurted out in a rather loud voice, which somewhat surprised me, "Better get some club members and get the club started" (p. 50)

The worker then met with school personnel, and the group was on its way to being formed.

As this final vignette illustrates, success in pregroup contact with adolescents includes *careful preparation, anticipation of ambivalent feelings, and patience and respect for the hesitance with which some youngsters may approach joining a group.*

SOCIAL AND AGENCY CONTEXT

Social/agency context refers to the conditions existing in the agency or host setting and the wider community that may have an impact on worker action and on the group that is being formed.

Reinforcing the Frame

The mission of the host agency and its philosophy, policies, culture, and attitude toward group work will all play a major role in the successful development or failure of a group service. The agency, in turn, is influenced by a broader context including the community in which the agency exists and the communities served by the agency, the institutions that provide funding for the agency (i.e., governmental, private, insurance), and the organization of the profession into fields of practice.[9]

How resources (i.e., human, financial, space, time, equipment) are allocated provides some insight into what an organization values. The worker's role in planning includes assessing the social/agency context as it relates to a proposed group service, understanding where group work fits

[9]See Northen (1988) for a discussion of social context and fields of practice including family and child welfare, neighborhood services, school social work, mental health, health, law and justice, and occupational social work (pp. 106–113).

into the agency's hierarchy of values, identifying obstacles that need to be overcome to provide a group service, and advocating for change as needed.

McKnight (1987) paints a fascinating portrait of the contrast between an institution's limitations and a community association's strengths. Although they are presented in general terms that fail to capture the unique character of the specific case, his insights are useful for group workers in assessing the agency context of their work. He contends that institutions are structured to control people and community associations to act through consent, with institutions aiming for perfection, and community associations accepting fallibility and embracing diversity; institutions organized hierarchically, and community associations allowing for shared leadership and mutual problem solving; and institutions responding to crises through bureaucratic design, and community associations responding quickly and creatively. McKnight concludes that such bipolarity may contribute to institutions providing the opposite of what they are intended for, that is, "crime-producing corrections systems, sickness-making health systems, stupid-making school systems" (p. 57). There are, of course, institutional exceptions in which the values he attributes to community associations are clearly valued in agencies (see Levine, 1991, as an example).

What kind of setting would be ideal for group work? Do any of the following elements of community life apply to the organizations in which you work?

- *Capacity:* the fullness of each member to contribute.
- *Collective effort:* shared work that requires many people's talents.
- *Informality:* authentic, unmanaged relationships, care, not service.
- *Stories:* reaching back into common histories and individual experiences for knowledge about truth and direction for the future.
- *Celebration:* associations in community celebrated because they operate by consent and have the luxury of allowing joyfulness to join them in their endeavors.
- *Tragedy:* the explicit common knowledge of tragedy, death, suffering. To be in community is to be part of ritual, lamentation, and celebration of our fallibility. (McKnight, 1987, as quoted in Lewis, 1992, p. 282)

Schwartz's (1971) vision of group work is "a collection of people who need each other in order to work on certain common tasks, in an agency that is hospitable to those tasks," with the practitioner's central function being "to mediate the engagement of client need and agency service" (pp. 7, 10). An agency's values trickle down to the group, either enhancing or contaminating the experience. When the values of the agency and the conditions required to meet the needs of the group are out of sync, it becomes the worker's function to seek common ground and help the group and the agency "to rediscover their stake in one another" (Gitterman, 1971, p. 49).

As the remaining chapters of this book unfold, it is the vision of community life, as described above, that I aim to reinforce and bring to life in the various and diverse settings in which the group worker and the adolescent meet.

CONCLUSION

Thoughtful and sound planning is indispensable for the development of a successful group. The seven components described herein—need, purpose, composition, structure, content, pregroup contact, and social/agency context—provide a framework for getting started and for troubleshooting once a group is in progress. A group begins with an idea imaginatively considered. Planning is all about nurturing ideas and taking steps to transform the imagined into reality. Good groups don't appear by magic or as the result of charismatic leadership. It takes great care and careful preparation to grow a good group.

APPENDIX 4.1. GUIDELINES AND CAUTIONARY NOTES FOR USE OF THE PLANNING MODEL

It should be noted that the planning model is not only useful for getting started, it is also an invaluable tool for ongoing assessment and trouble shooting in the group. Practitioners who use this model should keep the following four key points in mind (Roselle Kurland, personal communication, 1994):

1. Think about the components concurrently. A worker needs to think concurrently about the seven components as planning for a group proceeds. The seven components of the model are interdependent and overlapping. Decisions made in regard to one component will affect decisions about the others.
2. Don't use the model as a checklist. The model is meant to serve as a guide to the thinking of the worker in planning for a group. It presents areas for worker consideration, decision making, and action as plans for a group are made. It is not meant as a checklist. In fact, it is unlikely that the worker will ever be able to resolve completely the many decisions to be made around each component of the model.
3. Use the model flexibly. The model needs to be used with flexibility by the worker. In different groups, different factors contained in the model will assume different degrees of priority and importance. Not every factor will be of equal importance. In some groups some factors will assume great

importance, whereas in others, the same factors will be of little consequence. Such differences are related to the particular situation confronting
the worker and are also closely related to the worker's own theoretical
approach to practice.

4. Customize the model to suit the particular group. Using the worker's own
judgment and practice approach, the model needs to be individualized. It
is hoped that use of the model will help the worker to see which areas are
ones around which there is uncertainty in planning for a particular group.
If, for instance, use of the model highlighted the fact that group size was
a key factor in planning for a particular group, the worker would then
need to refer to the literature that addresses the factor of group size.

APPENDIX 4.2. ASSESSING PLANNING

The following is an exercise designed to assess the quality of planning for groups
in an agency and/or program.

- Identify your agency/host setting.
- State the agency's/host setting's mission.
- Describe the philosophy and attitudes toward work with groups (use both
  your experience as well as interviews with key agency personnel).
- Assess the agency's/host setting's group services from a planning perspective. What are the strengths and deficits of the way that groups are
  planned? How thorough is the planning process? Is it uniform or does it
  vary from worker to worker? From group to group? (Interview staff to
  make a determination.) Use examples to illustrate.
- Critique the impact of planning, as it is practiced in your agency/host
  setting, on the overall group program.

Please note: If your agency/host setting does not have a group program per se, you
should assess the group services that do exist. Or you may assess the group services
within a particular agency program (i.e., alcoholism program, eating disorders
program, adolescent program). If there are no groups at all, you can assess an
adjunctive setting with which you are involved.

The purpose of this investigation is to exercise your critical thinking capacity
as it pertains to group planning. As you move further into the field of practice,
you will experience various levels of care in the implementation of group services.
As practitioners with knowledge in the practice of group work, you will be
confronted with the challenge of influencing programs and institutions whose
group programs might benefit from a more thoughtful process of planning.
Assessing what exists with a critical eye is the first step in this process.

| Good Beginnings
in Group Work

Socializing Adolescents
into the Group Culture

The world is full of the sound of waves
The little fishes abandoning themselves to the waves
dance and sing and play, but who knows the
heart of the sea, a hundred feet down?
Who knows its depth?

—*E. Yoshikawa (1981)*

The process of socializing adolescents into the group culture can be a challenging and exciting experience for the group worker. It is quite often, however, a baffling and frustrating ordeal. To begin with, the younger adolescent who is somewhere between the fifth and eighth grades balks at the slightest scent of play therapy, suspicious of the ulterior motive that goes unquestioned by the younger child. Their suspicion about play is surpassed only by a profound distaste for talk, especially insight-oriented talk. If play and talk are taboo, then what is a group worker left to do when faced with what remains, often an unsettling montage of prolonged silences, contagious giggling, and cacophonous noisemaking?

As younger adolescents move gradually and almost imperceptibly into their middle and then later teenage years, their propensity for group discussion increases incrementally. However, no appearance of sophistication in adolescence—verbal, physical, or otherwise—can completely obscure their child-like spirit, if conditions in the group allow for its emergence. It is a force that alternately delights and frustrates group

This chapter is a revised and updated version of Malekoff (1984). Adapted by permission of The Haworth Press, Inc.

workers who are trying their best to "pull something meaningful together." Unfortunately, in too many young people today, there appears a kind of deadly seriousness born of lost innocence and doused spirits. The group can provide the impetus for rekindling the child-like spirit, a place where play and work merge, and fun is not dismissed as a meaningless pursuit. How the group begins is critical to the rise of a cultural and spiritual renaissance for such youngsters.

The purpose of this chapter is to sensitize readers to the experience of the adolescent who is about to begin a new group and to familiarize the group worker with a framework for acculturating new members into the group life.[1] The framework includes five interrelated themes:

- Discovering the group purpose.
- Searching for common ground.
- Awareness of the normative crisis.
- Promotion of playfulness.
- Establishment of group rituals.

Many workers involved with adolescents in groups have described experiencing a recurrent feeling of futility (Levine, 1979). One must come to realize that group meetings with adolescents will rarely proceed in accordance with *Robert's Rules of Order*. The experience is more akin to being exiled on to the canvas of an abstract painting during its creation or being hurled into the unpatterned harmonies of a jam session (Katz & Longden, 1983). Therefore the aforementioned five-point mosaic would be incomplete without acknowledging the constant static, the unchannelled energy that pervades the group meeting:

> A combination of the extreme use of denial and the seemingly chaotic process of adolescent groups lead many adults to despair that nothing meaningful is or can be accomplished. Practitioners have left many adolescent group meetings feeling that they could have been doing something more productive with their time. (Levine, 1979, p. 23)

Flashes

The worker must gauge him/herself in order to find the necessary balance between tolerance and over control. He/she must also move quickly so as not to miss what's flashing by, for it is the flashes that provide the spark to ignite the group. As one philosopher mused:

---

[1]See Appendix 5.1 for a detailed summary of the "beginning phase" of group work (compliments of Roselle Kurland).

That which is unique and worthwhile
in us makes itself felt
only in flashes.
If we do not know how to catch
and savor these flashes,
we are without growth and
without exhilaration.
—E. Hoffer (in Tomkins, 1968, p. 88)

Following careful planning and pregroup contact with prospective members and their parents and relevant others, the group begins. When the group meets for the first time there is much confusion about "what we're all up to." Typical opening remarks, despite careful preparation, include "Why are we here?", "When is this class going to be over?", "I told my mom that this is the last time I'm coming," and "Is this room bugged?" The nonverbal behavior may include the following: restrained restlessness (don't fret, unrestrained restlessness is on its way), darting eyes (searching for listening devices or the titles of the "shrink's" books), front legs of all chairs elevated about one foot off the floor and back rests planted firmly on the wall (the wall soon reveals an indelible signature of back rest compressions), and the subtle scavenger hunt for an object to hold on to (and eventually mangle and throw), are but a few. When the verbal and nonverbal behavior are integrated, one observes caution, apprehension, curiosity, suspicion, and restrained energy. All of this seems to occur instantaneously, yet perpetually. A glance at the clock reveals that only a minute has passed.

Down Home Group Work: Life on the Farm as a Frame of Reference

In a chemical dependency treatment and prevention program for youth at-risk in a low-income minority community, many of the staff in the agency, principally individual and family workers, expressed frustration with the slow start of the daily after-school group meetings. At a special team meeting to address their concerns, staff members did acknowledge that, in time, the group members would settle down. One of the group workers, an African American woman who had grown up on a farm, used a metaphor from her early life experience to help the staff tune in more empathically and become more patient (Nellie Taylor-Walthrust, personal communication, 1995). No measure of theoretical explanation could match the natural quality and wisdom generated from her narrative presentation. She began by asking the staff, "Did any of you ever live on a farm? . . . No? . . . Well, I did, and when you grow up on a farm, you notice certain things:"

"In the after-school program I've noticed certain behavior by a number of the youngsters each time they come to the group [typically groups of 8 to 15 members, boys and girls, mixed racially, and divided on separate days into younger and middle adolescent groupings]. Whether they arrive early, or after the group has already begun, they perform a certain ritual before connecting more consciously with what is going on in the group. It seems to go something like this: They move the chairs several times, place certain objects—coat, sweater, bookbag—in a certain position on or near the chair, collect objects from their pockets or begin to crumple paper and place it in the waste basket, and so on. When confronted by a group worker or other members about their distracting behavior, they often reply, 'Okay, just one minute,' meaning that they hadn't quite completed their 'settling in' process.

"After weeks of observation, recognizing that this behavior was consistent, I was reminded that I had seen chickens perform similar rituals before laying eggs. I often wondered why they didn't simply walk in, lay eggs, and walk out. But instead, they would survey the nest, scratch and peck some more, and sit down again. This behavior continued until they felt 'settled in.' When the process was interrupted, I observed, they would start the ritual all over again. All of this is not to say that some youngsters are like chickens, but there seems to be a similarity in their need to release a certain amount of energy in order to focus on the task before them." (Nellie Taylor-Walthrust, personal communication, February 1995)

The natural quality of her "down home" presentation captured the essence of the groups' waking moments, a phenomenon that has been referred to elsewhere as the "milling process" (Coyle, 1930, pp. 30–31). Unsettled beginnings have also been characterized as the "normal resistance" brought on by the "daily residue" of feelings either about home or school, all in the service of avoiding "getting down to work and becoming task oriented" (Hurley, 1984, p. 80).

By scanning the group—taking in the whole group with her senses—the worker perceived that milling was a natural and normal process to be respected and left alone (Middleman & Wood, 1990a). History taught her that the members eventually settled down and attended to task, as did the chickens. The narrative description registered what appeared to be a soothing effect on the staff, whose patience and tolerance increased as a result. In time, everyone aspired to cultivate good beginnings in their groups—the farm way.

DISCOVERING GROUP PURPOSE

The "Why are we here?" and "Where are we headed?" or the purpose of the group can be most easily discovered with young people if the worker respects the members' past group experiences and begins to educate through them. As indicated in Chapter 4, pregroup contact should include a discussion of the group's tentative purpose. However no discussion prior to the group actually meeting can ensure a fully integrated understanding of purpose. Workers will attest to the fact that young group members have a tendency to suffer selective amnesia when asked to recall anything from a previous meeting (with the exception of the promise of a special treat, of course). This may be a result of anxiety and/or ambivalence about the content.

Reaching for Outside Group Experiences

Reaching for outside group experiences involves helping the members to identify any past or present group affiliations that will enable the group members to make a cognitive link to the newly forming group. The following is an example of a group of five boys who were meeting for the first time in a mental health clinic. The boys were 12 years old and presenting needs for socialization experiences and skills and enhancing self-esteem. (GW stands for group worker.)

GW: Have you ever been in a group before?

UNANIMOUSLY: No [most likely inferring this kind of group].

GW: No, I mean any kind of group, not like here, like Little League, Scouts, a club, or something like that.

JAMIE: I'm in Little League.

IAN: I'm in the Squires.

DARREN: What's that?

IAN: My father is in the Knights of Columbus and the kids meet once a week.

In reaching for outside group experiences, the worker selects communication patterns purposefully, in this case by addressing the whole group and allowing whoever is eager and willing to go first (Middleman & Wood, 1990a). In this way, no one is put immediately on the spot. In another instance, members might be selected one at a time or through a structured go-round (Duffy, 1994).

What happens when there are those who cannot think of another group? The worker can encourage the group to help them to find one, even if it is as highly structured and formal as the school class. Eventually every member has a frame of reference, a group that he/she has belonged to. Once all have participated, the worker then selectively addresses individual members.

GW: Well, every group gets together for some reason, some purpose. Jamie, what do you think is the purpose of Little League; why do you play?

JAMIE: I dunno.

GW: Well why did you join?

JAMIE: To play.

GW: What do you other guys think might be the purpose of playing Little League? What do you think Jamie gets out of it?

Eventually, and with a little coaching, what can be drawn from the discussion are several purposes including: for fun, to learn skills, to listen to the coach, to meet new kids, and to cooperate with others. At some point the worker can summarize by saying something like this: "So the purpose of the Little League Group, I mean Little League Team, is to learn skills, to learn to follow directions, to learn the rules of the game, to work together with others, and to have fun." This way of approaching purpose can be applied to Girl Scouts, camp groups, clubs, and other teams or groups. Once this process has been exhausted, the next step is to begin to develop a sense that *this too* is a group and *this too* has a purpose. The reader might find the above to be simplistic, and it is; however the implications are profound. A clear purpose gives the group members a sense of direction and an opportunity to work together to reach common goals. It is in this mutual quest that the seeds of belonging and mastery are sewn. Using their recollections of familiar group experiences as a frame of reference, group members begin to understand the importance of having a group purpose, easing into the new group in a more well-grounded manner.

Group purpose need not be static; it can change over time. The initial purpose of the above group was simply "to make friends," and then "to learn how to cope with teasing," and later "to recognize when and how we provoke others," and later "to better understand our sad feelings." As the group developed, its purpose became, "to learn to think before acting."

When Does Clarity of Purpose Exist?

Group purpose, when first conceived during the planning phase is tentative and subject to later modification. In the group's beginning, the purpose is addressed collectively for the first time and is opened for mutual discussion. Let's review when *clarity of purpose* exists (Roselle Kurland, personal communication, 1994).

- *When the purpose of the group can be stated clearly and concisely by both the worker and the group member.* Adolescents' understanding of the purpose must be the same as the worker's, but the language used to articulate it might differ (e.g., *Worker:* "The purpose of this group is to help the members to put a reflective pause between impulse and action." *Member:* "The purpose of this group is for us to learn to stop and think before going off.").

- *When the stated purpose is the same for both group member and worker.* The worker should not have an ulterior motive or hidden purpose. That would be unethical. Purpose should be aboveboard. If a purpose cannot be discussed openly it has no place in the group. For example, to try to get members to reveal their feelings about stressful situations in the family in a group that has been billed only as "to learn arts and crafts" is wrong. However arts and crafts might be one of the activities used by a group who agreed to address "problems at home." The difference lies in whether or not there is mutually informed consent, the contract that the group agrees upon for what they will be doing together and for what ends.

- *When the purpose is specific enough that both client and worker will know when it has been achieved.* Evaluation is a critical aspect of purpose. The worker and members can periodically review progress through formal (i.e., pre- and posttest) or informal means. In a group aiming to improve to impulse control, a member might come into a group meeting and spontaneously share an incident in which he/she acted impulsively or delayed an impulsive reaction (e.g., "I felt like throwing my chair against the wall, but I didn't. Instead I walked out of class. I still got in trouble, but it wasn't as bad as it could have been."). Or the here-and-now of the group might provide a situation in which purpose is tested, such as a frustrating situation that generates a more reflective reaction than previously (e.g., *Worker:* "Anthony, I was really worried when Miguel said that he thought you were going to jump over the table and smash him." *Anthony:* "Yeah, I felt like doing it; I came really close, but somehow I stopped myself. I am really trying.").

- *When the purpose is specific enough to provide directed implications for the group content.* Remember that content is what the group does, the means it employs to reach its goals. If the purpose is "prevention of alcohol and drug abuse" or "prevention of pregnancy or sexually transmitted disease," for example, the content might include group discussion, education through videotapes, field trips, and outside speakers. The purpose informs the group about what it can do to meet its goals.

SEARCHING FOR COMMON GROUND

If the group purpose is "what brings us together and what directs us," then the common ground is "that which connects us." Whenever two strangers meet on a train, if they happen to strike up a conversation, and if it lasts, they eventually settle down on common ground whether it be politics, sports, fashion, or the poor service provided by the train and their current, accompanying discomfort. The common ground can be sought on different levels. It is the job of the worker to lead the search party and to make the elements that connect group members overt.

The following vignettes illustrate the search for common ground:

Mutual Feelings upon Entering the Group: Establishing Trust from the Inside Out

> In the young adolescent boys' group, a quick scanning of the group by the worker revealed the members' early anxiety and suspicion. The early meetings involved a search for "bugs" or tape recorders and questions about whether or not the walls were thin enough to be heard through. Ultimately this led to the crisis of establishing trust in the group.

As necessary as is the establishment of trust, it is secondary to the careful process of "getting there." Getting there for this group included apprehension in the here-and-now, fear that the intrusiveness of particular parents may preclude confidentiality, and certainty that the worker—like a teacher—would provide a periodic "report card."

Worker skills for trust building include *amplifying subtle messages* ("It seems like you guys are wondering if what we do in here and what we talk about might get out to your parents.") and *reaching for a feeling link* ("It's not easy starting a new group. Lots of people in new groups aren't sure if they want to be there. I guess it's no different for you guys.") (Middleman & Wood, 1990a).

Some of the group members' suspicions (i.e., the room being bugged) are simply observed by the worker rather than amplified. The silent observations are then kept in mind for possible verbalization at another time. The decision would depend upon what the worker knows about the members, their experiences with issues of privacy and trust, and where the group is developmentally. For example, group members living in circumstances with diffuse boundaries and low predictability require early reassurance that the group structure will provide privacy and safety from intrusion. In a group where the issue of trust reflects a less dire quality but where the natural suspicion about the motives of adults exists, the worker might take more of a wait-and-see approach, allowing the group to "sit" with the issue for a while longer and to openly confront it themselves. In any case, it is important for the practitioner to consider under what circumstances he/she might amplify subtle messages or remain an observer.

Sharing Outside Interests: Cultivating Socialization and Recognizing Ambivalence

In another group of five young adolescent boys ages 9 and 10, one of them—Drew—stated that he couldn't return for any more meetings because he'd be missing his favorite television show, *The Little Rascals*. Through the magic of cable TV, syndication, and video-cassette recording, all the others were familiar with *The Little Rascals*. The worker encouraged a discussion of favorite episodes and characters, inviting full participation. Although the boys seemed to feel awkward at this juncture, the worker's fortunate knowledge of the *Rascals* allowed him to model this kind of sharing for them, and they followed suit.

In this example, if the worker, intent on getting to the "deep stuff," had viewed the discussion of a TV show (or other seemingly trivial matters) as superficial, as only a sign of resistance, or as counterproductive, then he would have missed the opportunity to reach for the more profound aspects of the experience. The *Rascals* discussion does however represent an expression of resistance on one level—the members' ambivalence about the whole enterprise, a theme to be addressed more directly once the members have become better acculturated to the group and are more emotionally available to address their mixed feelings.

The sharing of outside interests, the experience actually being listened to, and the enjoyment of being a part of a discussion need to be carefully cultivated. *The Little Rascals* example has symbolic meaning in that it represents a group of mischievous and fun-loving kids. More importantly, however, was the sad possibility that this live experience would never approach the vicarious pleasure derived from watching the show. But there was also the hope that it would. As this group progressed beyond a year together, Drew began to playfully assign *Rascal* nicknames to the others and to himself. Perhaps this was his way of broadcasting his fantasies about what this group might become, to achieve the closeness he imagined in the *Rascals* group. The worker might also use this as an opportunity to explore the members' ideas about how the *Rascals* arrived at their nicknames and what it meant to them to do so. Such a discussion could be used as a natural avenue for "lending a vision" to the group, helping the members to begin to understand that it takes time for a group to come together and to feel a real sense of belonging, but that it can happen.

Emergence of Interpersonal Styles and Complementary Roles

Just prior to a "duo therapy group" (Fuller, 1977) with two 11-year-old girls, both girls sat in the waiting room not having been previously introduced. The worker was able to quickly scan the scene as he walked down the stairs to greet them. Caryn was wearing a Girl Scout uniform, and Marian was busy attending to the elastic bandage that was conspicuously wrapped around her right ankle. As the worker greeted them, he asked them to follow him up the stairs to the meeting place. Caryn, the Girl Scout, spontaneously went to the assistance of her soon-to-be partner, who managed to dramatize her "disability" just enough to draw attention. That moment on the stairs illustrated, interactionally, what was to become a major focus of the group: the complementary nature of the compulsive, dutiful helper and the histrionic, impulsive victim. Common ground was established: the need to move beyond their rigid roles. The challenge was to make it overt, enabling them to help one another practice and experience greater role flexibility. This was accomplished by suggesting that the group make two lists: one of group rules (structure) and the other of group activities (content). Guess who wanted to write the rules? Guess who couldn't think of any? As the group work proceeded it became Caryn's "job" to help Marian become less impulsive, less dramatic, and more down to earth, and it became Marian's job to help Caryn to be less compulsive and more flexible.

The Group Name: From Stigma to Valued Identity

Three girls, ages 9, 10, and 11, constituted a group whose purpose was to improve social skills. Ruthie displayed a tendency to withdraw from others, and was found frequently to lie and steal. Rosa had poor impulse control, was prone to bouts of uncontrollable behavior, and was quite self-centered. Dominique was noted to have difficulty getting along with peers and adults because of her extreme "bossiness," excessive demands, and the desire to always "get her way."

At the very first meeting, the girls were observably anxious and expressed anger at being brought together in this type of setting (mental health center). Rosa stated her position firmly at the outset, "I'm not crazy, I don't have to be here!" (a common cry of children and adolescents).

In addition to promoting some discussion of the girls' fears and then clarifying some basic group procedures, one of the interventions used by the worker to enhance formation of the group was to suggest that the girls think about a group name. The girls became interested in this idea and were able to shift the focus from reasons why they should not be together to finding some commonalities among themselves.

One of them suggested that they call themselves "The Crazy Mixed-Up Kids." The girls giggled about this, and suddenly, the notion that they had problems was no longer a ground for conflict, but a place from which they could begin to work together. One of the others, however, suggested that they think of other ideas, and the rest of them agreed. As they came up with names like "The Flowers" and "The Stars," they were able to find out about each other, their likes, and dislikes. Finally, one suggested "The Kittens," and the girls discovered that they all had a love for animals and that each of them owned a cat. They unanimously agreed that they be called "The Kittens."

Space Invaders and Hanging Judges: Establishing Trust from the Outside In

In a time-limited (12 to 15 meetings), older-adolescent group composed of five boys and girls ages 17 to 20, the members reviewed the group purpose in the first two meetings. The purpose included: "to develop strategies and skills to cope more effectively with stressful situations in the family, school, workplace, and with peers."

Moving to begin to identify specific goals the worker asked, "If you could snap your fingers and immediately change one stressful situation or relationship, which would it be?" It was the second meeting, and the members still seemed tentative and unsure about the protocol for responding to an open-ended question. In scanning the group, the worker noticed Louisa weakly gesturing with her folded hands, as if to request permission to speak. He nodded to her, and she became the first to respond. Louisa had recently dropped out of high school. "Definitely my father. He goes into my room, looks through my things, my drawers, my closet, my clothes, reads my letters, my diary, everything. I don't know what he's looking for."

The worker turned to Ariel who was referred to the group after having been truant from school for several consecutive weeks. She lowered her head for a moment and then looked up and said, "Yeah, my father is a problem too. He's so old fashioned, so set in his ways, always on my case, always checking up about every little thing, very overbearing. He's so annoying." A moment of silence and then Michael quietly revealed that his father, who is divorced from his mother, is an alcoholic and is so unstable that he cannot bear to be around him. "It's embarrassing to be around him when other people are around. He doesn't know how to act like a normal person. Sometimes I feel humiliated by him. He's so loud." Rick, who was on probation for an act of vandalism that he denied, said that he had no complaints about his parents, including his father whom he rarely had any contact with. When asked by the worker about other adults, he immediately thought of his girlfriend's father. "He thinks that he's better than me. I feel real uncomfortable around him. It's like he's looking down on me or something. It's like I'm on trial, and he's the 'hanging judge.' I feel like taking him outside and teaching him a lesson. I think he's afraid of me." Janine, who lived with her mother and younger sister and brother, said that she resented having to watch after her siblings whenever her mother went out. "She goes out and has fun, and I'm like her slave, her free babysitter." The worker tied together some of the common themes by adding, "So it seems like everyone in here has some trouble with at least one adult in your lives. For some the problem is having your space invaded, your time and privacy intruded on." Then turning to Rick, "For others it's a problem of being judged, maybe unfairly, because of your appearance, style, or reputation. And for all of you maybe it's some combination." And then to everyone, "But what's clear is that everyone here is bothered enough with these situations that you would like them to change." All heads nodded.

The worker was aware that the themes raised by the members constituted a common ground on more than one level. The themes of privacy, boundary intrusion, and being judged also might be related to their ambivalence about the group and the male group worker, who was roughly the age of the men they were referring to. Making a direct interpretation about latent content is unnecessary if the worker is tuned in and able to respond empathically to the members' feelings. In this situation, by tying together the common threads, the worker was able to validate the group members' experiences. If trust is carefully cultivated and specific problems are beginning to be addressed in some depth, the worker might periodically stop the action—timing it right so as not to break continuity—and ask the members how they feel about "What's going on in the group right now?" and "What's it like to share personal matters with people who not too long ago you didn't even know?" In so doing, the common ground shared by the members is then expanded from the space reported about *outside* of the group to the more intimate space experienced *within* the group itself. Members are then given the chance to reflect on their evolving relationships in the group. This will help the group to begin to see that it has to attend to both the group purpose and the evolving emotional life of the group. These have been termed the "task" and "maintenance functions" of the group (Benne & Sheats, 1948), also referred to as "goals" and "process."

These five case examples are but a sample of possible inroads to discovering common ground. Absent from the discussion thus far are other stressful life situations including parental separation, a death in the family, alcoholism in the family, placement in a "special class" in school, and being on probation for example. Geographical, ethnic, socioeconomic, medical, and other familial themes can also constitute common ground. The possibilities are endless.

AWARENESS OF THE NORMATIVE CRISIS

In the style of the four questions asked during the Jewish Passover Seder, the new group member asks him/herself, "How is this group different from all other groups?" The exodus or journey in this case involves the transition from a more traditional and/or comfortable set of values, to the experience of normative shock, and finally to a new set of values for a new culture. For example, many of the rules and regimens of the classroom, family, club, and team evaporate as the new group unfolds. For many adolescents, this is compounded by the worker's tacit acceptance of the expression of antisocial feelings, breaking down familiar restraints. "At the same time, the protection and expiatory comfort afforded by punishment are absent. The two conditions together make for an anxiety filled emotional vacuum" (Garland et al., 1973, p. 44).

It is important to remember that the worker is likely to have grown up in groups in which the presence of restraints and the demand for "normal" behavior were the norm. Consequently, no matter how experienced he/she may be, the worker may have all sorts of countertransference feelings arising from the "strange" circumstances of fledgling groups and the "odd" behavior of their members. The following is an example of the kind of internal dialogue that might be experienced by the adolescent embarking on a new group experience.

> This place is weird, it's the joint, the nut house. . . . What the hell is going on in here? . . . What am I doing here? . . . I raise my hand to speak and the teacher tells me I don't have to raise my hand to speak in here. . . . I ask how long the class is going to meet for and he tells me that this isn't a class. . . . That crazy looking kid in the corner of the room curses and gives the nerdy looking kid the finger and tells him he'll kick his ass if he doesn't stop smiling. . . . One of the kids called the teacher by his first name. . . . I don't even know that kid across from me and he's already snappin' on me, tellin' me, "Your mother is so fat she bleeds Ragu." . . . Ha! . . . I'll fuck him up good when we get outside. . . . Or was he talkin' about the kid next to me? . . . Maybe he was just kidding around. . . . I dunno. . . . What the hell is going on in here? This place is weird.

The group worker's awareness at this point, his/her empathy, allows him/her to gently move the group into new and ultimately more intimate territory as a new, normative structure is carefully constructed. The practitioner must acknowledge that it is likely to be different than in other groups. There are certain rules that the agency has, but the group will be responsible for developing many of the norms itself. The members must be offered hope, through the commitment and reassurance of the worker, that neither anarchy nor autocracy will prevail and that something new and special can be created. This is what is meant by "lending a vision."

THE PROMOTION OF PLAYFULNESS

> The reason you got scared and quit is because you felt too damn important. . . . feeling important makes one feel heavy, clumsy and vain. To be a man of knowledge one needs to be light and fluid.
> —C. *Castaneda* (1974, pp. 7–8)

Early on, reference was made to the younger adolescent's reluctance to use play materials or to talk insightfully in the group. For the worker, one integrative solution is to make use of playful talk. "Playful talk" is the language of the brain's right hemisphere that specializes in the "holistic grasping of complex relationships, patterns, configurations and structures"

(Watzlawick, 1978, p. 22). The timely use of playful talk can serve to mobilize the group during chaotic moments and to energize the group during more stagnant periods.

Play on Words

One example of this kind of language is the "play on words."

> A particularly withdrawn 13-year-old member of a boys' group turned to the worker in the middle of a discussion that obviously bored him, and he whispered, "I wanna leave now, please." The group was momentarily silenced, and Jay was asked to present his request to the group. Reluctantly, but to all, he repeated, "I wanna leave." The worker pointed to the plant on his desk and replied, "You can't have a 'leave,' for if you take one away, the others will miss it." This led to at least a moment of confusion, then laughter, and finally a spontaneous group decision to make the plant a group member. It was then decided to name the plant. The boy who had first requested leave named the plant "Lief Green," and instead of losing a member, one was gained.

A crucial factor in the development of relatedness to another is the creation of the *playful feeling*. This is to be differentiated from the activity of play, which may or may not require or generate a feeling of relatedness.

> Whatever direct discussions of significant problems, issues and feelings take place are all to the good, but they are not essential for growth and change to result from the process. The [worker] must enter the world of the adolescent; he cannot require [them] to function like adults in the group. (Levine, 1979, p. 23)

Preserving Social Informality and Spontaneous Play

In her "theory of play," Boyd (1971) emphasizes the preservation of social informality and spontaneous play in group work, for both educational and therapeutic purposes. Not all play requires special planning and equipment. Cultivating a playful feeling among fellow group members adds a lightness to the group that is invaluable when addressing difficult situations. If the worker can playfully accept the kaleidoscopic nature of adolescent groups, his/her repertoire of creative interventions will expand.

> Ruben is a 13-year-old boy who was referred to a group because he had no friends and was constantly scapegoated in school. Ruben's

defenses included intellectualization, rationalization, and isolation of affect. From time to time he would open a book and begin to read silently during group meetings. The authoritative approach to this problem led to many intellectual debates between the worker and Ruben, at the expense of the others. Interpreting his behavior led only to a shrug of disinterest. Mobilizing the others to confront Ruben led to the scapegoating that he was so accustomed to. Finally, the worker and members created a Greek Chorus, and whenever Ruben opened a book, they would chant, with tongues planted firmly in cheeks, "Once again Ruben is retreating into the world of literature." This placed Ruben in a bind. The familiar authoritative stance was missing, there was no scapegoating, and yet something was being communicated that seemed to short circuit Ruben's intellectual style of thinking. The collaborative "tongue in cheek" and "smile in voice" approach, coupled with a reasonable interpretation and an implicit request for him to stop reading confused Ruben. All he could do was laugh. The message that probably came through was "please join us."

In my experience, many professionals avoid working with groups of adolescents, particularly younger ones. One of the more common reasons given goes something like this: "Nothing happens in the group that they can't get on the playground. . . . I am not a camp counselor. . . . I am a therapist (and I have more important things to do with my time)." Maybe so, but if the worker gives the appearance of being too sophisticated for such work, one need only look a little further to find that his/her real aversion is to the anxiety stimulated by the prospect of losing control in the face of perpetual confusion. In Shulman's discussion of the "fear of groups" syndrome, he highlights some of the underlying feelings of new group workers (1992). One such fear is loss of control, which he illustrates through the reflections of one wary workshop participant:

> When I'm conducting an individual interview I know where it is going and can keep track of what is happening. In a group session, the members seem to take the control of the session away from me. It feels like I am on my motorcycle, pumping the starter to get going, and the group members are already roaring down the road. (p. 286)

Practitioners new (and some old) to group work with adolescents need to be reassured that the members' taking over control of the group is to be valued when complemented by the worker's letting go of control. This gradual process enables the members to increase autonomy and reliance upon one another and not solely on the worker.

ESTABLISHING GROUP RITUALS

Increasing the level of group distinctiveness can lead to greater cohesion among group members (Kavanagh, 1973). One method for fostering distinctiveness in the group is through the establishment of group rituals. Ritual, although often maligned, is not merely empty, repetitive behavior. Equating ritual with simple formality suggests an act of superficiality. Rituals are best established in groups when they occur spontaneously and with respect to mutuality. "Ritual is concerned with relationships, either between a single individual and the supernatural, or among a group of individuals who share things together. There is something about the sharing and the expectation that makes it ritual" (Mead, 1973, p. 89). Interestingly the word "spiritual" is comprised of the two overlapping words "spirit" and "ritual," both of which have meaning for group work.

The Pledge

In an after-school club composed of African American teens, aged 12 to 17 and dedicated to preventing alcohol and other drug abuse, the members recite a "drug-free pledge" at the beginning and ending of each meeting. The pledge is written boldly on the club's brochure and recited before any open community events that the group may sponsor (Walthrust, 1992).

> **Drug-Free Pledge**
> I pledge to remain drug-free. I
> will not use alcohol and other
> drugs. I will not smoke
> cigarettes or do anything that
> doesn't help me to live a clean
> life today, tomorrow, and
> everyday. I am proud to be
> DRUG-FREE, and I pledge to grow
> up that way. I will choose my
> friends CAREFULLY and not have
> friends who use drugs. I am
> going to be a role model for
> myself and my friends.

At first awkwardly recited, the pledge has since become a source of pride for the group, enabling members to openly affirm what they stand for, what they value. To encourage learning the pledge, the worker, in the early stage of the group, set up an informal competition of sorts. Individual members were encouraged to memorize and recite the pledge to the group. At first this resulted in lots of teasing and giggling. In time though, there were more attentive members than noisy ones. The peer pressure was for the noisy members to quiet down. Applause followed each successful and/or sincere effort to recite the pledge from memory. The exercise also helped the members, many of whom were struggling with little success in school, by providing them with an opportunity to speak publicly, increasing their poise and confidence in themselves. This was a *ritual* that helped to promote group *spirit*.

Graffiti Wall

A week-long retreat for adolescents was planned by staff from a university extension division for the purpose of educating the participants, roughly 30 youth of ages 14 to 18, about alcohol and other drug abuse and to learn and practice various life skills (i.e., problem solving, conflict resolution). Simultaneously another group, consisting of adults, parents, teachers, counselors, and administrators was meeting. Their focus was on how to ensure that the school was a protective environment for its students. The workers leading both groups worked in collaboration during this time-limited group experience.

In the youths' meeting place, newsprint lined the circumference of the room. This was, it was explained, a *graffiti wall*. Anyone could write on the wall at any time. The most prolific writing usually occurred ritually, just before the start and immediately following the ending of meetings. Some of the entries were original, and others were borrowed. The wall became a statement of the combined wit and wisdom of the group—a time capsule of sorts—capturing the members' thoughts and humor and the group's evolving culture (like cave drawings). As the adult group joined the youth for mixed activities, they discovered the wall and were, in time, invited to write on it. Some of the entries follow:

> If love is plentiful, pass some around. . . . The writings of the prophets are written on the bathroom walls. . . . Man who speaks with forked tongue should never kiss a balloon. . . . He who asks a question is a fool for a minute. He who remains silent stays a fool forever. . . . It is better to be silent and thought stupid than to open one's mouth and remove all doubt. . . . Nothing goes right when your underwear's tight. . . . Oh I'm tired!!!!!! . . . Love ain't love till you give it away. . . . Happy are those who dream dreams and are ready to pay the price to make them come true. . . . It's very dumb to write on these sorta things. . . . Save water, shower with a friend. . . . Life is too short to take it easy! Live it with intensity! . . . Sex is evil, evil is sin, so sex is in. . . . A teacher who fails to accept his student as his teacher fails to learn. . . . Let this flower bloom, even if it's ugly. . . . You are like my

oldest pair of blue jeans. I love you! My mother hates you—and you fit so well. . . . If at first you don't succeed, then you don't succeed at first; that's all. . . . Each person's life is like a piece of paper on which every passerby leaves a mark.

The Big Chair

Another example of ritual, of the more informally determined variety, is drawn from the "Kittens" group that was introduced earlier. One day Ruthie sat in the large leather chair where the group worker usually sat. The other girls became angry and decided that they too wanted to sit in the leather chair. Rather than engaging in a power struggle, they talked about the meaning of the chair, feeling important, and acting "grown up." The worker suggested that the group, including herself, take turns each week, sitting in the "big seat." This became a ritual.

In this instance, the worker's thoughtful and creatively simple intervention led to a meaningful ritual, which respected the girls' passage through a new phase of development. However one might ask, why should the group worker have a chair different than that of the members? Is this reflective of another kind of "unconscious countertherapeutic ritual" in which everyone knows where the seat of power is?

Passing a Ball: An Ending Ritual

> Ritual for its own sake is vanity. Ritual for the sake of
> the participants reflects a thoughtfulness, a concern for
> others. It is easy to perform ritual for its own sake. It is
> more difficult to perform it for the sake of the participants.
> —E. Fischer (1973, p. 170)

The end of the group session is an opportune time for creating a meaningful parting ritual. In another group of younger adolescent girls whose parents had been recently separated, the last 5 minutes of each meeting were reserved for passing a ball in a circle to one another, including the worker. This emerged after several meetings were marked by endings in which the girls either refused to leave or uncontrollably fought over a variety of objects in the room. The passing of the ball provided both an emphasis of their growing mutuality and a symbol for loss and retrieval, not unlike the experience of mourning.

Famous Last Words

Another parting ritual evolved after a worker asked a group of young-adolescent boys, as the group was about to end, "Any famous last words?"

One wise guy raised his finger and pursed his lips as if to prepare the others for a profound statement, and he then said: "the." The others followed in suit with their own "famous last word," giving birth to a weekly ritual. They ultimately decided to take turns recording the "words," which they strung into sentences, on paper. Thus the members established a ritual that allowed them to summarize their experiences through a playful process of free association. It also enabled them, in a creative way, to say good-bye.

CONCLUSION

Perhaps the greatest challenge in working with adolescent groups is that no matter how prepared one is, one is unprepared. One of your greatest allies and advisors is your creativity. The outline set forth in this chapter won't do as a bag of tricks, as a recipe for survival; rather it can serve as a framework in the beginning of the group (and beyond) within which one can create.

APPENDIX 5.1. THE BEGINNING STAGE OF GROUP DEVELOPMENT[2]

WHERE THE MEMBERS ARE

Anxiety about the unknown
Trust vs. distrust
Approach and avoidance:

Approach:
- Want relationship with worker and other members
- Want to accomplish purpose
- Want to reveal themselves
- Desire closeness
- Want acceptance

Avoidance:
- Fear of unknown
- Fear of not being accepted
- Fear of not succeeding
- Fear of being hurt
- Feeling of being vulnerable

[2]Reprinted by permission of Roselle Kurland.

- Fear of getting involved
- Fear that things won't be confidential

Wary
Exploring
Not committing themselves
Giving themselves a chance to draw back
Keeping their distance

WHAT NEEDS TO HAPPEN

Orientation
- Worker to the group
- Members to the situation
- Members to the worker
- Members to other members
- Members to plans for the group
- Members to time, place, frequency, content of meetings

A group must form and ways the group will work will become established: norms, values, patterns of communication.

Purpose of group needs to be made explicit, discussed, agreed upon, accepted; even if purpose was discussed with each member individually, this needs to be done with everyone so it becomes a reference point (this is important later on).

Commonalities need to be established and seen, a basis for cohesiveness established.

ROLE OF THE WORKER

To help what needs to happen happen.
- Members look to worker for direction, structure, approval, help at a difficult time
- Has to be more active now—group members more dependent on worker at this point
- To help each member enter the group, allay anxiety help members communicate and explore, yet keep some distance
- Needs to acknowledge anxious feelings everyone has, express confidence in group's potential to accomplish purpose.
- To discuss purpose, help members look at it, get agreement
- To make the connections among the members, help members see what they have in common
- To help establish group norms—to a great degree, it is through what the worker does, verbally and nonverbally, at this point that norms do get established

| # What's Going On in There?

Alliance Formation with Parents Whose Adolescent Children Join Groups

How can we best orient parents whose adolescent children are about to become group members? How do we communicate with parents over time about what is happening in the group while at the same time maintain privacy within the group? How do we explain the static that periodically seeps from the group meeting place reaching parents, piquing their senses, stoking their anxiety, and testing their patience? How can we promote and preserve trust within the group while we simultaneously maintain a working alliance with parents?

Parents must not be cut out of the helping equation when their adolescent children become group members. Balancing the tenuous relationship between parent, child, group, and practitioner requires great foresight and careful attention. In circumstances where a single parent is the only adult living in the household, the quality of that parent's relationship with the group worker is especially vital. For many parents, a relationship with the worker may be the only one available to them in which the well-being of their child is addressed in a meaningful way and on a consistent basis. By working closely with workers, parents can become partners who monitor changes in their children's behavior and attitude outside of the group, gather information, and participate in mutual problem solving (Vinter & Galinsky, 1985).

This chapter is a revised and updated version of Malekoff (1991b). Adapted by permission of The Haworth Press, Inc.

This chapter examines the process of forging a working alliance with parents of adolescents who join groups. Encounters between the parent and practitioner during three phases of a group's life will be used to illustrate. They are:

- Pregroup contact with parents as the group begins.
- The ongoing relationship with parents as the group progresses.
- The ending transition with parents as the group comes to an end.

PREGROUP CONTACT WITH PARENTS

To many a worker's chagrin, adolescents often come to groups involuntarily and resistantly. However it is not only the young person in trouble with the law or confined to an institution who is mandated to participate in groups. When parents electively choose to bring a troubled child to an agency for service, it is rare that the adolescent eagerly accompanies them. Ironically, many workers who are assigned to work with groups of adolescents view themselves as "mandated practitioners." One of the worker's jobs in any group composed of mandated members is to gently cultivate a commitment that will gradually overcome negatively weighted ambivalence (i.e., "I had no choice about coming into this group in the first place, but now that I've been here for a while, it's not so bad, it's kind of fun, and maybe it can help"). This has been referred to as "the second decision," a crucial one for the adolescent group member who is striving for greater autonomy and independence.

The worker's ability to orient parents effectively is a critical step in building the foundation for a working alliance. In group work, adolescents are seen in their natural environment—the peer group. This may be an unsettling reality for the parent who is all too familiar with the noise, static, and secrecy characteristic of groups of teenagers. (Incidentally, it has always surprised me to see and hear the reactions of colleagues to my "noisy kids" groups. They're hardly as loud, raucous, and profane as some of the livelier marital groups that I've witnessed.)

Pregroup contact with parents of adolescents is best handled in a family meeting that includes the prospective member. Adolescents do not appreciate being left out of conversations about them, particularly early on and before trust has been established. One useful approach in the orientation phase is to first meet with the prospective group member alone to emphasize his/her autonomy and then to ask parents to join the meeting. As the group meets over time, separate sessions with parents are more palatable to teens if they come to trust that no confidences will be broken.

Parents must understand that separate sessions cannot include divulging secrets to be kept from their child.

Tuning-in to parents' concerns prior to the group includes anticipating their ambivalence and some of the questions that they might have. Many parents will not or cannot articulate all of the questions that they might like to have answered. It is the group worker's responsibility to help parents to formulate and respond to such questions. Some of these orienting questions for the practitioner to keep in mind when first meeting with parents are:

- How can a group benefit my child?
- What actually happens in the group?
- What's special about group work?
- What is the purpose of the group?
- What's going on in there?

The preceding questions and following illustrative responses are presented as a framework for orienting parents. It is unlikely that the examples and language used will be suitable for all situations. Workers are encouraged to use the framework adaptively, taking into consideration different parents' level of sophistication, education, experience in groups, history with human service systems, and cultural heritage and values. Individually tailored responses are essential to the effective orientation of parents.

How Can a Group Benefit My Child?

"How can the group benefit my child?" is a universal concern that all parents of prospective group members deserve a response to. The trouble is that the answer is not a simple one. A good place to begin educating parents is through a familiar frame of reference. For example, the following approach was used with one family.

> "Let's first try and understand how any group might benefit someone, and then we can look at this specific group. Are you with me? Okay, picture this: A group of six kids who have never met before drift into the local playground. One of them is dribbling a basketball and begins shooting. One by one, with no words spoken, the others wander over and join in. A 'swish' is rewarded with the return of the ball for a free shot. In a while they pick sides and decide on rules ('game's to fifteen . . . you have to win by two . . . winner takes it out . . . '). As they proceed, they gradually begin to assess the strengths and weaknesses

of each player on each team. Some do this consciously, while others do it more intuitively. Spontaneous strategies are created, initiated, repeated, and modified. The players reward one another through both words and actions ('nice shot' or hand slapping). If the experience is worthwhile, they agree to play two out of three games.

"The group is much like the team. The members share something in common, and they've come together for a purpose. As in the example of the team, their strengths and weaknesses will emerge naturally, and they will learn from and lean on one another. They will discover that they each have different roles to play in different situations. Through experience, they will learn to complement one another so that their movements become natural. Can you see some of the benefits of a group now? Bear with me. We're going to move on from basketball to the real group."

In the above explanation, common ground, mutual aid, role differentiation, the use of activity, and the concept of promoting mental health through ego building are introduced using a natural group as a frame of reference. The knowledge base of group work is gradually demystified and the prospective group members depathologized. The value of the peer group is presented as a proactive force capable of confronting problems and providing mutual support.

The "choose-up" basketball game is but one frame of reference used to describe what happens in groups. The parents' own childhood memories of clubs, teams, and other groups, if they're willing to reveal them, are all excellent sources of consciousness raising and avenues for engagement with the worker. Workers can help parents to tell their own stories of group participation and use them to educate. Such personal examples can also be used to help parents to better empathize with their children as they journey through the long-forgotten transitions of youth. The next step is to begin to differentiate the specific group being offered from the more abstract illustrations or memories.

What Actually Happens in the Group?

Demystification is a great equalizer. Through the use of a story-telling or narrative style, the worker can share past encounters with agency groups to bring experiences with *this specific kind of group* a little closer to life for parents. The following case presents one example of a story used to tell the parents of a young adolescent boy, a prospective group member, about what happened in one group to help a boy with poor social judgment.

Several years ago I worked with a group in which there was a 12-year-old boy who had a terrific imagination. The trouble was that he sometimes mixed up what was real with what he imagined. This created great problems for him when he tried to socialize outside of the group. He had become a laughing-stock, often the butt of cruel jokes, which enraged him and led to many fist fights. When any adult challenged his far-out tales, he would curse that person and then withdraw. He would almost always end up isolated, misunderstood, angry, and lonely.

As is often the case with group members, he played out his problem from *outside* the group *inside* the group. In other words, he enacted his unique problem for all to see and experience firsthand. This real-life demonstration was far more powerful than any intellectual discussion *about* problems. As the demonstration continued on a weekly basis, another member who emerged as the group "bully" found his mark and mercilessly baited and taunted the "exaggerator." And soon the group learned why the "bully" also had trouble making friends outside of the group.

After some discussion, and taunting, and bickering, and more discussion, there finally came a solution. I asked the group if they knew what a "fish story" was. One of them, no doubt the lone fisherman among us, obliged the others by defining the term: "It's like when you tell a story that's not totally true; like you make it a bigger deal than it really is; you know, to make yourself look good. It's like, 'hey everybody look at me, look at how cool I am.' Except you're not so cool when everybody finds out it's all bullshit. You tell everybody that you caught a whale, and they find out that it was just a guppy. Know what I mean?" From that time on whenever the "exaggerator" started to get carried away, the others simply held their hands apart with palms facing one another as if to wonder, "howwww big?" And the "exaggerator" couldn't help but smile, and he would then proceed without further prompting to tone his story down.

So as you can see, a great deal can happen without any words at all. Sometimes when the group is involved in a fun activity, problems and difficulties emerge naturally and are opened for inspection. Sometimes after the members feel safe enough to reveal themselves naturally, valuable discussions follow. In this case, we talked about exaggerating and bullying and their relationship to making friends, fitting in, and feeling left out. The reality of their imperfections and the accompanying acceptance and support by their peers is a special feature of the group. They can push, criticize, and support one another in a way that no adult alone can. In the group, they bring their outside lives in, and they create something new that takes on a life of its own. In time it becomes *their group*.

If the worker cannot think of a fitting story from his/her own practice, examples from the literature may be adapted for orientation purposes. Some parents may even be eager to read some of the literature on group work if the worker provides a few appropriate selections containing lively illustrations. For example, I have provided some of the illustrations in this book to educate parents about group beginnings (see Chapter 5) and the use of nonverbal activities (see Chapter 8) in treatment groups. Selections should first be carefully reviewed by the practitioner and edited, if necessary, to ensure suitability for these purposes.

What's Special about Group Work?

Providing a "real" group work illustration provides an opportunity for the parents to *see* and *feel* the worker and group in action and the integration of nonverbal and verbal activity in the group. Beyond colorful metaphors and practice illustrations, it is useful to expose parents and relevant others—including collaborating colleagues—to selected group work principles. I recommend introducing some of the following core concepts (which can be found illustrated in a variety of contexts throughout this book), perhaps like so:

> "Group work is about inviting the *whole person* of your child into the group and not just the troubled or problematic parts. What this means is that there are specific problems that each member brings into the group that will be addressed, however, there are also special abilities and qualities—I call them strengths—that each member brings to the group [the worker then can provide some examples of specific problems and strengths as they apply to the situation]. Strengths need to be affirmed and given room for expression in the group. The group members need to know that they are more than the sum of their problems, more than a reputation they may have gained, and more than some diagnostic label that they have been assigned. It's also important for you to understand that *in a group there are more helpers than just the adult*. What I mean by this is that while I am responsible for getting things going and making sure that the group stays on task—that is, remains focused on why we're all together—the members also have a responsibility for the group's success. They are expected to help one another and to solve problems in the group. There is not just one expert in the room, but many. This may take a

while to grasp, but it is very important to understand. In time, the members must come to see the group as their own, a special place. Some people have referred to this as 'owning the experience.' If they come to feel that they have a stake in what goes on, in its success, then the chance of success increases. All of these things are a part of what being involved in the group can mean. I'm kind of like a coach helping them to do the job we set out to do, to reach our purpose and goals, and to help to evaluate how we're doing together as a group, how everyone is getting along and working together."

The group is described as a context in which the tools of social mastery are refined and in which gaining a sense of belonging is valued. Prospective members are viewed as individuals who will be enabled, through the group experience, to move beyond ascribed roles, labels, and negative stereotyping.

What Is the Purpose of the Group?

The group's purpose and goals should be discussed with parents and prospective members, with the discussion moving along to the specific situation and present reality. It is recommended that the group purpose be described along three dimensions, which are presented here and each followed by an example:

1. *Specific presenting problems/symptoms/concerns.* In other words, the group will address the problems that the members presented when they first came to the agency. For example, improving social judgment might be Joey's goal. Achieving it would help reduce Joey's problem behavior in school and improve his ability to get along with his peers. Another goal might be to find alternative ways for Joey to express anger instead of fighting with others or engaging in self-destructive behavior.

2. *Aspects of normal adolescent development.* A goal of all groups for adolescents is to become well informed and to prevent problematic behavior in areas that most concern all teenagers today. These areas include sexuality, violence, and alcohol and drug abuse. Kids' problems and needs are often interrelated, appearing in clusters rather than in isolation. In work with adolescent groups, it is a mistake to ignore areas of importance to the members themselves. By gathering accurate information, learning to solve problems and resolve conflicts, and making healthy decisions, young people have a better chance to be successful as adults.

3. *Systems impacting on the young person's life.* The group should try to find ways to help the members to get along better and work out

problems more effectively with parents, school personnel, and peers. During adolescence, kids may become alienated from others and unable to find the right way back; often, those whom they've become alienated from are also unable to "reconnect." In the group one goal is to reconnect the members and those who care about them, that is, those who have a stake in one another.

Parents' and their children's ideas about goals should be solicited and included in any discussion about group purpose. Despite any fantasies to the contrary parents must be informed that their children will do more than have quiet, civilized discussions in the group. But the fantasy lives on until the static begins.

What's Going On in There?

Time for a reality check. Despite careful preparation and a wonderfully erudite presentation on the value and benefit of group work, parents and relevant others are rarely prepared for the real thing. After an early "honeymoon" period in which group members tend to be on their suspiciously best behavior, sizing up the new situation and maintaining a safe distance from one another and the worker, the storm begins to roll forth. As the normative crisis in the group emerges and as members begin to test out for themselves what behavior is acceptable and what isn't, the levels of noise and movement accelerate rapidly, particularly with younger adolescents.

If the setting contains a waiting room, parents will inevitably hear or feel the static. They may begin to make eye contact with one another for the very first time. . . . And they will begin to shake their heads. . . . And they will begin to mutter to themselves . . . and then talk among themselves . . . and they will have found common ground: "What's going on in there?!?!" Laughter, banging, thumping, slamming doors, screams—all serve to reinforce their worst fears about their children and about this insane idea of a group. Embarrassment, shame, doubt, and anger—anger at the "genius" who sold them a bill of goods about what a wonderful experience the group would be for their children. This is often the point at which many parents will contact referral sources and any one who will lend a sympathetic ear including guidance counselors, school psychologists and social workers, probation officers, and others to try to initiate a process in which the group recommendation is reversed.

Parents' anguish at this point may be expressed in one of at least three circuitous ways, assuming that it is not communicated directly ("I'd like to meet with you to discuss the group"), which it frequently is not.

- The *I'm-fed-up, disappointed, what-did-I-get-myself-into look*. The silence and facial expression here are stronger than any words. The purpose of the look is to elicit an explanation from you. The group worker must transcend any defensiveness to provide reassurance for an angry and confused parent.
- The *you-go-wait-in-the-car, pivot-step, and corral-the-worker maneuver*. Here "junior" is sent ahead following the group meeting. The worker is cornered, usually in the presence and earshot of colleagues, receptionists, clients, and other witnesses to his/her "incompetence," and asked the magic question: "What's going on in there?!"
- The *this-may-be-my-last-meeting–courier canard*. Here the youngster becomes the parent's messenger. The purpose is for the worker to approach the parent to make the first direct move. This usually occurs during the meeting immediately following a particularly chaotic one.

Admittedly, these are generalizations. But they point up the fact that, as in any endeavor involving the welfare of their children, parents are legitimately and genuinely concerned about how things are going. The traditional model of the professional as "knowledgeable decision maker" and parent as "passive recipient" (Healy, Keesee, & Smith, 1985) is alienating and intimidating to parents and an anathema to true collaboration. The slapstick described above, in which parents are depicted as awkwardly trying to get the practitioner's attention, is more a reflection of the all too typical inaccessibility and aloofness of professionals than of any interactive inadequacy on the parents' part. Parents' concerns must be heard and addressed forthrightly. It is the alliance that is established with the worker, based on accessibility and trust, that will prove to be more reassuring than any explanation. If parents feel that their children are in capable hands, they will be able to weather the inevitable storms whipped up in the group. Capable hands mean collective hands—practitioner, parents, and involved others all in partnership.

THE ONGOING RELATIONSHIP WITH PARENTS

Once a reasonable level of trust has been established and the members have committed themselves to the endeavor, parents are less apt to dwell on "static" and more likely to be concerned with how the group is working to address the important issues facing their children. For the worker, a major dynamic issue that emerges is how to maintain an alliance with parents without sacrificing the trust of the group members. The contract with the members and all concerned others must be based on trust, not solely on the traditional notion of confidentiality.

The Family Secret I: Testing Trust from the Inside Out

In the following illustration, the issues of trust, confidentiality, and family loyalty are tested.

> Teddy had been a member of a younger adolescent boys' group for three years. He joined at age 13 when he was transferred from his home district to a special educational setting. At first he encountered daily beatings by other students on the school bus. As a consequence, he was excessively truant. Teddy lived with his parents and older sister who was the family "star," an excellent student and talented athlete.
>
> By the time Teddy reached his 17th birthday he was back in the home school district. He was gradually becoming "mainstreamed" academically, and he had become a varsity athlete. Despite his success, which he acknowledged made him feel proud, he continued to be anxious and unsure of himself. Adjusting to part-time employment, fitting in socially, and planning for the future beyond high school were all concerns of Teddy's.
>
> Teddy appeared extremely anxious and fidgety during one particular group meeting. He did not deny feeling disturbed about something but refused to discuss it despite the other group members' cajoling. Finally, he admitted that he had promised his mother that he would not discuss "it," whatever "it" was. Teddy's position was respected, and instead, the group discussed the predicament of keeping family matters private, a problem that each of the boys could relate to. As each of the others shared, Teddy was encouraged to describe the feelings associated with the bind he was in. "I'm all tied up inside," he revealed.
>
> The worker asked if the others had any advice for Teddy. They wondered if he, the worker, could talk to Teddy's Mom. Teddy was initially hesitant, fearing he had said too much already. The group rehearsed what might be said by the worker through role playing, emphasizing that Teddy had not revealed the secret to the group or worker. Experiencing how it might work through the simulation, Teddy then agreed to the plan. However, he asked not to be included in the meeting.
>
> [A meeting was arranged with Teddy's Mom for the next week.]
>
> Teddy's dilemma was reviewed with his Mom. Visibly relieved to have the opportunity to talk about it, she revealed the secret to the worker while softly weeping and exposing her feelings of shame and

fear. Upon her return home, she freed Teddy to share the secret with the group.

In the next meeting, Teddy revealed that his older sister had attempted suicide.

In this illustration the worker effectively intervened with a parent to gather information and to engage in a collaborative process of mutual problem solving. The family's boundaries were respected enabling the secret to surface in a respectful way, allowing Teddy to openly address the stress, anxiety, and fear that he felt.

The Family Secret II: Testing Trust from the Outside In

In the next illustration a "family secret" was discovered through yet another path.

Claude's father called and said that he had to see the worker. It seems that his wife had discovered something that greatly disturbed her while she was cleaning under Claude's bed. The worker agreed to the meeting with the proviso that Claude be informed that his father would be coming in to discuss something.

Mr. K entered the office holding a blue spiral notebook under his arm. He held out the notebook and declared, "This is what I'm here about." He then placed it on the chair beside him and went on to describe its contents. It seems that Claude, 16 at the time, decided to keep a diary of his sexual fantasies, which, according to his father were rather explicit. Mr. K remarked, "I didn't know he could write so well." Mr. K, appearing mildly forlorn, said that he didn't really think the contents of the notebook were that bad: "After all he is a teenager." He offered the diary to the worker who declined to read it, adding that he trusted Mr. K's judgment. He asked Mr. K if he thought that Claude might be looking to have a "man-to-man" talk. Mr. K thought that might be so, and he agreed to tell Claude about his discovery and the details of his meeting with the worker. The worker offered to make himself available for any further discussion on the subject, ensuring his accessibility to Mr. K.

Subsequent to the father–son talk, the worker met alone with Claude to affirm his knowledge of what had occurred. The purpose was to avoid any hint of collusion with his parents and also to reassure him that the choice was his about whether or not to discuss the incident in the group. He didn't reveal the details, however he actively pursued discussions related to privacy and sexuality as the group progressed.

Practitioners working with adolescents in groups must ask themselves if it is ethical to work exclusively with group members while consciously excluding from the process those who will also be affected (Moore-Kirkland & Irey, 1981). Rigid adherence to arbitrary standards of confidentiality work against the flexibility necessary to cultivate a working alliance with parents.

Being Responsive to Emergent Crises and Going Out on a Limb

As the above illustrations suggest, circumstances may arise in which the practitioner has a professional and ethical obligation to address a problem outside of the group itself. These emergent situations often require some sort of immediate response. In one case, a parent called to inform me that her 15-year-old daughter Marie, who was about to join a new group, had written a "last will and testament" that had been left conspicuously on her bed. The worker arranged a meeting with Marie, informing her mother that the act of preparing a last will and testament had to be taken seriously. The ultimate result of a quick and decisive response was a stronger bond among all involved parties—parent, child, and practitioner.

The intervention with Marie was fairly traditional. Any sign of suicidal or homicidal thinking or behavior must be taken seriously and must supersede any and all confidentiality agreements. Group members and parents must be informed of this exception from the start. However, earlier in my career, I made another intervention with a troubled and possibly suicidal group member. Except this time, the intervention wasn't quite so traditional, one that I can only laugh about in retrospect. It didn't seem so funny at the time.

Mrs. P called me at the office on a Monday morning. She sounded frantic as she informed me that her 14-year-old son, Marty, had been extremely depressed over the weekend and was home alone. He had been expelled from school for fighting. He had a history of alcohol abuse, and his brother had a history of depression, including being hospitalized following a suicide attempt. Mrs. P tried to reach Marty for a few hours, but the phone line was busy. She called the phone company and was informed that no one was on the line and that it was probably off the hook. My office was located only minutes from their home so I offered to drive by and look in on Marty. I had made previous home visits early on to get to know Marty when he first refused to come to the agency. So going to the home was not new for me. She was grateful for my offer and agreed with the plan. As I recall, it was a cold winter's day and snowing lightly. I was wearing a long blue Air Force overcoat that I had bought in an Army–Navy store for $10 during my college days (the best buy I'd ever made), a navy blue watch cap pulled down over my ears, and black leather gloves. I am a little over 6 feet tall, fairly broad shouldered, and I weighed in at about 220 pounds at the time. As I arrived, I pressed the door bell and then knocked. I knocked louder and louder and more rapidly when there was no response. *No sign of life,* I thought to myself. Unbeknownst to me, I was being observed all of this time by neighbors through the blinds of their picture window across the street and behind me. They must have really freaked out when I picked up a loose brick from the front walk and smashed it into the window adjacent to the front door. As I reached in to unlock the door, I could see Marty coming down the stairs. At the same time, through the corner of my eye, I saw the police car quietly pulling up into the driveway behind me. It didn't take long for me to realize that they hadn't come to check on Marty. They had come for me.

Can we say of this case, "All's well that ends well"? I don't know. Maybe I should have knocked on a neighbor's door first. But I truly believed that time was of the essence. Would I lose my job? Would Mr. and Mrs. P press charges? Actually Mrs. P told me that what I did was "the best thing anyone ever did for our son." I wasn't quite sure how to take that. I reported what had happened immediately to agency officials and was told to complete the standard State "incident report." And that was the end of it. Nothing like that has occurred since. I wouldn't recommend "breaking and entering" as an effective form of outreach, but I can't say that I regret what I did. I have learned from years of experience that outside systems are always testing a worker's commitment, competence, and ability to be trusted. Some tests are routine (e.g., returning phone calls in a timely fashion), some are more challenging and demanding (e.g., testifying in court or at special education hearings), and others seem inexplicable and constructed of a strange logic all their own. What they all seem to have in common is the question: "Can we count on you?"

Authenticity and Joining the Resistance: When Family Dynamics Are Replicated in the Helping System

It is not unusual for workers to feel challenged by parents and representatives of collaborating systems. However, "the fact that parents are anxious, aloof, on the brink of tears, or angry may show their reaction to the situation rather than their prevalent mood or style of interaction" (Chess & Hassibi, 1978, p. 149). Parents need to hear from practitioners that their expressions of concern are not out of bounds. The same respect needs to be afforded to collaborating colleagues from allied professions. The alternative is defensive maneuvering that may lead to an early demise of service. "Working oneself out of a job" is a valued maxim of social work practice. Practitioners must remind themselves that this applies to the successful completion of a service intervention rather than to premature flight by group members and families.

> In one case, I was confronted by a frustrated school psychologist who was questioning the efficacy of a group for one of his students. The student was functioning well academically, however, the boy's mother was frustrated with his behavior at home and had questioned the value of the group. She appealed to the school psychologist to confront me and to advocate for individual therapy for her son. As it turned out, the ongoing dynamics of an acrimonious marital separation and subsequent divorce between the mother and the boy's father were soon being played out in a new arena, with the group worker (me) and school psychologist as unwitting participants.

In the above illustration I, as the worker, entered into an adversarial relationship with the mother and school psychologist. In order to recover from this mistake, I had to step back and "join the resistance," inviting an open expression of concerns and doubts by all involved about how the group might help. Mistakes are an inevitable part of the work. A good recovery from a mistake, particularly one in which the practitioner becomes drawn in to a family's dynamics, can elevate the quality of a partnership with a parent who anticipates that the drama will lead to another separation. For the adolescent child caught in the middle, again, such a result provides a ray of hope that not all differences must lead to the demise of relationships.

False Arrest: When the System Fails

The next illustration begins in aftermath of the false arrest and imprisonment of a teenage group member. The group worker assumed the roles of advocate and broker, and in partnership with the boy's mother, worked toward his unconditional release from the criminal justice system.

> In an older adolescent boys' group composed of four members, one of the two minority members, a Haitian immigrant, came into the group one evening announcing that he had spent the previous night in jail. He went on to explain how he was confronted by a detective who accused him of selling drugs. He was frisked, handcuffed, dragged away, and jailed. The story didn't make sense to the worker

since this 18-year-old had no criminal history, juvenile or otherwise, and was singularly naive about drugs and alcohol, as evidenced by his many questions during group discussions. The group worker's suspicion that he had been falsely arrested, as a consequence of his color, was confirmed months later when the charges were dropped.

After the group meeting, the worker approached Willie's mother, expressing his concern about the events he had just learned about in the group. Mrs. G, a soft-spoken woman, had recently been widowed and was recovering from injuries she had sustained in an automobile accident. She was also distraught. "He was shopping for Christmas presents in the mall with friends of the family when they said he was selling drugs. I don't understand this."

A court-appointed legal aid attorney had been assigned to represent Willie. Willie might have had the "look"—baggy pants worn just below the waist in the current inner city style, wool cap, unlaced high-top sneakers, and dark skin—but he was no drug dealer. With the permission of Willie's mother, the worker contacted a lawyer–social worker who was known to do pro bono legal work. He was skeptical at first but finally agreed to meet with Willie and his mother to assess the situation. When he returned from his visit he told the worker, "There is no way this kid did it. I'm arranging for affidavits verifying his whereabouts at the time in question." He took on the case, advocating for Willie until the charges were dropped.

One's race or ethnicity can be a powerful determinant of one's social role. As the above example illustrates, young black males walking down the street are often at risk for being confronted by police and subject to false arrest and incarceration. How the judicial system might have treated Willie following his arrest would have also been influenced by his ascribed status, which was compounded by the fact that his family did not have the financial resources to engage a private attorney.

Collectively the above illustrations demonstrate the considerable work that takes place outside of the group itself. Practitioners working with adolescents in groups will find it necessary to be flexible and to assume a variety of complementary professional roles such as mediator, counselor, broker, educator, and advocate. Much of the work on these fronts involves intensive collaboration with parents and involved others.

It is ironic that those who are fond of extolling the "cost effectiveness" of groups fail to recognize the volume of work "behind the scenes" of the group meeting. The term "cost effective," when applied to group work with children and adolescents is often a euphemism for how many paying customers can be crammed into one service hour together. The reality is that work doesn't end after the hour. If it does, it isn't social work with groups. The only cost-effective group work with adolescents is the kind that contributes to a reduction in the social costs of neglected youth.

THE ENDING TRANSITION WITH PARENTS

The ending transition in the group signals a separation and impending loss for parents of group members as well. They have struggled through the earliest stages of the group's development, monitored their children's progress during the course of the group's life, provided data regarding their functioning outside of the group, and collaborated in solving problems.

Group members' reactions during the ending transition may include denial (acting as if the group is not really ending), regression (early group conflicts that were resolved suddenly reemerge), flight (preemptive measures such as leaving the group prematurely to cope with feelings of abandonment—"I'll leave you before you can leave me"), hostility (attempts to sabotage plans), and increased dependence on the group worker. For those youngsters who have experienced great loss in their lives beyond the group, parting may be especially painful as old feelings are reawakened.

Just as many parents are unfamiliar with what to expect in the beginning, they are equally unprepared in the end. By anticipating their children's reactions during this phase, the worker can help the parents to consider and rehearse appropriate responses (i.e., discouraging missed sessions; relating empathically to resistance to ending). The working alliance is reemphasized here as parents and group worker join in preparation for the ending.

Parting also represents a loss for the parent who has developed a relationship with the worker and a connection to the agency. As with the group members, the intensity of one's feelings during the ending transition are influenced by earlier losses. By exploring these feelings and working with parents to discover and support alternative outlets for their children, a healthy transition can be made.

Often parents will ask, "Can we come back if we need to?" By ensuring his/her availability, the worker offers support as new experiences are sought. There are those who never return, some who call to say "hello" and make contact to "refuel," and a few who do actually "come back."

Reunion: A Group Worker's Reflection

In the final illustration Kolodny (1992) provides a moving account of a group that was formed around a 9-year-old youngster who was being treated for hemophilia.

I had met weekly with the group for three years in the kitchen of this youngster's home, he being completely homebound. I had also devised program activities in which I tried to reconcile the needs of the members, including the referred child, for expressing aggression with the limitations on aggressive behavior dictated by the child's dangerous condition. The club had met under the watchful eye of his mother, who had remained in the living-room during meetings but would customarily come in to serve refreshments and chat with the boys at the meeting's end.

I was called by the family during the youngster's final hospitalization and remained with them until close to the hour of his death. Sometime thereafter I was a bit surprised to have the mother call and ask me if I could possibly get in touch with the five other former group members. She had not seen them in several years, most of them having moved far from the neigh-borhood. She wanted so much to see them. Through one of the former members who still lived nearby I was able to make contact with the others, now well into their teens, and, a week after the funeral, we met on the corner outside the house. They had not seen me in some four years, and a couple of them, lanky sixteen-year-olders, laughed and said, "Ralph, you shrank." We went into the house and sat in the kitchen with the mother. Her tears were matched by the warmth of her greeting. Where she found the emotional resources I do not know, but when I left the house she was still sitting with the boys and reminiscing about some of the lively and humorous incidents that had occurred in the group, four years and more before. (pp. 168–169)

CONCLUSION

All too often we experience parents and involved others as a thorn in our "professional" side. We overidentify with the youngsters, perceive parents' questions as "the third degree," and hide behind the inviolable cloak of confidentiality. To get beyond these barriers requires genuineness, a systems perspective, flexibility, courage, and humility.

CHAPTER 7

The Use of Problem
Solving in Group Work
Promoting Reflection, Critical
Thinking, and Mutual Aid

Growth in the beginning phase of group work is characterized by reduced anxiety, increased trust, growing commitment, clarity of purpose, and establishment of norms. As the group matures, the emphasis on these issues, while never completely resolved or immune from regressive pulls, lessens, and the group moves into a middle phase of development. In the middle phase, the unique culture of each group becomes more pronounced. Patterns of social interaction and communication need to develop. Members need to come to respect the similarities and differences among them. With a stable membership, a growing commitment to the group and its purpose, and the development of a more cohesive unit, the group becomes a place where the members can really work on problems— exchange, differ, confront, try out, really share.[1]

A thoughtful process of problem solving is a sine qua non of group work. Group work with adolescents requires special attention to promoting positive mental health, a counterforce to deficit model thinking in which the emphasis is on pathology. Promoting positive mental health can be equated with ego building and includes strengthening judgment, reality testing, regulation of impulses, mastery and competence, empathy, critical thinking, and any other behaviors that enable adolescents to deal more effectively with inner and outer realities. The small group is an ideal place for all this to occur. Membership in a group that values mutual aid implies a focus on strengths. In such groups, the message to each participant is,

[1]Many of the examples in this chapter occur beyond the groups' "beginning phase." See Appendix 7.1 for a detailed summary of the "middle phase" of group work (compliments of Roselle Kurland).

"You have something to offer in this group." Problem solving in the group is one avenue for the expression of what one has to offer. As Somers (1976) has so aptly stated, "Problem solving is so germane to social group work that the two are almost inseparable—one assumes the other" (p. 333).

This chapter outlines and illustrates the use of Dewey's problem-solving model in group work with adolescents through a variety of practice examples. The first example will provide a step-by-step illustration, integrating concepts of mutual aid along the way. The next three examples are presented more loosely, illustrating that not all problems can be addressed in a linear fashion. The final example is a verbatim transcript of an adolescent group, accompanied by the group worker's (my) commentary about the process as it pertains to problem solving and mutual aid.

A PRAGMATIC MODEL FOR PROBLEM SOLVING IN THE GROUP

John Dewey (1910), a pioneer in the progressive education movement, a major influence on the development of group work, created a scientific model for problem solving. The steps of the model, as applied to group work, are:

1. Sensing that a problem exists in the group.
2. Identifying the problem.
3. Exploring the problem in depth.
4. Identifying possible solutions and obstacles.
5. Choosing a solution, try it, and evaluate it.

Below is a presentation of the model using parallel descriptions of two groups to illustrate (1) a group of mothers of adolescents, and (2) a coed group of adolescents (ages 17–19).

PRACTICE ILLUSTRATIONS

Grappling with a Group-Internal Problem: Addressing Norms and Taboos

The mothers' group. This group consisted of 10 women, all who lived in the same affluent community. Most of them knew one another, at least casually, prior to the group. All had adolescent children who attended the same schools. The group met on a monthly basis in their own homes to address their concerns related to being parents of adolescents. The group worker, a male social worker from a local mental health center, had developed a network of similar groups for parents who were resistant to going to the local clinic (Malekoff, Quaglia, & Levine, 1987).

The older-adolescent group. This group consisted of five members, three boys and two girls, all of whom had been referred to the mental health clinic mentioned above. They were all in transition, about to leave or having recently graduated from high school. None of them had settled on plans for work and/or college. All of them had been involved in risky behaviors (i.e., physical fighting, carrying weapons, drug use, robbery, driving while intoxicated, unprotected sex, drug selling, vandalism). Arrests, jail time, pregnancy, abortion, drug dealing, and gang activity were all aspects of their experiences. The group was mixed racially and ethnically. The group worker was the same practitioner who met with the mother's group.

The two groups are presented consecutively, each illustrating the use of the problem-solving model to address a group-internal problem in the groups' beginning phase of development. Characteristic beginning phase dynamics exhibited in both groups included feelings of trust versus mistrust, approach-avoidance behavior, anxiety about the unknown, exploration, and preliminary commitment and consideration of group norms. The frame of reference influencing the member's perceptions and behavior at this stage of the group is societal. That is, "Members draw upon those past experiences which appear similar to the present one, and in so doing find continuity, and meaning . . . as well as a basis for orienting their own conduct in the group" (Garland et al., 1973, p. 36).

Sensing That a Problem Exists in the Group

Something is going on that requires some attention. The difficulty might be group-internal, that is, something related to the interactions, norms, or structure of the group; or it might be group-external, that is, occurring in the home, school, or community, that has not yet been clearly identified.

In the early meetings of the mother's group, one of the members habitually dozed off for several minutes at a time. At first the others surreptitiously made eye contact with each other, secretly acknowledging that something was going on. But no one openly addressed what everyone in the room could plainly see.

In the adolescent group, one of the members had what appeared to be a perpetual "head cold." At first his throat and nose clearing symptoms drew no reaction. In time, they became more pronounced and unusual. As Jerry's "sniffles" intensified in frequency and decibel level, the others exchanged furtive glances with one another, a grin now and again, but never a word.

Identifying the Problem

The group members must have a clear sense of the problem they are addressing, so that they're all headed in the same direction.

In the case of the dozing group member, the worker finally addressed the problem, turning it back to the group, so that it could be openly identified. He chose the communication pattern of addressing the whole group at once by asking the simple question, "Does anyone here notice anything unusual happening, anything out of the ordinary?" So accustomed to concealment, the group members' responses ranged from feigned surprise to dramatic expressions of bewilderment. Nevertheless, the worker pushed ahead, and finally the "secret" was out. The group soon learned from the sleeping member that she suffered from narcolepsy, a condition that involves a frequent and uncontrollable desire for sleep. They were, as one might expect, tolerant of their fellow member's condition. However, there remained the issue of the members' avoidance of something that was directly under their collective nose. To let the group off the hook, once the dozing member's condition had been "diagnosed," would have robbed them of an opportunity to explore, in greater depth, underlying issues of privacy, trust, self-exposure, and risk taking in the group. The worker suggested to the group, "Let's take a closer look at what's been happening in the group, at how we arrived at this point." As the group soon acknowledged, the problem in the group was not that someone had narcolepsy, it was that the group had danced around and avoided openly addressing an uncomfortable issue.

The adolescent group continued to avoid any direct mention of Jerry's "sniffles." Finally the worker stopped the action and said, in his most professionally tuned voice, undergirded with years of experience, "Something's going on in here." Everyone paused and then innocently pled ignorance: "What are you talking about?" That is, everyone except for Jerry, who by that time figured out what was going on. More comfortable with the taboo area than the others, Jerry informed them about the subject in which he was an expert, Tourette syndrome.

He explained that he had a neurological disorder characterized by motor and/or vocal tics (i.e., involuntary, rapid, sudden movements that occur repeatedly in the same way and might include any of the following: throat clearing, head jerking, barking noises, facial grimacing, vocalizing socially unacceptable words, and repeating a word, sound, or phrase just heard). He said that his tics were of a more simple variety and had improved over the years with the help of medication. The others listened respectfully and, in time, warmed up to the subject of Tourette syndrome, asking Jerry many questions about how he copes with various situations. However, there remained the problem, as in the mothers' group, of their avoidance of something that had been right before their eyes. Stated a bit differently than in the mothers' group, the worker said, "Okay, it's great that this is out in the open now and that nobody is hiding from what's right in front of us. We're all on the same page now. Why do you think it was so hard to get to this point? Why all of the secretiveness?" As the group soon acknowledged, the problem in the group was not that someone had Tourette syndrome, it was that the group had been unable to openly address something that was happening right before their eyes.

Exploring the Problem in Depth

This is the area that is most often neglected in problem solving. Too often, groups jump from problem identification directly to finding solutions, without an adequate period of reflection and exploration.

It was agreed that without trust, the group would be prevented from dealing directly with any problems of significance. They described the community in which they all lived as having a well-developed grapevine, along which information traveled fast. One member, Mary Ann, said that exposing personal and family problems in the group would be risky. Another gave a cryptic example of a betrayed confidence generated from another parents' group she had belonged to, under the auspices of the local school district. To amplify her and the others' feelings, the worker said, "It sounds like you're fearful that the same thing is likely to occur in here if you share something personal." They all nodded in agreement. Another member, Joan, deduced that the reason that so many in the community had avoided the local mental health center was because "no one wants to be seen entering that building by anyone else who knows them." Again the others nodded in agreement and, with the worker's prodding, talked about what it might mean to "go for help, to acknowledge a problem in the family." Further exploration revealed that many in the group had moved from the city to this upscale suburban community, in the hope of finding Utopia. For some, moving from the "old neighborhoods" had been particularly traumatic as the dream of Utopia became tempered with reality. Problems in the family, which seemed to become more pronounced and difficult to conceal as their children moved into adolescence, were experienced as a source of shame and embarrassment.

The discussion took an interesting turn when the worker asked the teen group how likely they might be to avoid other issues, however obvious or subtle, in the group. He enumerated familiar examples of dangerous behaviors such as drug use, fighting, use of weapons, and unprotected sex. Projecting ahead, he asked, "Will you just look the other way, maybe secretly smile at one another, when you get a whiff of something else important going on?" As the discussion evolved, they each confirmed some familiarity with a misguided code of peer group loyalty and silence, in which destructive behaviors are overlooked and the overriding norm is to "live and let live." The philosophy sounded, to the worker, like what might be a fractured version of a well-known cliché—"I'm okay, you're okay; (wink) okay?" The worker posed the question of whether such a code (norm) could be operative in a group where helping one another sometimes means challenging destructive behavior: "Are you saying that you'll look the other way in here, kind of like you did when you noticed something happening with Jerry?" He asked about the consequences of certain past behaviors (i.e., sexually transmitted disease, pregnancy, abortion, probation, incarceration, driving while intoxicated) and whether the outcomes might have been different if a trusted person confronted them before it was too late. This stimulated a dialectical process, an exchange of views and opinions among members. The essence of the discussion was whether or not someone "is gonna do what they're gonna do no matter what; so what difference does it make what anyone else has to say anyway." This seemed to reflect, more or less, the belief system that they brought from their outside experiences, into the group.

Identifying Possible Solutions and Obstacles

Imaginatively consider. Brainstorm. What options are available? What are the strengths and limitations of these alternatives? Is what the group is setting out to do, in fact, do-able?

Using the "third person" (a less threatening alternative than the "first person"), the mothers' group imaginatively considered "arbitrary" circumstances and issues that they might find difficult to confront in the group. They shared a variety of "embarrassing" scenarios (e.g., child's suspension from school, drinking and drugging behavior, the need for special educational services, sexual activity, interracial dating). Reviewing and reestablishing group norms for privacy and confidentiality helped to emphasize the issue of trust and how open members might be in the group. They rejected one brainstorming suggestion of moving the group to a more neutral site such as the school or church. They agreed that meeting in their homes, as opposed to an institutional setting, may have contributed to their concerns about the group's boundaries. However, they decided to continue meeting there, since the informality of the home was valued. The group affirmed the norm of respecting each other's privacy and using discretion outside of the group.

In the adolescent group the members considered how they might address problems that seemed easier to avoid. How would they deal with issues and concerns that were not quite so obvious as Tourette syndrome (e.g., personal, family, peer problems)? Jerry revealed what it was like for him growing up, being alternately ignored, teased, and rejected by other kids, and never knowing for sure if it was the Tourette syndrome or something else. He said that it was a relief for him to have it out in the open in the group. Seeing their options as continuing to avoid and ignore emergent problems or trying to be more direct, the members agreed that they would make an effort to be more forthright as the group moved ahead. Through this mutual agreement, they took a step toward establishing a different kind of norm for helping one another.

Choosing a Solution, Trying It, and Evaluating It

The solution in the mother's group was to continue meeting in their homes, take risks to be more open, and be sensitive to members' privacy needs. Only the test of time would determine whether or not the members would feel free and trusting enough to share difficult issues in the group and to handle them with discretion. When one of the members revealed the "secret" of her son's prolonged truancy from school and then another shared the history of alcoholism in her family following her husband's relapse, the group was put to the test.

In the adolescent group, the solution was to pay attention and respond to what was happening inside the group itself and to reach beyond politeness and risk being straightforward with one another. This solution provided the members with a chance to practice being more direct rather than politely avoidant. Trying out this kind of communication with one another helped the group to learn that confrontation and aggression are not synonymous, and that being diplomatically direct or tactfully honest were alternatives to raising one's voice or shaking a threatening finger in someone's face. This was the kind of solution that later enabled the group to confront another "sniffling" member, who they suspected was at risk for cocaine addiction. By not politely avoiding his problem or colluding with him out of some misguided code of peer group loyalty, the members were able to supportively confront him and reinforce a recommendation that he enter a drug rehab program.

The two illustrations demonstrate the importance of identifying problems, exploring them in depth, and not simply jumping from a loosely defined concern to a flurry of poorly conceived cookbook solutions. Directly addressing strange and/or unknown conditions and behaviors (e.g., narcolepsy, Tourette syndrome) was taboo in these groups, as it is in much of polite society. To break a taboo the practitioner charts a course aimed at mentioning the unmentionable (Middleman & Wood, 1990a). These groups mirrored the norms that their members brought into the groups, drawn from their outside experiences. When such norms are not challenged in the group, they are likely to constitute a significant obstacle to the group's reaching its goals and to the individual's and group's ability to reach out to one another, a significant feature of mutual aid. Each group must create its own unique culture, including norms that enable members to address taboo subjects. In both of these groups, addressing norms and taboos helped to cultivate what all mutual aid groups must—a culture for work (Shulman, 1992).

Implicit in the problem-solving model is the process of stopping the action, reflecting, critically thinking, and imaginatively considering. Use of the "scientific method" in problem solving does not suggest abandoning spontaneity in the group. The contrary is the case. The problem-solving model supports and values spontaneous and creative thinking, by providing a structure within which the imagined can become real.

In the next example a boys' group struggles with the problem of getting accurate information related to sexual activity and protecting oneself and one's partner. In this illustration, as with the ones that follow it, the problem-solving model is presented less as a step-by-step guideline to problem resolution and more as a framework to be kept in mind, coupled with the principle of enabling the members to help one another by fostering mutual aid in the group.

Grappling with "Myth-Information" in the Group

Beyond the internal life of the group, there are those problems and issues that arise from the members' experiences outside of the group. In one of my groups of 15- and 16-year-old boys meeting in a child guidance center, the topic of discussion was sexually transmitted diseases (STDs). All were either sexually active or involved in relationships in which sexual activity appeared imminent.

> The boys were trading information about what they knew (and didn't know). The room was filled with a curious combination of fact and fiction, not unlike typical conversations of natural groups of teens. For example: "Herpes? That's when your dick blows up." "No, that's when there's all little animals inside you and shit." "No, you're talking 'bout crabs." "What about gonnorhea?" "I know this girl who got gonnorhea of the throat—she was sucking a man's dick." "You can tell if a girl has an STD by putting your finger in your ear, digging out some wax, and then putting your finger inside her. If it stings then she's got it. Don't laugh. I saw it in a film in health class." "You can tell if a girl has an STD by her smell. If she smells nasty down there, then she got something. Don't mess with her." When the worker first suggested that they seemed confused about certain things, they became defensive, dismissing and challenging him—"Wanna bet? I'll bet you five dollars, right now." "What would you know?" "Andy [the worker] probably has the sex life of a rock." In time, though, they became more open to listening to and exploring different sources of information, gradually acknowledging their need to know.

Practitioners should take note that it is normal for their adolescent groups—once the members get to know one another, size up the situation, and decide to stick around for a while—to have the look and feel of informal groups of youth gathered on their own natural turf (i.e., school yard, street corner, park, or wherever they hang out). The banter, the language, the posturing, the style—it's all a part of a culture that they are familiar and comfortable with. For adolescents to be expected to adjust their relational style to some standard held by adults is a mistake. The key is to allow their culture to emerge naturally and to join it rather than attempt to change it. Joining it doesn't mean becoming a part of it; it means understanding and respecting it. Of course good judgment and discretion are always paramount. The above conversation was held in a private meeting room. Had the same conversation been held in a more public setting like a waiting room within earshot of others, then confronting their use of language and lack of discretion would be in order.

Let's return to the group of adolescent boys seeking accurate information about STDs.

It turned out that, in a round-about way, they were also seeking information about how to get tested for HIV. The worker tried to inform them about the local testing site and procedures. They all talked over him, effectively short-circuiting anything of value that he might have had to share. That is, all except for one of the boys, who made fleeting eye contact with the worker and seemed to be responding in concert with him, obviously familiar with the information he was trying to impart.[2] The worker, recognizing that the group was not focused on him, remembered that he wasn't the only one available to provide help to the members. He asked, on a hunch, "Has anyone here ever been tested for STDs?" The boy who seemed to be responding, Frank, raised his hand high, obviously anxious to share some information with the group. He started off quickly, as if in a race to get to the finish line. The worker stopped him momentarily, to help him to help the others, and suggested that he start from the beginning. The worker coached him as follows: "Okay, you walk into the clinic and then what happens, travel us through it, take your time." He was able to take this direction and did a masterful job of carefully explaining the testing process from beginning to end. There wasn't a single interruption. He had succeeded where the worker had not— that is until it dawned on the worker that success didn't rest upon him being the central helping person.

One of the time honored traditions of good group work is that group members are respected as helpers. Problem solving should not rest solely on the shoulders of the practitioner. If it does, it's not group work. It is worth reminding oneself that, if you find that you're working too hard in the group, there is probably something wrong. As the preceding example illustrates, problem identification–exploration and solution generation–implementation don't often develop in linear fashion in adolescent groups, or in most other groups for that matter. The problem-solving process is more of a circular one. "In reality, themes and problems may emerge only partially in early sessions and then reemerge later in new forms when group members become more comfortable with each other and the worker" (Shulman, 1992, p. 419).

It is useful for the worker to have the problem-solving model in mind

---

[2]By the way, be careful about making prolonged eye contact with adolescents. While one cannot generalize here, many teens don't seem to like it—"You lookin' at me?" Maybe it's too intimate, too intimidating, or a combination of both. Of course this can change over time, possibly indicating an increased level of trust and/or intimacy.

but not expect the members to conform to a rigid step-by-step protocol. (However, teaching the model itself—as a tool—to a group that can handle it, may be a worthwhile activity and use of "program" [see Chapter 8].) In the boys' group, the problem was a lack of accurate information. Frank's competent description of how to get tested for HIV/AIDS provided the others with vital information and reinforced the importance of valuing the members as helpers.

The next illustration highlights the work of the group in solving problems that move from the near things of individual change to the far things of social action.

Problem Solving and Social Goals: Finding a Public Voice through the Group

Although not always operative, in social work groups there are the traditional dual foci in which members are (1) working on their own behalf and (2) developing and promoting responsible citizenship and social goals beyond the group. This was the case for one group of 12- to 15-year-old African American adolescents who were concerned with the problem of violence in their community. Early in the group's development, they were faced with a serious challenge. A local newspaper reported on the escalating tension between blacks and Hispanics, including a string of violent events. The most recent had been the murder of a Mexican immigrant who was walking home from work. Violence was on the group members' minds even before this well-publicized incident.

> In recent weeks they talked about how insecure they felt in school. They spoke about students carrying weapons and apathetic security guards who, they insisted, were selling drugs to students. They feared that, "No one will listen until someone gets hurt or dies." The issue of bigotry was raised as they recounted a recent attack against a Haitian immigrant in the high school boy's room. On one occasion, as if to bring the reality of their stories to life in the group, two of the members brought in their 13-year-old friend. During the course of the meeting, with the gentle encouragement of her friends, she raised her skirt to reveal welts across her thighs. She reported being beaten with an electrical cord by her mother. The worker and group worked collaboratively to establish trust and reach out to her and her mother.

Following the murder of the Mexican native, community activists from various neighborhood groups banded together to form a coalition. They worked in earnest to prevent anticipated rioting and unite the area's ethnic groups.

A short-term goal of the fledgling coalition was to organize a "March for Unity." The group members got wind of the plans and seized the opportunity to organize youth in the community. They saw this as a chance to make a public statement about violence, to let their voices be heard. They constructed banners and signs and decorated the program's van. As it turned out, they organized the largest youth contingent that marched in the parade.

Organizing and marching in the parade didn't solve the safety problem in the school. It didn't address some of the individual concerns of the group members either. It provided, however, a chance for the members to participate in the life of their community and to practice and gain experience with thoughtful and responsible citizenship. The immediate problem facing the community was the growing unrest and potential for rioting and physical clashes between ethnic/racial groups. The decision to participate in the march was one solution to the problem of violence. It allowed the group to move beyond talking among one another, enabling them to express themselves in a public arena. The fact that rioting and further violence were averted told them, as they evaluated the experience, that their efforts contributed to a constructive alternative to violence.

In another group, it was the parents of younger adolescents who decided to couple their individual needs with social justice.

A group of parents who shared the horror of their children having been sexually abused by a trusted scout leader joined together for emotional support under the auspices of a local child and family guidance center. Through the group experience they discovered that they had even more in common, as one mother put it, "a sense of betrayal by society." They talked about their ongoing victimization at the hands of insensitive child protective and criminal justice systems and about a news media more concerned with sensationalizing their stories than joining them as advocates. During the ending phase of the group, the members decided to recontract and add advocacy to the group's activities. A new purpose of the group would be to reduce the risk of insensitive treatment at the hands of outside systems for future victims and their families.

By going through this transformation—from support to advocacy—and becoming effective advocates, the members also sent an important message to their children. They taught their children, through their living example, how one can remain hopeful by fighting injustice.

In the next illustration the group helps a member to rehearse what is anticipated as a difficult meeting with a school administrator. The use of experiential learning is demonstrated as a means of transferring learning from inside the group to outside of the group.

Rehearsal in Problem Solving and Mutual Aid: The Value of Doing in Learning

While problems are identified and explored within the group, solutions are often implemented outside of the group. Rehearsal, a feature of mutual aid, can help group members to prepare for implementing solutions outside of the group (Shulman, 1992).

> In a middle-adolescent, coed group of 15- and 16-year-olds, one of the members, John, was anticipating a meeting with the chief administrator, the principal of the "special school" he attended in the district. He had been sent to the school 2 years earlier as a result of his chronically disruptive behavior. Finally reaching the opportunity to return to his home district to complete high school in his local public school, he had to first make it through this "parole hearing," with the same administrator with whom he'd locked horns in the past. The problem was identified as his "short fuse." Exploring the problem involved (1) understanding the history of his temper and impulsive behavior, (2) identifying high-risk situations or "red flags" that often led to his losing control, and (3) sizing-up the upcoming situation, the meeting with the principal. The group helped John, by anticipating the event and role playing various scenarios, to practice how he might respond to subtle provocation, intended or not, by his "tormentor." For example, one group member took on the principal's role and said, "John, tell me why I should let you out of this school. I've reviewed your past record, and I've come to the conclusion that you don't even belong here. No, you belong in a cage with the rest of the animals." Everyone in the group cracked up laughing. But John couldn't deny, when asked, that he had a "twinge" to go on the offensive, even though he knew it was an imaginary scenario. It was the "twinge" (impulse) that the group identified as the "major thing" that John needed to control so that it wouldn't continue to control him. (A member in another group with a similar problem described his "twinge" as an "adrenaline rush.") In any case, helping adolescents to identify physical sensations leading up to impulsive, violent, and out-of-control behavior is critical to addressing behavioral problems.

In this practice illustration, experiential learning, a critical aspect of whole person learning, is emphasized. "Learning experiences are deliberately constructed to emphasize many sensory, information-receiving systems (touching, moving, visualizing, tasting, and so forth), as contrasted to merely hearing and reading" (Middleman, 1990, pp. 2–3). As Dewey (1938) asserted, "Amid all uncertainties there is one permanent frame of reference: namely the organic connection between education and personal experience" (p. 12).

The final illustration is a transcript of a group addressing the normative adolescent problem of separating from family and increasing autonomous functioning. The process described represents an integration of problem solving and mutual aid and provides the reader with a glimpse of the evolution of a particular problem through the verbatim interaction of the group supplemented by the worker's (my) reflections about what is happening along the way.

"She's Very, Very Bossy": Integrating Problem Solving and Mutual Aid

The following practice illustration is of a middle- to older-adolescent boys' group meeting led by me in a community mental health center. James, Bruce, and Tony, three of the group's five members are present. The group is in its middle phase of development, characterized by mutual revelation and a greater demand for work and expectation to move forward with their ideas and plans. All three members have been, in the past, either suspended or expelled from school and/or have spent time in jail. The group purposes include helping the members to put a reflective pause in-between impulse and action, to learn to better mediate the various systems impinging on their lives, and to address normative adolescent issues that they might be struggling with or find to be of interest (e.g., sexuality, drug and alcohol use, intergroup relations).

James is a 16-year-old African American who lives with his older sister who is his legal guardian; Bruce is a 17-year-old Ecuadorian American who lives with his father; and Tony is an 18-year-old Portuguese American who lives with both parents. Interspersed in brackets are my thoughts as the group process unfolds. Comments related to the problem-solving model and dynamics of mutual aid are *italicized in bold print*. (GW stands for group worker; the author.)

> [The boys come in together, and James is in an obviously semiagitated state, shaking his head. A quick scanning of the group reveals that *something's up*. James looks a bit agitated. Better check it out.]

GW: What's going on?

JAMES: My sister, she's very, very bossy. I don't know how her boyfriend puts up with her. I mean she calmed down on him. But she's very, very bossy. She's been with him for a couple of months. He must really, really like her because anyone else would have let go (*snaps his fingers*) like that. I mean she's very, very bossy; very, very bossy.

GW: But what you're saying, that "she calmed down on him," is that she knows she has a problem with this.

[I have a *sense that there is a problem* and that it has something to do with James. James had made the transition from head shaking to the articulation of some concern. Could it be that he is simply concerned about his sister's love life? Nah!]

JAMES: Why should I suffer? She's always telling me, "James, these are the best years of your life."

TONY: These are the best years of your life, and you should live your own life.

[Hmmm, James appears to be talking about himself and his sister. The boyfriend angle was just a lead in. While not a universally *taboo subject*, bringing private family matters into the group might be considered taboo for some. Let me check out where the others are with this theme, and *search for common ground*.]

GW: Tony, do you think that what he's talking about is unusual, being a junior in high school and getting angry at your parents?

TONY: When I was a junior in high school I was crazy. I was flipping tables and throwing chairs whenever I got pissed off.

BRUCE: Yeah and you got a PINS petition [Person in Need of Supervision status from Family Court] for that stuff. You know what I'm saying. He doesn't have a PINS right now.

[Sounds like Tony's been *in the same boat*, unfortunately in the brig.]

JAMES: I'm going to be independent. She wants to do everything for me, and I don't want her to do that because she always works. She's always saying she's stressed and everything. She's mainly stressed over me. I mean, she wants to buy my school clothes and she wants to worry about Christmas and all that stuff. *I can get a job!* I can do this shit myself. Goddam. She's making things hard for herself, and she's bringing me down with her. I'm not going down.

[The *problem is gradually moving more clearly into focus*. Back to the boat. The boat I'm referring to here is the *we're-all-in-the-same-boat* phenomenon, an important part of establishing mutual aid in the group.) I have to keep trying to *seek common ground* and avoid running a *casework-in-the-group* number on them.[3]]

GW: (*to Tony*) Is that the same thing you have to deal with or is it different?

TONY: I just want to do it all, whatever I want. There's no question about it.

GW: How long did it take for your mother to change?

TONY: I used to do whatever I wanted to, but now she doesn't scream as much when I do something. Like if I were to go out and come in at 3 in the morning.

BRUCE: My father doesn't say anything to me. The only time he gets pissed at me is when I don't go to school or if I cut classes. If I come home late he doesn't care. He knows I can take care of myself. I know how to take care of myself. When I was little . . .

TONY: (*cutting off Bruce*) I'd do all that shit. All the time she used to kick me out of the house, and I used to go out and sleep over my friend's house, and I used to always call up—you know—and they would come get me and shit. Finally I got wise. I just went and slept on the grass.

BRUCE: I never got kicked out of my house, and I never got grounded. Never been grounded. My father says I do get grounded, but then he forgets.

[Looks like Bruce is not fully committed to boarding this boat. He's intimating some of the same problems—"I do get grounded but then he forgets." I'll give it a shot; see if the boat is ready to pull out.]

GW: So what you guys are talking about is something that's universal— like everybody at this age deals with this, right?

[Did I say "universal"? Is this too jargony or what? Acchh! I should have used another word. Maybe I should have said, *"It seems like you're all in the same boat."* Yeah. The second guessing never ends. Sometimes when I speak, they all laugh and say, "EWW." James invented that. EWW stands for "educated-white-way." James likes to mimic me with an exaggerated "nerdy" voice. Hey, I'm no nerd. It's actually pretty funny. Can't afford to be too defensive with adolescents. Somebody once told me that *"seriousness is the root of all mental illness."* I like that.]

TONY: If your parents don't care about you, then you don't have to worry about that, you know. They're usually afraid to let you do something.

---

[3]Casework in the group: That's where the worker has what amounts to an individual meeting with a group member in the presence of the rest of the group, occasionally asking the others to pitch in (Kurland & Salmon, 1992).

[Nice supportive *reframing*, Tony. I can't believe he said that. It never fails to amaze me what these kids produce. Not only a nice reframing, but an opening for James to proceed without too much guilt about "bad-mouthing" his sister. His statement also represents a further *exploration of the problem.* The impact of this coming from the guys is greater than had it come from me. It shows how *tuned in* they are. James doesn't often ask for help. He is available for others but tends to be stoic about what's bothering him. What Tony's comment suggests is that maybe James's sister is not *just* bossy. Let's check it out.]

GW: So what James is describing about his sister shows that she cares?

JAMES: Yeah, yeah she does (*hesitates and softens for a moment*). But that shit is not right, it's not right (*more agitated again*) What do I do when I get old and in college? She still going to buy my school clothes? It's my second to last year of school man, you know . . . and I still feel like I'm in middle school.

[*Exploring his feelings in greater depth.*]

BRUCE: Bein' in at 8 o'clock at night. Good TV shows don't even start at that fuckin' time. It's so stupid. I don't come in 'til 2 A.M.

[Yeah right! (as my 8-year-old son is fond of saying). Thanks a lot Bruce, that was a real help. Let's explore the family context and history a bit further.]

GW: Did you ever ask your parents (*to Bruce and Tony*) or your sister (*to James*) what it was like for them when they were your age?

JAMES: See that's another thing . . . my brother tells me—he's older and doesn't live with us; he has children. My mother [who died when James was 9] didn't treat *him* that way. You know she gave him leeway. She understood that he was 16 years old and had to go out and see the world.

GW: Your mother treated the boys different from the girls, but your sister treats you . . .

JAMES: (*finishing my sentence*). . . . *the way she was raised!*

GW: So in other words, what she learned about being a mother for someone who's 16 is how she was raised? And now she's trying to bring you up the same way?

JAMES: She used to tell stories about how she would get in trouble if she didn't come in at the right time. And usually the time she came in was early. The only thing that my brother had to do was tell my mother where he was, and he never got in trouble. You know, I can't tell her where I'm going. I mean I could tell her where I'm going. I have no problem with that. But I've got to use some kind of excuse to go out. I tell her I got to walk the dog or some shit.

TONY: What time did you have to go home when you were 12 years old?

JAMES: Twelve years old? Shit. Well that's when I lived in Brooklyn, and I didn't really like going out, so that was no problem.

GW: And this, when she does this, it makes you feel like you're a middle school kid?

TONY: What's the earliest you had to come home for curfew?

[Don't you just love it when you ask a question and the group totally ignores you? It's so affirming, so validating. Thanks, guys.]

JAMES: Before dark in the summertime.

BRUCE: Shit, my earliest curfew was 12 o'clock.

GW: What would you suggest, Tony? You're a little bit older now. You're 18, right?

TONY: Yeah.

GW: (to James) You're 16, right?

JAMES: (nods yes)

GW: (to Tony) So you're a couple of years past that. What would you suggest?

BRUCE: Have fun!

[Time to begin to consider possible *solutions and obstacles.*]

GW: No, in terms of how to deal with this. You know he's saying, "I got to run away . . . I got to take off."

TONY: That's what I did, and then they caught on. And my friend ran to his mom's. She's all fucked up though, so he had to leave there and go back to his dad's.

[Doesn't make running away, under the circumstances, seem too appetizing.]

GW: Is this the guy that you were talking about, in an earlier meeting, whose mother was a cocaine addict?

TONY: Uh-huh, he moved back with his dad and left her.

GW: So what you're saying is that James . . .

TONY: I don't think that he should—like—just go run away, you know?

[Nothing like an emphatic statement by a contemporary, a fellow group member, to hammer home the point. A lot more persuasive than I am, I bet.]

BRUCE: He doesn't know that.

> [Now you're getting it, Bruce. You want to make sure James gets the point that this is a **poor solution.** Great!]

TONY: I don't know [if he does or doesn't get it].

BRUCE: I think you have to be 18 to get off a PINS petition [intimating that James's sister might take him to Family Court if he runs away].

TONY: Wait a minute, you might be right.

BRUCE: 'Cause you have to be an adult to get off a PINS petition.

JAMES: (*obviously frustrated, reflecting on the absurdity, as he sees it, of his dilemma*) But what if I do stay out past curfew? She can object to any crime I might commit, but staying out late is no crime! This is not a crime at all! I'm not even thinking about crime! This is not near crime!

GW: It sounds to me like this is something you have to work out somehow with your sister. Not with the legal system or anything like that. It sounds like something you and she have to work out. She knows that it's a problem. She already said to you that she's having difficulty letting go.

> [Another **possible solution** suggested. **What are the obstacles?** The idea here is to move in the direction of helping James and his sister **to reach out to one another, to rediscover their stake in one another.**]

TONY: He should just call up and tell his sister what he's doing. If she says no, that's messed up. I mean I did that with my mother.

> [**Another solution**—checking in.]

GW: So you're saying that if you check in, that that makes a difference sometimes.

BRUCE: Like just call up and let her know.

GW: What about that?

> [Seems simple and logical enough.]

JAMES: I already do that!

GW: And what, she doesn't accept that?

JAMES: Basically, I'm not out on the street. I'm staying wherever I go. You see, that's the one thing, I joined this new choir; it's a youth choir, you know we still have fun like we're in the street but we're singing in church. And she doesn't approve of me being out late, but she lets me go. But sometimes I have to beg her to go to rehearsals. I gotta worry about asking her. I shouldn't have to worry about that. She should be glad I'm not on the street.

GW: So what you're saying is that she's just having a terrible time letting go of you.

[A little *more exploration* appears in order.]

JAMES: And she gives me a curfew. When I have rehearsals she gives me a curfew, but we practice long. And I have to rush the whole choir to make sure that somebody takes me home. And I'm a lead singer in the choir, *so I have to be there.* So that's another thing.

GW: So what do you think, what do you think you want to do about this? Do you think she should come into the group?

[A wild suggestion.]

JAMES: (*with his head hanging and shaking*) She needs to seek therapy. She needs therapy. She needs some *let-go* therapy.

[*Let-go therapy*—it has a nice ring to it. I love it!]

BRUCE: Why don't you bring her in? Why don't you bring her in and have a one-on-one session?

[These guys are pretty focused and working in concert at this point. As a result *my role feels less central.*]

JAMES: (*pointing to me*) He's going to have a one-on-one session with her.

[Who, me?]

GW: Why wouldn't you want to be included? I'm not going to make you do it of course; I can't, but I'm just wondering why you wouldn't want to do that.

[*Exploring obstacles.*]

JAMES: 'Cause I get so mad. Andy, I've changed. I've changed.

GW: Changed in what way?

JAMES: I have an "I don't give a fuck attitude." One thing she'll tell me—that she doesn't like my attitude. That's one thing. Because that's the kind of face [attitude] that I give her now. It'd be hard for me last year to think about hitting her. But this year, I would actually knock the hell out of her. That's how much she gets on my nerves.

GW: Let me ask you guys this question. What are the advantages and the disadvantages of him coming to discuss this with his sister together, or having her come in on her own?

BRUCE: One thing he's saying is that if she doesn't like what they talk about in here, then later she's going to start yelling at him.

JAMES: Eventually we're going to talk about it when we get home, and that's exactly why I don't wanna talk about it with her here.

[*More obstacles.*]

BRUCE: You'll probably get a stricter curfew if you go against her. What do you call it when somebody does something and you're not supposed to?

TONY: Disobey?

BRUCE: No something else, a different word. You know, you do it just because the person said not to.

GW: Do you mean oppositional, rebellious?

BRUCE: Yeah, rebellious. She's going to be like "Oh I give you a curfew at 11 and you don't follow it, how about now you come in at 9?" She's going to do that.

TONY: (*motioning to me*) You and her should just meet. You should go to his [James's] side and tell her like how he feels and that he should be able to do things now that he's 16.

   [*Another solution offered.*]

GW: But why don't you think he should be included in that?

   [*Searching for obstacles, consequences.*]

TONY: I think they'll be getting off the track.

JAMES: We'll tell each other off, then you won't get anywhere. If we're both talking , we'll throw you off and you won't get the understanding. Then I'll lose. *I will lose.* You should talk to her, then tell me what she said, then eventually we're going to talk about it when we get home. Eventually we're going to have to talk about it.

BRUCE: It's better that both you guys argue it out together, because he [James] could state his own feelings about her and she could state her feelings to him about it while he's [referring to me] here.

JAMES: Hold on, hold on . . .

GW: Wait, we're talking about pros and cons, so let's just keep going with that.

BRUCE: And also it's better for you because that means that she knows that you're worried about what she's doing. . . . And you state what you think about it—your opinions. . . . Did anyone see the Oprah Winfrey show, anybody here today? There's a mediator or something like that, that doesn't take sides, she can't take sides. But if you do it at home, your brothers and sisters, whoever is at your house, they're going to take her side and someone might take your side, and it's not going to be even fair.

   [Nice *reframing*, Bruce. Thanks for the consultation, Oprah.]

JAMES: But look, you can do the same thing that you're talking about here. Because he'll [referring to me] talk to her about how I feel. I'm not hiding anything from her. I'm telling Andy to tell her that I said that that's not right [referring to curfew, rules].

BRUCE: She is going to think that you're afraid of her.

[Bruce is really *confronting* James here and *holding the focus* in a *direct and supportive manner.*]

JAMES: We're going to talk about it eventually when I get home. I just don't feel comfortable.

GW: You're saying that Bruce is right?

JAMES: (*leaning forward, head hanging and slowly shaking, and responding in a whisper*) He's right.

GW: So what do you think then about meeting together?

BRUCE: (*looking intently at James, tuning in to his feelings*) You still don't want to do it?

JAMES: I know better, but I'm not going to do it.

TONY: When I was younger, I used to go to my guidance counselor—you know—because my mom was such a bitch. She would call my house and have a meeting. And she would talk to my mother and my mother would just shut up.

[*Emotional support* and *subtle demand* from Tony.]

JAMES: Yeah, she'll tell me, "Shut up and let me talk," and I'll never get anything out. That's how she is.

BRUCE: Yeah but you see that's why you should do it here, because if she comes by herself she might say something that you might not like and . . .

JAMES: Andy will tell me.

BRUCE: Sometimes I don't even like that, having—like—Andy involved. . . . I mean telling parents what to do. . . . People don't want other people telling them how to raise their kids, what time they should come home, you know, all that. They want their kids telling them what's bothering them. That's what my father said. He wants me telling him. You know—he doesn't want anyone else telling him how to raise me.

[I like that, Bruce. Nice point. And now for an attempt at an integrated solution.]

GW: Do you want my opinion about all of this? (*they're silent; I continue*) My opinion is that if you don't feel comfortable meeting together with your sister, and if you would like me to meet with her, I can meet with her. But what I want you to know is that if this is going to get resolved down the road at some point, I think you'll have to come in with her. Maybe not right away. I'm just saying this because you agreed with what Bruce was saying before [referring to Bruce's point about James's sister thinking he is afraid of her], and I think that you (*facing Bruce*) had a good point there. But what do you think about this—and let me get Tony's and Bruce's opinion too—what if I did meet with her and explained to her that, "We talked about this in the group, and James felt most comfortable with the idea of me meeting with you alone but eventually, to try to work this out he agreed—you know—that we should have a meeting together, all three of us, because it's not my place to tell you what to do."

BRUCE: You know how I bring my father here sometimes?

GW: Yeah.

BRUCE: James, this is what I'm saying, she's probably going to be hurt knowing that you can't talk to her.

JAMES: Well that's her fault.

BRUCE: Yeah, but it's not her fault because it's your fault because you're telling somebody else to talk to her first before you do it. James should actually talk to her first and then set up a meeting with you. Let her know about it first and talk to her about it.

   [Bruce, who just talked about parents not wanting to be told what to do, is able to make a subtle shift and demand. He supports James, without minimizing the value of his own earlier statement.]

GW: In other words, James should let her know rather than me. What do you think about that?

JAMES: Yeah, I'm telling her that Andy is going to set up a meeting. Yeah, I'll tell her that tonight as soon as I get home. That's what I'll tell her—"Andy's going to set up a meeting with you tonight."

   [James is beginning to *imaginatively consider* what he might say, to *rehearse* to himself how he might approach his sister. A role play might have been worth a try, but I didn't think of it.]

BRUCE: First you should tell her why.

JAMES: She should know why.

TONY: Not everybody would know why. She might think you're in trouble.

   [Tony working in tandem with Bruce, intimating that his sister isn't a mind reader. (Go team go!)]

GW: I'll try to arrange a meeting as soon as possible. You're going to hold out, right? You're not going to run away from home or anything like that? Or lash out or anything? You feel like doing it, I understand. But it's not something you're likely to do? But sometimes it feels good just to say you can do it, because you can kind of imagine what it would be like. I've gotta hand it to you guys. You guys did some pretty good thinking on this. You came up with some stuff that I know I couldn't have come up with alone.

Aftermath

In the aftermath of this meeting, I met with James's sister and then with the two of them together. Both of them were struggling: James for responsible independence and his sister for a way to let go. Negotiating boundaries through more open communication was the goal. Added to all of this was the pressure on James's sister to be a mother to her brother and, at the same time, to build her own life beyond this role. James, despite his anger at what he perceived to be his sister's inflexible limits, had a deep abiding love, respect, and devotion for his sister that was dissonant with his angry feelings. The structure of the meetings with her—the direct result of the group's problem solving process—enabled James and his sister to come together to confront a normal developmental issue in the family life cycle. Furthermore it was done in a manner that did not undermine his sister's authority, acknowledged her role as a caring "guardian" to James, and supported James's autonomy in the process.

As time went on, the others, Tony and Bruce, would often inquire of James, "What happened with you and your sister?" opening a door for reviewing and evaluating the solution to the problem that they, along with James, helped bring to life.

CONCLUSION

To paraphrase Bernstein (1973), the outcome of a problem is less important than the development of the ability to deal with the problem on a more mature level (p. 74). Were the solutions to the above problems ideal? Perhaps not. However, in each case, the group members were afforded an opportunity to work together, in a focused way, to find a better way to deal with something distressing. Problems might be group-internal (i.e., reflecting the socioemotional climate in the group); group-external (i.e., reflecting goal achievement and/or individual needs of members); or they might reflect an interesting amalgam of both. Each problem-solving process serves as a frame of reference for the next opportunity that arises to address a problem, increasing the maturity of the group and strengthening the members' competence along the way.

APPENDIX 7.1. THE MIDDLE STAGES OF GROUP DEVELOPMENT[4]

WHERE THE MEMBERS ARE

In the beginning (of this stage) members are still:

- Exploring and testing the situation
- Seeing where they fit
- Sizing up each other
- Struggling for power
- Competing for leadership
- Finding their roles
- Determining their status

By the end (of this stage) they:

- Have found their place in the group
- Have found others they like (subgroups may form)
- Feel more accepted and understood
- Better accept and understand other members
- See themselves and the other members as distinct individuals
- Recognize similarities and differences and see differences as useful
- Acknowledge each other's uniqueness
- See their own particular contribution
- Feel some affection for and desire to share with other members

Members:

- Seek to understand the perceptions that the worker and the other members have of the group
- Begin to understand the meaning of the group for them
- Begin to clarify their own goals and what they want to achieve in the group
- See that their goals can be met within the group

Members test the worker, seek proof he/she cares about and accepts them, how worker will protect them.

Members begin to understand and accept the worker's role, become less dependent on the worker and develop more reliance on each other, begin to see worker as a unique person.

As they become more sure and comfortable, members:

- Begin to express themselves more
- Share more of themselves, their experiences, their feelings, their opinions
- Are willing to risk more exposure of themselves and their ideas

[4]Reprinted by permission of Roselle Kurland.

Discussion becomes less scattered and more focused; members are able to do more sustained work on problems, to help each other more.

As they experience success, they are more and more willing to bring problems, to look at themselves.

They begin to attach prestige to a person's efforts to express him/herself and work on problems.

As members communicate more freely they recognize even more where they are similar and different.

The group becomes more and more important to the members; they see this group experience as unique.

WHAT NEEDS TO HAPPEN

Group culture, style, way of doing things, norms of group behavior need to be recognized, understood, and accepted by the members; norms that define the way conflict (difference) will be expressed, managed, and resolved, norms that encourage experimentation, flexibility, responsibility for supporting and stimulating each other.

Patterns of social interaction and communication need to develop.

Structure of interpersonal relationships emerges: status, ranking, leadership, roles.

A realistic purpose needs to be reclarified and redefined; each person's needs and goals must be understood in relation to the group purpose; there needs to be continued clarification of the goals that individuals seek for themselves as these are similar to and different from those of others in the group; harmony needs to be achieved between the way each member perceives the group and the way the worker does.

Members need to test the worker and other members and come to trust that they can express their feelings and bring problems into the group without being rejected or punished.

Members need to come to respect the similarities and differences among them.

Stabilization of membership needs to occur; people need to get involved, committed to the group, its purpose, other members, the worker.

Cohesiveness needs to develop; the group needs to be seen as a place where members can really work on problems-exchange, argue, confront, try out, really share.

ROLE OF THE WORKER

To help what needs to happen happen:
- To support the patterns, to play a less and less central role to maximize group leadership and functioning
- To evaluate what is going on: where the group is at; how it is moving; what the stresses and strains are

- To assess each individual member: attitudes, relationships, behavior, motivation, goals, how each person is doing in the group
- To help reclarify goals, purpose, encourage members' questioning, engage members in making decisions about the group and their use of it
- To encourage the development of positive group norms
- To recognize the commonalities: how one member's goals are similar to those of others; how different goals can be accommodated in the group; how one individual's concern can be related to the concerns of others
- To recognize the differences among the members, between the worker and the members
- To help members get to know each other, see how they can help each other, help identify common interests, concerns, and feelings
- To permit testing of him/herself, of rules, but to maintain limits, are not to let people hurt (demolish) each other
- To promote flexibility in roles so that members can experience and try out and modify ways of contributing to the group, relating to others; may need to confront the members directly if they are tending to stereotype others
- To work toward improving communication in the group, to point out when people aren't hearing or listening to each other, that it is OK to get angry, to encourage members to support or question the comments and behavior of others and to bring things to the group
- To step in and regulate conflict if it gets too threatening (conflict and disagreement are to be expected at this stage)
- To confront members re: irrational thinking, unacceptable behavior
- May need to work with members individually, to encourage them to express themselves in the group or to increase their understanding of something that happened in the group or if there was much conflict and person wants to drop out (run away, avoid a difficult situation)

| # The Use of "Program" in Group Work

Cultivating a Sense
of Competence, Belonging,
and Creativity

TWIN ANCHORS

Whenever I'm with a group of children or adolescents and in the midst of the swirl of noise and action, I try to imagine what the dance is asking on behalf of the dancers. Most often I hear the same two questions:

"Am I ever gonna fit in?"

"Am I ever gonna be any good at anything?"

"Am I ever gonna fit in?" suggests the hunger for belonging and the need for attachment, so critical for human growth and development. "Am I ever gonna be any good at anything?" suggests the thirst for a sense of competence, a desire to be considered trustworthy and reliable, and the hope of becoming intimate with a feeling of self-confidence. All these represent the need for growth-oriented experiences in the group.

Belonging and competence are like twin anchors. Far from weighing me down, they help to ground me when, sometimes in the midst of chaos, flight seems so inviting. The twin anchors remind me to "hang in there" and not "bail out" as too many an adult already has. And they help in the building of a foundation upon which something new may emerge, a platform for creative expression and for extending the bonds of belonging beyond the group itself.

INTRODUCTION

What is necessary to cultivate a sense of competence, belonging, and creativity in the group? The answer begins by relying on traditional group work principles to guide the group. These are principles rooted in turn-of-the-century settlement, progressive education and recreation movements, and which include

- Attention to helping the members gain a sense of their groupness.
- Understanding and valuing the group process itself as a powerful change dynamic.
- Valuing the group members as helpers (enabling them to become a system of mutual aid) rather than viewing the practitioner as the sole helping person.
- Inviting the whole person to participate in the group (i.e., strengths, talents, and special interests) and not just the troubled or hurt parts.
- Relating to the group members in context and not disregarding the various systems impinging on their lives.
- Respecting the growth-enhancing power of play as opposed to the exclusive use of play for diagnostic and psychotherapeutic purposes (Breton, 1990; Middleman & Wood, 1990b).

The planned and spontaneous integration of discussion and activity to promote members' strengths constitutes a recurrent theme running through this chapter. A flexible approach is offered to counter the ambivalence experienced by young group members who are likely to reject the exclusive use of one or the other of these modes of expression. A companion theme is the worker's commitment to play and embracing of a child-like spirit (Malekoff, 1987).

PLAY AS CHILDREN'S AND ADOLESCENTS' WORK

An air of condescension often surrounds the use of nonverbal activities in groups. When the activity of the group is other than earnest discussion, parents, referral sources, administrators, and colleagues too often arch a collective eyebrow of disapproval as if to say, "This is nice but when does the real work begin." The skepticism and sarcasm reserved for anything that strays from more formal discussion and talk reflects a perception of such activities as lacking in intellectual depth and professional sophistication. This attitude may lead to the unfortunate consequence of discouraging aspiring and experienced practitioners from being open to innovation.

Hear ye! Hear ye! Adolescents don't join groups prepared to engage in the mode of discourse expected by many an adult.

In his treatise on little league baseball and young-adolescent culture, Fine (1987) comments on the infusion of joy in one's work, adopting a playful attitude toward it, and transcending the formal rules of an activity without breaking them. To the extent that group work, like little league baseball, is task oriented it is a form of work; to the extent that it is flexible, free, and involves choice, it is play. It is, in fact, both. Each metaphor contributes to our understanding of "program." Work and play in young people's groups are inseparable.

Children's and adolescents' play activity in natural settings (i.e., school yard, playground, playing field, street) provide an excellent frame of reference for group workers to learn from and to model. Boyd (1971) encourages group workers to free themselves from "the limitations imposed by an overemphasis on verbalized aspects of expression." She concludes that "only in spontaneous, uncalculated response of human beings to each other can sensitivity to undefined subtleties function" (p. 149).

A FRAMEWORK FOR THE USE OF ACTIVITY

• Program is the group's breath, its expressiveness. It can be used to scream, gasp, scold, exalt, tell, sing. . . . Like the sorcerer's apprentice, it can get out of hand and do its own thing. But it is a vital sign, at the core of group life. Although constantly happening it cannot be taken for granted. Some discipline and control must be exerted over its expression, but as with the human breathing system, we can't restrain it for long without dire consequences.
—*R. Middleman (1981, p. 190)*

Activity is more than a "tool," more than programmed content, more than "canned" exercises, and more than a mechanistic means to an end. Middleman (1985) aptly described the "toolness of program more as putty than a hammer, i.e., as a tool that also changes as it is used" (p. 4). In addition to a wealth of structured resource material available (e.g., games and exercises), there are the activities that grow spontaneously out of the living together that the group does. These are the creative applications, the member- and worker-initiated innovations that can be cultivated and brought to life in the group, contributing to a growing sense of *groupness* and rich history of experience together.

A well-conceived use of program, what the group does together, can add texture to the group experience, fueling its capacity to transform itself into a unique entity, something new and special that has never existed before. Program is the unbreakable, malleable stuff that real life groups are made of, creating "something-ness" from "nothing-ness." The following four-dimensional framework is presented to illustrate the use of program with adolescents for:

- Promoting a sense of competence.
- Promoting a sense of belonging.
- Promoting self-discovery, invention, and creativity.
- Extending the bonds of belonging beyond the group itself.

The illustrations that follow are organized using this framework, the components of which should be viewed as interrelated and overlapping.

PROMOTING A SENSE OF COMPETENCE

Can you recall a time in your childhood or adolescence when you felt that you would never be any good at anything? What probably helped you to move from that awful place was the completion of a task of some kind, a task that called upon your dexterity, intelligence, and/or perseverance. It is likely that someone was there to observe and offer encouragement and praise in spite of any flaws in execution. Collectively, such experiences amount to a feeling of competence, what Erikson (1968) refers to as "the lasting basis for cooperative participation in adult life" (p. 275).

Tho Paint Job

The following practice illustration demonstrates the use of program to begin to change the self-images and self-esteem of the members of a young-adolescent boys' group. The boys' experiences outside of the group proved inadequate for developing feelings of trustworthiness, reliability, and competence. Through the group experience, a spontaneous decision, thoughtful plan, and well-implemented activity developed, all of which contributed to the emergence of a series of newly reflected images, accentuating the members' growing capabilities.

> Five 9- and 10-year-old boys had become members of a weekly group at a community mental health center after being referred by school personnel for problems defined as immaturity, poor social judgment, and low self-esteem. Socially, all were said to have been scapegoated to varying degrees. They were described as academic underachievers

and as overly dependent on adult supervision to complete assignments.

By the time the boys were together for about 3 months, it had been established that the room was not bugged, that hands needn't be raised to talk, and that no member could strike another in anger. Following a bittersweet moment of mutual discovery in which each of the five boys revealed a detested school-yard nickname representing either physical, intellectual, or temperamental Achilles' heels, one of the boys, Vincent, revealed that he felt "untrusted" by his parents. When encouraged to elaborate, he explained that his parents had refused to let him contribute to a recent household paint job. After some discussion, it became clear that these boys experienced little autonomy in the presence of their parents or any other adults for that matter.

As this information emerged, the worker rediscovered that his room was in dire need of a paint job. Over the years young "decorators," including these boys, had adorned the office walls with reclining chair backrest compressions, assorted hand prints, multicolored soda-pop blotches, and the dried remnants of not-quite-scraped-off-the-wall chewing gum. Since the agency administration had ignored all prior requests for a fresh coat of paint, the worker seized the opportunity to solicit the members to do the job. There was spontaneous unanimity in their decision to perform the task. As a result, discussion was slowly transformed into an activity that was intended to support the group's sense of competency and autonomy.

The painting of the office required several steps: (1) making a list of supplies and tasks (planning), (2) studying a paint color chart (decision making), (3) organizing a trip to the hardware store to price and purchase materials (environmental competence), (4) learning the functions of the equipment (skill development), (5) committing time to a weekend day to do the job (time investment), and (6) deciding on the workday plan—break time, lunch time, salary—(negotiating).

The job itself, which lasted roughly 6 hours, was completed with great care. An older adolescent, a participant in the agency's vocational training program, agreed to serve as job foreman. This pleased the younger boys and provided them with a role model not too far beyond their reach. The worker, who was present during the job, intervened minimally and primarily to "inspect" the work in progress and to praise the boys' effort and skill.

In addition to the job and life skills indicated above, patience, judgment, problem solving, and cooperation were highlighted as the work proceeded. The aftermath provided an opportunity for review (work inspection) and the chance to show off their good work to their parents and to Center staff (public affirmation). As the weeks unfolded, the boys basked in the glow of their cleanly painted meeting place.

The "paint job" demonstrates the integration of discussion and activity to promote a sense of competence and belonging, build ego strengths, and enhance the self-esteem of a group of young-adolescent boys. The worker served as a catalyst, mediator, and resource to the boys until they gradually came to rely on one another to complete their tasks. The project also stimulated the boys' capacity to enjoy one another and increased their openness and ability to use adult assistance to complete a task. As each group member's mastery of this new situation grew, so grew the competence of the group, and the members' sense of pride in one another as well as their parents' pride in what they had accomplished.

Before moving on try to imagine for a moment what the young-adolescent boys' group might have looked like if, instead of the activity described, the worker had insisted on the exclusive use of discussion to probe what it is like not to feel trusted by one's parents. Yawn . . .

International Cultural Celebration

The following is an account of The Youth of Culture Drug-Free Club composed of 20 African American youngsters, boys and girls, ages 13 to 17. The purpose of the group is to prevent alcohol and drug use, to promote a drug-free lifestyle, to encourage other youths to remain drug-free, and to develop a sense of personal pride through social, cultural, and educational activities (e.g., trips, recreation, parties, community service projects, and learning about alcohol and other drug use and sexuality).

An alcoholism counselor (an African American woman) and social worker (a Chilean American woman) are the group workers who staff the club. An array of other volunteers and staff also contribute to the program through a variety of roles. The club is open to all young people from 12 to 18 years old who live in the community. Unlike the more formal chemical dependency services offered that require a DSM diagnosis for access, there is open admission and universal access to the club. Beyond age, the only criterion for admission is an interest in participating and a commitment to remain drug-free.

The group, roughly a year old, decided that a community-wide celebration was in order to mark their first anniversary as a group. They had previously planned dances and parties, had taken field trips, hosted invited guest speakers, played games, and held group discussions. They seemed ready for a more ambitious endeavor and decided to plan a gala event to become known as the "international cultural celebration." The members saw this as an opportunity to address proactively the issue of diversity and living in a changing community (i.e., one with a growing Latino and Haitian population).

As the group brainstormed and shared ideas, they soon discovered that planning an event of this magnitude would demand increased togetherness and a greater investment of time. In addition, the division of labor would require that some tasks be performed alone and others in small groups. As the idea took shape, the International Cultural Day promised to feature a panoply of cultural music, dance, clothing, artifacts, food, and prepared speeches, all highlighting diversity. This required rehearsal, homework, gathering resources, and enlisting the support of parents and others in their families and community.

The skills involved in successfully carrying out this endeavor promised to be considerable. They included dancing, singing, modeling, delivering prepared speeches, and cooking and baking. Beyond these content-oriented skills were the socioemotional demands of planning, decision making, problem solving, conflict resolution, frustration tolerance, and impulse control. All of these skills are key to building ego strength, positive mental health, and preventing drug abuse and other destructive behavior. There were difficult challenges that faced all of the members at one time or another. For example there were a few members who were embarrassed by their inability to speak articulately in front of a large group.

During a rehearsal Shirley volunteered to recite the group's "drug-free pledge" by heart. She stumbled a bit and was soon exasperated when Matthew and Freddie, two of the five boys present, began taunting and mimicking her. Their antics led to a gradual contagion of snickering and then laughter among the others. In furious frustration, she threw down her paper and stormed out of the room in tears, only to be followed by two other group members. The remaining members sat by quietly until Malcolm, at 17 the oldest male in the room and someone who had worked hard to overcome a difficult early life, confronted Matthew, Freddie, and the rest of them making it clear that the taunting was unacceptable. Shirley returned to the room a bit more composed, arriving just in time to hear Malcolm declare, "Look here, Shirley is the only one in this group who has memorized the pledge and who has the guts to stand in front of everyone and recite it. We should be proud of her instead of laughing at her. I'd like to see any of you try it." Matthew and Freddie and the others were instructed by Malcolm that if they couldn't refrain from putting others down that they could leave. Shirley was encouraged to continue. She proceeded with some trepidation, successfully completing the pledge and receiving the spontaneous applause of the entire group. Tested every step of the way, the group worked within the context of the activity to reinforce the norms of respecting one another and helping one another rather than hurting one another.

This was a critical step in the process of preparation because soon others would reveal their own sources of discomfort. There were those who were self conscious about their changing bodies as they anticipated modeling clothing in front of a large crowd of people. There were those who had extraordinary talent yet little patience for those who weren't as gifted. There were those who were always accustomed to having their way who were faced with having to compromise. With the stakes higher than usual, the challenges were more difficult to evade.

The final rehearsals, as well as the event itself, were videotaped allowing the Club members to see themselves in action, to critique their performance, to celebrate, and to giggle and laugh with one another. With the lights dimmed and a plentiful supply of popcorn and juice, as in a family-style gathering, they watched the videotapes repeatedly for weeks, enamored with what they had accomplished.

PROMOTING A SENSE OF BELONGING

In addition to developing a sense of mastery, activity can provide an important doorway to addressing obstacles to belonging and promoting a sense of good will, fellowship, and affection in the group.

A Familiar Game

In the following illustration, a familiar game naturally leads to discussion about a problem in the group.

A group of five 10- and 11-year-old girls had been meeting for about 2 months at a local community center. The members were African American, attended the same school, lived in the same neighborhood, and shared many of the same friends outside of the group. During one meeting, one of the girls was absent, and the others initiated a game familiar to all of them requiring that each group member write the names of four boys, four houses, and four cars that they like, and the number of children they each hoped to have one day. The person who has made the selections then chooses a number and the others, using a special formula, count to that number crossing off items on the list as she counts. What remains represents the future husband, house, car, and number of children.

While engaged in the game, one of the girls said that the only reason she could play this game was "because Sara isn't here." She went on to say that she doesn't trust Sara because she's always "saying things about people and running at the mouth too much." She said that Sara tells others, outside of the group, "what we do and what we say in here." The other girls agreed with this assessment, and each added a personal incident that substantiated the charge that "Sara can't be trusted." As the theme of confidentiality was further explored, it was agreed that Sara had to be included in the discussion. They were hesitant to confront Sara, afraid of "hurting her feelings."

It turned out that secrecy, sharing, and trust were recurrent themes not only in the group but also in the context of the girls' lives. The need for privacy and firmer boundaries in the group was underscored by the fact that the girls all knew each other. Once these issues were universalized, each member could identify beyond Sara, and they grew more comfortable with the prospect of continuing the discussion upon her return. One of the members, Shontelle, agreed to act as spokesperson.

At the following meeting after the usual chit chat, snacks were served, and Shontelle opened the subject. She began by saying, "Sometimes it's hard for me to talk about certain things in the group because some people can't be trusted." After an anticipated pregnant pause the others, including Sara, joined in on the discussion. Shontelle's contention was then supported as each member took turns expressing her feelings of inhibition. After Sara spoke one of the others addressed her directly, recounting times that she felt betrayed by Sara. Sara became quietly defensive; however she did not deny the charges. The others, who were poised to attack, softened as the worker stepped in to renegotiate the group contract regarding confidentiality to which Sara agreed. The worker supported the girls' openness and maturity in confronting a difficult problem. She then generalized the discussion to allow for further exploration of the underlying issues of trust and confidentiality in the girls' lives outside of the group.

In this illustration, the worker's comfort in allowing the members to introduce a familiar game into the group, created a natural opening for the exploration of feelings about privacy. This resulted in the effective mediation of an emergent scapegoating process.

Dungeons and Dragons

> listen here,
> drop the sneer,
> lend an ear,
> free a tear
> cause
>   we
>   all
>   been
>   there
> —A. Malekoff (1994g)

The following illustration from my own experience demonstrates the use of another game, this time as a pathway for an isolated group member to gain status and to find his place in the group. As in the illustration above, the game transcends itself and becomes an avenue for belonging.

At 14 years old, Pete was referred to the mental health clinic after setting the family garage on fire and refusing to attend school. After a formal evaluation, he was referred to an early-adolescent boys' group where one of the purposes was to learn to put a reflective pause between impulse and action. At first he refused to attend the group but soon softened when his mother bribed him with the promise of a new bicycle. The other members had been briefed and were prepared for a new member to the group. What they weren't prepared for was Pete's locking himself in an outside shed and refusing to come out. When the other group members were informed of this turn of events, they quickly decided, perhaps out of curiosity, to go outside and survey the situation.

Where the worker and mother had failed, the boys were successful in cajoling Pete from the confines of the shed and into their meeting place. However, nothing could have prepared them for the tirade that followed. Without as much as an introduction, Pete started to berate the group—"waste of time"; "assholes"; "worthless group." To the worker's surprise, their response was quick, controlled, forceful, and precise. They told him, in no uncertain terms, that "in this group, we care about one another," and if he didn't want to be a part of it, "you can leave right now! Get the fuck out of here!" The worker took a deep breath, kept his mouth shut and waited,[1] expecting Pete to take

[1] I have learned the hard way that three of the most important words in my own internal dialogue during group meetings with adolescents are: "Shut up, Andy." How ironic it is that in a group in which improved impulse control is a goal, this worker often had trouble sitting on his own words.

his cue and take a powder (leave, that is). Amazingly, at least to the worker, he stayed.

Pete's tenure in the group was longer than a few weeks, and he struggled to find a way to fit in. Week after week, he brought in an armful of books and papers that he would conspicuously shuffle throughout the group meetings. In time, perhaps as he had hoped, the others became curious. Little by little, he revealed to the others a fantasy game that he enjoyed playing known as *Dungeons and Dragons*. In time, the others asked if he would teach them and asked the worker if they could play the game during the group time. An agreement was made about how to structure the time in light of their interest in the game and Pete's willingness to teach them.

While negotiating the time frame to play the game in the group, Pete, in a clever attempt to preempt what he anticipated would be the worker's negative response to *Dungeons and Dragons,* presented him with a magazine clipping about the fantasy game. The item was about a father who was outraged that a school library carried a publication entitled *Dragon Magazine.* According to the report, the father confronted a library official demanding, "Don't you know young people have committed murder and suicide over playing *Dungeons and Dragons?*" The premise of article was, however, to neutralize some of the fears that adults, and particularly parents, have about such fantasy games.

The worker couldn't help but be impressed with Pete's rather sophisticated negotiating style, but what else might he be trying to tell the worker? That he wasn't suicidal? That his interest in this game wasn't pathological? That he should be given a chance to find his place in the group? That the worker should be more accepting of him than other adults, including his father, had been? Or all of the above? It is unlikely that such questions would have emerged had Pete's pursuit of playing the game in the group been squashed or ignored by the worker. What all of this suggests is the need for practitioners to be sensitive to adolescents' interests and pleasures and to consider how these can be brought into the group with open arms.

PROMOTING DISCOVERY, INVENTION, AND CREATIVITY

As the preceding illustrations suggest, in addition to cultivating a sense of competence and belonging, the use of program is a vital tool for tapping the strengths of group members, enabling them to solve problems creatively, discover new ways to have fun and be inventive, and find new pathways for expressing obscured parts of themselves.

The Video Camera

The building in which I work has one room with a built-in video camera. The camera is located in an upper corner of the room and can be operated from an adjacent room. While a group was deciding whether or not to allow themselves to be videotaped through this means, a member of this group took one look at the contraption and declared, "It looks like the X-ray machine in a dentist's office." Struck with the image, I had a vision of my adolescent boys' group members being outfitted with protective lead jackets to guard against overexposure. Needless to say, the metaphor signaled the anxiety of the members. After some discussion, only one member nixed the idea, but, as agreed, just one "no" vote was all that was needed to scrap the idea. The lone dissenter may have been the unconsciously anointed group spokesperson, since the others raised no opposition.

The idea of using a camera continued to intrigue me. I came to see that rooms outfitted with cameras in this manner, tantalizingly beyond the reach and control of the members, both stimulated self-consciousness and denied access to the technology itself. As an alternative, I decided to add a camcorder, a hand-held video camera, to a shelf in my room. The group included five middle-adolescent boys, racially and ethnically diverse, who had been referred to the agency after getting into trouble for a destructive act of one kind or another. Some of the transcripts of group meetings appearing elsewhere in this book were drawn from videotaped and recorded meetings of the group. The transcripts themselves highlight various themes in the group (i.e., problem solving, sexuality, violence, race and ethnicity). What the transcripts don't reveal is the use of the camera as an activity.

When they first realized that they could use the camera, the members all excitedly took turns. I learned that none of them had ever handled a camera of this kind before. At first, the camera took on an awkward presence in the group, but before too long, it became a natural part of the process. The camera was available for anyone to use, including me, during the weekly group meetings. Sometimes it sat quietly in its place, and other times it was activated, providing the group with much more than a distant record of an hour's time together.

One of the frequent themes in the group was sexuality. During one interchange, the then-recent death of a rock-and-roll star was mentioned. Freddy Mercury, the lead singer of a popular band from England known as Queen, had been diagnosed with AIDS. Following his death, one of the band's earlier songs ("Bohemian Rhapsody") was discovered by a new generation of youth when it appeared in a teen-oriented movie and subsequent music video. The song was introduced in a scene from the movie that featured a group of older adolescent boys lip-synching along with their car radio. During the group discussion, one of the boys commented on the irony of the renewed interest in the song. He remarked, "It's a shame that you have to die to be popular."

In forthcoming meetings, the group exchanged myths, debated issues, and shared information about AIDS, sexually transmitted diseases, and protecting oneself. They also brought in audio cassettes of Queen and decided to perform their own music video version of "Bohemian Rhapsody." I brought in a "boom box" (cassette recorder), and after a brief rehearsal, they were ready to go. Their 5-minute performance was exciting, full of energy, and it progressed along group developmental lines. As the opening notes jumped from the speakers, I observed, through the lens of the camera:

- An initial tentativeness and ambivalence as they self-consciously warmed to the task, catching quick glances at one another as if unsure about whether to plunge in.
- A preliminary commitment by the group's indigenous leader who stepped forward and, on one knee, passionately played "air guitar" in synch with the band's rhythms.
- Deepening their commitment to the group (the singing group that is) as each of them followed the leader and began to sing parts that they determined through split-second nonverbal cues.
- Evidence of the determination and growing competence necessary to see the task through to its completion and without let-up, hesitation, or any further sign of ambivalence.
- Creative expression, as they differentiated themselves through a free-form dance segment, spurred on by one of the only purely instrumental riffs in the song.
- A reunion that calmly brought them back together from the frenzied dance phase.
- A graceful ending that featured the boys with arms draped around one another's shoulders, swaying to the closing notes (the only time they had touched one another affectionately up until that point in the group) and "re-experiencing their groupness at the point of termination" (Middleman & Wood, 1990b, p. 11).

What I hadn't realized until seeing the group members through the lens, and then on videotape, was that in 5 minutes, the singing group (the group within the group) had passed through every stage of group development in a clearly discernible manner.

The video added texture to the group, heightening the members' enjoyment and uncovering their talent and capacity to be a productive unit. It was as if they had been "discovered," or at least a part of them had been. The members were able to look back at their performance and marvel at their skill in "pulling it all together" and working so well together. Perhaps the performance was also an unconscious tribute to a kindred spirit who "had to die to be popular." As this illustration demonstrates, the camera was used for more than distantly capturing content. It breathed life into the group and it captured the group's depth. The ready access of the camera enabled the members to discover different and inventive ways to use it in the group, often with unexpected and wonderfully creative results.

Succeeding videos provided more opportunities for physical contact as the members carefully choreographed their movements to match the mood of the music and, perhaps, their feelings about one another. When the boys handled the camera, another dimension of talent and affect was added. The creative use of the camera's zoom feature (making the images closer or more distant for the viewer) enriched the emotional quality of the product. For example, in one case, the cameraman (a group member) effectively captured the boys' innocence (and perhaps his own reflected innocence) by intuitively training the camera on their eyes during solo segments of the song. The emotional quality was such that one of my colleagues, after viewing the tape for the first time, remarked that she couldn't "get those boys out of my mind." The videotaping activity allowed the boys to portray parts of themselves that were most often obscured from others and themselves, a new way to communicate that words alone wouldn't satisfy.

During another group meeting a heated conflict between two of the boys raged. The others gradually took sides. Try as I might, my interventions were essentially ignored. Another group member took the camera and started filming the conflict. As he did, he assumed the voice of a television commentator, consequently capturing everyone's attention and assuming leadership. In a grand interviewing style, he moved the camera from member to member probing each of them about the events that led up to the conflict, infusing humor into his remarkable inquisition. Having been supplanted by a worthy and more effective replacement, I gradually relaxed, marveling at the group's ability to take over. The camera gave the bearer the power to speak (reminding me of the conch that permitted the holder to speak in Lord of the Flies). When the videotape was viewed afterward, the cameraman's grasp of the situation and leadership was even more impressively displayed through his movement of the camera, which reflected his ability to catch and direct the action.

As was demonstrated by the example above, the use of video can have a tremendous impact on adolescents.

- They look at the video immediately after the taping, often wanting to view it several times, and they experience themselves intensely.
- They learn about creativity and technical production (e.g., that a video can be edited, that scenes can be recorded and assembled in logical order rather than chronological sequence).
- By seeing the possibility of doing something creative and then acting on it, self-esteem can be enhanced.
- They experience a sense of power in handling the camera. (Simonetti et al., 1996, p. 324)

The Robot

In this vignette, the use of program for inventive purposes helps to transform the quality of life in a difficult group.

Four boys, ages 10 and 11, all diagnosed as chronically depressed, although exhibiting different symptomotology, were referred to a mental health center. All were functioning below their academic potential, two had histories of aggressive acting-out behavior, and three lived in single-parent families. The group was mixed racially and socioeconomically. During the early months, a power struggle with the worker raged. Structure was defied, rules were broken, and proposed routines were challenged. The chaos that prevailed was punctuated by swearing, explicit sexual posturing, "gas-passing" competitions, and unsolicited brandishing of assorted sharp or flammable objects. In one meeting, one of the members, loathe to leave the room to relieve himself, urinated into a drinking cup in the corner of the room.

A turning point came when Glen, the indigenous leader and the most aggressive member, had broken an electrical wall outlet. Uncharacteristically, he mobilized himself and volunteered to repair the damage he had caused. The group soon discovered that he had access to an extensive tool collection, his father's. He brought in the tools and proceeded, with great skill and care. Although unexcited about the repair job in which they remained observers, the others were more focused than at any prior time. The worker seized the opportunity to shift the group to an activity in which the use of the tools would be central.

With some ambivalence they discussed the worker's idea and jumped at one member's suggestion to build a robot. This became the central activity for the next few months. By virtue of his know-how, the previously most-destructive member became a leader. He brought in a huge tool box that became a permanent fixture in the corner of the room. In order to proceed, safety rules were developed, instructions about the use of the tools were discussed, and turns were taken in order to master the use of the equipment.

As time passed and as the robot neared completion, the atmosphere in the group changed. Structure was more clearly defined, rules and limits were more readily accepted, and impulse control began to improve. A gradual metamorphosis took place in which weapons were replaced by tools, chaos gave way to order, and a sense of pride prevailed over self-disdain. Once completed, the robot was installed, by the boys, in the Center's reception area. The members constructed a sign bearing their names and the warning: DO NOT TOUCH. Periodically, one by one, they checked in with the receptionist to learn about weekly reactions to their wonderful creation.

By enabling the members to solve a problem in the group—the repair job—the worker made an important discovery freeing her to move the group along a new path, one in which their creative invention provided them with a sense of group identity that had eluded them just weeks before.

Self-Discovery in the Wild

Project Synergy was a program in which early- and middle-adolescent youth living in a low-income minority community were recruited to become a part of a community service project. Ten African American youths, boys and girls, participated. One of the group's activities was wilderness trips (hiking, camping, canoeing). The trips were staffed by two group workers, a male and female.

Each wilderness outing was preceded by several preparation group meetings held at the local middle school on Thursday afternoons and group meetings at The Place (Project Synergy's host agency) on Friday afternoons. Group meetings were also held following each wilderness outing at the same locations so that the group could debrief. The preparation meetings included films and videos, discussion, instruction in the use of equipment, and wilderness skill-development activities. Attendance at the meetings was mandatory for all those who intended to participate in the wilderness outings.

During the planning meetings, a few of the boys dominated the time and space through physical posturing and verbal banter, appearing to position themselves as the leaders of any upcoming outing. However, once the group drove for 2 hours to the site and departed from the van, we found ourselves immersed in the forest, with no pavement, stores, traffic lights, or any of the usual trappings of the home neighborhood. It was interesting to note that the boys did not volunteer to lead the way. The boys followed the girls, who became the models of leadership that the boys had expected to be. It took several hikes for their bravado to catch up with their behavior. And by that time, it was with a strong dose of humility.

The boys seemed not to want to take the responsibility of searching for the trail markers and to make sure that the group was following the correct path. They seemed much more comfortable falling back into the middle of the group to watch and silently learn from the girls, who volunteered to lead the way. Little by little, the group learned how to read trail markers located on trees and rocks, indicating the direction of the trail. Relying on their growing aware-ness of themselves and the direction of the workers, the group members gradually learned to hike at a controlled, measured pace, rather than starting out in a sprint and tiring as the day wore on. This was also emphasized during preparation meetings. It was, however, in the "doing" that this learning was integrated by the hikers, who soon learned how easy it was to get worn out.

As the group became more familiar with the wilderness environ-ment, different aspects of the members' personalities were revealed. The boastful, self-assured boys, who surprisingly had abdicated their leadership role on the first hike, assumed more assertive, controlling postures on the second and third hikes. Nevertheless, they never strayed too far ahead of the group or the adult group leaders.

The group also developed a noticeable respect, admiration, and affection for its members. This was evidenced after the first hike, which challenged them to walk for many hours on rough terrain, past what they probably considered to be their physical and emotional limit. We took a photograph of the group on that day toward the end of the hike. Tired and done-in, the group gathered around some rocks, leaning on one another for support, warmth, and belonging.

Self-discovery took another turn on a canoeing trip by the same group. This time they didn't reach their destination. As one worker recalled:

"On our canoe trip, the group was faced with strong winds and an unfriendly current, as the participants learned the basic canoeing skills in Long Island Sound. All canoeing dyads experienced a great deal of frustration, disappointment and anger as they struggled in teams to control the direction and progress of their vessels. They also learned to recognize that the elements and obstacles proved too formidable on that day [for us] to reach our destination, when after three hours of tiresome paddling, our group needed to turn around and paddle back to our starting point, rather than continue to our original destination, six miles away."

They learned that when the challenges of the wilderness became tiring and frustrating and weather conditions on the river became burdensome and oppressive, they had to reach inside themselves to summon up additional strength to overcome frustration, anger, and fear. By doing so, they could focus clearly and immediately on the situation confronting them, remembering the new skills that they learned and finding a way to communicate with their partner or the group in order to ensure their success.

The process of the wilderness outings from preparation meetings, to excursions on both land and sea, and to debriefing sessions had the affect of incrementally preparing the group for unknown challenges ahead. One such challenge took place in a dramatically different kind of environment and one that extended the bonds of belonging beyond the group.

EXTENDING THE BONDS OF BELONGING BEYOND THE GROUP

Where does belonging end? If group work values working within the context of members' lives, then the concept of belonging cannot always be reserved to group membership. Membership can include the possibility of a special kind of belonging, the bonds of which may be extended beyond the group itself at times. To belong beyond the group does not imply group-internal membership status or privilege for those outside of the group. What it does suggest, as the following illustrations attempt to demonstrate, is a reaching out to the environment and making new connections born of need and driven by mutuality. For adolescents, reaching for connections beyond themselves and their peers is a critical step in making the transition from the lonely odyssey of youth into what will soon become adult life.

From One Landscape to Another

During a discussion in which the Synergy group was planning a Christmas party for themselves, they chose to launch a community service project to be carried out on emotional terrain as challenging and grueling as the natural landscape of the wilderness.

Several group members shared that they had relatives, or knew someone, who was infected with the HIV virus or who had died from

AIDS. The group unanimously agreed to take on a project related to this problem—a visit to a local nursing home. In the course of planning, the members talked about how the disease had impacted on their lives. They also identified and dispelled some of the myths about the disease that arose in the discussions. The educational phase of the activity included learning all of the pertinent facts about the disease, including how someone infected with AIDS might be feeling. The group discussed different stages of the disease and what to expect on their visit to the nursing home. Their focus was on empathy not sympathy. In addition to a personal visit, the members each agreed to contribute $2 of their own money and to collect bottles and cans from home and the neighborhood for deposit. Through the sale of recyclables and their personal contributions, they hoped to raise enough money to purchase a gift and holiday card for each patient they would visit.

The A. Holly Patterson Geriatric Center, which houses a 35-bed AIDS unit, readily agreed to the visit once the details had been shared by the worker. In the meantime, the members busied themselves shopping for gifts and cards. They were vigilant to ensure that there would be enough gifts for everyone they would visit. As the day of the visit approached, a few of the group members chose not to attend. Despite their preparation, they said that they could not handle seeing people in such a deteriorated state, that nothing could prepare them for that.

Upon arrival, group members and leader were welcomed by the director and assigned nursing staff to help with our visit. The members, working in teams of two or three, visited each patient and presented each with a gift and card. For those patients who could talk, the members spent some time with them, 5 or 10 minutes, to offer hope and encouragement. When the group returned for debriefing, the most memorable stories that they shared were the ones about those patients who told them that they felt abandoned by family and friends, that no one came to visit them, let alone give them a gift. The youth were moved by the experience, realizing that the gift of brightening someone else's day was perhaps the best gift that they, the young people, themselves received during the holiday.

In the end, the field trip to the nursing home was no less stressful or exhilarating than the wilderness excursions. The nursing home residents seemed to enjoy the gifts. But mostly they liked the time spent with the teens—the sitting, the talking, and the caring. By visiting the nursing home, the group made a powerful statement about the importance of sharing responsibility for the community and for the welfare of all its members, extending the bonds of belonging beyond their small circle.

CONCLUSION

Activity and discussion must not be viewed as polar opposites, rather as two sides of the same program coin. What the use of program is about is what the group does to create its life together. The group lives through its program and not by its program. Do you get it? Not sure? Well, I'll leave you with this to ponder: As you weave your way in and out of this book and through its many practice illustrations, try to come back to the idea of program from time to time, and ask yourself, is the group living through its program, or is it being programmed to death? The following poem illustrates what a group of young people might look like when the use of program is structured to invite the "whole person."

Group Work with Children and Adolescents

Playing, planning, confronting, creating,
fighting, protecting, joking, berating;
Burping, sleeping, farting, snacking,
cooperating, disrupting, insulting, attacking;
Listening, ignoring, teasing, supporting,
resolving, deciding, defying, conforming;
Pondering, clowning, denying, admitting,
talking, laughing, standing, sitting;
Yelling, crying, touching, hugging,
opening, closing, coming, going;
Dancing, singing, grabbing, poking,
mimicking, acting, threatening, stroking;
 Revealing, hiding,
 prying, confiding,
 Stretching, crawling,
 jumping, falling;
 Taking, giving,
 thanking
 and
 living.

     —A. Malekoff (1993)

CHAPTER 9 | Leavetaking, Moving On, and Looking Back

The Ending Transition
in Group Work

> What we call the beginning is often the end
> And to make an end is to make a beginning.
> The end is where we start from.
> —*T. S. Eliot (in* Oxford Dictionary
> of Quotations, *1979, p. 203)*

Endings in adolescent groups cannot be taken for granted. Too many young people today have already experienced a number of unceremonious separations throughout their short lives. Relationships with loved ones seem to come and go in revolving-door fashion. Moreover, there is the toll that loss exacts, a result of poverty, disease, and violence, on a growing legion of youngsters. Adolescents need supportive environments to help them to work through the painful feelings generated by loss. As any group of adolescents approaches the end of their time together, its members move through a natural process of separation, facing loss in both the present and past tense. There is, naturally, the impending loss of the group experience itself and attendant relationships. In addition, there is the emergence of residual feelings that flow out of the echoes of past losses. A skilled group worker will use the separation stage of any group to help its members through an ending transition that is sensitive to these echoes, which often go unheard and unanswered in the course of everyday life.

As the group moves into the final phase of their time together, the worker can expect to experience mixed feelings of relief and concern. There is the relief stemming from the knowledge that the intense fatigue of years (or less) facing youngsters who are so often emotionally in pain and socially in trouble is about to be over. The concern arises around the worker's uncertainty as to whether his/her impressions of positive gains are illusory or fear that they're unstable gains at best. These of course are the conscious feelings. The worker's unconscious feelings spring from the echoes of his/her own history with separation and loss.[1]

GROUP DYNAMICS IN THE SEPARATION STAGE

As the end of the group draws near, there is a gradual weakening of interpersonal ties, characterized by behaviors such as irregular attendance (e.g., "I can't make it to group anymore. This is the only free time I have.") and self-weaning through increased involvement in extra-group affiliations (e.g., "I've joined a basketball league, so I can't come to group every week"). The internal group behavior during the ending phase reflects the members' ambivalence and difficulty accepting the reality that the end is rapidly approaching. This may be expressed in any of the following ways:

- *Reawakened dependency needs.* The need to be taken care of is expressed through increased dependence on the worker (e.g., to set limits and provide structure in areas that the group had been handling maturely or self-monitoring; pleas for the worker to provide help in areas that have been previously mastered) or by symbolic means (e.g., one 13-year-old group member brought a dying baby squirrel into the group, proclaiming his determination to nurse the creature back to health).
- *Excluding the worker.* The worker is left out the discussion/activities of the group, as if to suggest that the group has already been abandoned (e.g., one school social worker reported that, to her dismay, a group of young-adolescent girls walked out, in unison, in the middle of one of their final meetings).
- *Regressive behavior.* This may take the form of a variety of group resistances to termination including, "exaggerated problems, lateness, absenteeism, subgrouping, helplessness, excessive pairing, splitting, denial, and generally, an overall increase in acting-out behavior inside and outside the group" (Hurley, 1984, p. 77). Gains made in the group seem to vanish, often evoking an impulse in the worker to postpone the ending (i.e., in response to the behavioral message: "We still need the group").

---

[1]See Appendix 9.1 for a detailed summary of the "ending phase" of group work (compliments of Roselle Kurland).

- *Devaluation of the experience.* Any positive feelings about the group experience are dismissed. To ease the pain of ending the members take the position that, "This group sucks; we're glad it's finally over."
- *Flight.* Some members leave the group before the ending, sending the message: "We'll leave you before you abandon us!" Close work with parents, in preparation for separation, is needed to prevent early departures. This is particularly so in families with a history of separation and loss. Remember, an ending in the group is also an ending for parents who have had a stake in the success of the group and collaborated closely with the worker (see Chapter 6). When parents are ignored during termination they are more likely to collude with their child's attempts at preemptive flight to avoid the painful feelings associated with abandonment. Another variation of flight is a group's flight to health, in which the worker is presented with near perfect behavior, representing the inviting behavioral proposition "If you let us continue, we'll show you that we can be really, really good."

As these dynamics suggest, ending is likely to arouse powerful emotions and memories associated with past separations and losses. Group members employ the above "strategies," albeit unconsciously, in an effort to short circuit the ending process. Garland and Kolodny (1981) point out that "the most delicate part of what the worker does in effecting the separation may be the area of helping the members to express and come to terms with the ambivalence that is involved in termination" (p. 247).

THE WORKER'S ROLE IN THE SEPARATION STAGE

A good ending experience in a valued group is a powerful counterforce against the impact of growing up in a capricious environment, in which unpredictable comings and goings (i.e., separation, divorce, dislocation, death) seem commonplace. A good transition from the group must be well timed, thoughtfully conceived, and sensitively facilitated (and in collaboration with parents whenever possible). The worker's focus on the four themes that follow will foster a good transition for adolescent group members in the separation stage.

- Preparing the group for separation in a timely manner.
- Focusing the expression of feelings through review and recapitulation.

- Helping members reexperience their groupness through shared activity.
- Providing availability for support beyond the group (Henry, 1992; Middleman & Wood, 1990b; Rose, 1989; Garland et al., 1973).

PREPARING THE GROUP FOR SEPARATION IN A TIMELY MANNER

Adolescent group members must be afforded sufficient time and preparation for leavetaking and working through feelings related to the separation. Although no specific formulas exist, notice of ending must not be so close to the end as to prevent the opportunity for a full expression of feelings or too far in advance of the end as to induce enough anxiety to impede the work of the group in the middle phase. Good timing is essential, not only for final partings, but also to ease the transition at the end of individual group meetings.

In short-term groups, where the ending is imminent, separation is a significant theme from the beginning. The worker must tune in to the coming separation early on so that he/she can begin to prepare the group for its leavetaking.

In an older-adolescent group meeting in a mental health clinic, one of the members, having just learned that a close friend tested positive for HIV, recalled the multiple losses she had already experienced (e.g., divorce of her parents, suicide of a friend, and death of a cherished pet). The group was approaching the half-way point of their contract (15 meetings). As the theme of group discussion continued to revolve around loss, the worker reminded the members, "I don't know if you're aware of it or not, but we have about another 2 months to meet. Then we'll be leaving one another." To that one of the members responded, "Yeah, but it's different; we're all strangers, and we'll probably never see each other again." And another said, "Yeah, it's like meeting somebody on a bus, having a conversation, getting off the bus, and never seeing them again."

Respecting their ambivalence, expressed by minimizing and denying the potential impact of loss within the group, the worker asked, "Do you feel like strangers to one another?" One of the others responded, "Well, not really strangers, but it's different than friends on the outside." The others nodded in agreement. The girl whose friend was diagnosed "HIV positive" said that "I'm always a little wary about becoming too close with anyone, because I've been hurt too many times already." However, she did acknowledge that she had already taken some risks in this group by sharing personal feelings and experiences, as had the others.

Not wanting to push too hard, or attempt to move the group prematurely into the separation stage, the worker summarized with a modest prediction intended simply to keep the end in sight: "However you describe things in here, I think that we just might end up becoming a little more than strangers to one another. Maybe when we finally say good-bye, it will be a little different than getting off the bus." In each succeeding meeting, it became inevitable that someone would ask, "How many weeks do we have left?" In this particular group, more focused attention on separation took place in the final 3 to 4 weeks.

In adolescent groups, when the group ends may be subject to rigid parameters that are outside the control of the group. For example, the end of a school group may be dictated by a change of semesters (when all of the members' class schedules change) or the end of the school year. In hospital or residential groups, insurance coverage is likely to influence a group member's departure date. Externally imposed limits may not reflect the fact that group members' needs require special attention. The practitioner must take responsibility at the outset to inform the members of when the group (or group meeting) will end and to provide adequate time to prepare the members for the transition.

Preparing the members for the transition applies to endings in individual group meetings as well as to the life of the group. The ending time of a single group meeting in a school is likely to be controlled by a daily class schedule. In school settings, the ending time and meeting place is often variable, changing from day to day and week to week. Meetings don't often conclude with advanced notice. Instead there is a sudden transition signaled by a startling array of bells, buzzers, or disembodied voices blaring from the intercom system. The following case example illustrates the impact of a poor transition.

In a training session with 12 group workers from a special high school for troubled adolescents, the participants identified a universal problem: Group members were reported to be out of control following each meeting, disrupting the succeeding class, much to the chagrin of the awaiting teachers. As the training group explored the problem in some depth, what became clear was that the workers hadn't given much thought to the issue of transition. The groups simply ended at the sound of the bell, and the members poured out pell-mell, into the hallway and on to the next class. After some discussion about the lack of structure and healthy boundaries in the lives of many of these students outside of school, it was agreed that they needed to have another kind of experience in school, one that provided a sense of order, predictability, and consistency. The training group decided that the solution was to modify the structure within the groups to allow for a calmer transition. Workers agreed that they needed to be more aware of the time and the intensity of the meeting. They decided that a 5-minute period (or more, depending upon the process and content of the meeting) for debriefing and unwinding, in advance of the bell, would reduce the risk of spill-over beyond the group.

Although the primary focus of this chapter is on endings related to the life of the group over the "long haul," workers must pay attention to ending transitions in individual meetings, as illustrated above. If the setting in which the group meets is structured to move the members from activity to activity, as in a school, inpatient setting, or camp setting, for example, the transitions between shifts require special care to reduce the impact of impulse drainage beyond the group. No transition, however, can totally eliminate the fallout from a previously intense activity. The agency personnel (i.e., teachers, therapists, counselors) at the receiving end of a recently concluded group meeting, must consider how to structure their activity (i.e., class, program) to ease the transition in.

To achieve smooth transitions, wherever they occur in the life of a group, collaboration and open communication among colleagues are essential. While informal interaction is of great value, the agency/institution must allow time for the planning and evaluation of group services. The consequences of poorly coordinated transitions are growing resentment and misunderstanding among all parties, development of unhealthy staff coalitions, finger pointing, increased use of the grapevine to process information, and inconsistent boundaries, all leading to the gradual development of a dysfunctional helping system (which too often replicates what group members experience in their lives outside of the agency). Group workers have a duty to advocate for what is needed in order to provide effective groups for adolescents.

FOCUSING THE EXPRESSION OF FEELINGS THROUGH REVIEW AND RECAPITULATION

During the ending transition, it is essential to provide group members with the opportunity to look back at their time together, evaluate their experience, and express what it has meant to them and what they mean to one another. In the case of an individual member (or worker) leaving the group, the remaining members' feelings must also be addressed in the aftermath of the separation. It is a mistake to attempt to move ahead without acknowledging the loss that the group has just sustained.

Approaches for reviewing and evaluating the progress of the group can be more or less formal. One early-adolescent boys' group developed a unique form of evaluation that served them well as members left the group.

> A group of young-adolescent boys (13–15 years old) meeting in a counseling center developed a special approach for evaluation. They used it throughout the life of the group to review progress and to identify goals. The process involved each member taking turns quietly listening while the others offered their assessments of the individual group member's *strengths* (+) and *areas that need work* (–). The worker (the author) was assigned the role of recorder, taking verbatim notes to be transcribed later for distribution and review. Following each critique, the subject was invited to share his reaction. Once this periodic process had been "perfected," it ascended to a level of ritual status, which lent an almost sacred quality to the activity, calming the typically rambunctious boys, at least until the evaluation was complete. The following is an example of one member's written evaluation illustrating the themes of the discussion that contributed to its development:
>
>> Bernard (+): Good conversationalist; he's been the foundation of the group; "imagine what the group would be like if he wasn't here"; he's a good explainer; knowledgeable; the heart of the group; the glue of the group; a caring kind of guy; always has good ideas for topics and parties; tries to liven the group; the kind of guy you'd like to have for a priest.
>>
>> Bernard (–): Overtalkative; he needs to look at things from different points of view and not only his own; sometimes laughs at the wrong time; sometimes exaggerates.
>>
>> Bernard's reaction: "I'm deeply touched."

By supporting this process, the worker helped the boys to express their feelings openly about one another, recapitulate and reminisce about the group's time together (as each item in the evaluation is backed up with examples), and evaluate goals achieved and remaining.

As indicated earlier in the chapter, when the reality of the ending is near at hand, it is likely to stir up feelings and reopen old wounds from past losses. Therefore, a good ending is essential not only to address the loss within the group, but it is an important step in working through residual feelings from the past. This is not to suggest that separation from the group is a time to open up new problems that cannot be fully addressed in the time remaining (i.e., doorknob communications). However, the group worker must be prepared to acknowledge any tender feelings associated with past losses and separations that are reawakened in the here-and-now of the group.

If bereavement has been an issue for group members, feelings about separation from the group are likely to merge with feelings of grief. Those "youngsters for whom loss is a major life happening will find themselves catapulted back to reliving of the familiar trauma associated with these events or themes" (Garland & Kolodny, 1981, p. 240). The following case example illustrates one group member's separation from the group, framed by the recapitulation of a devastating loss and the event that brought it to light in the early days of the group, some 4 years before.

Practice Illustration: When Bereavement and Separation Intersect

> Where John?
> John gone.
> John gone?
> Gosh darn,
> John gone.
> —A. Malekoff (1994f)

In one of my young-adolescent boys' groups, a 12-year-old member who was referred for his aggressive behavior, surprised the others by revealing that he liked writing poetry.

> "The school newspaper is putting one of my poems in the next issue," he casually told the others. The group soon discovered that poetry had become an avenue for Jack to express his feelings about the death of his father. Four years later, at the age of 16, Jack decided that he was ready to leave the group. His ties to the group were loosened gradually, over several months.
>
> When Jack had first joined the group, however, he told the others about his problems in school following the death of his father. There were daily fights with other students, often provoked by cruel "jokes" about his deceased father. Jack spent lots of time in the principal's office and in the detention room. He had been no angel before his father died. However, it become evident to the worker that the emptiness that followed him, in the wake of his great loss, had not been met with compassion but, rather, by an insensitive environment.

In a short time, the school labeled him as "emotionally disturbed" and transferred him to an out-of-district "special education" setting composed of a population of teens with serious behavioral problems.

Grieving teenagers, upon their return to school, are often "subject to considerable social pressure to demonstrate a resolution of grief, and to do so according to an unrealistic time table" (Allen, 1990, p. 39). They're also expected to "be strong" for the surviving parent. Group work can help adolescents to understand what is happening emotionally (e.g., "I know it's normal to think about my father's dead body and what happens to it"; "I know someday I will be happy again"; "Talking about memories and good times helps"; "I don't feel embarrassed to cry"; "There is no right or wrong way to grieve"; Allen, 1990, p. 40). To return to the case of Jack, allowing time for grief was crucial.

The practitioner's work extended well beyond the group itself, as it often does (and should). In Jack's case, this meant advocating for a return to his home district, which took 2 long years to achieve. By the time he reached the eleventh grade, Jack had become a full-fledged member of the junior division of his local Fire Department. He had also become a member of the high school basketball team. His return to the local school and growing involvement in outside activities contributed to his gradual drifting away from the group. He started to miss meetings and then asked to cut back to attending every other week. Finally, after some discussion in the group and consultation with his Mom, a date was agreed upon for Jack to leave the group.

As Jack's final meeting unfolded, some 4 years after he had joined, the group filled themselves with pizza, Cokes, and memories of Jack's time in the group. There was lots of laughter as they reminisced, mostly about the humor that Jack brought into the group. The worker walked them through some of the turning points in Jack's life and how the group responded to these events, inviting their recollections. So as to ensure a "last chance" for everyone, he invited the boys to share any final thoughts or "words of wisdom" for Jack (and Jack for them). The round-robin approach seemed to make the boys feel a bit awkward. When it was his turn, the worker told Jack that he would miss him. Jack smiled and the others responded with an hilarious spell of exaggerated sobbing.

Four years earlier, when Jack had revealed to the group that he wrote poetry, he was encouraged to bring in a sample of his writing. He brought in just one poem, shared it with the group, and agreed to let the worker keep a copy. During one of the final interchanges of Jack's last meeting, the worker asked him, "Whatever happened with your poetry? You seemed to have a real talent." He shrugged off the complement and informed the worker, "I don't do that anymore." The worker said, "You know I saved the poem you gave to me years ago." Jack looked pleasantly surprised. One of the others asked, "Can we see it?" The worker responded, "It's up to Jack." Then he added, "But if he says it's okay, I'd like him to read it to you before we end today. You don't have to Jack. What do you think, will you?" A mild shade of red covered Jack's full cheeks, but he said, in his typically self-effacing manner, "Sure, why not?" As he unfolded the piece of paper that was handed to him he first read quietly to himself, smiling ever so slightly. "Yeah, I remember this," he finally said, breaking the waiting silence. He then proceeded to read his poem to the group.

The Man Upstairs

There was a man 86 years old
that lived upstairs from me
who would tell me how he used to
climb a tree,
and how he told me about the war
with spectacular galore,
but he told me sounding sore
that he was not in the war,
so he told me how he was with
the girls
he even brought one
real pearls,
until he passed away
and I was at his grave
that day,
and then I knew
that day,
the man upstairs
went away.

The others listened patiently. One of them volunteered to interpret the poem: "I know what it means," he offered. He started off by saying, "See it's about this guy that Jack knew who died . . . " While Jack's father was not mentioned, the recitation of the poem in his final meeting seemed fitting. The group had come full circle as they said good-bye to their friend.

In the aftermath of Jack's departure sadness dominated the emotional space of the group. "We better get some new members in this group," declared Alex. "This is really getting boring as hell," added Paul. The energy level in the group was hovering on empty. There was little talking, lots of slumping, occasional dozing, and none of the characteristic horsing around. The worker wondered aloud, "When do you think things changed in here?" No answer. Silence. And then out of the stillness came Marty's voice, Marty who had given his interpretation of Jack's poem, "It was when Jack left the group." The others eagerly nodded. With gentle encouragement, the group proceeded to share their memories of Jack . . . the energy gradually building as they laughed, shook their heads and slapped hands . . . continuing to reminisce about their time with Jack . . .

HELPING MEMBERS REEXPERIENCE THEIR "GROUPNESS" THROUGH SHARED ACTIVITY

The introduction of a shared activity, something that the group can do together, helps the members to reexperience their "groupness" at the point of termination (Middleman & Wood, 1990b; Middleman, 1968). To illustrate this phenomenon of bonding is a familiar recreation group to which thousands of children and adolescents have belonged for years and which holds its "meetings" in the natural setting of the community—little league baseball.

> One Little League coach instituted an annual ritual of a postseason combination barbecue and parent–child softball game. As the end of the season approached, the players (boys and girls), their siblings, parents, and grandparents would start buzzing about the barbecue, making plans from the sidelines. Compare the feeling in this leavetaking scenario to that of the team whose ending would come and go as swiftly as the final pitch of the final game of the season.

Every year millions of children and adolescents are involved in recreational programs just like little league baseball (e.g., drama groups, school clubs, choirs, bands, and countless other activities). Many of these groups are led by adults (coaches, teachers, parent–volunteers) with some technical knowledge of the activity. In most cases, they have less knowledge about the developmental needs of their group members, and even less about how to work with youngsters in a group and handle the interactional aspect of the activity. Group work skills, not the least of which is the importance of facilitating a decent ending, are applicable to all of these groups as well as to the so-called "problem-oriented" groups (e.g., therapy/treatment groups). After all, don't adolescents with problems partici-pate in normal group activities? Don't "normal" adolescents who participate in these groups sometimes have problems? Don't all of these young people, however they might be labeled, participate in some of these groups together? When they do, don't they develop relationships with one another? Don't they have feelings about separating from one another when the baseball season ends, when the concert ends, and when the final curtain closes? Yes. Yes. Yes. Yes. Yes. The adults who work with children and adolescents in these groups need to know more than how to turn a double play, hit a high note, or deliver a line.

Group workers can play an important role as consultants to community leaders involved with youth. For example, in one community, several group workers organized and developed the Long Island Institute for Group Work with Children and Youth.[2] The Institute's mission is: "to promote and enhance effective group work practice with children and youth through advocacy, education and collegial support." Some of the Institute's activities include producing a quarterly newsletter, launching a research project on the training needs of professionals and nonprofessionals (e.g., little league coaches, camp counselors) who work with young people in groups, and organizing peer supervision and training for practicing and aspiring group workers.

The next case example is of a group whose final meeting was held at a restaurant for a final meal together, emphasizing the transition beyond the group.

Practice Illustration: Transitional Spaces and Places

Meeting outside of the confines of the agency can help to make the connection to the world beyond the group (Malekoff & Kolodny, 1991). In one school group of 12- and 13-year-old boys, the members had spent 3 years together when they were about to end. As the worker (Kolodny) recalls:

> The final meeting was held at a local restaurant. As parting time drew near, one of the boys, Joey, said he wished he could just sit there after supper and talk. The prior three meetings had been highlighted by the force of the boys' denial and regression matched against the worker's efforts to encourage the boys to evaluate and recapitulate their time together. There was the recurrent, haunting question, posed in a variety of ways, of whether the experience and people would be

[2]The Long Island Institute for Group Work with Children and Youth, c/o North Shore Child and Family Guidance Center, 480 Old Westbury Road, Roslyn Heights, NY, 11577. Readers are invited to write to the author, Andrew Malekoff, at this address for more information or for a copy of the Institute's newsletter, *Huh?!?*

forgotten. Would the boys forget one another? Would the worker forget the boys? Would the whole experience be lost? One boy declared, "You'll forget us, you'll forget who we were." And then he asked "Do you have a card file?" This question suggested a combination of mixed feelings ranging from "We're just names on a card to you" to "You need to have concrete suggestions to remember us." In response, the worker simply said to them that he would remember them and that when people had been together like this, they don't forget each other.

Maybe he should have said to the boys, "I wonder if you'll forget me?" Doubts about whether the experience would be lost forever was just one manifestation of their feelings about the ending. There were also expressions of their anger and deprivation enacted through regressed behavior and sarcasm.

During one trip in the worker's car after a meeting, the boys started to throw things out of the window. They talked about what a lousy group this has been, that they had all been "gypped" and how they're all still "mental." At one point, one of them poked his head out of the window, laughing and calling out, "Help, we're orphans, we're orphans!"

Without pressing the issue the worker remarked that he would still be available to the boys and that his interest in the boys and their families didn't end with the ending of the group. He also made it clear that people could get angry and then get over the anger, giving them permission to express such feelings.

Most of their anger was directed at the worker and the agency. There was little intragroup hostility during the separation phase of the group.

The worker planned the final meeting at a pancake restaurant with some trepidation. He told the boys that since they'd been together for 3 years that he thought that they could handle it. In fact they did handle it in fairly good humor although not without the usual younger-adolescent comments and gesturing. One of them acted as if he were throwing up at the thought of eating pancakes in the evening. He said that it was okay to eat them in the morning but crazy to eat them at night. As a group, they actually approached the trip with great maturity. One of them even showed up wearing a sports coat.

On the ride over to the restaurant there was some yelling, but the boys confined it, for the most part, to inside the car. The worker tried to connect their behavior to their anger about the ending of the group. Denials of anger were immediately forthcoming. Once in the restaurant, one of the boys meekly commented on the occasion being a sad one. He declined to elaborate. The worker supported his expression by commenting that a person can talk about sadness and tell people about it, that he doesn't have to try to tell people about his sadness by doing a lot of angry things without saying anything. The boys wondered aloud about the new group that they learned the worker would be forming. By that time, their last hour together, they discussed the subject quite calmly and pleasantly, as "veterans" perhaps. And they talked about having a reunion (every five weeks, one boy suggested). And in the end, after supper, it was Joey who said he wished that they could just sit there in the restaurant and talk.

On the ride back from the annually attended and agency-sponsored summer camp a year earlier, Joey's shutting off of positive memories was so immediate and powerful as to be overwhelming. He was a bright kid, much abused at home by a probably psychotic father and an often nasty stepmother who had lost her left leg in a car accident. He was the school bully when he was referred to the group. Shutting off memories of camp may have been a way of protecting himself from these happy times being "taken away" from him at home through disparagement of them by his parents. Or maybe it represented his "hunger" that the pleasant experiences he had just consumed would no longer exist for him. Whatever the case, he couldn't bring himself to remember, wouldn't do so. A year later, he, of all the group members, was the one who wanted to bask in the warm glow of conversation about what they'd all done together.

Regarding the value of the work in the end, "a substantial statistical underpinning may be required by researchers and educators seeking evidence of the efficacy of a particular approach. For the practitioner immersed in the work itself, however, it is his or her impressions of the potential of the approach, as revealed at moments of its optimum impact on one or more group members, that persuade him/her of its worth" (Kolodny, 1992, pp. 158–159).

PROVIDING AVAILABILITY FOR SUPPORT BEYOND THE GROUP

A part of our commitment in providing meaningful help often involves continuing postgroup support for the individual and family. This may take the form of a periodic "check up," assistance in accessing resources (e.g., job, school placement), conferring with parents, or friendly visits. Workers who subscribe to the myth that relationships developed with individuals in groups are "less intensive" than those formed in one-to-one relationships, tend to minimize feelings of loss that group members and worker experience at the point of termination.

A Personal Reflection:
Just Like That—Tribute to a Group Member

The final case example is a personal reflection, by the author, of the transition beyond the group for one former adolescent group member.

> Eddie maintained periodic contact with me after his time in the group. From time to time he'd call to check in, ask for advice, or just make contact. On occasion, his Mom would call with a question or for clarification of some issue or another. I started to feel like a part of the extended family. Occasionally Eddie would stop by for a brief visit.
>
> I first met Eddie when he was 13 years old. He was what some people euphemistically referred to as a "special-ed kid." What first impressed me about him was his smile. It was a closed-mouthed, but genuine, smile. I knew it had to be because his eyes were smiling too. His cheeks were always red, from allergies he told us. The photograph of Eddie that appeared in the newspaper, some 10 years later, captured *the smile.*
>
> Eddie stayed with the group until his junior year in high school. It was about that time that he had returned to his home school district, after years of exile in a much detested special education placement. He especially hated the bus rides and the inevitable attacks, verbal and physical, from which there seemed to be no protection. During one stretch, he was truant from school for 2 weeks before anyone noticed. All this to avoid the bus rides. I remember when Eddie was caught calling in false fire alarms from his home telephone. "I wanted to see what would happen," he told the group. We learned that the Fire Chief showed up at his house after the calls were traced. What a remarkable turn of events followed. It seems that Eddie's brother had been dating the Fire Chief's daughter, apparently a source of concern for both sets of parents who had never met one another. The "false alarm" created the pretext for the parents to become acquainted, beyond addressing Eddie's actions (I guess it wasn't a false alarm after all). Another one of Eddie's many "experiments" was throwing crayons into a big pot of boiling pudding in the school kitchen. When

confronted, again he said, "I just wanted to see what would happen." Knowing Eddie, that was really all there was to it.

As Eddie progressed I felt so proud of him, as did his family, when he made the high school swim team and then when he became a high school graduate. I remember one time in particular when Eddie came in to see me, years after the group had ended. He was so upset. It seems that a group of men almost clobbered him when he drove down their block and smiled and waved to a group of neighborhood kids. How could they have known about Eddie's smile? They called the police. To them his smile meant something else, something to fear and protect their children from. The police rousted Eddie and threw a real scare into him. Eddie continued to struggle as a young adult, but he was determined and pressed ahead, always trying his best to navigate the rough waters of work and relationships.

Eddie continued to call me from time to time. He agreed to join a young adult group being formed by a colleague in the same agency. The group met in the same room as had the adolescent group that Eddie had left 6 or so years before. Having had a positive experience in a group as an adolescent, the transition back to group for him wasn't as difficult as it otherwise might have been.

From time to time I'd see Eddie in the waiting room and chat with him briefly before his group meeting. Then I would see him no more. The photo in the newspaper really did capture the smile. The headline read:

Man, 24, Found Dead in Whirlpool

The newspaper account stated the following:

> . . . According to Nassau police, Edward, 24, was found about 5:45 P.M. after another member of the Health Club told employees that she felt something at the bottom of the pool . . .

"Something?"

The news was shocking. Workers must find ways to address their own feelings about separation in the group, as I had when Eddie left the adolescent group at age 17. But there was no saying good-bye to Eddie this time. There was only the emptiness of an ending that shouldn't have been. Sometime very soon thereafter I remembered the boy with the special smile in a poem. It was my opportunity to reminisce about my time with Eddie.

Just Like That:
Tribute to a Group Member

enter smiling
always did
friendly greeting
special kid.

terror ridden
school bus
understated
no big fuss;
stayed home
had to hide
folks asked
Eddie lied.

false alarm
no fire
curious Ed
live wire;
station bound
faced chief
promised folks
to turn a leaf.

dropped a crayon
in the stew
disappeared
not a clue;
teacher asked
tell me why?
Eddie shrugged
no reply.

years pass
same face
water baby
nice pace;
made team
olympic pool
nice stroke
feeling cool.

cap 'n gown
Eddie passed
folks proud

moving fast;
stepping out
strange world
finding work
meeting girls.

in his car
passing by
confrontation
angry guys;
cops approach
Ed confused
friendly smile
misconstrued.

found a job
Eddie tries
struggles through
silent cries;
occasional drink
social reprieve
magic elixir
instant relief.

feeling better
joins gym
lays back
takes a swim;
stretches out
cools down
whirlpool nice
Eddie   gone.

exit smiling
always did
tragic parting
special kid.
    —A. Malekoff

CONCLUSION

In the end, the worker must reach for his/her own feelings about the impending separation, including one's own personal history as it relates to loss. Awareness of associated feelings and experiences can greatly assist the worker during the separation stage. The practitioner's openness and authenticity about the coming loss, expressed with good judgment and timing, will contribute to a meaningful parting, under almost any circumstances. Conversely the worker's unacknowledged ambivalence about separation can greatly compound the process (Hurley, 1984).

The consolidation of experiences through recapitulation and review serves, in the end, to accent the memories charted during the life of the group. The memories then become the historical landmarks revisited in the sentimental journeys to come. The once empty reservoirs, brimming at the moment of departure and subsiding some with the passage of time, will never drain completely. Always available will be the nourishment of reminiscence to be savored in solitude or swapped with others during times of nostalgic recollection.

APPENDIX 9.1. THE ENDING STAGES OF GROUP DEVELOPMENT[3]

WHERE THE MEMBERS ARE

Members begin to talk more about their successful efforts to try new things or change their patterns of behavior outside the group.

Communication is free and easy.

Members begin to move apart, find satisfaction in relationships outside the group (simultaneously they may break ties between members in the group and cohesiveness within the group may weaken), find new activities.

Members talk about some of the changes that have taken place in themselves and in the group; they review experiences, reminisce, evaluate, show desire to repeat earlier experiences (to show they can do better now).

Most members view termination with ambivalence and anxiety, it is an acknowledgement of improvement, yet they fear loss of support of worker and group; group experience may have been so good and so gratifying that people may want to continue.

Many reactions are possible:

- Denial of termination and of the possible meaning of the group experience
- Regression: Return to earlier patterns of behavior, inability to cope with relationship and tasks previously mastered; behave as they did in earlier stages, negative symptoms may recur as if to show "We're not better and still need the group and worker"
- Flight: Miss meetings, quit before the official end, show hostility toward worker and other members—I'll leave you before you leave me
- Constructive flight: Move on to new groups, other relationships, etc.

[3]Reprinted by permission of Roselle Kurland.

WHAT NEEDS TO HAPPEN

Ending needs to be discussed.

Gains that have been made need to be stabilized.

Members need to be helped to leave the relationship with the worker, with each other, with the group.

This group experience, if it made a significant impact on the members, needs to become a frame of reference for the members in approaching new groups and other situations.

Service to the group needs to be discontinued.

ROLE OF THE WORKER

To help what needs to happen happen.

- To prepare members for termination
- To assess desirability and readiness for termination; can members continue to improve outside of the group?
- To assess progress toward achievement of goals
- To help members stabilize the gains they've made
- To inform members of reality of termination (need for ending should be discussed well in advance)
- To anticipate responses of individuals to ending; To set goals for period of time that remains before the end
- To plan timing and content to make maximum use of remaining sessions
- To help members express their ambivalence about ending
- To help evaluation of the group experience
- May need to support a member who has not made as much progress as he/she hoped for as other members made
- To share observations of progress and confidence in ability of members to get along without worker and group
- To support members' efforts to move away from group, to develop new relationships outside the group, find other resources
- To indicate nature of any continuing relationship he/she may have with group or with individuals; may need to make him/her self available for help on an individual basis
- To communicate with others (staff, family members) who may need to be involved
- To help members tie their group experience more directly to their subsequent life experiences
- Worker too may be ambivalent—may be pleased about progress but feel a sense of loss and regret not having been more helpful to more members; there is a tendency for the worker to try to get everything in at the last minute

PART III

Contemporary and Age-Old Themes in Group Work

Guidelines, Applications, and Practice Illustrations

CHAPTER 10

Prejudice Reduction,
Intergroup Relations,
and Group Identity

Spontaneous and Planned
Interventions to Address Diversity
in Group Work

A good group experience can provide adolescents with a unique opportunity to explore the typically taboo areas of race and ethnicity, exposing deeply ingrained or loosely formed beliefs and attitudes. The mature group, through the development of its own history and culture, becomes a special frame of reference for its members, influencing their perceptions and behavior in the world outside of the group.

The focus of this chapter is on the use of group work to reduce prejudice and bigotry, promote intergroup relations, and enhance ethnic group identity in adolescence. Group work, with its emphasis on mutual exploration and discovery, is uniquely suited to address these issues. In such groups "each person responds to a situation he/she helped create a moment ago, and to which the response is always to a relation. I respond, not only to you, but to the relation between you and me" (Follette, 1940, p. 45). This deepening spiral of circular behavior, characteristic of group work, is the bedrock for the development of human relations.

PRACTICE PRINCIPLES FOR ADDRESSING DIVERSITY

What follows are principles for addressing diversity in group work with adolescents. They may be adapted for confronting other forms of diversity in groups (e.g., religion, gender, sexual orientation, age, disability). Practice examples from a variety of settings are then provided to serve as illustrations.

- *Address diversity as a normative adolescent issue in the group.* Encourage interaction about group identity, prejudice, and intergroup relations as a normal part of adolescent development and not only in reaction to emergent conflicts or crises.
- *Help the group to tune in to ethnically and racially charged events impacting on youth.* This includes an awareness of local, national, and international events with racial–ethnic overtones (e.g., O. J. Simpson trial; Persian Gulf War; defacing of synagogues, churches, and schools; Rodney King case/Los Angeles riots; boycott of Korean grocery in New York; Million Man March on Washington, DC). When such stories dominate the media and youth's consciousness, stereotyping and polarization are often reinforced. A healthy and spirited exchange of ideas and opinions about controversial subjects in a safe environment enables young people to test out their beliefs and attitudes, to practice listening to others' views, to respectfully express differences, and to discover common ground.
- *Confront prejudice, stereotyping, and oppression in the here-and-now of the group and workplace.* Confront issues such as stereotyping and the use of racial/ethnic slurs as they arise in the here-and-now of the group. Facilitative confrontation involves addressing issues and problems in a direct, caring, and forthright manner (Shulman, 1992). When the group or workplace replicates the oppressive or prejudicial behavior of society, the practitioner must skillfully intervene to raise consciousness, stimulate interaction, foster understanding, and motivate change.
- *Use cultural self awareness to model effective cross-cultural relationships.* Tune in to personal feelings, experiences, attitudes, and values related to one's own group identity and views about different groups. Model respectful and effective cross-cultural relationships in the group and workplace (Hurdle, 1991).
- *Promote understanding and respect for the world view and values of culturally different members.* Help group members to develop, if not an emotional affinity with different ethnic and racial groups, a cognitive empathy and cultural sensitivity that can lead to a deeper understanding of culturally different group members (Sue & Sue, 1991). This may be developed through "self-awareness, elimination of stereotypes and unfounded views, and acquisition of objective knowledge about and actual interaction with members of a particular cultural group" (Soriano, 1993, p. 443).
- *Tune in to the differential experiences of ethnic group members within their own particular culture.* Help group members to understand the different experiences of members of ethnic groups that may customarily be

perceived through an undifferentiated lens (i.e., "They're all the same"). For example, in one group of adolescent boys, one of the members was sure that the worker, a Jewish American, was rich because "Everyone knows that all Jews are rich." So convinced was he of this common myth, he couldn't accept the reality or empathize with the pain of a fellow member, a Jewish boy whose family had been homeless and was struggling on public assistance. He was flabbergasted when he finally realized the truth.

• *Open pathways for intercultural communication and socialization.* In addition to advancing an understanding of cultural differences, reach for commonalties experienced among adolescents across cultures to open intergroup pathways for relating (Bilides, 1990). For example, it is not uncommon for groups of culturally different adolescent group members to discover some common ground in their experiences of negotiating with parents or other authority figures for greater freedom and more privileges.

IS TRUTH STRANGER THAN FICTION?

This section presents a boys' group in a mental health clinic as its members struggle with themes of prejudice, group identity, and intergroup relations. An example of a time-limited structured group approach, "ethnic sharing," to addressing these issues concludes the section.

Jimmy, a 16-year-old African American member of a boys' group formed in a community mental health center, made this statement at the outset of one of the group's meetings:

> "Now this is true. I was chilling one day—right—drinking a Tropical Fantasy because it was hotter than a mother-fucker outside. Somebody came up to me and said, 'Yo'—and he was a white guy too. He was like, 'Check this—that stuff you're drinking is real bad for you.' I said, 'Why?' He said, 'Think about it, it's really cheap.' He told me that the KKK made that kind of soda and put it in almost every black community and sold it really cheap—fifty cents. It's like a quart of milk (gestures with his hands to indicate the size of the bottle). No soda that big should cost fifty cents. They're running it *really cheap.* It should cost over a dollar. And they're selling it everywhere, EVERY-WHERE. If you think about it—anything with that quantity that sells *really really really cheap* and it's *really really really big* and it's *really really really good*—I mean it's good as hell—it's better than a Mystic. Why would something so big and so good be so cheap? There's spermicide in there to kill sperm. They put it in the black community—you know?"

This was not the first time Jimmy and other group members had raised the specter of conspiracy. He and the others also speculated about the origin of AIDS:

"What I was trying to figure out—what they were saying is that AIDS came from a monkey in Africa—a green monkey at that—this is what my health teacher said—well I think AIDS is synthetic—it's a man-made disease—and they don't have any antibiotics to stop it—a lot of black friends of mine say the white man made it to eliminate black people—I don't know—first of all they'd have to inject into themselves—if they knew it was killing everyone they'd have an antibiotic to stop it—I don't know . . . "

In recalling Jimmy's statements I'm reminded of the gag line, "Just because you're paranoid doesn't mean that they're not really out to get you." Some weeks after the discussion about the Tropical Fantasy soft drink, the worker spotted the following headline in a local newspaper (*Long Island Newsday,* September 2, 1993): "Snapple Tries Putting Cap on Ugly Rumors: Combats Tale about KKK with Advertising Campaign." The article began: "Snapple Beverage Co., the Valley Stream-based maker of iced teas and fruit drinks, launched a five-day media campaign in the San Francisco area yesterday to combat rumors that the fast-growing company supports the Ku Klux Klan," and continued by explaining that the company's senior officers took out full-page ads in the San Francisco area newspapers, stating that the claims against Snapple were false. The ad, which took the form of a letter, said that Snapple was not involved in any way whatsoever with the KKK or any other type of pressure group or organization. The letter stated that the rumors circulating were false, wrong, and outrageous.

This article put Jimmy's presentation of a tainted soft drink into a new perspective for the worker and the group members, who poured over reprints of the article. Although a variation on Jimmy's theme, the news item highlighted the insidiousness of hateful propaganda and the need for critical thinking to differentiate fantasy from reality. The group had also discussed police brutality after having been exposed repeatedly, through television, to the videotaped footage of the Rodney King beating. As if this didn't confuse the boundaries between fantasy and reality enough, closer to home there was the false arrest and jailing of another black youth who later joined the group.

As the above gag line about paranoia confirms, often profound truth is revealed in humor. As Greir and Cobbs have noted "Black men have stood so long in such peculiar jeopardy in America that a *black norm* has developed—a suspiciousness of one's environment which is necessary for survival. Black people to a degree that approaches paranoia, must be ever alert to danger from their white fellow citizens" (1968, p. 206). Indeed, the phenomenon of adaptive paranoia is not at all uncommon to other ethnic minority groups who have experienced this historically.

Moments like the ones generated by Jimmy's reflections on Tropical Fantasy and the origin of AIDS provided the group with the chance to confront powerful issues that arouse deeply felt emotions. For many, such opportunities are thwarted by societal taboos, "reflecting a general consensus to block or prohibit discussion in areas of sensitivity and deep concern" (Shulman, 1985/1986, p. 54). One observer noted that "ethnicity can be equated along with sex and death as a subject that touches deep unconscious feelings in most people" (Levine, 1982, p. 4).

Minority adolescents must often deal with the double crisis of normal developmental stress and society's reaction to their ascribed status as perceived by the majority community (Irizzary & Appel, 1994; Brown, 1984). Addressing this double crisis requires attending to group members' outer sociocultural reality as well as to the inner world of psychological processes. The complexity of belonging to two cultures—one's ethnic culture and the dominant culture—cannot be underestimated (Davis, 1984). Minority youth often face the daily challenge of moving between cultures, a process of intercultural socialization in which the primary socialization occurs within the minority group world and a secondary socialization takes place in the mainstream white society (Wilson, 1991; Bilides, 1990). Yet, along with a deeper understanding of cultural factors comes the realization that "All ethnic labeling is an oversimplification and falsifies the degree of variation and nonconformity in any social group" (Spiegel, 1965, p. 583).

In the two earlier illustrations, the worker encouraged an open exploration of Jimmy's statements in the group, validating the concerns raised and enabling the group members to probe issues that they later confirmed were denied a serious airing anywhere outside of the group. The others didn't see Jimmy's theories as too far fetched. All expressed a degree of general cynicism about government. Perhaps this was reflective of their feelings about authority in general. But Jimmy's concerns were not about authority in general, they ran much deeper than that, as the following case example illustrates.

PRACTICE ILLUSTRATIONS

Ethnic Sharing:
A Time-Limited Structured Group Approach

To enhance the group program beyond spontaneous discussions of intergroup relations and to emphasize issues of group identity and diversity, the worker, with the members' agreement, invited a special guest, Irving M. Levine, to join the group for one meeting. Levine, also a group worker, identified himself as a Jewish American with a lifelong commitment to civil rights, intergroup relations, and group identity. To model sharing for the group, he talked about his own youth, including his early experiences with race relations and participation in the development of a social agency known as the Brownsville Boys' Club (Sorin, 1990). His plan was to facilitate "ethnic sharing" in the group by probing the members' experiences, feelings, and ideas about their group identity and encounters with prejudice and bigotry.[1]

Research shows that the factors leading to the formation of an individual's attitudes of prejudice are related to group membership, that is, "to adopting the group and its values as the main anchorage in regulating experience and behavior" (Sherif & Sherif, 1953, p. 218). The most frequent source of prejudice "lies in the needs and habits that reflect the influence of in-group membership upon the development of the individual personality" (Allport, 1958, p. 39). The special significance and influence of the peer group during adolescence necessitate addressing racism and other forms of bigotry through the group.

Ethnic sharing, an approach to prejudice reduction, was designed as a group intervention because, asserts Levine (1995), "It is impossible to confront prejudice without a planned attack through the group process." In one exchange he asked the boys—Jimmy, African American; Rob, Latino; Jack, Irish–Latino; and Kevin, German–Italian—about incidents in which they had been victims of prejudice. Jimmy was the last to respond.

GW[2]: Any dramatic instances in your life where anyone picked on you because you're black?

JIMMY: I'm not sure.

GW: Like when you shop in stores.

JIMMY: Thank you, yes, yes, thank you, thank you! In this store where I go to play video games—I go in and the guy [storekeeper] comes to me the other day and says "excuse me"—he didn't know who I was, and there were lots of customers in the place—and he says, "Please don't harass or scare my customers. If you do I'm going to have to kick you outta here."

GW: How did that make you feel?

JIMMY: I was very frustrated, but I controlled myself.

[1]See Appendix 10.1 for a detailed description of an "ethnic sharing" workshop; see Appendix 10.2 for a list of references on diversity and group work not otherwise referred to herein.

[2]GW refers to the guest group worker.

GW: Are you proud of yourself, that you controlled yourself?

JIMMY: Yeah, no reason to do that, normally I'd explode, but I controlled myself, told myself—"Don't do it."

ROB: I couldn't do that. I'd explode. I've exploded too much.

GW: Do you regret it?

ROB: No, 'cause it shows that you're not a person who's willing to be put down. If you keep getting put down and you don't do anything about it, they'll keep it up.

GW: (looks to Kevin and Jack) You two are white; do you think your situation—racially—is as serious as theirs as an African American and a Puerto Rican?

JACK: It's who you hang out with. I get followed around too when I hang out with black kids.

GW: Because?

JACK: Because I hang out with black kids. And I hang out with black people. Once this kid came up to me and called me a "wigger." He said, "Why do you hang out with all those niggers? You should hang with your own kind."

GW: How did you feel?

JACK: At first embarrassed, then angry!

GW: Has this made you a better person because you understand more deeply the experiences of people other than yourself?

JACK: Yeah, I guess.

JIMMY: (indicating empathy) So you can see what we're talking about.

KEVIN: If they're following you around, I have to defend the store owner because I watch people in the store I work at in the mall. It's the people you hang out with. And it is your attitude. When you're with your friends, you have a different attitude than when you're with your mother.

GROUP: (laughter and affirmative expressions) True, true.

KEVIN: You see a bunch of kids walking together. They could be black, white, Spanish, whatever. They could be walking together. They look like they don't have a care in the world. They've got book bags. They touch everything, and most of them don't buy shit. The store owner gets worried because, you know, it's his merchandise, and he wants to protect it. He's only being cautious. They're not directing it towards a certain race. And if they do, that's wrong.

JACK: You could be walking in a store and someone could be asking if you're looking for something to buy. Yeah, that might be fine. I'm looking for something, and if I need help ask me, but not every time. You walk around, and they have two people following you, walking up and down the aisle.

GW: I understand, but mostly it's racial. I have no question about that. Everybody reports it all over the country. Black teenagers report it everywhere you go. You hear the same thing all over. But do you think part of it is because you're teenagers, that there's prejudice against teenagers?

JACK: I think there's prejudice against race, but there's also prejudice against age.

In the process thus far, common ground is sought by asking each of the members to share his experiences as targets of bigoted attacks; racism is addressed directly and personally in the interchange around Jimmy's experience with the storekeeper; and intercultural pathways for communication are opened by broadening the focus to include discrimination against teenagers. Beyond asking the members about their own experiences as victims of prejudice, the ethnic sharing provided an opportunity for them to recall if they had ever acted in a bigoted way toward another person or a group.

GW: Think of a time when you performed an act of bigotry against somebody else . . .

JACK: Right after Crown Heights broke [Crown Heights, a neighborhood in Brooklyn, New York, was the site of black–Jewish conflict touched off by the vehicular death of a black child, subsequent rioting, and the murder of a rabbinical student by members of a black mob] we were in Queens, and we saw some Jewish kids, and we crowded around them and started staring them down.

GW: What did you think was happening?

JACK: I don't know.

JIMMY: It's like blaming kids here [in New York] for what happened in L.A. [riots following the Rodney King verdict]. Something I'm not proud of was making fun of a disabled person. I made fun of him, but deep in my heart I said, "Jimmy, stop doing that."

GW: Why did you do it then?

JIMMY: My friends were there, we were all doing it.

GW: How much guts does it take to tell your friends that it's not right?

JACK: A lot!

Jimmy's revelation about ridiculing people with disabilities led to a few moments of nervous laughter among all of the boys and opened the discussion of diversity beyond race. Jack exposed his antipathy toward gay people when discussing his ambivalence about whether they should be permitted to march in the St. Patrick's Day Parade, a well-publicized and perennial controversy among several competing groups in New York City. All of the boys admitted telling ethnic jokes and poking fun at people with disabilities and gays. Jimmy, assuming the role of spokesman, downplayed these actions stating, "Everyone jokes around, it's not like we mean to hurt anyone." The others nodded in agreement. The consultant, tuning in to their need to clarify and explain asked, "Am I to get the impression that even though you make fun of the handicapped, gays, blacks, Puerto Ricans, that you don't mean it deeply, that you don't consider yourself heavily bigoted?" This allowed the members to move beyond defensiveness and to acknowledge their ambivalent feelings without denying responsibility for their actions and attitudes.

KEVIN: No, I don't think I am [heavily bigoted]. There is a sign someone made in my school that I agree with. It says there is only one race: the human race.

GW: Do you think that what you believe other teenagers believe?

KEVIN: No, no.

JIMMY: It's not their fault they're that way. If you get a black parent that doesn't know a white parent and a white parent that doesn't know a black parent and you get their children and sit them down to play, they don't know nothing, they don't know the color, they don't. If you raise your kids like that, you don't say black and don't say white (*struggling for words*) . . . people don't seem to want to touch each other.

Reaching for strength and possibility the consultant then frames the boys revelations in a hopeful context.

GW: Okay, you (*referring to all of the boys*) don't appear to be as bigoted as many people your age. Any reason why you're less bigoted than others?

ROB: The hurricane in Puerto Rico.

GW: Interesting. How do you mean?

ROB: It brought lots of people together.

GW: Did you do anything?

ROB: I sent $50 [to the relief effort].

KEVIN: Take the Fire Department [Kevin is a junior member]. You can be any race or color. What it comes down to is there's somebody who needs help. No matter what's up here (*points to his head*) it's here (*points to his heart*) that counts. It's just all the same. When somebody needs help you are all one.

GW: How important do you think this issue of racism, anti-Semitism, bigotry, prejudice is? How important is it?

GROUP: (*several voices*) Big!

GW: On a scale of one to ten?

GROUP: (*in unison*) TEN.

JIMMY: It's killing our people. It's a plague, an invisible plague.

JACK: If people keep doing what they're doing, pretty soon there's not going to be an America.

ROB: It'll be a ghost land.

As the meeting came to a close, the guest worker asked the members if they feel capable of making a difference, intimating that they have the power to influence change.

GW: Do you see yourselves as potential leaders?

ROB: I want to be like Malcolm X or Martin Luther King.

KEVIN: No, I don't see myself as a leader, but I'm someone who can stand up against prejudice.

JIMMY: Yeah, I wouldn't have the patience.

JACK: We should accept each other.

GW: In other words you want to be an example but not push too hard.

KEVIN: Yeah.

During the meeting, the group's regular worker assumed a less directive role, enabling the group to have the space to function more autonomously. Participating in the discussion sparingly, he positioned himself as a validating audience urging the members on and reinforcing their competence nonverbally with a smile here and a nod there. At the close of the ethnic sharing, the guest consultant commented to the boys on their ability to work together and confront important and difficult issues in an intelligent manner, emphasizing their competence. The ethnic sharing soon became a new frame of reference for the boys, an historical landmark for the group to draw on from time to time.

Disrespecting People You Don't Know: Integration or Conformity?

The following four illustrations touch on issues of diversity from a variety of vantage points. These include addressing the use of dehumanizing language in the group, confronting self-imposed segregated seating in a racially mixed group, the worker's use of self when his own childhood memories of being a target of prejudice are evoked in the here and now of the group, and the use of program to promote group identity and inter-group relations.

The members of a life skills group composed of nine Caucasian girls ranging in age from 11 to 13 years met weekly in a community center. The purpose of the group was to help the girls to navigate early adolescence by addressing normative issues such as puberty, sexuality, peer pressure, gender roles, diversity, drugs, and career awareness. The group had been discussing issues of racism in the community, and the coworkers (GWa and GWb) had some concerns about the language the girls were using to characterize members of minority groups. They didn't want to cut off the discussion prematurely.

GWa: Before we get into today's activity, I want to discuss for a bit the stuff that was brought up last week about people of other races.

GWb: We wanted to let you know that we are happy you feel comfortable enough to talk with us about what is on your minds, and we want you to continue to do so. However, remember the rule you made that said respect each other?

CHRIS and JEAN: Yeah.

GWa: Well, we think that should include respecting all the people that we may discuss in here, including people who are different and from different races.

GWb: Last week, several people referred to African American people as "niggers" and Spanish or Latino people as "spics"; these are very hurtful words, and when they are said, they are hurtful to us (*referring to coleaders*).

ANNA: Why? You're not black?

GWa: That's true, but I respect African American and Latino people, and to hear them called "niggers" and "spics" hurts me.

JEAN: We say it all the time; it is just going to slip out in here.

GWa: Well, maybe this group is different from other places you hang out.

GWb: Yes, and in the group it is OK to say black people or African American or Spanish, but not the hate words.

In this illustration the workers clearly and directly, and with emotion, shared their values and expectations for group behavior with the aim of teaching the members that discussions about different groups, racial and otherwise, can occur without disrespecting and stereotyping entire groups. The girls did test the limits, "slipping" several times, but the workers stood fast, consistently and firmly reinforcing their expectations. Gradually the discussions reflected what the workers were aiming for, as stereotypic language was shed from the discourse.

Had the group members really integrated and internalized the changes reflected by their behavior or were they merely conforming, doing what the workers expected of them? An alternative approach would have been for the workers to wonder aloud why they were using these words and whether or not they were curious as to why the workers never seemed to use them. This might have led to a more penetrating discussion of the feelings that lie beneath the surface of the words.

Being with People You Know

In his treatise on race, color, ethnicity, class, and multicultural experiences in school-based adolescent counseling groups, Bilides (1990) describes how the groups "become microcosms of struggles and prejudices played out in larger social contexts" (p. 45) including the host institution itself. This gets enacted, in part, through seating arrangements, group attendance, and cultural typecasting. One principle Bilides recommends to address these issues is to confront them, as he illustrates below.

> In one career exploration group, the members had divided themselves along a narrow table into two subgroups: the Spanish-speaking students at one end, and the Black students at the other. The members of each subgroup were conversing among themselves, with the Spanish-speaking students using Spanish. The group leader interrupted and said, "It looks as though we have two groups: the black kids here, and the Spanish-speaking kids here. What do you make of that?" The students at first protested that it wasn't a matter of two different groups. The group leader persisted by asking them to explain the seating arrangement. A discussion ensued about "being with people you know" and how people get to know other people. The members spontaneously changed their seats to create a more mixed arrangement. (p. 51)

Knowing Oneself

The worker must tune in to his/her own feelings, experiences, and attitudes regarding cultural diversity and to model respectful and effective cross-cultural relationships (Hurdle, 1991). This should include one's self-acknowledgment of discomfort around certain issues. In our 1991 article, Kolodny and I (Malekoff & Kolodny, 1991) describe a preadolescent boys' group on an outing to an urban downtown area during Christmastime. At a certain point, one of the members climbed out of the van and ran to the corner of a brownstone with a piece of chalk in his hand and, with an angry smile on his face, drew a swastika. The worker (Kolodny), in his best therapeutically neutral voice asked, "What's that mean Billy?" Kolodny continues:

> But was there the slightest quaver in my voice? Even hints of anti-Semitism have a way of disconcerting Jewish workers. For me it always brought me back to the sandlots and playgrounds of a New England mill town where I grew up in the 1930s. . . . For me the happy memories of the playing field on the heights would always be marred. Twelve years old, I was happily wrestling with my close friend Bucky—and then the voice of mean Mike McD., 17 years old, all five-foot-ten of him: "What are you doing playing with that Jew bastard Bucky?" At 12 one is not allowed to be a coward. Thus the inevitable. Several futile, furious swings up at the tormentor, the arch anti-Semite, followed by a terrible beating. . . .
>
> But the four-foot-seven 10-year-old standing in front of me defiantly with the chalk in his hand was not Mike McD. He was Billy, who lived in an alley tenement near the bus station, whose mother rarely showed emotion of any kind, and whose well-meaning father considered himself, and was considered by others, a total failure, as he had lost one menial job after another. What must have been Billy's thoughts and feelings on being taken into the sumptuous world of downtown at Christmastime.
>
> His siblings were undoubtedly envious and must have let him know that they were. They must have had questions as to why he, the one who had brought particular shame to the family by his antic behavior in school and by being practically unable to either read or write, was being singled our for what to them simply appeared as interesting activities and 2 hours of fun, weekly. Under these conditions, Billy could not have escaped feeling a sense of separation from his family and strong ambivalence whenever a particularly pleasurable time was being offered him through the group. The drawing of the swastika was likely an expression of the ambivalence brought on by the gift of a good time, rather than a hostile personal attack. . . .
>
> In control of myself now, I pressed my question, "What's that mean?" Back came Billy's retort, "It means I'm a big shot." Hands on hips he waited for his chastisement. . . . "You really don't have to get yourself punished for having a good time, Billy," I replied. "It's okay for you guys

to be here. You're supposed to have a good time." My assessment of the situation and comments seemed to be on the mark, as Billy and the others relaxed. . . . To this day, however, I wonder whether Billy had learned anything about another important lesson, the one about the swastikas. . . . Didn't Erik Erikson write something about wedding clinical dispassion to moral indignation? Somehow I always have difficulty remembering which Erikson intended to come first, the clinical dispassion or the moral indignation. (Malekoff & Kolodny, 1991, pp. 96–97)

Use of Program to Promote Group Identity and Intergroup Relations

Where appropriate, the practitioner should encourage activities that accent cultural traditions and values in the group. Such activities help to promote identity development, raise consciousness about differences, and encourage intercultural socialization. Aponte (1994) points to the impact of slavery (African Americans), conquest (Native Americans), and colonization (Puerto Ricans) on the loss of traditional culture for many of the poor in the United States and contrasts their experiences from those of other immigrant groups.

> [The] European and Asian immigrants to the United States, who were not subjugated, were accompanied by their cultures into the American scene. Their ghettos, even with poverty and discrimination, became nurseries that fostered identity, social role, personal values. They contended with American society from a core that affirmed who they were, what they were worth, and why they should strive. (pp. 2–3)

This statement affirms the importance of integrating history and tradition into the group experience. In *Los Seis,* a coed Mexican American group (see Chapter 4), in addition to drug- and alcohol-prevention activities, the group purpose included learning about Mexican history and culture. This was accomplished by practicing traditional Mexican dance; wearing traditional Mexican clothing; reading, studying, and reciting an epic poem of the Mexican American people, *I Am Joaquin* (Gonzales, 1967).

In The Youth of Culture Drug-Free Club, the members, all African American, planned an International Cultural Day featuring clothing, music, artifacts, food, and speeches identifying the history and customs of various ethnic groups. In both *Los Seis* and Youth of Culture, the program involved great preparation and family and community support and participation, all culminating in community-wide presentations, enabling the members to publicly share their work and to receive the affirmation and validation so significant to developing a sense of competence and cultural pride.

The final three illustrations address the plight of immigrant youth.

While illustrated with groups of Latino/Latina youth, the themes of separation, loss, acculturation, alienation, isolation, and misunderstanding may be generalized to others as well.

Images of Immigration I: *"Vendidos!"*

> "Yeah, that's the problem, they don't really care. . . . they never listen to us, right? . . . That's true, see, they think that just because we are different, we are garbage, right?"

So declared a member of a special high school group composed of six Latino immigrant youth from El Salvador, Guatemala, and Puerto Rico. The teenagers, ages 14 to 18, are referred by assistant principals and teachers because of their poor academic performance and violent and acting-out behavior. The student body includes many recent immigrants to the United States from Central America who speak very little or no English. The group members share similar histories of physical and psychological abuse, abandonment and neglect by primary caretakers, and the difficult task of adapting to a new cultural environment that is perceived by them as hostile and threatening.

The purposes of the group included the desire to improve their social skills and academic performance, improve the social functioning of group members, reduce their acting-out and violent behavior, learn to be more reflective and less reactive when confronted with stressful situations, identify common stressors in their lives—particularly oppression—and to cope with them more successfully, identify and access support systems, and learn to effectively mediate the various systems impacting on their lives.

All of the members complained that the school was insensitive to their needs. The school authorities reportedly related to the immigrant students in a distant, impersonal, and authoritarian manner. The concept of *personalismo* (a preference for relating to people rather than impersonal structures) was missing from their experiences in the school.

The worker, himself a Latino, had gained the trust of the students. He had introduced, advocated for, and successfully implemented an idea for a group to be composed of these students. In one of the early meetings several group members referred to the school principal, another Latino, as a *vendido*—a sellout.

ANDRES: Yeah, that's the problem, they don't really care. . . . They never listen to us, right?. . . . That's true, see, they think that just because we are different we are garbage, right?

MARCO: That's true.

GW: Wait a minute, I think that there is some exaggeration on that assumption. It may be true that because of the language and the culture some vice principals may not be able to fully understand your side, but to say that they see you as garbage . . .

ANDRES: (*interrupts*) It's true, though.

(*Silence*)

Somewhat defensively the worker has jumped the gun by challenging the members' statements. This could have the effect of shutting down communication if perceived as a challenge or as disapproval. Exploration of their feelings and whether or not there is consensus would help to better understand and develop an idea of where they are coming from. It should also be emphasized that, in the beginning of a new group, establishing trust is critical. Members are typically wary of the new experience, not yet committed to the group, and maintaining a safe distance. Once he/she is viewed from this perspective, the worker can search for common ground and discover whether or not the other members share the sentiments of their fellow member. The worker might also wonder whether or not the statement suggests something about his own role in the group. Can he be trusted? Is he a *vendido* as well?

GW: Don't you have anything else to say about that?

(*Silence*)

GW: Marco, you sounded like you agreed with Andres, can you explain why?

A nice recovery here by the worker who initiates exploration. "Recoveries" are common in group work with adolescents. Just because the "perfect" intervention does not occur when you think it "should have" doesn't mean that you don't get a second and third chance to get it right. Group members often provide workers with a "second offering" on a theme of concern that might have been overlooked or denied adequate attention in the first place (Shulman, 1992).

MARCO: Yeah, I think it's true.

GW: Why?

MARCO: Because it happened to me, and not once but several times. You know that, right?

GW: Yes, I think we talked about that before. Do you want to share it with the group? [The worker continues to encourage exploration.]

MARCO: Hmm, well, yes, for instance, everyone knows that Ms. O [teacher] is a racist. She hates me; she has told me several times: Marco, I'll get you out, I gonna get you out. She knows I can't speak English, but she keeps talking to me, and she knows I don't understand, but she says: "I know you understand Marco, you just pretend you don't so you can get away with this." That completely annoys me, I mean, the way she talks to me. My mom once got upset with her, and she said that she would complain to Mr. V [school principal]. She did. She talked to him. He said he would look into it.

ANDRES: He is a *vendido* anyway; he is just like them.

GW: What makes you say so?

Now the worker appears to be settling in to the group's rhythm at this early stage of group development. The members continue to denigrate the school administration. While the worker can relate to their complaints, he is also a member of the school staff. The questions the worker must ask himself is: How do I encourage an open airing of the group members' needs and experiences and not become overly identified with them? And, how do I represent the school without becoming just another *vendido*?

ANDRES: Because he is [a *vendido*], he works for the school; he thinks like them. I liked him when I first met him, but now I don't like him anymore. He wants to get me expelled. I know that. Mrs. P has told me that; he told that to my sister too, that I will be expelled.

GW: Actually, Andres, it was he who personally decided to give you one more chance, remember? The vice-principal recommended that you be expelled immediately after you came high to class, and Mr. V said you should be given another opportunity.

In admission to the reality of the assistant principal's attitude toward him, Andres expresses some anxiety that his days in the school are numbered and that his chances for a successful future may be threatened. There are also the realities of immigration that all of the members are reminded of daily as they struggle to adjust to a new world. This needs to be addressed as well by the worker, perhaps once a basic level of trust is established and the members have made a clear commitment to the group.

ANDRES: He accused me of being high. I wasn't high.

GW: All right, I don't know that, but let's go back to the principal. If Mr.

V is as mean as you say he is, if he is a "sellout" as you describe him, why does he care about you?

ANDRES: I don't know. I don't think he does.

(*Silence*)

GW: Does anyone else have anything to say about that?

ALBERTO: Yeah, well, I think he has to do his job. He can't just throw you out, he has to look good, you know, to keep his job. But he works for the school; he is one of them. I wouldn't trust him, no, I don't trust him.

GW: So now it isn't just a matter of race or being Anglo or Latino; now it all comes down to working for the school. If you work for the school, you have to be mean to these kids. Does it really make sense? Am I also one of "them" to you? (*smiles, pauses*) Does anyone want to respond to that?

The worker's distinction lays the groundwork for an important area for the members to sort out. Are school personnel insensitive to them on the basis of their cultural backgrounds? If so, are they all that way? Are there areas that the members need to take responsibility for themselves? Does the cry of *vendido* create a smoke screen, an obstacle to the work the group must do? The worker asks the members what he realizes they've been wondering all along, if they think they can trust him: "Am I also one of 'them' to you?"

ANDRES: No, you are not.

GW: Why? What makes me different? I also work for the school, you know.

DONALD: Because you know how to listen to us.

GW: Well, maybe I'm just "doing my job" as you said.

MARCO: No, we know you care.

GW: Well, then perhaps the fact of me being here talking to you is proof that the school wants to help you, right?

(*Silence*)

Images of Immigration II: Gang Intervention and Cultural Sensitivity

Although gangs have existed throughout the 20th century, there is growing concern over their increasing numbers and participation in violence (Doherty, 1995). Gangs are no longer confined to inner cities or isolated regions. A recent survey revealed that gangs are present in all 50 states including Alaska, Hawaii, as well as in other U.S. territories, including Puerto Rico (Spergel et al., 1990). It is reported that more than two-thirds of gang members are ethnic minorities (Spergel & Curry, 1990). This reinforces the need for cultural sensitivity in any gang prevention or intervention project (Soriano & De La Rosa, 1990).

In one case, an outreach worker participating in an agency peer supervision group presented her account of a "secret" meeting held in a local high school. The student body in the school is predominantly African American with a growing population of Latino and Latina youth, many of whom are refugees (some undocumented) from Central American countries. The worker, a Salvadoran immigrant, had successfully developed groups throughout the school district. She described to her colleagues in the supervision group how she was called, without being briefed, into a school meeting. The following is her account of the meeting.

> "I was surprised to be called to the meeting. When I walked in, there were about 25 high school students I didn't know personally. In the front of the room were the school principal and two men, who I soon learned were police detectives. The students were told that investigations revealed that they were members of a gang, that it was known that they were involved in illegal activity (drug sale, burglary), and that they were going to be closely watched. I was told that I must work with this group and to report back on anything I 'find out.' The meeting was very upsetting. At the end, they left me alone with all of the students. Surprisingly, the youth didn't seem angry. There was only a silent sadness in the room. Among the 25 students, I found that about two-thirds of them had arrived in the United States within the previous 2 years. Almost all of them had been separated from family members for some length of time. Many had relatives who met violent deaths as the result of war and political unrest. Those students who lived with their parents rarely saw them, since they had to work two or three jobs just to survive."

The location? Not the inner city, but a "poverty-pocket" set in the midst of a suburb adjacent to New York City. The worker reported being shocked by the school's response to these students. She had heard rumblings about such a gang, but this was her first introduction to the alleged members. As far as she could determine, no prior attempts had been made to understand these students with respect to where they had come from, what they had come to, and what they struggled with on a daily basis. The school's message, at least as it was delivered in the meeting described above, was for social control and containment. Absent were any messages about helping the students to adapt, to express their needs, to deal with a new language and culture, to negotiate the myriad of systems that confronted their families, to cope with fears of deportation, and to reach their academic potential.

The supervisory group helped the worker to devise a plan that included the following goals: (1) broadening the focus of the problem beyond social control; (2) helping the school and the students to seek common ground no matter how obscure it had become by obstacles; (3) enabling the students to amplify their voice to raise consciousness about their plight; (4) identifying and addressing the school's legitimate concerns for a peaceful environment; and (5) stressing cultural sensitivity at the administrative level of the school (Pederson, 1988). All agreed that much more was necessary than "keeping an eye on a gang" or "keeping them in line."

Images of Immigration III: The Journey Back Home

Another Latino worker, in recalling his work with immigrant Hispanic youth, expressed the lament of many parents who "observe the 'Americanization' of their children as they attempt to separate and to belong by experimenting with many of the dominant culture's values. For many, the higher the level of adaptation and acculturation to mainstream, the greater the distance from the family of origin" (Lopez, 1991, p. 54). In one group of immigrant youth, a plan was set into place for a far-away trip.

> The introduction of the opportunity to plan a trip elicited fantasies of being out in open fields, simply running and jumping. Memories of their homelands, swimming in rivers and of catching wild birds were juxtaposed with the limitations of where and when they could go. Funds were needed. Lost memories collided with stark realities. What followed was a series of events, planning a new trip that perhaps symbolized the reconstruction of their original trip to America. What was different now was that this trip was to be to an open, green and safe place. This old place in New York was Bear Mountain. . . . As a way of fostering affectional ties through the group, those who were to be attending the trip were asked to extend an invitation to their parents. A goal of the group is to strengthen identity development. By inviting parents, intergenerational differences could be bridged. The group initially resisted the idea. They felt that the parents would hamper their style, inhibit their expressive behavior, and ultimately embarrass them. It was interesting to note how ineffective they envisioned their parents to be. They no longer felt that they needed their protection. Perhaps they felt they had been without it for too long. . . . On the day of the trip, as the bus departed for Bear Mountain moving from the coolness of the Manhattan skyline to the mountainsides of north New Jersey, one could feel the bus relax. The mood was

playful and the mixture of current popular music and the frenetic meringue filled the air. The bus rocked right on up to Bear Mountain. When the young travelers arrived, they resembled little rabbits let loose into the open countryside after having been caged. . . . As a small group hiked up through a trail, they remembered childhood games such as *al escondido*—hide and seek—and memories of looking for frogs and snakes and how many different types there were. . . . A young man spoke to the worker about his current dilemma of maybe having to drop out of school. They were happy, at least for that day. The parents who participated also seemed to be overwhelmed with the experience of being out in the open, in a different place. They spoke anxiously about getting groups of their friends to come together and on their own and they pressed the worker for directions to return. They felt happy that their children were safe, protected by the environment and they were glad to be a part of it. (Lopez, 1991, p. 38)

The worker recalled his own childhood migrating from Cuba to the United States:

Having come from Cuba's tropical climate, I was unprepared for the harsh winter. I had no winter coat, no warm hat, no gloves, no boots, and scarf. It seems like I spent the remainder of my childhood fighting off colds and the flu and well, much more. Beyond the brutality of the winter was the sound of a strange language that heightened the chill. It was clear then how different I felt and how different everything was. To others I spoke another language, one that they did not understand. I did not eat their food nor dress like them. I had not realized until then that I had been "left out in the cold." (Lopez, 1991, p. 29)

Years later, after the trip to Bear Mountain the worker reflected back and forth over the landscape of time:

As an immigrant with over thirty years of acculturation, my awareness of my own frustrations in negotiating outside systems enabled me to tune-in to the members' sense of helplessness. Beyond that it helped me to lend a vision that served to empower the youth with a renewed sense of mastery. Memories and building new bridges helped the members and me to discover common ground. The *white blanket* of snow that I encountered so many years ago became a guide to opening doors and taking a journey to a free and open place. (p. 39)

CONCLUSION

The essence of diversity, with its emphasis on our stake in one another is captured in this concluding passage.

Diversity is not about "us versus them." And neither is it about easy agreement among different cultural, ethnic, and racial groups. And neither is it about easy community living among the different groups. It is a bold, rich, and complex tapestry. It has to do with being different in values, traditions, and speech, and the same in human need, suffering, and love. It has to do with living in separate neighborhoods, and together in the larger common community of nation. Diversity of culture, ethnicity, and race gets its significance and specialness in the context of our universal identification as human beings. (Aponte, 1994, pp. 239–240)

Group work is a special arena in which the problems of diversity may be confronted openly, honestly, and safely and where the richness of diversity may be celebrated.

APPENDIX 10.1. STRUCTURED WORKSHOPS FOR GROUP IDENTITY AND PREJUDICE REDUCTION

The following are outlines for two structured group workshops addressing group identity and prejudice reduction (Ethnicity and Mental Health Associates, 1992). The model has been described it as an "in vivo experience to help participants to gain an emotional understanding of the difference and similarities between themselves and members of diverse cultural groups . . . with the purpose of: 1. Achieving understanding and 2. Reinforcing attitudes and behavior that respect differences among people" (Pinderhughes, 1989, pp. 211, 218).

A cautionary note: These exercises should not be attempted without adequate preparation. In addition the worker–facilitator should use the following guideline to determine readiness for the endeavor:

- Skill in group process
- Relative comfort with conflict
- Flexibility, creativity, patience, and openness
- Willingness to share one's feelings and prejudices, thus modeling risk-taking behavior
- Modeling a secure sense of ethnic and racial identity
- Appreciation for differences in others (Pinderhughes, 1989, p. 232)

Practitioners interested in using this model are reminded that in social work with groups the "use of program" relates to what the group does and not what is done to the group. Therefore, as with the introduction of any activity, it must be viewed as an integral part of the purpose and culture of the group and not as an out-of-context exercise to manipulate or keep the group busy (see Chapter 8).

ETHNIC SHARING[3]

Objectives

- For participants to increase their awareness of how their ethnic, racial and religious backgrounds can influence their personal and professional identities, behaviors, and attitudes
- To help participants become more aware of and sensitive to similarities and differences among people

Activity

Ethnic sharing exercise

Group Arrangement

Participants seated facing each other either in a circle or around a table. If the group is large, it should be seated facing the trainer. Five to six chairs should be up front for a panel selected from participants representing a diversity of ethnic/racial backgrounds.

Content and Process

The following steps should be taken to stimulate interaction.

1. The trainer explains to participants that this is going to be an ethnic sharing experience and that everyone will have a turn to speak. Each participant is asked to address the following questions:

    - Identify yourself ethnically (black American/African American; Jewish American; Irish American; Italian American, etc.).
    - Describe the area in which you grew up (geographic location, kind of neighborhood).
    - Tell us about your family. What are your parents ethnic backgrounds? Where were they born? What do (did) they do for a living?
    - What were some of the attitudes and values you would identify derived from your ethnic/racial/religious background?
    - Have you ever experienced bigotry or heard an ethnic/racial/religious slur about your group?
    - What do you like most about your ethnic background? What do you like least?

2. Model by sharing your background in detail first. Relate in-depth personal

[3]Adapted from Ethnicity and Mental Health Associates (1992). Copyright 1992 by Ethnicity and Mental Health Associates. Adapted by permission.

experiences through appropriate anecdotes. This will give everyone permission to talk about personal stories and feelings. Participants sitting next to you speak next, followed by each person in turn around the circle.

3. After four or five people have spoken, ask others of the same ethnic background how their experiences have been similar or different. You may want to ask someone how he/she felt about what he/she heard from a member of a background different from his/her own.

4. Discourage participants from speaking abstractly or offering generalizations. They should speak about themselves initially, relating personal experiences, anecdotes, and feelings.

5. Listen carefully for specific ethnic characteristics or ambivalence and interrupt to ask for elaboration. Probe to clarify and help individuals relate to their feelings.

6. Leave some time at the end of the exercise for participants to process the experience.

Materials

Microphone for trainer and panel if it is a large group.

Time

Sixty minutes

RACISM AND OTHER FORMS OF BIGOTRY[4]

Objectives

- To raise awareness that everyone holds stereotypes
- To understand the nature of racism and bigotry and their effects on individuals and intergroup relations
- To deal with incidents of racism and bigotry in personal and professional relationships

Activities

- Exercise—Prejudice awareness
- Video excerpts on the effects of racism and stereotyping
- Role play—Dealing with prejudice

Group Arrangement

Group facing trainer. Small groups of four to seven participants; return to larger group to present role play.

---

[4]Adapted from Ethnicity and Mental Health Associates (1992). Copyright 1992 by Ethnicity and Mental Health Associates. Adapted by permission.

Content and Process

1. The trainer introduces this activity by telling participants that he/she would like them to think about any time in their lives when they personally experienced racism/prejudice/ethnic slur or witnessed such an incident, or participated in one. The trainer can explain that the session's objectives are to raise awareness of the effects of racism and bigotry and to try to learn how we can handle these incidents more effectively on a personal, professional, and organizational level.

2. To get more "into" this issue, the trainer starts with racial/ethnic stereotypes. If a video is available, participants can view short excerpts of various people sharing their stereotypes about different racial and ethnic groups. This is followed by excerpts from adults and children sharing the hurt they feel from these remarks. If a video is unavailable, a written exercise and or a group participatory activity also is effective. Participants will discuss their reactions to the exercise.

3. The trainer asks participants to return to the question raised at the session's beginning and to divide up into small groups of four to seven people. He/she calls upon participants to recall a story or incident in their lives when they experienced or participated in an incident of bigotry. Participants are asked to write the gist of their stories on a worksheet. Everyone then is requested to briefly share their stories with the group. After hearing all the stories, the group is asked to select one, to role play the incident, and to present it to the entire group.

4. The trainer leads a discussion on what was presented and what could have been handled more effectively.

Materials

1. Video/VCR
2. See References for articles on racism, prejudice, and stereotypes.

Time

Sixty to 90 minutes

APPENDIX 10.2. ADDITIONAL REFERENCES FOR DIVERSITY AND GROUP WORK

African American youth and the use of improvisation (Pierce & Singleton, 1995)
African American families and incorporating traditional strengths into group work practice (Lewis & Ford, 1990)
Arab and Jewish youth (Bargal & Bar, 1994; Bargal, 1992)

Asian clients (Lee, Juan, & Hom, 1984)

Asian-Pacific Americans (Chue & Sue, 1984; Ho, 1984)

Biracial and bicultural issues in the clinical treatment (Gibbs & Moskowitz-Sweet, 1991; Chau, 1990b)

Caribbean adolescents in Canada (Glasgow & Gouse-Shese, 1995)

Chinese, Malay, and Indian in Singapore (Anderson, 1990)

Cultural issues and adolescent pregnancy (Dore & Dumois, 1990)

Cultural senstivity and competence training in group work (Rittner & Nakashini, 1993)

Gay and lesbian adolescents (Morrow, 1993; Jacobsen, 1988; Sancier, 1984)

Hispanic inner-city adolescent males (Millan & Chan, 1991)

Latinos (Acosta & Yamamoto, 1984; Delgado & Humm-Delgado, 1984)

Low-income black youths (Brown, 1984)

Mixed membership—race and gender (Brown & Mistry, 1994)

Native Americans (Edwards & Edwards, 1984)

Puerto Rican youth (Costantino, Malgady, & Rogler, 1988)

Southeast Asian refugee adolescents (E. Lee, 1988)

Transracial foster care (Mullender, 1990)

Vietnamese refugees adolescents (Tsui & Sammons, 1988; Chan, 1990)

CHAPTER 11

Violence and Youth

Dimensions and Interventions in Group Work

DIS WAY

shoulders colliding
eyes all ablaze
each one
committed
to not losing face

*tired'a takin shit—always on my back—tryin ta hold it
    all together—another cuttin crack;*
*acts like mr. big—thinks that he all that—worthless lit-
    tle nuthin—insignificant gnat;*
*ever in my face—mockin' snarling smirk—love to wipe
    it off—mutha-fuckin jerk;*
*blood boilin over—phony poser's strut—can't take it
    any longer—gotta kick his butt;*
*gonna call his bluff—prove i aint afraid—end it now
    for always—time is now to pay . . .*

patterns carved in blood
mounted on the street
not the first
not the last
certain to repeat

legacy of vengeance
passed to next of kin
unsuspecting
little ones
to
take it on the chin

—*A. Malekoff*

KILLED FOR A QUARTER

12-Year-Old Shot by Teen Over 25 Cents

So read the headline of the *New York Daily News,* July 19, 1995. The story on page seven began:

> At gunpoint, tough 12-year-old C_____ refused to hand over 25 cents—and laughed out loud as a backed-down bully slunk away. . . . A day later C_____, nicknamed Junior by his friends and family, was cut down by five bullets—killed the night before his 13th birthday, cops said yesterday, over nothing more than a quarter's worth of disrespect. . . . Junior was shot once in the back; he ran a few feet and then got another bullet in the back of the head. He then fell to the ground and received three shots in the rib cage—one above the heart. . . . C_____ was a sixth-grader at School _____. "He was so happy to officially become a teenager," said his aunt. . . .

VIOLENCE AND YOUTH: DIMENSIONS OF THE PROBLEM

From "Put Down" to "Snuffed Out"

Violence—random, sudden, illogical, and lethal—has become a fact of life that many practitioners address daily in their practice. It is scary. Years of social and economic injustice have resulted in large numbers of people who are frustrated and without hope for the future, to whom bravado, especially for teenagers, is everything, and for anything that seems the slightest bit threatening—a put down, a disagreement, a dirty look—it demands immediate retaliation (Kurland & Malekoff, 1993b).

> You know I'll tell you what the whole shouting match came down to. *Dis.* It was all about *Dis.* [He] disrespected me by raising up in my face. I dissed him by throwing him up against the fence . . . he dissed me by walking off . . . I dissed him by flicking his hat . . . He dissed me by giving me a shove. . . . Everything is *dis.* . . . Because, you know, out there all you got to your name is your heart. (Price, 1992, p. 30)

As Bell and Jenkins (1990) have written, "Most homicides occur as a result of altercations among acquaintances, fueled by emotion and anger. Violence erupts as individuals get locked into an escalating situation from which it is difficult to extricate oneself without loss of face, and for which they lack skills, other than violence, for defusing" (p. 148).

Youth suicide and homicide account for 30% of all deaths among adolescents and young adults ages 15 to 24, in the United States (Holinger et al., 1994). Despite adolescents' ability to successfully carry out violent acts, their conception of death remains child-like. An inadequate conceptualization of death coupled with a sense of invulnerability can lead to both suicidal and homicidal behavior that the young person believes somehow will not be fatal.

Witness to Violence: A New Role for Children and Youth?

Among those who are left in the wake of violent acts are the survivors—friends and family members of victims, who live with the emptiness, frustration, and rage of incomprehensible death by violence. In addition there are estimated to be at least 10 million children who are witnesses to violence, observing a physical assault between parents. Many of these children suffer from posttraumatic stress that impacts profoundly on their day-to-day lives in any number of the following ways:

- Interferes with normal social growth.
- Causes a numbing of responsiveness.
- Causes a lack of interest in spontaneous play.
- Impacts on a child's future orientation.
- Generates flash-backs and/or reenactments of the traumatic episode.
- Causes frequent nightmares and sleep disturbance.
- Precipitates increased states of arousal.
- Causes irritability and anger in the child.
- Produces poor concentration.
- Causes an exaggerated startle response.
- Precipitates "failure to thrive" symptoms and diagnoses among the youngest witnesses.
- May lead to a worsening of asthma and other conditions and illnesses. (Zuckerman, 1995)

Beyond violence survived and witnessed in the family is the incremental trauma experienced by young people who are fed a regular diet of horrific episodes of violence through graphic media accounts of crime, child abuse, terrorist acts (e.g., Oklahoma City and World Trade Center bombings), and war both close and far from home. The coupling of technology and the media opens the populace to a steady stream of violent images, real and fantasized, on a daily basis. Can children and adolescents easily differentiate between what's news, what's documentary, what's docudrama, and what's pure drama? Can we?

In Northern Ireland, the constant exposure to danger, violence, and death left many children so insecure and frightened that high dosages of tranquilizing medications were deemed necessary (Berkovitz, 1987). How different is the experience for many of our young people growing up in inner cities where the drug trade is the number one industry, where the sound of gun shots has become almost as commonplace as the cadence of crickets in the outlying communities, and where drive-by shootings have turned our urban streets into a modern-day version of the "Wild West?" Are these young people not also witnesses to violence? Do they need to be tranquilized as well?

Intervention and Prevention: A Public Health Approach

Public health advocates suggest three levels of intervention to address violence, all of which suggest prospects and possibilities for group work practice:

- *Primary prevention.* Don't allow violence to start; help people to prevent violence through the use of education and the development of problem-solving and conflict-resolution skills.
- *Secondary prevention.* Help people learn how to stop violence once it has started, and use problem-solving skills to intervene and stop a situation that may be escalating toward violence.
- *Tertiary prevention.* Provide "postvention" treatment for people who have been involved in violence, either as a victim, perpetrator, or witness. This is especially critical, for example, in the aftermath of adolescent suicide to reduce the risk of "contagion" or "cluster suicides" (Holinger et al., 1994; Prothrow-Stith, 1995).

Aggression in adolescence may be ignited and lead to violence as a consequence of numerous circumstances and conditions including individual stress related to family problems, child abuse, poverty, crime in the neighborhood, gang involvement, inappropriate rules and unsympathetic authority in school, unrealistic academic expectations, unemployment, media violence, and conditions of war.

Society expects parents to do everything—to counter the violent messages in the media, to teach children problem-solving skills, and then keep them physically and emotionally safe. These are unrealistic expectations. Too many parents lack the information and wherewithal to accomplish this alone. A public health mandate to address the prevention of violence is what is needed, an approach that involves parents, peers, community, and media. Group work with adolescents can play an important role in any such public health initiative. Groups are where the action is in adolescence.

PRACTICE PRINCIPLES FOR ADDRESSING VIOLENCE

The following are practice principles that are critical in providing group services for adolescents, particularly when confronting destructive values and behavior is a goal.

- *Group interventions to violent events must occur as close to the actual event as possible.* There are an increasing number of structured programs and exercises intended to prevent violence by teaching life skills such as "effective conflict resolution." While such efforts are of great value and are most often introduced in a group context, of equal importance is the need to catch aggression and violence in process. That is, the practitioner must position him/herself, with due caution, to respond to violence as it is about to erupt, and/or during, and just after it has occurred. Variations on this idea have been referred to as "life space encounters" (Redl & Wineman, 1952) and "counseling on the go" (Garfat, 1985). What these concepts all share in common is a commitment to mediating between the child and what life holds for him/her as close to the moment as possible (Maier, 1991).
- *Youth need order and consistency in their lives and, therefore, in the groups to which they belong.* Children who grow up in dysfunctional environments become uncomfortably accustomed to living with chaos, uncertainty, unpredictability, and inconsistency. Practitioners must construct group environments absent of the dysfunctional conditions likely to spur violence in the group.
- *Alliance formation with parents and other involved systems is needed to contribute to a sense of grounding, particularly in times of crisis.* In group work, the group may be the hub of the experience, however, it is the careful construction of a network of spokes that provides the stability necessary for responding to crises and encouraging growth. The effectiveness of any violence prevention or postvention group initiative will be hampered if important systems in the young person's life—parents and relevant others—are left out of the process (see Chapter 6).
- *Conflict must be addressed with a recognition that the outcome is less important than an adolescent's capacity to deal with conflict on a more mature level* (Bernstein, 1973). There is an evolutionary path to the way people attempt to resolve conflicts. Ranging from more regressed responses to more civilized and democratic ones, the path might look something like this if one begins from the more primitive end of the continuum: physical violence, verbal violence, subtle verbal contest, finding allies, seeking authoritative decision, creating diversions and delay, and respect for differences (Bernstein, 1973). One vital purpose of conflict resolution in groups is to help to move young people along on this continuum.

- *The group purpose must include addressing members' needs arising out of the sociocultural context of their lives—the situational surround.* Whether brief or long-term, all groups of adolescents must address the impact of the situational surround on its members. Local and distant events with violent content or implications must be acknowledged and addressed in a way that is appropriate to the group members' level of development and capacity for integration. Such events include war, rioting, terrorism, and murder, for example. They include events that personally impact on group members, such as the death of a classmate or teacher. They include events that periodically grab the attention of the masses such as the death of a child who has been severely abused or the aftermath of a terrorist bombing. The practitioner must thoughtfully determine what level of intervention is appropriate. Most importantly, practitioners cannot deny or ignore the potential impact of such events on their groups. Because an event is geographically distant doesn't mean that it isn't emotionally close to home.

- *Provide protection, support, and a safe climate in the group.* Youth need safe places to go, with worthwhile things to do, and opportunities for belonging. And they need relationships with competent adults who understand and care about them. Growing up with the ever-present threat of violence can contribute to a pervasive sense of fearfulness, hypervigilance and despair. Group settings must serve as a counterforce to fear and violence. Group workers must carefully attend to the structure of the group to ensure a basic level of physical and emotional safety that help to cultivate a sense of trust. This requires both practice savvy and ongoing advocacy with policy makers, funding sources, and agency boards and administrators to ensure sound environments for group development.

CLOSE TO HOME: THREE PRACTICE ILLUSTRATIONS ADDRESSING VIOLENCE

The following three examples represent variations on the theme of violence. The first is a transcript (with running commentary) of a middle-adolescent boy's mental health group. The account illustrates the aftermath of a violent confrontation that occurred just hours prior to the group meeting and that left one member seriously injured. The second is a description of an after-school, coed drug-prevention group's preparation and implementation of an alcohol- and drug-free dance, the unexpected mayhem that followed, and the aftermath. The third is a narrative account of an early-adolescent boys' group's attempt to cope with their growing anxiety just minutes before and then during and after the commencement of the 1991 Persian Gulf War. What these examples have in common is that the group intervention occurred as close to the actual precipitating events as possible.

"I'm Not Goin' to the Emergency Room"

The following is a transcript of group of middle- to later-adolescent boys—Manny, Kyle, and Eddie—meeting in a mental health clinic for about a year together. A fourth member was absent. All of the boys were referred for aggressive, impulsive, and antisocial behavior. The worker (GW; the author) entered the waiting room to greet them. Only Manny (Italian American) and Kyle (Salvadoran) were present at the time. Eddie (African American), 16, would show up later along with a surprise guest. The boys are all from working-class backgrounds. As he approached the waiting room, the worker observed Manny, a lanky 16-year-old whose every movement seemed carefully choreographed to create an image of being "with it" or "hip," standing with his back to him and engaged in animated discussion. Seated facing Manny was Kyle, a 17-year-old with a painful childhood history. Kyle's slight stature and angelic features belie the reality of his early years, giving him the appearance of much younger and more innocent child. Seated next to Kyle was an unrelated woman who appeared to be in her mid-40s. Her eyes seemed to be "bugging out," growing ever wider, as she peered at Manny, eavesdropping on his lively monologue. As they departed from the waiting room, the worker observed Manny spitting something into a tissue. As they walked up the stairs together at 6:00 P.M., the worker learned that there had been a fight just hours earlier. It was blood that Manny was spitting into the tissue.

GW: How did this whole thing develop?

MANNY: This kid hit me with the bat. He took the bat and said, "Get out of my house." I was sitting there playing pool. He told me to get out of his house, right.

GW: Who is this guy?

MANNY: This rich kid, that we . . .

KYLE: Andy [GW] should know about rich.

Here Kyle is sounding a familiar refrain about "all Jews being rich." This and other stereotypes are regularly confronted in the group. As a Jewish American, I'm momentarily stung by the comment but choose to pass on it. There is a more important agenda to get to. It is not at all uncommon for the group to take you down several roads at once. The questions are always—Which road to follow? When to take a detour? How to get back on the main road? and How to avoid or recoup from dead ends?

MANNY: We all hang out with him because he has all this shit in his house. He lives in, you know, like down Parsons off Main Street, where the rich people live.

GW: Yeah?

MANNY: Tulip Gardens. He lives in there. They have a pool room; they have a Jacuzzi. We always bring our girls. He's ugly looking. We always bring our girls over there and hang out in the hot tub with them.

GW: Why did he tell you to get out?

MANNY: I don't know. He had to go walk a dog or something.

KYLE: Did you leave the first time he asked you to?

MANNY: He said, "Get out of my house." I said, "Hold on a second." Oh, I remember, I was coloring in something, a picture he drew.

KYLE: Manny, you can't do that.

MANNY: I was coloring in a picture . . . I said, "Hold on a second." He said, "Get out now." And he picked up a bat . . . I said, "All right I'm leaving."

GW: Was he angry with something you were doing?

MANNY: No, he had to leave. He had to go walk his dog.

GW: All right, so he told you to leave.

I have two things in mind (at least two, that is). First, does Manny need medical attention? Second, how did this happen? Impulse control is not Manny's strong suit. One of the goals of the group is to help the boys put a reflective pause between their impulses and actions. By probing, I'm attempting to try and understand Manny's role in the fight, his thinking. But there is the nagging question in my mind, "Is he OK, should he go to the ER right away?" I'm torn. I don't want to use strong arm tactics. But if he's really hurt badly I know I must. I don't want to undermine his dad, who is waiting outside in his car. I'm not sure how to include him in the decision making, at least not yet. I need to get Kyle in the mix, find some common ground, see if he can help me to break through.

MANNY: So I said, "Hold on till I finish coloring it in." Then he went to go hit me with the bat on my hand but he was just playing around. He missed my hand on purpose. So I walked out and me and my friend Jim were playing around. We were wrestling because he's on the wrestling team. He has a match coming up this weekend.

KYLE: You were wrestling on his property?

MANNY: No, it was in his hallway. He lives in a big building. We were in the hallway waiting for the elevator to come up.

GW: The guy who lives there is on the wrestling team?

MANNY: No, my friend. This kid lives in the building. That was my friend Jim. We were wrestling and then Jim tried to pick me up to body slam me. And he slammed me, and it hurt so I pushed him, and he bounced into my friend Edgar. And so then Edgar went up and hit me in the ear.

GW: He punched you?

MANNY: Yeah, and then I beat up Edgar, and he ran into his house and I hit him like three more times. He came out of his house and I said, "What you're going to hit me with the bat?" and he picked it up like he was going to hit me. And I said, "Hit me then, hit me." And he said, "I'm going to hit you in your head." And I punched him because he was going to hit me with the bat. I thought he was going to hit me in the head. I thought he was going to fuck me up. I thought he was going to hit me on the head with the bat so I punched him, shit! If somebody picked up a bat. If someone tells you they're going to hit you with a bat and had a bat in their hand all raised up to hit you, wouldn't you try to fuck them up?

GW: Wait a minute. When he held the bat up, what were you saying to him?

MANNY: I was like, "Hit me then if you're going to do it."

GW: But what's that? You're saying to us, "What would you do if someone was going to hit you?" It sounds like he was holding the bat without the intention of really hitting you.

MANNY: No, hold on, he went like this (*miming a threatening motion with an imaginary bat*).

GW: But you kept saying, "Hit me, come on hit me."

MANNY: I said, "What? You're going to hit me?" He said "Yeah, I'm going to hit you dead in your head."

GW: You didn't provoke him?

MANNY: No, I actually thought he was going to hit me. I said, "What? You're going to hit me with the bat?"

GW: (*to Kyle*) You think he was provoking him? Taunting him?

KYLE: Yeah he told him, "Hit me, hit me."

MANNY: But he said he was going to hit me.

KYLE: Yeah but . . . he only said that to make you scared.

MANNY: He said he was going to hit me on the head, so I said, "Fuck it." So I hit him, and then I ran down the hall because he was chasing me with the bat and he hit me in the ribs. Oh shit, and he hit me in the ribs!

GW: So what happened after that?

MANNY: So I hit him, and then I flipped out.

GW: And what did you do when you flipped out?

MANNY: I went crazy, I was going to kill him. My friend sat on me. My friend's, like, 170 pounds and my other friend is, like, 150 pounds. And they both sat on me. They pinned my arms against my back because I was going to kill him. I was foaming out of my mouth. My eyes rolled back. They were telling me all this shit. It was funny. I wish I would have gotten a picture of it. It would have been funny as hell. I was flipping out; I was going to kill him.

A picture might just help Manny. In a previous group meeting Manny almost came to blows with another group member. That particular meeting was videotaped. The following week, the group was able to review the incident on videotape to see how the altercation started and what roles the two adversaries had played. Manny, in watching the replay, saw himself getting worked up and pointed to the screen saying, "There, I can see myself getting worked up, I'm getting that adrenaline rush." The use of video can be both a valuable activity for enhancing the group program and capturing here-and-now process of the group for review. In a group where impulsivity and violence seem so commonplace, it is inevitable that the impulsivity will get played out in the group. Catching them "in the act" enables the group to review the thinking, feeling, and doing attached to behavior to try and learn and practice alternatives to destructive behavior.

In this case, however, the fight was off-premises, and outside of the group. My job includes holding the members to focus by engaging in facilitative confrontation (e.g., asking probing questions) aimed at recreating the circumstances that led to the current situation and partializing the problem. The repetition involved in trying to change certain behavior feels like an endless and draining process at times. Yet there is no shortage of high-risk situations to bring into the group for inspection. To be fair, Manny had made some progress in walking away from potentially dangerous situations and in reducing his provocative and intimidating behaviors, which had led to weekly and sometimes daily fights. But obviously he was unable to walk away from this one. As the group meeting proceeds, I am aware of my growing concern about Manny's medical condition. Internally, I am continually weighing the urgency of the situation against the value of self-determination. Should I move quickly and decisively to get him to an emergency room? Or should I use the group situation to influence his decision? This is not the first time I've faced this dilemma in the group. But more on that later.

GW: Did you go to the doctor?

MANNY: Yeah.

GW: And what did the doctor say?

MANNY: Nothing, he said I might have cracked ribs. He said I didn't mess up my kidneys because he gave me a urine test and then took a blood test. And he was, like, "They didn't mess up your kidneys; you should go to the hospital because you might have cracked a couple of ribs . . . "

GW: He told you to go to the hospital. So why didn't you go?

MANNY: Because I stopped coughing up blood.

GW: Was your father there when he told you to go to the hospital?

MANNY: Yeah. I told my dad, I told him, "Dad I don't want to go to the hospital." If I don't want to go, they can't make me go. How's he going to make me go?

KYLE: The doctors can.

MANNY: How are they going to make me go?

KYLE: They'll call the EMS.

MANNY: So I won't go.

KYLE: They almost did that to me.

MANNY: I won't go.

GW: What's the reason that you won't go? Why?

MANNY: (furiously biting his nails) Because what if they find out my fuckin' ribs punctured my lungs, it ain't like they're going to save me. I'm dead anyway. So why should I find it out? After group I should go and hang out, and if I wake up dead in the morning, shit I'll wake up dead in the morning anyway.

The denial here is palpable. I'm wondering what, if anything, it will take to break through. I'm also wondering to myself, "Why did Manny come to group?" Did he come thinking that this is an alternative to the ER, and as if by magic, he'll be all better when the meeting is over? Did he think, unconsciously, that by coming here he'd end up having to go to the ER? He obviously wouldn't go on his own volition, and his father wasn't pressing the issue. So he came here. Sometimes when people are in denial, they'll search for someone who will make them do something because they know that they can't break into their own defenses. It's like the kid who fights tooth and nail about an unrealistic curfew time and then secretly feels relieved when a limit is set. It's as if a healthy part of the person seems to be saying, "I know somebody who'll take care of me."

KYLE: You can't even walk up the stairs good.

GW: You hear what you just said? You just said . . .

KYLE: He said, "I don't care if I wake up in the morning."

MANNY: I know I didn't say that. I said if I'm going to wake up in the hospital, I'll wake up dead with my friends. Where will I rather be dead at?

GW: If you go to the hospital, and they find out there's something wrong, they can help you. You're not going to be dead. If you don't go to the hospital . . .

MANNY: (*incredulous*) How can they fix a punctured lung? It's impossible!

KYLE: You've got cracked ribs. The bleeding is from the ribs you got cracked. But Manny, you gotta understand, if you don't go to the doctor, they got to do an X-ray. They can find even much worse than what you think; and if that happens, with that bat, and if it went right through your system and went right in where your lungs are, where the blood circulation goes, you can die from a blood clot like that. Trust me, because that's what they said could have happened to me. Because I got hit with a bat, got kicked, and they threw the bike on my ribs when it was already cracked. And I didn't want to go to the hospital because I didn't think nothing would happen to me, and then I went, and they said I had a concussion. That's why this eye (*pointing*) is even more messed up than it was before.

MANNY: What's wrong with your eye?

KYLE: I can't see far away with this eye. They messed it up real bad. And that could happen to you. So Manny, you better go. If I was Andy and you didn't go, I swear to God, you know I'm not telling you to do this, but I'm just saying if I was you, [I'd have you] go right now.

GW: What did your doctor actually recommend?

MANNY: That I go to the hospital and get an X-ray.

GW: For the possibility of what?

MANNY: Cracked ribs.

GW: OK, your doctor didn't say anything about the possibility of you having a punctured lung or anything like that. He checked you out, and he said that the thing that you have to go to the hospital for is to find out . . .

MANNY: No, he said go to the hospital and see if you have any. . . . He said, "Your kidneys are fine. Go to the hospital and get X-rays so they can find out if you have any internal injuries or not." He said, "All I • know is that your kidneys aren't fucked up."

GW: OK. You know I'm going to recommend to your father that he take you to the hospital.

KYLE: (*laughs nervously trying to disassociate himself from my authoritative statement*) I ain't telling you that!

Here it is obvious that Kyle is trying to reassure Manny that, while he is concerned, it is not he but the adult in the room who is threatening to bring Manny's father into the decision. Kyle also appears to be ambivalent, struggling with the issues of "urgency" versus "self-determination," yet he seems relieved to have me to point to, and to rely on, when the ante is raised. There is no reason on my part to confront his contention. In fact he can be more effective if he sees me as willing to back him up and enforce any recommendations, to do the "dirty work" that is. This is all a very complicated dance.

MANNY: I said I ain't going, Andy.

GW: That's between you and your father. I'm just saying that I'm gonna recommend to him that he take you to the hospital.

MANNY: Why? The doctor recommended it too; I don't want to go.

GW: Well that's between you and your father, OK, but I'm gonna recommend that to him.

MANNY: I ain't going. Shit!

KYLE: You think people our age wanna go to the hospital?

Manny seems pretty connected with Kyle at this point. Thankfully I have Kyle here to help. I wonder where Eddie is already. Manny really respects Eddie. Eddie is the group's indigenous leader, someone who commands respect from all of the others. He could really help. All of this process thus far emphasizes both the paradoxical nature of adolescents and the need to differentiate the words from the music. It's like Manny is saying, "I came here so that you [the group] will make it happen for me to get help . . . and my father has to be a part of it to make it right." That's the music behind the words. Now, we need to find the right dance to get us there, to get it right. Right?

This is also tricky because it's difficult for adolescents to enter into a dependency relationship, you know, to accept help. This has to be done without "losing face." Meeks (1986) writes about this process in addressing suicidal adolescents. He says, "Many of these youngsters are extremely threatened by their intense dependency wishes. The [practitioner] must often utilize humor, extreme tact, and vigorous support of independent behavior to help the adolescent tolerate being helped" (p. 259). I am keenly aware that some critics will say I should have hauled him into the ER as soon as I saw the blood. But I'm not so sure about that. It's not as easy a call as it might seem from a distance.

The dialogue continues for a while in a back-and-forth (dialectical) fashion, with Kyle and me trying to uncover obstacles to Manny going to the ER and Manny offering reasons why he doesn't need to go. Finally Kyle gets out of his seat and heads for the door, saying he's going to find Mannny's dad.

GW: (to Kyle) Go ahead, go talk to his dad. You can tell him to come up here if he wants. Tell us what happens.

(Kyle leaves, and Manny and I are left alone)

Kyle made the move on his own, and I gave him the nonverbal go ahead. Manny did not object, silently permitting Kyle to seek out his father. Now I've got to wonder what his father will do. His father must know that I am concerned and that I won't drop the issue. He's got to remember the time I called the police and reported Manny when he threatened to shoot someone outside of the group. What happened was that Manny reported to the group that he had been ripped off by another kid. He came to group claiming to have access to a hand gun and threatening to shoot the kid. When given the chance, he refused to recant, even in the presence of his father. I told him that he left me with no choice but to call the police and report him, which I did. They investigated. I was certain he'd never return to the group. But he came back the next week, sloughing off the whole incident. (A famous court case known as *Tarasoff v. Board of Regents of the University of California* [1976] led to a number of court decisions holding mental health practitioners responsible for reporting threats of serious harm against third parties.)

(GW alone with Manny)

MANNY: I ain't goin' to no hospital.

GW: You don't like the idea of being helpless there, right? (*Manny gets up to throw a tissue in the trash can and then sits down slowly, grimacing*) You can't even sit down without being in pain. If you have something wrong inside of you have to have it checked out.

MANNY: My ribs hurt, that's all, shit. They [at the hospital] ain't gonna do nothing.

GW: Or you could have something worse than that. I know what you mean when you say you don't want to go. You don't want to think that there's something that could be wrong. You want to kind of just wish it away. It's like, "I'll go home to sleep and I'll wake up and everything will be fine."

MANNY: It will!

GW: That's what you say but you don't know that. I had something like this happen to me. You see this (*tilts head to side, separating hair to reveal a two-inch scar*). I had something like this happen to me. You know what happened? How old are you?

MANNY: Sixteen.

GW: Well, I was 17. I got hit on the head and the blood was gushing out of my head and my friend who was in the car put a T-shirt, you know, on top of it. And he wanted to go to the hospital and I said "No." So we went back to his house and my head was still gushing blood (*at this point, for the first time, Manny stops biting his finger nails*). We weren't going to the hospital. And then finally we realized that there was something wrong here, and we went to the hospital and it took them about. . . . I think about half an hour to close it up with clamps. I ended up getting about 25 stitches in my head, and my hand was broken also cause I got hit twice. And what they [the doctors] said was that I was about this close (*holds thumb and forefinger slightly apart*) to dying.

MANNY: Why?

GW: Because we delayed the time going to the hospital, and they had such trouble closing it up, and there was an artery that was ruptured, you know, split open.

MANNY: Damn.

GW: You should be going right now as a matter of fact. So I think what we gotta do is walk downstairs now and arrange for that.

My own experience was lurking in the back of my mind the whole time. At first I wasn't aware of it, and then it came into my consciousness. The question of self-disclosure is always tricky. I don't think it is a good idea to self-disclose in an effort to try and be "one of the gang," to be accepted. Nor is it a good idea if your purpose is to subtly (unconsciously) encourage some kind of acting-out behavior that you might vicariously live through or relive. In this case, had I suffered some permanent disabling injury, it wouldn't have been a good idea to disclose. It might have been far too frightening for Manny. The level of self-disclosure seemed to work OK. He stopped biting his nails and seemed able to maintain his defenses. He could gradually listen to the reality presented by others, from Kyle and me (and later from Eddie and his dad), but his denial kept him from hearing his own voice.

MANNY: No I wanna stay in group, hang out with my friends.

GW: All right, then you have to make an agreement with me that you're not gonna put up a fight with your father about going.

MANNY: If he asks me to go I'll go.

GW: All right, do you give me your word on that?

MANNY: (*equivocating*) I don't know.

GW: I need your word.

MANNY: Why? Look (*draws up phlegm and spits into a tissue*) I'm not spitting up blood anymore.

GW: I don't wanna see that. You can either go now or go later.

MANNY: Where is he? (*referring to Kyle or perhaps his dad*)

(*At that moment Kyle comes through the door*)

KYLE: (*smiling, relieved, announces*) You're dad's coming!

MANNY: Why's my dad coming?

(*Manny's father, followed by Eddie—the missing group member— walk into the room. I ask if everybody knows one another. Introductions are made. Eddie slaps five with the other guys and shakes Manny's dad's hand. Everyone sits.*)

Uh oh, did I break a cardinal rule of some kind here, mixing group work and family work? The cues I'm picking up tell me it's okay to bring the dad in. Now my job is to support the competence of the "executive subsystem," as a structural family therapist might say, to help the father to make the decision to get the proper medical attention for his son. It needs to come from his dad, not from me.

GW: (*to Dad*) He told us that the doctor said he should go to the hospital.

DAD: He said for X-rays.

GW: He said to rule out any internal damage?

DAD: He ruled out internal damage.

GW: What did he say?

DAD: He ran a blood test and a urine test and said everything seemed to be normal. He was just concerned that there might be a rib broken or something.

GW: So he said that there is a possibility that a rib could be broken?

DAD: Well he [Manny] said he wasn't in that much pain; it really wasn't bothering him.

GW: (*directs Manny to get up from his chair*) Stand up.

MANNY: Why?

GW: Just stand up please.

> (*Manny, seated next to his dad, stands up grimacing in pain; his father's gaze fixed on his son.*)

GW: Sit down.

MANNY: (*sits down slowly, painfully, grimacing*) Yeah, so it hurts.

DAD: (*somberly*) Maybe we'll stop back there [the hospital] on the way home.

GW: I mean all I'm saying is that he doesn't want to go, and the only way he'll go is if you insist. I'm only going by the fact that the doctor recommended that he get an X-ray.

MANNY: I'm not going to the hospital. That's it.

DAD: (*turns to son dismissively*) Oh be quiet, you're going.

GW: I hope you don't feel like I'm intruding.

DAD: No, no.

GW: He's gonna make it seem like everything's okay—"I'm not gonna go"—and so forth. I don't know what kind of experiences you've had. But at this age you sometimes think you're invulnerable.

DAD: True.

GW: (*turning to Eddie who is busy chomping on his fast food*) What do you think Eddie? To make it brief . . . (*summarizes the meeting thus far*).

EDDIE: (*to Manny*) You got hit today?

MANNY: Yeah.

EDDIE: (*without equivocation*) Then go to the hospital.

Eddie's input is important here. By validating the decision, he makes it more acceptable for Manny to go. Let's see if everyone has been in the same boat.

GW: (*to Dad*) Did anything like this ever happen to you when you were a kid?

MANNY: What is this (*commenting on the new composition of the group*) group with my pops?

(*Manny's question seems to cut through the tension in the room as everyone breaks up laughing*).

DAD: (*Proceeds to tell a story from his youth when he accidentally threw a knife into his leg during a game of "chicken." He said that it had been bleeding badly, but he didn't go for help.*) I lived through it.

GW: You're not saying to Manny, "You'll live through it, so don't get it checked out."

DAD: No, this is different.

EDDIE: I once broke my collarbone . . . (*goes on to tell the story, including how he went to the hospital*)

GW: (*to group*) Do you guys ever think, that you'll live forever? Like, "I can do stuff and I can't get caught, I won't get into trouble, I won't get hurt, I won't die. . . . "

MANNY: Yeah.

GW: You agree with that?

MANNY: Yeah.

GW: You've had that experience with other things too?

MANNY: Yeah.

GW: Like what?

MANNY: Like my dad's here.

GW: Yeah?

DAD: (*chuckles*) He doesn't want to go into it with me in the group.

The group comes to an end with Manny making a declarative statement emphasizing the boundary between the group and his father, as if to ensure that his dad won't return to the group. In his own way he said,

"OK, my dad did what he had to and now he can go." And his dad responded in kind by acknowledging the reinstatement of the generational boundary. . . . And, in case you're curious, they *did* go to the hospital, after all, and no, his ribs weren't broken. Better safe than sorry.

"Shall We Dance?"

After several highly successful social gatherings sponsored by a neighborhood club composed of African American youth living in a lower income community, an unexpected act of violence erupted at the conclusion of a party attended by almost 100 young people ranging in age from 13 to 18 years old. As in each previous activity, the group had held several planning meetings that focused on violence prevention. The themes of the planning sessions included the following:

1. No use of alcohol or other drugs.
2. No weapons are allowed.
3. Only age-appropriate students currently attending school can attend.
4. Adult staff and parent supervision are required.
5. No vulgar or seductive dance or music is allowed.
6. Each member is responsible for maintaining self-control.

Various scenarios were presented in order to bring life to these points. An occasional impromptu role play was used to enact potentially high-risk situations.

As the event came to a close, winding down to the last dance, all of the careful planning seemed to have achieved its purpose with a good time had by all. As the party ended everyone left the building in an orderly fashion. And then suddenly and without warning, the front door flew open and several young people began running and pushing their way into the building to seek safety and avoid injury from a fight that had broken out on the street. In the midst of the whirlwind, a young girl, an innocent bystander, was seriously injured. It had happened so suddenly and so unexpectedly that she hadn't even noticed until a friend called out to her, "What happened to your hand?" As she lifted her hand she saw a deep cut that extended across three fingers, dripping a steady stream of blood. The workers moved quickly to stop the action, restore order, defuse the situation, prevent further injury, and determine what had happened.

Once the chaos had been contained, the workers moved quickly to identify and calm the feuding youths, get medical attention for the injured victim, make sure that everyone got home safely, and notify parents about the disturbing events that had transpired. However, this was far from the end. The two adversaries, one a Club member and one a guest, vowed to continue the feud in school or on the street, whichever situation came first. The workers knew that this was likely to provoke additional violence against others in the community and, quite possibly, violent behavior between the feuding youths' families, as well as the injured girl's family.

Outreach was the next logical step. The timing had to be just right. Parents wanted answers. The community needed to get the facts about what had happened, to mount a counterforce against further eruptions resulting from any misinformation or gossip generated by the local grapevine. The outreach included home visits, first to the injured victim and then to the adversaries. Parental support was enlisted to help defuse tension between the youths. Parents were able to communicate effectively with one another and to accept responsibility for their children's behavior. Most importantly, the parents were willing to work on a resolution to bring closure to the incident without further violence on the street or in school.

The antagonists seemed calm, at least for the time, but it was uncertain what might happen the next time they bumped into one another. The workers agreed that this was too great a risk to leave alone. Therefore the next step involved contacting school personnel immediately with details of what had happened at the Friday evening party and to assist them with a plan of action to prevent any potential outbreaks on school grounds. An early morning meeting was held with the principal who was briefed about the steps that had been taken up until that moment.

Because of the immediate response by the workers to bring together the parents, community, and school, the crisis had been put to rest. However the debriefing process had only just begun for the Club members who just wanted to put the incident behind them and "move on." For the next several weeks, the Club members explored each phase of the dance in an attempt to understand what had happened and to prevent a repeat in the future. The phases reviewed included the planning phase, the activity itself, the aftermath, and a look at the possibility of future events.

Most difficult of all was reviewing the "aftermath." Mixed feelings were expressed in the group. Some of the group members wanted everything to be over. "How long do we have to keep talking about this?" and "This is boring," had become familiar refrains. Others were angry and advocated strongly for severe measures to be taken against the principal group member who had been involved in the fight. Their sentiments included, "Throw him out of the group!" and "We don't need him; he ruins it for the rest of us." They were flabbergasted when told that they, the Club, would have to pay for the hole in the wall, another casualty of the evening, "Why do *we* have to pay for it and with what money!" Still others expressed concern about violence involving weapons and questioned if there was any safe place for them to go. Meanwhile others matter-of-factly justified carrying a weapon for protection. "Yeah, I carry a knife to school. So what? What do you expect, everyone carries. I have a right to protect myself. Last year a kid got stabbed with an ink-pen. A pen!" But they all agreed that no weapons should be brought into the Club. They wanted it to remain a safe haven, despite the unfortunate event. The role of the workers was:

- To make a *demand for work* in light of the ambivalent feelings and frustration generated by this process and to make it clear that the subject wouldn't simply be dropped.
- To help the members to *partialize* the events or break them down into their component parts for examination.
- To enable the group to *move beyond scapegoating* the group members involved in the fight by recognizing and accepting their collective responsibility for events sponsored by the Club.
- To help the members to *tolerate ambiguity* in light of the mixed feelings generated by the intensive examination of events—the frustration of no immediate clear-cut answers.
- To encourage *problem solving* around the planning of future events, arriving at reasonable consequences for the members who participated in the fight, and determining who would pay for a hole in the wall, another casualty of the fight.
- To *clarify the values and purpose* of the group, reminding the members what the Club stands for, and all that they had accomplished, including organizing the largest youth contingent participating in a community-wide March for Unity following an interracial murder in the community just months earlier.
- To *lend a vision* that the group could and would overcome and rise above the adversity they were experiencing to become an even stronger Club (amidst their openly articulated fears that they would be forced to disband in the manner that other good things in their lives had come to an end).

Beyond addressing the Club members, the parents, the community and the school, program staff and agency administration needed to review the incident and evaluate their own roles. This included reviewing policies and procedures. The workers knew that they had to model a "practice what we preach" approach to any postvention activity. The agency resolved to provide individual counseling to group members, to provide additional help with impulse control and anger management, provide counseling and support to the youths' parents, and not to restrict the activities of the Club but to solicit increased parental involvement.

All of the above might seem rather tedious and time consuming. It was. The alternative is, however, the grim probability of an escalating cycle of violence. Incidents like this are inevitable if you go to where the kids are or if you create a context for them to bring their culture to where you are. Good planning is a necessity but not a panacea. Structured exercises and socioeducation programs for conflict resolution and anger control are valuable preventive tools that schools and programs can adopt. Of equal or perhaps even greater value is for a program to be prepared itself to "catch them in the act" offering "life space interviews" and "counseling on the go." The practitioner with a systems perspective is uniquely qualified for such a role.

So when a group member brings in his bruised ribs for our inspection, instead of going directly to the ER or when a fight breaks out at a dance, group workers must view these events as unique opportunities for change and growth. These are the special moments amidst the madness of many chaotic lives. They are moments in which group work can serve all involved to move to a higher level of functioning. And sometimes, they're moments where world events intersect with the group.

Where the World Stage and the Group Intersect

While teaching a university course on group work in the spring semester of 1995 on the day following the Oklahoma City bombing, I asked my students how the agencies that they were placed in, and how they themselves, were dealing with the impact and aftermath of the bombing with their clients and group members. The long silence was broken by a lone voice accompanied by a growing wave of nodding heads. "This is the first time anyone has mentioned it," was the sole response. In the discussion that followed, class members shared their reactions and feelings about the event, speculated about their group members' reactions, and considered ways of bringing it into their groups.

Violence, directly experienced or witnessed, close to home or far away, can have an emotionally deadening affect on people, a psychic numbing. We cannot afford to ignore violence on any level. Safety, while a luxury that some enjoy, has become increasingly elusive. I can recall a radio interview in the early 1980s in which a prominent peace advocate addressed the subject of the nuclear arms race. He said that when one is aware of critical and life-threatening issues that require advocacy, the individual must ask him/herself the following two questions:

1. Why am I awake?
2. How do I relate to those who are asleep?

These questions suggest a step toward addressing psychic numbing, an emotional deadening spawned by violence (Straus, 1994). During the course of the class discussion, I shared an experience I had had, one that brought the violence of far-off war closer to home for a small group of boys (Malekoff, 1991d, 1995).

On a foggy evening on January 16th, 1991, at 6 o'clock, my early-adolescent boys' group arrived for their weekly meeting. Sometime soon thereafter and during the course of our meeting, the allied forces in the Persian Gulf started bombing Iraq. I wondered how tuned in to these events the boys were. There was growing anxiety reflected in the media and in conversations picked up almost anywhere one ventured.

Just days earlier, a member of a past boys' group had showed up at the front door of the Center accompanied by a uniformed naval officer. He was about to enlist and was requesting copies of his record, a prerequisite he informed me. He was just a few years older than the boys in my group.

Following a brief and impassioned debate about the upcoming football playoffs leading to Super Bowl XXV, the talk shifted to the prospect of war. The January 15th deadline given to Saddam Hussein to leave Kuwait had passed 18 hours earlier. Too young to have experienced the war in Vietnam, yet old enough to know about indiscriminate terrorism and to have viewed innumerable movies and television programs featuring American mercenaries in action, the boys engaged in animated discussion of their country's military capacity.

They strutted their knowledge of the American arsenal of air power much like they might debate a forthcoming sporting event. Cruise missiles and B-52s, stealth bombers, F-15s, and "tomahawks" filled the air. The pride in their perceived strategic acumen was evident as each one tried to outdo the other. Especially confident with his knowledge was Rick, the physically imposing 13-year-old who recently had bragged about shattering a glass door in school. He informed his fellow "Nintendo" warriors that, "They [the Iraqis] only have MIGs." He went on to declare that, "The New York State Police could beat Iraq!" His conclusion was left unchallenged.

Fully recognizing the protective nature of their discussion to that point and not wanting to assault their defenses with a lecture on the realities of war, I asked them, "Are any of you worried?" They actually startled me with the swiftness of their response, a stark contrast to the macho posturing that had preceded it: "I'm afraid we'll be bombed. . . . We might be hit. . . . I can see World War III. . . . What if there's a nuclear war . . . ?" Jack, whose father had died 2 years earlier and who was referred to the group after several reportedly indiscriminate acts of physical violence against classmates, was the last to respond. He spoke of the consequences of nuclear war in human terms. Without missing a beat he described a book he had recently read, *Johnny Got His Gun,* about the impact of war through the experience of a single soldier trapped inside of a severely damaged body.

Matthew, the group's self-described "intellectual," told the others about "the prophecies of Nostradamus." He carefully detailed a prediction that he attributed to the 16th-century French astrologer: "At the end of the 20th century, a large man with a mustache wearing a blue coat and brandishing a large sword will conquer North America. . . . "

On the prospect of terrorism, the boys doubted that there would be any real protection. An irate Jack yelled about the planned layoff of scores of New York City fireman. He then reported the deaths of "two retarded boys" who "would have been saved if the local firehouse, a block from their house hadn't been shut down." (Within the year, Jack became a junior member of the local firehouse.) He and the others railed on about "how everything is falling apart." Jack's illustration seemed to highlight their diminishing faith in adults and in the power of "authorities" to protect them.

As their earlier defensive posture gave way to a more open expression of anxiety and fear, I asked a second question intended to engage group members in finding the resources within themselves and in the group to cope with their growing terror. I pointed to an empty chair and asked: "If a boy about your age walked in here now and sat down in that chair, and he was shaking and asking for help to deal with the threat of war, how would you help him?"

They said that they would tell him not to worry because "The bombs could never reach us," and if they ever got close "They would be blown out of the sky." Then there was a pause, and Rick, the most "arsenal savvy" of the group said, "You guys will think I'm a wimp, but I'm scared shitless." He punctuated his confession by grasping the fingers of both hands behind his neck and then burying his head between his knees. This was a curious sight. It reminded me of the frequent air-raid drills I'd participated in as an elementary school student in the 1950s ("duck and cover"). The other boys silently studied Rick's metamorphosis back to the innocence of childhood.

I asked the others if they thought Rick was a "wimp." Their response was a resounding "No!" and they revealed that they, too, were scared. I told them that they had nothing to be ashamed of, that war is scary and that it took a lot of courage for them to be as forthcoming and supportive as they had been. And then I tried my best to reassure them that they would be safe.

The room fell silent following my attempt at reassurance. They asked to play a game that Matthew had brought in for the last 10 or 15 minutes of the session. The game, *Advanced Dungeons and Dragons,* is a fantasy game in which characters are created to battle various enemies and life-threatening obstacles. Matthew had prepared character profiles for each of the boys. The profiles described their assets in such categories as special abilities, armor, hit points, wounds, weapons, ammunition, and more.

For the remaining minutes of the group meeting, they played the game. Perhaps they were expressing their fears through another avenue, one that gave them temporary mastery over their demons. I felt no need to contaminate the activity with interpretation but simply allowed them the space to relate to one another in the coded language of the game, language that kept me at a distance. I was an outsider who was allowed to bear witness to their attempt to cope with horror.

As the meeting ended, the boys bolted out at a few minutes past 7 o'clock. I instinctively flicked on the radio only to hear the President's press secretary, Marlin Fitzwater, announce, "The liberation of Kuwait has begun." Moments later two of the boys, Rick and Kenny burst through my door yelling, "They've started dropping bombs, they've started dropping bombs!"

Rick, who earlier had gloated that he had a "hot date" planned for the evening, seemed to change his plans: "I'm going home to hide in my basement." Kenny remained. His eyes started to fill up and he said, "My mother's not here yet, and I'm scared. Can I stay with you until she gets here?" I gestured to Kenny, who had been brutalized as a child, to sit down. We heard an airplane overhead, and the tears began to roll down Kenny's cheeks. "Every time I hear a plane, I'm afraid it will drop a bomb. You know I was afraid of the dark when I was younger. I live in the top part of our house, and I'm afraid that the bombs will drop whenever I hear a plane." My reassurances were soon interrupted by the buzz of the telephone and the message of the arrival of his mom—his former foster mother, who would hang in with Kenny and adopt him, finally providing him with some stability and consistent care. Without hesitation Kenny, about half my size, gave me a bear hug and, burying his head into my midsection, said, "Thanks, Andy, I hope to see you next week." I assured him that he would, and as I escorted him down the winding staircase with my arm around his shoulder, I could feel him trembling. Or was it me?

When I was in the seventh grade, the news of President Kennedy's assassination came to us through the classroom intercom. Twenty-eight years later, as I approached my 40th birthday, the news of the war with Iraq arrived again from a disembodied voice, this time through my office radio. At age 12½ the news was followed by no human interaction, only blank stares and a gasp-punctuated silence. We were dismissed, and I returned home to an inescapable eeriness that I remember sharply to this day. And now the world stage was again intersecting with a gathering of seventh graders. As I look back to this particular boys' group, I feel privileged to have been in a place that provided us with more than blank stares and silence.

What is it that these group members fear when they get caught up in the news of American involvement in war as in the Gulf? Of the adolescents, some, to be sure, if they are emotionally more primitive, may literally fear being attacked. But I wonder if for some others, all of the excitement of the news of these events makes them frightened, as if they really can't handle the strong, and socially shared, feelings of aggression and hatred toward the "enemy?" I also wonder about the desire of a young person like Rick to be a "part of things," the identification with soldiers in combat, with its resultant enhancement of self-esteem (even if this enhancement is both transitory and illusory). In the group Rick can be "one of them," a hero, "unafraid to be afraid," while actually there is no realistic danger to be confronted. What do you think, reader?

Some months later I wrote a letter to an unknown soldier in the Persian Gulf. I learned that the letter-writing program was launched to provide human contact "back home" for soldiers who "weren't likely to get mail." I wasn't sure where to begin, so I wrote to the then unnamed soldier about my boys' group's reaction to the war. Weeks and months later, I received letters from a soldier who I'll refer to as Sam. The return address on the envelope read, Desert Storm. Sam was a 19-year-old Cavalry Scout in the U.S. Army. He told me that he enlisted in the military to help pay college tuition. "On my own at 15," he wrote, "I needed to grow up fast in order not to get brought down by the overwhelming competition of society."

Despite the considerable stress he was enduring, Sam's letters reflected an uncanny sensitivity to the boys in my group. Referring to his own fellow soldiers, he wrote about watching "adult kids" become men at the outset of the war. In one letter, Sam described an army buddy watching his *Dungeons and Dragons* books go up in flames when the bombing began. With a link to his childhood before him in ashes, Sam reported that his

26-year-old friend simply said to him, "I guess this means we're growing up, huh?"

I shared my letters with the boys' group. In my next letter to Sam, I included their questions for him:

- How did it feel being in the war?
- When the war was over how did you feel?
- How did it feel not to be on US territory?
- How did it feel fighting alongside foreigners?
- What do you think of Saddam Hussein and what he did to the people of his country?
- How did it feel looking up in the sky and seeing all the flashes of light?
- What did you think about the Super Bowl?
- Who is your favorite team?

CONCLUSION

In the three practice illustrations, violence is addressed in the group as close to the actual precipitating event as possible. A group member requiring medical attention after being injured in a fight attends a group meeting rather than going to the emergency room for X-rays; a coed youth group struggles with the aftermath of the violence that marred their otherwise well-conceived and well-executed community dance; and a young-adolescent group wrestles with the excitement, fear, and anxiety evoked by impending war. In addition to the immediacy of the interventions is the undeniable value of group affiliation in addressing these issues. Manny chose to go for mutual aid before first aid; the Youth of Culture Club banded together despite fearing they'd be torn apart; and the boys' group shared a moment that no measure of solitude could have satisfied.

CHAPTER 12

Adolescent Sexuality
and Group Work
Variations on a Theme

If ever there was a time to be tuned in to the theme of adolescent sexuality, there is no time like the dawn of the 21st century. The Centers for Disease Control and Prevention (1996) report an escalating pattern of adolescent AIDS cases, from 1 in 1981 to almost 2,700 by the end of 1996. HIV/AIDS has risen to become the sixth leading cause of death among 15 to 24-year-olds in the United States. Since it can take up to 10 years for the HIV infection to result in AIDS, it is obvious that many young adults contracted the virus while they were still teenagers.

As AIDS and other sexually transmitted diseases (STDs) continue to grow at unprecedented rates, the proportion of teens who get pregnant has remained steady for nearly 20 years. Among those teens who have had sexual intercourse, the pregnancy rate has gone down almost 20% since the early 1970s (Alan Guttmacher Institute, 1994). Nevertheless there remains a large proportion of teens who do not have ready access to contraception as the result of the freezing and cutting back of funds for the federal Title X family planning programs. Consequently, several million teen women each year are prevented from getting the most effective contraceptive, the birth control pill (P. Scales, personal communication, 1995).

There remain a few vocal critics who claim that sexuality education and family planning are failed programs that promote sexual activity among teenagers. The problem is that despite the relatively small percentage of those who are against these programs, when it emanates from powerful interest groups, the opposition can be difficult to overcome. Such was the case in Wisconsin in 1987 when the governor vetoed legislation to fund school-based clinics after advocates were able to obtain a $2 million appropriation (Dryfoos, 1994). In any case, suggesting that sexuality education causes sexual behavior is like saying fire stations cause fires (Scales, 1996, p. 6).

How adolescents who are achieving physical maturity get most of their information about sexuality is a critical question for policy makers and youth workers. Recent research findings show that adolescents who received a comprehensive sexuality education course early enough, and with enough depth to make any difference in behavior, are more likely to postpone having sexual intercourse or to use contraception when they do have it (Portner, 1994).

A 1988–1990 survey by the National Institute on Drug Abuse (NIDA) found that 50% of U.S. students engaged in intercourse after using alcohol and or other drugs (Anderson, 1992). Problems and risky behavior during adolescence (e.g., physical fighting, carrying a weapon, drug abuse, early sexual intercourse, school failure, poverty) cannot be addressed in isolation. Since the needs and concerns of adolescents are interrelated, solutions must take into account the whole picture, and group interventions must be structured to invite the whole person and not just the distressing parts.

There is concern that involvement of peers and the media in these matters overrides the influence of parents (Zelnick & Shah, 1983). Sex and birth control tend to be discussed most often among friends and peers, often leading to exchanges of inaccurate or misleading information (Rosenberg, 1980). In adolescence, as the peer group's values compete with the family's, the former may more strongly influence one's decisions about early sexual behavior.

Despite their influence, which is quite often positive, peers are only one part of a four-part community that also includes family, larger community, and media influences, all of which have demonstrable effects on adolescents' sexual attitudes and behavior, and which all act together in a complex way. For example, beyond the peer group are "images and information conveyed by the media that may embody values that are inimical to young people's self-image and health" (Carnegie Council on Adolescent Development, 1995, p. 29). In families where sexuality is not a taboo subject and related discussions occur quite naturally throughout childhood, pathways are forged for ongoing dialogue about all aspects of sexuality (Cicarelli, 1980). If parents' influence is strong enough (i.e., if their relationships with their children are warm and close and their parenting style is authoritative), it can be a powerful protector against negative peer influence.

PRACTICE PRINCIPLES FOR ADDRESSING SEXUALITY IN GROUP WORK WITH ADOLESCENTS

Sexuality is a vital area to be addressed in group work with adolescents. Beyond information about the physical aspects of sex, adolescents need to learn that sexuality is about feelings, skills, norms, and values. Recommended practice principles for addressing sexuality in group work with adolescents are:

- Provide accurate information about sexual functioning (e.g., biology, conception, childbirth, and a focus on preventing pregnancy and disease).
- Reinforce values and group norms against unprotected sex that are age and experience appropriate (e.g., abstinence, contraception, and their consequences; Kirby et al., 1994).
- Confront narrow perceptions of sexuality and broaden the focus by providing information about the relational nature of sexual activities (e.g., helping group members to learn that well-rounded relationships reflect a blending of affection, interdependence, intellectual stimulation, mutual interests, responsibility, and sexual satisfaction; MacLennan & Dies, 1992, p. 157; Carrera, 1996, pp. 75–82).
- Encourage exploration of attitudes and values about sexual identity (e.g., what it means to be a man or a woman).
- Provide opportunities for the acquisition of cognitive and behavior skills needed to prevent high-risk behaviors and their consequences (e.g., developing problem-solving skills and reducing barriers to safer sex through the use of discussion, education, and experiential and skill-building activities).
- Confront social influences and pressures (e.g., negative peer influence, confusing messages communicated through the media).

CLARIFYING VALUES: PRACTICE ILLUSTRATIONS ON THE DIALECTICAL PROCESS IN OPEN DISCUSSION GROUPS

The following are practice illustrations of group work in which diverse themes of adolescent sexuality are addressed. In these illustrations of three discussion groups—younger-adolescent girls (seventh grade; 12 and 13 years old), middle-adolescent boys (tenth grade; 16 years old), and a mixed-age adolescent coed group (eighth to twelfth grades; 14 to 17 years old)—demonstrate the dialectical process involved in attempting to clarify one's values in the group.

The workers in all three cases ask probing questions intended to clarify what the members believe in, and how strongly. Group members are faced with the challenge of affirming what they believe, which may differ from the majority. Therefore, the process also creates an opportunity to test one's ability to go against the majority and to stand up for what one believes. For the majority, there is the chance, in listening closely and carefully considering another's views, to change one's opinions and to try out new values.

The three examples also illustrate the meandering conversational style of adolescent groups that requires some patience and getting used to for workers. In the first record of service, the girls consider what attracts them to boys; in the second, the boys debate their differential approaches to becoming involved sexually with girls; and in the third, a group that developed a newsletter questions the policies of the agency regarding publishing sexually frank content (Brandler & Roman, 1995).

Sixth-Grade Girls' Lunch Group

Just prior to an open discussion group on normative adolescent issues, a new girl joins the group and is greeted with a recitation of group norms including: respecting one another, taking turns to speak, and upholding confidentiality. The worker (GW) begins by asking the girls if they recall where last week's discussion left off. "No one remembered so I reminded them that the topic had been 'boys.' " One of the girls picked up the discussion.

JULIE: Oh, I think you were asking what we liked about boys, but we didn't finish talking about it.

GW: How many of you would like to continue talking about this? Could you raise your hands? (*all raise their hands*). OK. I think we left off when I asked you to tell me what you look for in boys or what you like about them. . . . Who would like to start?

JULIE: I like boys who are honest.

CHRIS: Yeah. Someone who's nice but also sincere.

JACKIE: Someone who doesn't fool around.

GW: What do you mean, fool around?

JACKIE: A boy who won't cheat on you with another girl.

CHRIS: Someone you can trust and talk with.

GW: Wait a minute, so when you look at a guy you like, is his physical appearance important?

[The worker redirects the discussion, intimating that the girls are glossing over something—physical attraction. Just how important is appearance? More than respect and fidelity? The girls' values are probed through this informal process.]

CHRIS: It's not that important.

GW: So none of you worry about what the guy looks like?

ALL: Yeah we do!

GW: Then, what kind of physical characteristics do you look for in a boy?

JACKIE: He's got to be cute!

ALL: Yeah!

GW: What do you mean cute?

JACKIE: Like he's got a nice face and a nice body.

IRIS: Yeah. Someone who dresses nice and looks neat and clean.

JACKIE: A boy you can be with all the time—like a boyfriend.

CHRIS: Except if he's a nerd.

GW: Why?

CHRIS: Because you'll be embarrassed when you're with him.

GW: Why would you be embarrassed?

CHRIS: 'Cause. Especially if you're really popular and a lot of people know you.

GW: Why is it bad to be popular and have a nerdy boy as a boyfriend?

RUTHIE: 'Cause people could make fun of you.

GW: So, you all would be afraid of what people say about your boyfriends?

IRIS: I don't think you should worry about what other people think as long as you love that person—why should people care who you go out with? You shouldn't be ashamed of the boyfriend you're going out with.

GW: What's the difference between liking a lot and loving?

IRIS: When you get to know a guy, then you like him.

GW: How about the rest of you? What is the difference between liking and loving someone?

RUTHIE: I used to like a boy . . . no, I used to *love* him. He was in Puerto Rico, his name was Jose. He was cute!

GW: And how did you know you loved him?

RUTHIE: 'Cause I liked being with him all the time.

GW: So, you're saying that if you're with a guy all the time, you'll fall in love?

RUTHIE: Maybe.

GW: And how do you find out if you're in love with that guy?

CHRIS: When you want to spend time with only one boy and you're not looking around for another boy.

GW: Do you think that now, at you age, you could fall in love?

IRIS: Right now I don't think so because, for me, I have a boyfriend, but I just met him 2 weeks ago, and I like him, but I can't say I love him yet.

GW: Why not?

IRIS: I think we're still too young to say that we love a boy. I mean, right now, you really don't know if you love or like a guy. Love is such a strong word.

GW: What do you mean, it's such a strong word?

IRIS: 'Cause you really can't tell just yet if you're in love unless you go out with a guy for a long time.

GW: When you first meet a guy you like, do you like him because he's cute or because of the way he treats you?

> [The worker gradually brings the group back to the themes touched on earlier, demonstrating that detours are sometimes necessary for getting back on the main road. By winding her way around the subject of relationships with boys, she reapproaches the question of how the girls expect to be treated on a stronger foundation.]

CHRIS: You ask a lot of difficult questions.

GW: (*laughs*) I do?

ALL: Yeah.

In the above process, the worker is fairly directive using a question and answer format. There are important issues being addressed, however the following questions must be considered regarding the worker's role in the interaction: Why is there no room for silences, hesitations, or group member-initiated questions? Is the group worker trying to discover how the members feel or trying to show them how they should feel?

What a group does may vary in its degree of structure from group to group (i.e., from loosely structured informal discussion to highly structured program exercises). In any case, it is important to consider whether the members are afforded enough time, space, and freedom to explore their feelings, ideas, beliefs, and values in any depth and for the worker to understand what his/her role is in making this happen or in preventing it from occurring.

Middle-Adolescent Boys' Group in a Child Guidance Center

The following is a transcript of a group composed of middle-adolescent boys who were referred to a mental health clinic for a variety of acting out behaviors. The group consists of five members, three of whom are present for this meeting. The purpose of the group includes helping the members to be more thoughtful and to use better judgment in their behavior. It has also been agreed that the group will address normative adolescent issues including sexuality.

The discussion begins with one of the members, Miguel, addressing me, "You've got to get me some condoms, Andy, my father won't get them for me. You've got to get me some. Or should I get them myself?" As the discussion unfolds, Miguel reveals that he is thinking about becoming sexually involved with a girl he likes. When I ask if he and his girlfriend have discussed this, the other two group members, 16-year-old boys, break up laughing.

NICK: (*incredulous and sarcastic tone*) You don't go discussing fucking with the girl—"Yo, baby, we gonna go fuck tomorrow night, all right?"—You don't say that!

GW: How do you do it, Nick?

NICK: She's supposed to think it's happening spontaneously, like it's romantic or something.

GW: That's what she's *supposed* to think?

NICK: (*smiling*) You plan that stuff out carefully. You plot and make out charts and everything . . .

GW: So it's never something that gets worked out ahead of time?

NICK: Hells no. Then you never get the ass. Like Andy [GW]. Andy never gets the ass.

MIGUEL: He [GW] has children.

NICK: Andy doesn't have children. How many?

MIGUEL: I think he has two.

NICK: (*laughing*) I guess the condom broke twice.

GW: (*playing along with ribbing*) Actually, I only had sex twice in my life.

NICK: (*looks puzzled, unsure how to respond*)

Up to this point the group seems to be testing the waters to see far how they can take this discussion. Miguel and Nick are laying out their positions. Nick, not for the first time, tries to rattle me with a well-placed put down, questioning my sexuality. I guess it's difficult for Nick to see me, the worker, as a sexual person. I tell myself, "Andy, don't take yourself too seriously and get caught up in a power struggle with Nick." He's great at doing that, getting into power struggles with adults (and with kids for that matter). Maybe I should have asked them what they think having this information (about my sex life) would do for them. I'll play along in as good-natured a manner as I can muster and forge ahead with this theme. But I really have to watch out about being seduced into participation and competition like when I played along with the ribbing, saying, "I only had sex twice in my life." It seemed OK at the time, but I really don't need to interject myself in this way. Anyway, I think we're on to something here. Let's see what happens next.

GW: Is there a time that it doesn't happen like a game? Where you work it out in advance?

NICK: Yeah, after I fuck her the first time.

GW: What about you guys?

MIGUEL: See if she's ready.

GW: So Nick's way is not the only way.

Here I'm trying to establish that there are alternatives. Rather than directly attack Nick's crude language and insensitivity, the idea is to help the group to explore, in dialectical fashion, different values and to see if they'll join or challenge him. Realistically, I'm aware that they're far more influential with one another than I am with them at the moment. Ironically, this includes not assuming that they're not taking in whatever I might have to say despite their dismissive posturing. Adolescents do want information from adults, but they rarely want to openly project their dependency needs. A tough facade or impervious manner doesn't preclude an open ear.

NICK: My way is the only way.

GW: (referring to Miguel) He says you can talk [to a girl] first . . .

MIGUEL: (as if to finish the sentence) . . . to see if she's ready.

NICK: (incredulous again) To see if she's ready! Like some kind of dog getting ready to mate?

GW: Nick, it sounds like you've got special training in this subject.

NICK: Yeah, when I was 13, I fucked a 16-year-old ho, that's where I got my training.

GW: So, there's no other way than your way?

NICK: Sometimes. Maybe.

MIGUEL: I have a sister I try to set the right way . . .

GW: (to Nick) What if you had a sister? Let's say an older kid your age came on to her?

NICK: Is she fly looking [attractive]? If anyone touches her I'll kick his ass.

GW: But you're that 16-year-old guy with someone else's sister; do you deserve to get the shit beat out of you?

NICK: (scratches and shakes his head)

GW: Things getting a little too complicated, Nick?

I feel like I've become a little too involved in trying to knock Nick down a peg. The power struggle seems to have walled off the other members transforming the group, temporarily, into a dyad between Nick and me. On the one hand, I want to neutralize Nick and emphasize that there are other beliefs and attitudes worth considering. But on the other hand I want to defeat Nick, which only leads him to withdraw. Drawing the group in earlier and allowing them to do the work would've made more sense, in retrospect.

GW: [Attempting to broaden the focus by drawing in Jamal, who has been silent thus far] What do you think?

JAMAL: (shakes head quietly as if to say, "I don't know")

NICK: (to Jamal) Which way is right, mine or his?

I'd like to say I planned this, but I'd be lying. By going to Jamal, Nick becomes reengaged after his temporary retreat. I'd better back off here and let the group do some of the work.

MIGUEL: (before Jamal has chance to answer) Nick, what you don't understand is that I'm Catholic. My family values from my grandparents tell me that you just don't go too quick with a girl. That's not right.

The influence of one's religious beliefs and values is as significant a theme for the worker to be tuned in to as are sensitivity to ethnicity and to race. Issues of premarital sex, masturbation, contraception, homosexuality, and abortion have powerful meaning to many people within the religious context of their lives. For example, masturbation might be discussed as a good alternative to sexual intercourse, but for some it may be viewed as even more "sinful" than intercourse outside of marriage and, therefore, deserving of much exploration by the worker and group.

NICK: So what? I'm Catholic too.

JAMAL: If the girl is right here (*gestures to an empty chair*) and you start kissing on her and kissing her titties and she doesn't say anything, then you keep going. . . .

MIGUEL: (*interrupting*) . . . I would ask the girl.

NICK: (*loud, raucous, ridiculing laughter*)

GW: [Trying here to reinforce a norm for discussing differences in the group] Nick, instead of putting someone down, why don't you just say you don't agree with his opinion and then state yours. [This is offered as a suggestion, not as an order.]

In reading this process you may be wondering about the use of foul, dehumanizing and sexist language. As offensive as some of the language is, it is secondary, in my opinion, to getting at the theme of the relational nature of sexuality as experienced by the boys. Getting caught up in words that are consonant with their reference groups would be diversionary. If as a worker you find this language to be intolerable and no rule had been previously set, you might say something like this to the group: "I know that this is your way of expressing your views about things. I want you to feel free to say what's on your mind. But I find some of the language offensive. I'm sure that there are other words you can find to express yourself, and I would appreciate it if you would." Or a reasonable facsimile, something framed as an "I-message" rather than as a controlling demand. I'm not contending to be "right" by not confronting the language, however I'm also wondering whether the tenor of the discussion might naturally moderate and humanize the language as the clash of values continues. One consequence of confronting this language, which is quite natural among groups of adolescent (and adult) males, is that to put a stop to it provides members with a way of attacking you (the worker) by continuing to use profanity and using you to punish them and relieve their guilt.

GW: (*to Jamal*) So what you're saying is that you can communicate by touch *and* you can communicate by talking. Do you agree that you can communicate by talking?

JAMAL: If you ask a girl, "Pardon me, do you wanna fuck?" she'll be embarrassed.

GW: Would you agree that both talking and touching are OK?

JAMAL: One or the other.

GW: Can't be both?

JAMAL: If I really like a girl and respect her, I would ask her first. But girls can take advantage of you too. Girls like sex as much as boys do.

As the group meeting continues, it weaves in and out of a variety of themes: touching and talking, sexual enjoyment, and the difference between consent and date rape. Did anything get resolved? Discussing this taboo area candidly opened the door for further discussion and the expression of difference allowed group members to explore their own values and consider those of others.

The Newsletter Group

In the next illustration, an adolescent group struggles with the censorship of a newsletter they produced by the agency that sponsored the activity. The group includes five teenagers, four girls and one boy, ranging from 14 to 17 years old and all of different racial and ethnic backgrounds (Puerto Rican, African American, Dominican, Jamaican, Polish American). The worker is 23 years old and Irish American. The purpose of the group is:

> To produce a newsletter that is distributed to various settlement house sites; to address developmental tasks of adolescents including identity formation and gender issues, self esteem building, mastery of specific skills, development of positive peer relationships, separation and individuation issues, and cooperative work skills; and to encourage creative expression (Brandler & Roman, 1995, p. 26)

The following vignette from Brandler and Roman (1995) captures the group's discussion soon after learning that a story written by one of the members had been censored. The content of the story included, "a highly explicit, stark, and powerful commentary on teenage sexuality, misogyny, and the possible consequences of unprotected sex—pregnancy and HIV transmission" (p. 26). The agency executive director reportedly held up publication fearing repercussions from board members and the community.

> YOLANDA: What you wrote about is really real. I know a lot of boys that say "I bagged this girl" or "I got that one last night." They're really nasty sometimes.

ED: Yeah, guys are always talking crazy-like. They say "Man, I had this girl and her leg was all up by her ear," or "Oh yeah, well this honey I was with, I had her wrapped up like a pretzel."

ELLEN: [the author of the controversial piece] I know. The boys I hang out with are always talking like that, but they don't want me to write about what really goes on.

CINDY: No, but it's the truth. What should we write about? Fairy tales and butterflies?

KEISHA: You know, I hear a lot of boys near my house who talk just like that or who make bets about how many girls they can be with. It's just a game for them. Guys always be dissing on girls.

ED: Naw, not all of them. I know guys who really like girls, but they won't even look their way.

YOLANDA: No. Boys are just trying to be cool with their friends and try to show off by saying "Yeah, I been with her. She's good," or "Aah, I can't believe you did that ugly girl! You can't get nobody better than that?"

ED: Not every boy. Some of them, yeah.

GW: So, Ed, you're saying that maybe different people experience this issue in a different way. Your experience is that not all boys act this way?

ED: Yeah, not every guy's like that.

ELLEN: No, but most of them are. I hear boys talk about girls all the time, just like in my story.

GW: You know, how this relates to the newsletter group may be in learning to think how our readers will take what we write about. In Ellen's story, she means to let everyone know that if you mess around you might get hurt, like get pregnant or get AIDS, but what if someone reads that story and thinks that Ellen meant only to say all boys are dogs, even though Ed said they aren't? What if someone doesn't understand what Ellen meant to say? One thing that we'll learn in doing the newsletter is how to be responsible for the kinds of messages we may be giving our readers. Well, maybe we should talk about what we want to do in the newsletter group this year. Let's try to come up with some ideas about how we would like the newsletter to be. (Brandler & Roman, 1995, pp. 27–28)

In discussions in which a focus of the group is clarifying values, the worker ought to be aware of the thinking, feeling, and doing components of values. Once dissected, a true value, which represents something of deep significance, must stand the test of having been freely chosen from a variety of alternatives, openly and publicly affirmed, and acted upon in a repeated and consistent manner. Probing questions can help to clarify one's choice of values and willingness to stand for what one believes (i.e., does one "walk the walk" or simply "talk the talk"?). In the three illustrations above, the young people involved are provided with rich opportunities, through the dialectical process of group work, to take a closer look at their own values and to test them out in a supportive environment.

The use of group activities can help adolescents struggling with sexual identity issues to overcome resistance to material that is painful or too uncomfortable for discussion. For example:

> A co-ed basketball game may be a way to bring boys and girls together in a game which involves some physical closeness with clear rules for conduct. For adolescents less able to tolerate the physical intimacy of a game like co-ed basketball, another sport like baseball may be appropriate. The recreational element can lessen the discomfort and provide an arena for discussion later. (Brandler & Roman, 1991, pp. 129–130)

MUTUAL AID: THE MEMBERS AS HELPERS IN PROVIDING INFORMATION AND SUPPORT

In the succeeding three examples the importance of valuing the members as helpers is highlighted. The variable role of the practitioner in positions of lesser and greater centrality in the group is emphasized.

> In a coed group, a 16-year-old girl tried to downplay the risk involved in her preferred method of birth control and protection—"pulling out." When another member reminded her that she had become pregnant using the same method, she maintained her facade attesting to how considerate her boyfriend is—"I know he pulled out in time." But behind her self-assured front, the other girl tuned in to the underlying anxiety and passed along her telephone number and an invitation to call, "If you don't get your period."

In an older-adolescent boys' group, the subject of discussion was AIDS, other STDs, modes of transmission, prevention, and detection.

> The worker (the author) tried to explain how one could determine if he has transmitted an STD, where to go in the county to get tested, and what the process entails. Amid the constant chatter of the members, which camouflaged the group worker's message, there was one member whose body language suggested that he was tuned in. It became obvious to the worker that this 16-year-old boy had some knowledge to share. Rather than try and maintain his centrality, an obvious mistake, the worker asked, "Has anyone here ever been tested?" With that question, Gary raised his hand high and proceeded

to describe the process in detail. The others became quiet and attentive, asking questions as he went along. He was far more effective in his "blow by blow" presentation than the worker had been in his failed attempt (see Chapter 7 for details).

In a coed group of middle adolescents, the group was confronted with an unexpected discovery about a fellow member.

Ruthie, a 16-year-old, typically vivacious member, appeared to be uncharacteristically morose and quiet. After a while, the others seemed to notice the "loss," and one of them questioned her with "What's wrong?" She replied with an unconvincing "Nothing" and a shrug of the shoulders. The worker asked her if she was aware that she seemed to be "different," today, than usual. She half smiled and nodded affirmatively but swore that she didn't know why. The worker asked the group, in an attempt to universalize, if that ever happened to any of them, drifting into unexplainable moods. All nodded and some shared examples. The worker suggested that sometimes we are reminded of things that we are not even aware of, milestones or anniversaries, that might evoke strong feelings in us, feelings with unknown origins. Another member asked Ruthie, "Is this some kind of anniversary or something?" With that question she paused, looked down and then up, revealing her tear-filled eyes. She told the group that it was a year ago to the week that she had terminated her pregnancy through an abortion. Intermingled with the feelings of loss was the guilt exacerbated by what she described as her parents' (and in all likelihood, her own) lack of forgiveness.

Supportive services for teens following abortion are invaluable, and especially for those adolescents who are in the midst of a separation struggle with their parents (Horowitz, 1978).

DETOURS, ANXIETY, AND ADOLESCENCE

As with other taboo subjects, discussions and activities in the group related to the theme of sexuality are likely to evoke some anxiety. This is especially the case when two taboo areas such as sexuality and death are intermingled, as is the case of group content about AIDS (Malekoff, 1994e).

In a discussion on sexuality among a group of 15- and 16-year-old boys, the subject of STDs was the focus. The boys, all purporting to be sexually active and expressing differing views about the meaning of "protecting oneself," turned the discussion to the question of "Where did AIDS come from?" and "Why is there no cure?" The discussion was lively, their concerns real, and their anxiety palpable. An unexpected turn occurred when the lack of a cure for AIDS was compared to the problem of household roach control. "You can't get rid of roaches," proclaimed Aaron. This led to an invocation of the names of various well-known products—Raid, Combat, and others. In no time, the members proceeded to analyze and debate the strengths and weaknesses of each product in rapid-fire fashion: "It kills the roaches but leaves their eggs behind," said Charles. "No, it kills the roaches *and* their eggs," argued Darnell. And Gregory, adding a touch of reality to the surreal proceedings concluded, "The only thing that will kill roaches is your hand." To which the worker (the author) said, "That might be a good way to prevent STDs as well. You know, using your hand." After a pause the boys smiled at one another understanding the reference to masturbation. And Aaron said, "He's right" and "high-fived" Darnell. And the great roach debate, true to the tradition of theater of the absurd, continued.

The worker sat by in amused disbelief at the discussion's transition from AIDS to roaches. "What is going on?" he wondered to himself. "Should I make some kind of interpretation about anxiety and avoidance or should I play with this analogy about roach control? Or should I get them 'back on track' with AIDS and STDs? Or sit back and allow this to continue—they were so engrossed—and see where it goes?" Finally breaking into a pause in the action, the worker simply stated, "This is amazing, I've never heard a discussion about AIDS linked to roach control." They all cracked up laughing, not seeming to have realized where they had journeyed.

In this illustration, I viewed my choice of intervention as the least intrusive of the alternatives short of saying nothing. In adolescent groups "a sensitive and strategic approach to resistance is required rather than a purely interpretive or confrontative approach that may lead to further resistance and hinder the work of the group" (Hurley, 1984, p. 80). In this situation, the subtle use of humor enabled the members to reconnect to the original theme without forcing the issue, and it allowed them to appreciate, together with me as their worker, their creative and humorous departure into the land of roach motels. Soon they returned to the more realistic aspects of the issue: contracting STDs, protecting oneself, and seeking testing for HIV infection. The great roach debate was a detour that, in retrospect, seemed inevitable.

In adolescent groups, detours are not uncommon. Nor is resistance.

Resistance should not be negatively interpreted or challenged directly. Patience, sensitivity, and flexibility in dealing with difficult subjects are necessary to tolerate the detours that epitomize the meandering conversational style of adolescent groups. The give and take of conversation with its repeated opportunities for social mastery is a critical feature of group work with adolescents. Free-wheeling conversation accents the "normal" in the group members, supporting and building on their strengths.

In the same group, the discussion later took another turn. The members discussed under what circumstances, if any, intercourse without a condom was safe. They debated the pros and cons of using a condom and when they would or would not use one.

> The debate centered around ejaculation, with Darnell declaring, "As long as you don't come, you know—pull out in time, there's no harm." This also led to a revelation of myths about masturbation, including whether the practice can result in "running out of sperm." While permitting plenty of room for open expression, as worker, I tried to provide accurate information and expose myths. However, the group was intent on rejecting my arguments, cutting me off at the pass. Was this a case of denial, avoidance, rebellion, or maybe an example of that old adage that says, "You can't be a prophet in your own land"? Frustrated with my inability to get through to them, I suggested that they consult a higher source—the AIDS Hot-line, a national 800 telephone number. With that they asked, "Can we call now?" Fortunately the office had a speaker phone that would permit all of them to participate. One of them volunteered to be the spokesman. As I dialed the phone, they laughed nervously. Once a connection was made, the volunteer spokesman, perhaps embarrassed or thinking that he was protecting his anonymity, changed his voice to "avoid detection." As the disembodied voice from the speaker filled the group room, the boys seemed to feel encouraged to ask the anonymous voice a number of questions, until they were satisfied.

This example demonstrates the importance of the practitioner's maintaining a sense of humility in relation to what he/she has to offer. The group worker cannot know everything about everything. Authenticity enables the worker to lose his/her centrality and to lead the members in another direction when necessary. Knowing about resources and how to access them is critical in discussions about sexuality. As the above example illustrates, the group worker was able to bring a temporary "coworker" into the group, enabling the boys to double-check his information and to scout out an easily accessible resource for future reference.

VARYING CONTEXTS

Gay, Lesbian, and Bisexual Youth: Group Work and the Coming-Out Process

Lesbian and gay youth who become aware of their sexual orientation and come out during the high school years experience significant stresses including social stigma, isolation, invisibility, harassment, physical and verbal violence, and family rejection (Morrow, 1993; Hanley-Hackenbruck, 1989; Hunter & Schaeder, 1987; Sancier, 1984). This group, despite political gains, remains a hidden minority in most schools. The coming out process of acknowledging one's homosexual identity occurs independently and without major complications for some youth, but for many, the stress places them at risk for psychological disturbance and self-destructive behaviors including suicide (Holzhauer, 1993). Among the needs of gay and lesbian teens are:

- The need to be accepted for who they are.
- Protection from harassment and discrimination.
- The right to have family acceptance.
- The availability of positive role models.
- To have access to supportive services.
- To be seen as whole people with strengths and weaknesses. (Jacobsen, 1988)

Comprehensive information and positive role models are in scarce supply for struggling gay, lesbian, and bisexual youth striving to establish a positive identity (Dempsey, 1994). In addition to the emotional cruelty of their contemporaries, there are legions of uninformed and insensitive teachers, counselors, and school administrators whose attitudes approximate the general attitudes of a homophobic society (Martin & Hedrick, 1988).

A recent study confirmed the importance of social support for gay youth (Anderson, 1993). In one program, services are provided to gay, lesbian, and bisexual teens through a variety of groups—social, educational, and support. One of the open-ended membership groups addresses the problems of isolation, stigmatized sexuality, and the process of coming out. The purposes include providing a safe place for members to socialize and to establish a peer network to negotiate the coming out process. The group program includes socioeducation (e.g., sexuality, self-esteem, alcohol and other drugs, dating, HIV and AIDS, safer sex, gay history, political activism), discussion, and role playing. The group meets for 2 hours weekly. The first hour is for discussion of current concerns and the second hour is the educational module. The members, in different stages of the coming-out process, provide mutual aid for those who are struggling with the issues of coming out. The worker's role is to help to encourage mutual aid and to lend a vision, emphasizing that coming out is a life-long process as opposed to a terminal event.

In the following illustrations Kate, 21, expresses concern about her parents finding out about her attending the group. Also present are Marcy, 16; Jody, 18; Richard, 19; and Mandy, 18.

RICH: You're not out to your parents?

KATE: No.

RICH: I told my parents a year ago. My mom was fine about it. My dad wasn't so great at first. He told me I'd grow out of it, or something like that.

JODY: That's what my father keeps saying to me. He says, "You're going to find yourself a nice boyfriend some day."

MARCY: Yeah, my father used to say the same thing. But he's OK with it now. My brother was the one who gave me the hardest time. At first he was OK, but he keeps saying things like, "When are you going to get a boyfriend?" and stuff like that.

KATE: I get that all the time, and my parents don't even know.

GW: A frequent kind of coming out reaction by parents is this kind of denial or disbelief . . .

[The members establish that they're "all in the same boat," and the worker universalizes the experience, supporting the members sharing their coming out experiences. This provides great support for closeted members who are eager to hear the others' experiences.]

GW: Kate, I'm wondering what you're thinking hearing about these coming out experiences.

KATE: I don't know. . . . I don't think I'm ready to tell my parents.

MARCY: That must be really hard. . . . I mean, I remember what it was like before I told anyone—I was really depressed and had no one to talk to about it.

JODY: I couldn't keep it to myself—I told one of my girlfriends and then my brother.

MARCY: So like, do you get depressed and stuff?

KATE: I guess so. Yeah, I'm pretty depressed . . .

[Participants find comfort in the fact that they are all going through the same struggles in dealing with homophobic parents and friends.

But Kate's original problem was what to tell her parents about where she was when attending the group.]

RICH: Just tell them you went out for a little while—that you wanted to be alone. That's what I always tell mine.

MARCY: Yeah, or you could tell them that you went out to get something to eat. Just stop by Taco Bell on the way home.

JODY: I used to say I was going out with friends.

RICH: Or just tell them that it's none of their business.

GW: From the ideas that have been thrown out, it sounds like everyone has been in the position of having to make up excuses in order to attend the group.

Awareness of the stages of gay, lesbian, and bisexual identity will help the practitioner to tune in to where in the process of coming out their adolescent group members might be (Troiden, 1988; Hanley-Hackenbruck, 1989; Dempsey, 1994) . The stages are summarized as follows:

1. Some awareness of gender-related peer difference, most often before puberty.
2. Growing inner turmoil as the early sensitivity to differentness becomes associated with being gay, lesbian, or bisexual, most often during adolescence.
3. Homosexual identity is assumed and attempts to find belonging in the gay community are made, most often during later adolescence (into early 20s).
4. Commitment to homosexuality as a way of life including readiness for disclosure to a wider heterosexual audience, most often during early- and mid-20s.

Teen Moms' Group in a Residential Setting

A group of girls living in a residential facility for pregnant and parenting teens constituted a group formed to help the members to get off to a good start as mothers. On the site of the residence is a clinic where babies receive well care and check ups. Prenatal, postpartum follow-up, and gynecological care are offered to the residents as well. The group to be described is a short-term (six sessions, 1½-hour-long meetings), closed-membership group consisting of five teenage moms who are 13 and 14 years old. The girls are Italian American, African American, West Indian, Puerto Rican, and Salvadoran. Their babies range in age from a few days to 10 months.

The coworkers are African American and Jewish American women. The purpose of the group is to enhance parent–child bonding.

One advantage of coleadership in this group is the modeling provided by the workers who move freely among the girls and their babies helping them with feeding, comforting, and holding the babies, and assisting in interpreting the babies' signals. Early on, the girls often misinterpreted the babies' cues. In the following excerpt the baby is 2 weeks old.

MARY: (*to her baby*) Why don't you stop? I just fed you 2 hours ago.

GW: Mary, babies have very small stomachs and need to eat quite often.

MARY: No one used to feed me all the time when I was little.

GW: That must have made you feel really angry.

MARY: Yeah, but I don't care.

KEIRA: Fuck you! You kiddin' me? I know you get pissed all the time if there is no food here.

MARY: Well, they should've taken care of me when I was hungry.

JADE: Well, they didn't. But, you stupid or what? You gonna be mean to her too? (*gestures to one of the workers*) If they were mean to her [Mary], will she always be mean to her baby?

GW: No! That is not always true. That is one of the reasons we have these groups. There are many young moms who agree that they can take care of their babies now even if no one did it for them.

MARY: OK. I'm gonna feed her to make you all happy, but I still don't see why she has got to have all the luck. What about me?

GW: Well, we can't give you a bottle (*smiling*), but I'm sorry that no one was there for you then. But maybe we can help you feel better now?

As you the reader review this sequence, you might imagine yourself working with this group and consider some of the following questions: Is the worker showing her anger toward Mary for revealing her own needs? Are any unmet needs of workers likely to be aroused in this type of group? Does Mary need to talk further about what wasn't done for her? Introspection is critical in connecting the thinking, feeling, and doing components of the work. All questions might not be easily answered, but the practice of posing such questions is a critical part of the ongoing tuning in process. In groups with coleaders, such questions can be shared and discussed when debriefing following a meeting, and during supervisory conferences.

MARY: (*deep in thought*) OK, when I feed her, can I have some more juice?

> [With this request one worker poured her juice, the other offered her a snack, and she slowly settled in to feed her baby.]

As illustrated above, the workers are attuned to the babies and the mothers. Both workers had been holding babies during the interchange, one fixing a bottle and the other soothing Mary's baby with a pacifier. When Mary signaled that she was ready to feed the baby, each of them put the babies down and tended to Mary so that she could tend to her baby. Feeding is just one theme that signals the mothers' feelings of having been deprived of the same things that they must now provide for their babies. Another is learning to stimulate the babies through play.

JADE: Why should we play with our babies? No one ever played with us. These babies get to play all the time. It don't mean nothing.

GW1: Would you rather have activities for *you* all the time?

ARNELLE: Yeah. That was for them. There was nothing for us to do.

GW2: It must be hard to want to give these little guys something that you feel you didn't get, and wanted.

In another interchange, one of the group members, Keira, became angry with one of the workers. She withdrew, and the other worker talked to her. The discussion led to Keira's revealing how she typically expresses anger with someone—violently: "I beat them up real bad." Once Keira realized that physical force wasn't an alternative in this situation, the worker suggested that "in this relationship, talking might help." With that suggestion Keira became visibly alarmed—"*Relationship*?!? This ain't no *relationship*! I ain't *that way* ya know. I got a baby and everything!" Recognizing that Keira interpreted "relationship" to mean "sexual relationship" the worker reframed, "There are many different kinds of relationships. You can have very strong and loving relationships with women as well as men. It doesn't mean you are attracted to each other sexually."

Group work programs have proven successful for helping pregnant teens and teenage parents. This includes programs supporting fathers in the prenatal care of their infants (Barth, Claycomb, & Loomis, 1988) and helping teenage mothers to develop the interpersonal skills necessary to effectively negotiate the various systems—parents, family, peers—impacting on their lives through role playing in a cognitive–behavioral training program (Barth & Schinke, 1984).

STRUCTURED GROUP APPROACHES

Games: The Teams–Game–Tournament Approach

Social learning theory posits that if a behavior is learned in the context of a group it is more likely to be generalized to a broader variety of interactional contexts. The Teams–Game–Tounament (TGT) approach is small-group teaching approach, based on social learning theory, which consists of a detailed curriculum on adolescent sexuality. The use of this group-learning format rests on the following key points (Wodarski & Wodarski, 1995).

- In adolescence, high-risk behaviors often occur in group settings.
- Knowledge acquired in the group setting is more likely to be used when in similar peer-group settings, as compared to knowledge acquired through individual, separate means.
- The group method allows for a broader range of learning experience (i.e., students have the opportunity to learn while interacting with peers in a friendly exciting game).

Group work is an integral part of implementing such a curriculum when students: (1) understand that they share a common purpose/goals of gaining basic knowledge and skills about adolescent sexuality and developing positive peer relationships and (2) recognize that the learning process involves helping one another to learn the knowledge and skills as opposed to being fed information.

Small groups of students of varying strengths are teamed together, preceding the educational games and tournaments to follow. The TGT curriculum is divided into six weekly sections:

Week 1. Sexual Identity: Being a Girl/Boy. Who Am I?
Week 2. Dating: Parent and Peer Relationships
Week 3. The Biological Me
Week 4. Conception, Pregnancy, and Childbirth
Week 5. Teenage Pregnancy
Week 6. Sexually Transmitted Diseases

An accompanying and complementary six-section curriculum for parents is included to address their special needs.

Learning takes place primarily through a game/tournament format in which the teams of students prepare and compete against one another in small groups. Although the curriculum is very precisely designed it includes only about 80% of the structure (J. Wodarski, personal communication,

1995). There is room for the creative use of program to enhance what the curriculum offers. For example, one homework assignment involved carrying around a 10-pound bag of bricks for a week. The instructions were: You cannot get rid of the bag. This helped to simulate one feature of being pregnant, eliciting feelings associated with physical and emotional changes and demands. Guest speakers are also invited to the program. One especially powerful guest speaker was a 15-year-old mom who had been actively alcoholic during her pregnancy. She described what it meant to have a baby born with fetal alcohol syndrome.

By probing the belief systems of the participants and identifying informational needs in a stimulating manner, the game format is structured to promote more responsible sexuality and improved decision making. Assessment measures can be used to evaluate the curriculum including the following tests: Sex Knowledge Test, Attitudes and Values Inventory, and Instructional Evaluation for Students (Kirby, 1984). The last enables the participant students to evaluate the experience from a variety of perspectives including how the course affected their (1) knowledge, (2) understanding of personal behavior, (3) clarity of values, (4) attitude toward birth control, (5) communication about sexuality, (6) communication with parents, and (7) probability of having sex.

Pregnancy Prevention (and More) through a Socioeducational Model

Another socioeducational model (Moyse-Steinberg, 1990) uses the following value base as a guideline:

- Being a teen parent is not a good idea; it brings with it social, emotional, educational, and medical problems.
- No one should be pressured into a sexual act against his/her will or against his/her principles.
- The double standard for males and females, which still exists in our society, is not to be condoned.
- Postponement of sexual intercourse should be encouraged until after high school or until marriage.
- If a couple decides to have sexual intercourse, there should be no sex without birth control.

Underpinning these values is the social work value of self-determination, allowing room for expression by those group members who might differ with the philosophical base laid out above. Groups are organized by age and emotional maturity and may be single-sex or coed. The purpose of these groups is to help teenagers prevent unintended pregnancy by mastering decision-making skills. The standard curriculum includes the following content: (1) reproductive anatomy and physiology; (2) family planning and birth control; (3) sex roles; (3) relationships; and (4) sexually transmitted diseases. The program is flexible enough to allow for a wider range of discussion topics including virginity, double standards, orgasm, masturbation, homosexuality, pornography, self-image, and others.

Abstinence is promoted; however, sexually active teens are not excluded or ostracized. Three interrelated components, education—values clarification—practice, are used to reach the group purpose. The program includes discussion and giving and receiving information, all within a democratic context. Long-held attitudes and feelings blocking the acquisition of new knowledge can be explored by examining myths such as the girl who believes that menstruation is evil, adversely affecting her self-image and ability to care for herself physically and emotionally, or the boy who believes that "the gap between a woman's upper thighs represents a loss of virginity will assume that he can make judgments of others by the way they look until he is confronted with evidence to the contrary which makes sense to him. In the group, members can dispel myths for one another, since they never share all the same myths" (Moyse-Steinberg, 1990, p. 63).

In addition to learning new information and challenging myths, the program enables group members to identify values and to probe them in some depth to determine whether they are consonant with the way they live their lives. For example, "the member who professes to value loyalty but in fact tolerates infidelity is challenged on the contradiction but supported in the feelings of being without a boyfriend, of being alone on a Saturday night" (Moyse-Steinberg, 1990, p. 66).

The practice component of the model provides group members with opportunities to role play various scenarios (e.g., being pressured to have sex on a date) and to complete homework assignments (e.g., visiting local resource centers with information and services about reproductive health care). This, the doing component, enables the group members to gain experience with threatening and or unfamiliar situations, what it feels like to confront them, and what it takes to move from thought to action. Together the components of education, values clarification, and practice, provided in a group work context, support the participants' problem-solving and decision-making capacities. A 3-year study revealed that the program had a significant impact on promoting responsible sexual behavior.

CONCLUSION

Inclusion of the theme of adolescent sexuality is a critical component of any group that is structured to invite the whole person. As the illustrations in this chapter suggest, there are many variations on this theme. In dealing with a typically taboo subject, there are likely to be barriers—intrapsychic, interpersonal, and systemic—for both member and worker in moving ahead freely in this domain. The group can become a place where conversation and program around taboo areas are permitted, providing young people with a new frame of reference to thoughtfully consider these issues and to shape their behavior in a physically and emotionally safe and healthy way.

CHAPTER 13

Group Work as a
Counterforce to Alcohol
and Other Drug Abuse

The problematic use of alcohol, drugs, and tobacco is unquestionably the nation's number one health problem. While all segments of society are affected, the future of young people is most severely compromised by this epidemic. A recent study by Brandeis University's Institute for Health Policy (1993) revealed the following use rates for eighth graders: alcohol (70%), tobacco (44%), marijuana (10%), and cocaine (2%). For twelfth graders, use rates were alcohol (88%), tobacco (63%), marijuana (37%), and cocaine (8%).

Beyond use rates for youth are the staggering findings of the National Council on Alcoholism (Hosang, 1991): There are 28 million children of alcohol- and drug-abusing parents, or 1 in every 4 children. The council has estimated that 50% of children who grow up in these homes are likely to become alcohol or drug abusers themselves without intervention.

The pervasiveness of the problem extends well beyond the individual. Alcohol and drug abuse play a major role in "destroying families, crippling U.S. businesses, terrorizing entire neighborhoods, and choking the educational, criminal justice, and social service systems" (Brandeis University, 1993, summary p. 1). As practitioners committed to youth and the families and communities in which they live, we cannot escape the need to address the problems of alcohol and drug abuse regardless of the setting of our work. Where there are people, there is alcohol and drug abuse. Where there are youth, there are youth-at-risk. The purpose of this chapter is to highlight group work as a protective factor, a powerful preventive tool for

This chapter represents a modified, updated, and integrated version of Malekoff (1994a) and Malekoff (1997a). Adapted by permission of the National Association of Social Workers and the Oxford University Press..

youth who show early signs of alcohol and other drug abuse and who are at risk for alcoholism and drug addiction.

RISK AND PROTECTIVE FACTORS

What differentiates people with negative outcomes from those who grow up in similar circumstances and bounce back from great adversity? This question has stimulated much speculation and a dramatic growth of literature on vulnerability, resiliency and risk, and protective factors (Garmezy, 1991, 1983; Werner, 1990, 1989; Werner & Smith, 1992; Schorr, 1989; Rutter, 1979; Sameroff, 1988; Anthony et al., 1978; see Chapter 1).

What differentiates youth who become alcohol and drug abusers from their contemporaries from similar backgrounds who do not? This question points to the special concern of those interested in understanding the relationship between risk-reduction strategies and substance abuse prevention (Vega, Zimmerman, Warheit, Apospori, & Gil, 1993; Hawkins, Catalano, & Miller, 1992; Benard, 1991; Werner, 1986).

Risk factors may be driven by constitutional (i.e., physiological) and/or contextual realities (i.e., the physical, cultural, social, political, and economic environment) in the individual's life. Examples of risk factors for youth include: has a history of alcohol and drug abuse/addiction in the family; lives in a disorganized neighborhood; is a victim of child abuse; has become pregnant; has a chronic history of school failure; is economically disadvantaged; has attempted suicide; associates with drug-abusing peers (see Table 1.1 in Chapter 1).

Protective factors are the individual's constitutional assets (i.e., intelligence, temperament) and family and environmental supports (i.e., a close life-long bond with an adult relative or mentor) that have the potential to mitigate against risk. The importance of bonding has been emphasized as a key protective factor: "Antidrug attitudes are strengthened by promoting adolescents' bonds, including relationships with non-drug users, commitment to the various social groups in which they are involved (families, schools, community, prosocial peer groups), and values and beliefs regarding what is healthy and ethical behavior" (Hawkins, Catalano, & Associates, 1992).

Some of the settings in which group approaches have been used to address and study the preventive needs of youth at risk include: the school (Brown, 1993; Bilides, 1992; Hansen, 1992; Kantor et al., 1992; Shields, 1985/1986); the public housing development (Schinke, Orlandi, & Cole, 1992); the community mental health center (Malekoff, 1994a; Walthrust 1992); and the criminal justice system (Friedman & Utada, 1992; Smith, 1985). Comprehensive approaches have been described by Hawkins,

Catalano, and Associates (1992) and Felner, Silverman, and Adix (1991). Beyond the physical setting of the service is the cultural context of substance abuse (Vega et al., 1993; Wallace, 1993; De La Rosa & Adrados, 1993; Catalano et al., 1992; Bachman, Wallace, Kurth, Johnston, & O'Malley, 1991; Bilides, 1990); and the family context (Gross & McCane, 1992; Knight, Vail-Smith, & Barnes, 1992; Treadway, 1989; Emshoff, 1989; Efron, 1987; Deckman & Downs, 1982; Black, 1970).

A protective network of supports has the potential to increase the individual's resistance to risk, placing him/her in a better position to avoid and/or overcome alcohol and other drug problems. Group work can be an important part of constructing such a network.

PRACTICE PRINCIPLES AND COMMON THEMES FOR GROUP WORK PRACTICE

The following are practice principles and common themes to use when addressing the issues of alcohol and other drug abuse in groups.

Practice Principles

• *Alliance formation with parents and other involved systems is a prerequisite to establishing an engaged group membership.* Adolescents cannot be seen in a vacuum. Sanction from parents and cooperation with related systems (e.g., school) are necessary for ongoing work with adolescents. By establishing working alliances with these "significant others," the practitioner models collaboration and establishes the groundwork for mediating with the various systems. Working relationships with parents help to reduce the guilt that children often feel about betraying the family. By establishing working relationships with all involved systems, the possibility of dysfunctional interactions being replicated in the helping system itself is reduced (see Chapter 6). "Prevention programs seem to work best when they address the total life of the young person and focus on the factors that place him or her at risk" (Dryfoos, 1993, p. 3). In this era of categorical funding for human services, it is not always a simple task to provide comprehensive services. Therefore, collaboration among the various systems that serve youth is essential.

• *An appreciation for paradox and an ability to differentiate the words from the music is essential to working with adolescents in groups* (Malekoff, 1994e). Just beyond the surface of the strident facade or apathetic veneer that many adolescents project are the deeper meanings that not many adults are privileged to discover. Oftentimes the familiar refrain of "Leave me alone!" carefully conceals the cry for help. It's not always easy to hang around to hear the music underneath the static of the words. Yet to work with adolescents one must hang in there. Too many an adult has already bailed out.

• *Cultural awareness and sensitivity are essential for practicing social work with groups in a society of ever increasing diversity.* Social workers must be aware of racism, sexism, and homophobia as well as other cultural issues and values and how they impact on group members and how they have affected their own lives. Bilides (1990) suggests some guidelines for moving one's multicultural awareness into practice with groups. These include the following: " . . . discuss stereotypes at all levels (personal, familial and societal) . . . point out commonalties . . . explore the meanings of words and language . . . recognize and acknowledge your own discomfort about race, color, ethnicity, and class issues" (pp. 51–56) (see Chapter 10).

• *Use of self and access to childhood memories are important.* Awareness of what the group experience evokes in oneself is invaluable, especially with a population in motion. This includes conscious memories of the social worker's earlier years and struggles during adolescence (e.g., personal and/or familial experiences with alcohol and drugs). The worker's feelings that inevitably bubble up in the lively context of the adolescent group must not be ignored. Feelings and experiences can be disclosed at times, however only with good judgment. For example, the purpose of disclosure should never be to gain the acceptance of the group or to tacitly encourage acting-out behavior for a vicarious thrill. This is where good supervision enters the picture.

• *Don't go it alone.* Social workers working with at-risk adolescents in groups need support from colleagues. Too many an adult (professional or not) looks awry at the group modality when adolescents are involved. They question the efficacy of the work when confronted with the noise, action, and attitude that seem absent in the adult talking-group. Colleagues with a track record and an inclination to work with youth can be invaluable partners. Such partnership might include good supervision, peer or otherwise, and opportunities for teamwork (e.g., when one practitioner works with the adolescent in a group and another sees the parent[s] in some other context). Coleadership of groups is an approach that must be very carefully considered. Adequate time for planning and reflection must be set aside. Too many human services workers, without adequate group work training, operate under the false assumption that more is better, easier, or less stressful. Maybe. It depends entirely on the match, commitment and honesty that develops in the partnership. Simply throwing people together to run groups is to be avoided at all costs. As suggested above, having a partner(s) outside of the group is some insurance against the pitfalls of going it alone and a viable alternative to coleadership within the group itself. Work with children and adolescents requires involvement with other helping people and systems.

Common Themes

Groups may be formed specifically for children living in families with a present or past history of alcohol or other drug abuse. Other groups may be composed of youth who evidence a variety of related risk factors. Substance abuse prevalence rates (and practice experience) suggest that in either case the social worker must have knowledge of the impact of alcohol and drug abuse (including alcoholism and addiction) on the individual in the family.

What are the implications of growing up in a dysfunctional family system? How might this impact on the individual in the group? How might it affect the group as a whole? (Although the attention here is to substance abuse, these questions may also apply to families in which there is child abuse, domestic violence, or severe mental illness). The following six themes will address these questions.

• *Children who grow up in families with alcohol and drug abuse/addiction learn to distrust to survive.* Attention to the beginning phase of group development is critical in building trust. By using anticipatory empathy to tune in to the group, the practitioner takes an important step in helping to create a safe environment for mutual exchange. The social worker's focus in the beginning is to allow and support distance, search for the common ground, invite trust gently, establish group purpose, facilitate exploration, begin to set norms, and provide program structure (Garland et al., 1973; Malekoff, 1984). Beyond a good beginning in the group, the theme of trust/distrust must never be too far from the practitioner's consciousness in working with adolescents from families with a past or present history of alcohol and/or other drug abuse. When unpredictability has dominated an individual's life, he/she is likely to be wary, always sensing disappointment lurking nearby.

• *Children growing up in alcohol or drug abusing/addicted families become uncomfortably accustomed to living with chaos, uncertainty, unpredictability, and inconsistency.* Children growing up under these conditions have to "guess at what normal is." The group experience must provide a clear structure with norms and reasonable limits. Issues of membership (i.e., is it an open or closed group?; if open, how do new members enter?; how do members exit?); space (i.e., is there a consistent meeting place?); and time (i.e., does the group meet at a regular time for a prescribed period?) are all important considerations. Group rituals might be considered to reinforce a sense of order, establish value-based traditions, and promote bonding. For example, in one group a "drug-free pledge" was recited at the beginning and ending of each meeting. Because people tend to learn incrementally, one step at a time, real stability in the group develops gradually and not only as the result of an externally imposed structure, no matter how thoughtfully conceived and humane. The practitioner must be prepared for the unexpected, including the likelihood that group members will reenact aspects of their lives outside of the group, in the here-and-now group itself. When the result is unpredictable and chaotic behavior, it creates a live opportunity for exploration and establishing order and consistency in the group. (Redl & Wineman, 1952, referred to this as the "clinical exploitation of life events.")

• *Denial, secrecy, embarrassment, and shame are common experiences of children who live in alcoholic or addicted families.* Joining a group of "outsiders" might in itself be experienced as an act of betrayal, a step toward revealing the "family secret." The worker's awareness of members' pain allows him/her to gently invite trust, paying careful attention to the group members' bruises (emotional and otherwise), and to concerns about trust and confidentiality throughout the life of the group.

• *Growing up with the ever present threat of violence (verbal and physical) contributes to a pervasive sense of fearfulness, hypervigilance, and despair.* The group must become a place where differences are safely expressed and conflicts need not be a matter of life and death. Conflicts can be resolved and differences respected in a thoughtful and increasingly mature manner in the group. The group is a place where members can practice putting a reflective pause between impulse and action and where despair can be transformed into hope.

• *Children who grow up in alcohol- and drug-abusing/addicted family systems become rigidly attached to roles.* Many of those growing up in alcohol- and drug-abusing/addicted systems construct a wall of defenses and repressed feelings by adopting rigid family roles (Wegscheider, 1981). Accompanying these roles are stultifying family rules and unspoken mandates, such as "Don't talk, don't trust, don't feel." A group experience can provide members accustomed to enacting rigid roles with an opportunity for practicing role flexibility, broadening their intrapsychic range and interactive repertoire, and gaining competence in coping with the environment.

• *Growing up in an alcoholic and addicted family system leaves youths with little hope that things will ever change.* The group is a social system that assumes a life of its own, marked by an evolving culture, a history of events, and a developing set of relationships. As in any human relationships, there are decisions to be made, problems to solve, and crises to surmount. If a dysfunctional family system is the only frame of reference for a young person, he/she may have little experience in successfully resolving conflicts or overcoming obstacles. The group can provide members with a growing sense of confidence that difficult and frustrating circumstances can be overcome. The group worker must be tuned in to the sense of hopelessness that such members bring to the group so as not to get easily discouraged him- or herself. It cannot be emphasized enough that group work with this population requires hanging in for the long haul and modeling a sense of hope.

The following sections present two practice examples. The first illustrates an innovative prevention approach combining group work and action research. The second portrays a short-term multiple-family group. The setting for both examples is an outpatient chemical dependency treatment and prevention program for youth and their families.

PRACTICE ILLUSTRATIONS

Action Research: An Approach to Preventing Substance Abuse and Promoting Social Competency

"I have a friend. He drinks, smokes, and I found out that now he is taking drugs. I'm really worried. Sometimes he talks about suicide. I really don't know what to do."

Above are the written words of a 13-year-old, one of several hundred young people and adults who participated in an action research project addressing the problems of alcohol and drug abuse in a small suburban community (New Castel) in Nassau County, just east of New York City.

Action research is an approach combining various social work methods to raise community consciousness, stimulate intergroup and intergenerational interaction, and motivate people to work toward change both individually and collectively. The central theme of investigation was local youths' perceptions about drug and alcohol abuse in their own lives. A group of youths, in partnership with professionals, surveyed their contemporaries with a questionnaire of their own creation. The community meeting (referred to later as the intergroup conference) that followed was designed to stimulate the youths through reflection, dialogue, and planning for action. This practice illustration is divided into the following parts:

- A description of action research.
- A description of the local community.

- A description of the project itself (development of questionnaire, results of survey, structure and process of the intergroup conference, aftermath of the conference).

This approach implicitly incorporates aspects of traditional substance abuse prevention such as values clarification (Smith, 1973), affective education (Slimmon, 1975), positive peer influence (Vorrath & Brendtro, 1974), and social competence building (Bell, 1990). However, the method of involving the study target group in the investigative process was distinctive, enabling the youths to become teachers as well as students.

Action Research: Legacy of the Settlement Movement

Many social workers are drawn to specialized clinical fields organized around individual services. However, it was within the settlement movement that people were perceived as more than individuals, as "members of social groups and cultures affected by the social, economic and political conditions in which they lived" (Breton, 1990, p. 22). The pioneers in this movement saw people not merely as victims but as potential activists capable of bringing about change through collective, democratic involvement. One tool used for these purposes was the social survey, a forerunner of what is known today as action research. Combining research, community organizing, social work with groups, social action, and social policy formulation, action research is guided by the spirit of the settlement movement.

The action component and the direct involvement with the local community in the creation and implementation of research distinguish action research from more formal research (Malekoff, 1990). Rather than expanding knowledge for its own sake and maintaining value neutrality, action research attempts to expose social problems and effect changes (Wagner, 1991).

Much of what is written about action research is found in the community organization literature (Bilken, 1983; Chamberlain, 1987; Kahn, 1982; Neikrug, 1985; Rubin & Rubin, 1986). Some recent examples extend beyond this tradition (Children's Defense Fund, 1983; Malekoff, 1990; Malekoff, Johnson, & Klappersack, 1991; Wagner, 1991; Chesler, 1991; Sarri & Sarri, 1992a, 1992b; Donovan, Kurzman, & Rotman, 1993).

The action research described in this chapter represents an effort to mobilize youths and adults living in a rapidly changing, culturally pluralistic, low-income community to begin to confront the impact of drug and alcohol abuse in a context of mutual respect and support.

A Community on the Edge

As in most American suburbs, black people in Nassau County live in primarily segregated communities (Wilson, 1991). A local study found that 82% of Nassau County's black population resides in 10% of its census tracts (Smothers, 1986). In New Cassel, two-thirds of the population is black. The Hispanic population in New Cassel increased dramatically between 1980 and 1990. During this same period, the black population was held to a virtual standstill. The African American population decreased, and a growing number of black immigrants identified their origin as West Indian. With a steady increase in immigration, chiefly from Central America and Haiti, New Cassel is in the midst of a transitional crisis. New Cassel residents of all backgrounds reported being troubled about welfare dumping, blight, lax enforcement of building codes, increases in crime, and overcrowding of residents. The number one concern, however, according to a local study is an increase in the prevalence of illegal drug use (Government Subcommittee of the New Cassel Task Force, 1986) .

It had been the experience of the host agency, a community mental health center founded in 1953, that the leadership of New Cassel was factionalized. Various groups and individuals had historically battled over turf and special interests. This process intensified with the recent population shifts in the community, further reducing the probability of people collaborating on mutual concerns.

The project described here did not adhere to traditional protocol but attempted a new approach. The attempt was to bring people together in a new way that enabled them to engage in an exciting investigation based on reciprocity of action (Freire, 1982).

Action Research, Mutuality, and Prevention

Although the community is predominantly black, drugs are not a "black problem," as is often portrayed in the media. In 1988, studies by the Federal Bureau of Investigation and the National Institute on Drug Abuse concluded that "blacks make up only 12 percent of the nation's drug users and whites 80 percent" (Fresco & Peracchio, 1990, p. 37). Nevertheless, Bell (1991) suggested that "every issue on the black agenda today—employment, education, crime, housing, health care, teenage pregnancy—is affected in some way by substance abuse" (p. 1). Addressing these issues, which extend beyond the concern of the black community in New Cassel, requires prevention efforts that reach across the generations and cultures and that are designed to build social competency (Bell, 1990; Caetano, 1986).

Opportunities for socialization in groups are a profound developmental need and primary prevention strategy for children and adolescents (Middleman & Wood, 1990b). The action research process relies primarily on group involvement, not primarily as a developmental tool but as an avenue for joining the generations and people of different cultures in a search for common ground, mutual problem solving, and collective action.

In his discussion of "problem-solving education," Freire (1982) promoted the need for human beings to "become jointly responsible for a process in which they all grow" (p. 67). The essence is to bring people of different ages, genders, and origins into an arena of learning that stimulates true reflection, critical thinking, creativity, action, and most of all, humanization.

First Steps

From September 1990 to June 1991, several small groups of seventh- and eighth-grade students from two local schools met on a weekly basis with an outreach worker from the host agency. The groups, which met in the schools, had been previously formed by the outreach worker and were composed of Latino immigrants from Central America. The original purpose of the group meetings was to discuss issues related to immigration, acculturation, and coping with life in a new country and community. The youths in these groups were invited to participate in this action-oriented project. They enthusiastically agreed because there had been much prior discussion regarding the impact of alcohol and other drugs on their families and in their lives.

The purpose of the project, they were told, was to discuss their concerns about drug and alcohol abuse and then to generate questions to be refined into a questionnaire to be completed by local youths. A core group of the youths volunteered to refine the questionnaire, a process that also included the input of a small group of agency staff. The next step was for the two groups to identify a target group and make arrangements for the questionnaires to be completed, collated, and analyzed. The outreach worker served as liaison to both groups. Ultimately an all-day conference was organized, and the results were shared with the community for the first time at the conference.

The preceding summary of events is essentially the blueprint for an action research project, "a systematic gathering [and dissemination] of information by people who are both affected by a problem and want to resolve that problem" (Rubin & Rubin, 1986, p. 151).

Questionnaire

The group planned to distribute 450 questionnaires to seventh, eighth, and ninth graders from two schools. A random sample of these classes was selected. The outreach worker informed the school principals of the project as it was developing and received their cooperation in distributing the questionnaires.

A total of 235 students completed the questionnaires. Forty-eight percent (*n* = 215) were not completed because of a planning error. Several classes did not receive the questionnaires, and because it was the last week of school, a modified school-day schedule prevented redistribution of the remaining questionnaires.

The questionnaire included a combination of short-answer and Likert-scale items as well as two open-ended questions. The questionnaires were printed in English, Spanish, French, and Creole so that no student would be excluded. Of the 235 who responded, 42.7% described themselves as immigrants to the United States.

Results

The questionnaire was intended not solely as

> an instrument to inform but also as a tool to join the generations in dialogue and action. . . . The creation, implementation and analysis of the survey represent a preliminary event in the process of community engagement. The action-oriented research approach, sustained at the grass roots level, stimulates the process of raising community consciousness. . . . The survey results are not static conclusions to be passively mulled over, but a warm-up exercise purposefully intended to energize people at the collective and interactional level. (Malekoff, 1990)

The following are some of the results of the structured portion of the questionnaire:

- 26.0% (*n* = 61) reported having smoked cigarettes.
- 41.3% (*n* = 97) reported having used alcohol.
- 3.6% (*n* = 8) reported having used other drugs.
- 9.8% (*n* = 23) reported that others think they have a problem with alcohol.
- 20.9% (*n* = 49) reported that a friend has a problem with alcohol.
- 20.4% (*n* = 48) reported that a parent has a problem with alcohol.
- 71.1% (*n* = 162) reported that they tune in when their parents want to talk about alcohol or other drugs.
- 79.3% (*n* = 172) reported that they tune in when their teachers want to talk about alcohol or other drugs.
- 83.9% (*n* = 187) reported that they have someone who they can talk to about alcohol and other drugs.

- 64.6% (n = 152) reported an interest in joining a group to talk about alcohol and other drugs.
- Those who reported having a relative with an alcohol problem were more likely to have a friend with an alcohol problem.
- There appeared to be a correlational relationship between cigarette smoking and drug and alcohol use. A much greater percentage of those who smoked also used alcohol. All eight who reported having tried drugs had smoked.

Of the two open-ended questions, the first asked the respondents to advise their parents about how to help youths deal with drug and alcohol abuse. Responses included "Talk to me, be my friend," "Give me accurate information," "Don't have it in the house, and don't use it," "Punish me," "Hands off!", "Change the neighborhood," and "Understand me."

The second open-ended question asked the participants what they were deeply concerned about. Naturally, the single most referred-to topic was substance abuse. However, the youths also reflected their thoughts and feelings about AIDS, homelessness, violence, crime, hatred, racism, divorce, death, suicide, child abuse, teenage pregnancy, and abortion. What follows is a sample of responses organized by themes. The responses are reflective of many of the common themes identified earlier in the chapter. Particularly salient are the fearfulness, distrust, despair, lack of hope that things can change, uncertainty, and chaos that are expressed through these passages. There is also evidence of strength, as asserted through the youths' expressions of common sense, values, passion, and hopefulness. The age of each respondent is indicated after each quotation.

Drug and Alcohol Abuse

- "I hate what drugs are doing to the world; so many families have broken up. . . . I wish it could be stopped, but where would I begin." (age 14)
- "My mother just started smoking again. . . . She just got over an operation and the doctor thought she might have cancer . . . and now she starts smoking again." (age 12)
- "My uncle took drugs and hit my father. . . . It's not the first time. We called the cops. They never came. Then two days later my uncle comes and asks for help and forgiveness. My father forgives him. . . . Now he's in a rehab center." (age 13)
- "I have an uncle who parties and gets drunk. . . . then he drives home. . . . This makes me scared." (age 11)
- "Once my Stepmom got really drunk and my Granddad too. They were both really out of control and they almost started doing stuff together. I couldn't believe it." (age 13)

- "Lately I have drunk a lot of alcohol and get drunk quite often. I know alcohol can harm you, yet I drink it anyway. This troubles me very much." (age 14)
- "An old friend of mine was killed long ago because of drugs. Somebody shot him in the head." (age 14)
- "Why don't people in this country pass a law which would close the factories that manufacture alcohol and cigarettes?" (age 16)

Sex, AIDS, and Pregnancy

- "You never know who to trust. I mean a boy can just go with one thing on his mind. And act like he cares for you and then—bang, pow! He asks you, and you say you are not ready. He calls you every name in the book, then leaves you with nothing." (age 14)
- "Nowadays young people are doing it just to see how it feels, and I think that's the wrong reason to do it. . . . I think at our age we are responsible enough to have a relationship but not responsible enough to have a physical relationship." (age 15)
- "AIDS concerns me because I don't know who has it, and when I get to high school, I'm afraid if I start dating I might date someone who has AIDS." (age 13)
- "I know I'm too young for it but . . . me and my best friend made our plans for the future and the first thing we said is that we are going to have our first child at the age of 16 or 17." (age 13)

Self-Respect, Popularity, and Dignity

- "Why do girls want to be popular? I don't find nothing with wanting to be popular, but the thing is, to get to the top, some girls will do just about anything. Me, I let time tell if I'll be popular, but I'm not going to go around like dough that anyone who wants to touch can dig in. No, the day that I'll be popular will be when [I'm] best known as respected and serious . . . not needing to impress anyone. Because if anyone is going to count you, let them count you for what you really are, don't let anyone change you and [think] you've got a big rep. . . . Be number 1, not the last one on someone's list." (age 15)

Race, Ethnicity, and Bigotry

- "If everyone goes around being judgmental and picking on everyone's faults and looking at the color of skin . . . then how could we conquer our problems? People won't even gather together to discuss these problems. . . . How could we even unite and become one nation and have peace and understanding?" (age 15)

The Future

- "We should take actions in our own hands to build up the bonds that keep our community together." (age 13)

The results of the survey, including the open-ended responses, were prepared for inclusion in the intergroup conference booklet. In addition to the results, the booklet included a history of the project and resource information. Preliminary results were shared with the local media in the form of a press release, so that a still wider audience could be reached.

Intergroup Conference: An Exercise in Democratic Participation

The development and implementation of the intergroup conference is a critical feature of the action research project. During the conference the process of consciousness development moves from the information-gathering stage to awaken people to a sense of collective identity (Breton, 1991). Thoughtful and thorough preparation and planning for this conference, which relies heavily on group involvement, is crucial. To review, the elements to consider in planning are: agency and social context, need, purpose, composition, structure, content, and pregroup contact (refer to Chapter 4 for details on the planning model). Need had been assessed through the surveys and would be expanded in the conference; the purpose was to raise consciousness, stimulate intergroup interaction, and to motivate change; the composition was intergroup (intergenerational and cross-cultural); the structure was a time-limited, single day, and integrated large- and small-group format (Peck, 1983); the content included formal presentation and small group discussion; pregroup contact was through formal invitation; and the social and agency context involved sanction by the local schools and support from the host agency. What follows is a more detailed description of the process.

The conference was planned by project staff from the host agency. As the conference day drew near, additional staff from the agency were recruited to fulfill a variety of roles (clerical, set up, registration, audiovisual, small-group leaders). It became critical to involve more of the staff in the conference planning process because it was hoped they would feel a sense of ownership in the success of the project. (Remember, don't go it alone.)

The conference was held at the host agency's branch office located in the target community, which is known to most participants. The conference was structured in an all-day, large- and small-group format. All participants received formal invitations and were expected to respond. The planning committee and the agency's central administration decided which adults to invite. Involvement in local community affairs was the major criterion for the invitation of adults. The youths were selected by the planning committee and school personnel. The major criterion was that they represent a cross-section of the community. A few selected individuals from neighboring communities were invited as well. Approximately 35% ($n = 60$) of the adults and 85% ($n = 40$) of the youths who were invited attended.

Youth involvement represented the greatest hurdle in the intergroup conference planning. The logistics involved (transportation, formal permission) required a working alliance with key school personnel. Failure to "deliver" the youths would have dealt a serious blow to the success of the day. Youths required both parent and school permission to ensure ongoing collaboration with the system. All participants were asked to sign releases because the event was to be filmed. An edited videotape of the day was later used for ongoing education, prevention, and early intervention activities.

The adults who attended included parents, professionals, and community leaders, several of whom attended in dual roles. The youths in attendance represented roughly 40% of the 100 conference participants. Although the majority of attendees were residents of the local community, there were a handful of participants from neighboring communities who had heard about the project and asked to attend.

The atmosphere that was created enabled the participants to experience one another with a level of mutual respect that is usually lost in the more formal world of rigid roles and arbitrary status. One sign of a healthy family is appropriate role flexibility among the members. The conference represented an attempt to extend this concept to the community. Thus, the youths were able to inform, enlighten, empathize, and confront; the adults were able to listen, learn, and follow. Such an experience promises the best of democratic functioning, intergroup integrity, and mutual support.

Large Group

The large group provided participants with an anonymous and non-threatening structure in which to get "warmed up." Time was allotted for getting oriented to the physical space, participants, and program format. Following introductory remarks and brief formal presentations that summarized the project and the research findings, the audience, seated in auditorium-style rows, was invited to join the discussion. Within minutes, one young participant, a 13-year-old black youth who had been joking around just moments before, stood up and spoke. What he said moved the group to more intimate ground in an instant. He revealed that his friend, a sixth grader, had taken his own life just days before. There were groans of shock and disbelief and finally a spontaneous moment of silence that followed the young speaker's rhetorical conclusion: "He should've thought about it. He didn't realize how many people he has hurt."

Adults and youths responded. Another friend of the sixth grader, a 13-year-old girl, responded by charging, "He did tell a few of his friends, but nobody said anything about it." This was followed by a remark from one of the panelists, who were seated facing the crowd, revealing how hard it was for her at times, as a parent, to respond adequately to the pain of her own children:

> "Sometimes what people tell us is so powerful and so scary we just go like this [she covered her ears with both hands]. . . . If he's telling his friends, 'Look, this is it, I'm going to die,' what are they going to do at 11 and 12 years old? Once we communicate, then what? We all need to do much more work around supporting parents and children. I think it is an unfair burden for an 11-year-old to have to carry this secret and not know what to do."

Her use of self helped to deepen the discussion, stimulating other responses from adults in the room. A black businessman, a deacon in his local church, expressed his sorrow and validated the purpose of the project by reaffirming his commitment not only to the day but beyond the day. Finally, a social worker who helped to found a local bereavement network offered his services to the school and community.

This early interchange illustrates the beginning of the consciousness-raising process. People were "awakening to a sense of collective identity and solidarity" (Breton, 1991, p. 95). Beyond consciousness development directed to emotional catharsis (Staub-Bernasconi, 1991, p. 44), action research is designed to stimulate interaction and democratic participation and to motivate people to work toward change. The first instance of this occurred when the businessman and the bereavement worker were seen huddling during the lunch break. The bereavement worker revealed the content of their discussion—aid for suicide survivors—later that day.

All of this was stimulated by the moving disclosure of a 13-year-old, who took the risk to reveal the somber music behind his otherwise cheerful facade. In a dysfunctional context, where the numbing effects of secrecy, fearfulness, denial, and despair might rule the day, the powerful feelings evoked by such devastating news would not have had as safe and healthy an outlet. A supportive environment, reinforced by a carefully planned structure, allowed for this unanticipated and public expression of grief. Three generations of people, many strangers to one another and representing a variety of diverse cultures, modeled open communication in an unexpected situation. It was in this sense that the day began by reinforcing norms that asserted: it is okay to talk, it is okay to trust, and it is okay to feel in this group.

Small Group

The small group, a less anonymous setting, provided the participants with a greater opportunity for face-to-face sharing. The groups were all inter-generationally composed before the conference. Each group was led by an agency staff member. All of the leaders met before the conference for an orientation and brief training in time-limited group work. Bringing the culturally diverse program staff (African American, Haitian, Salvadoran, Chilean, Jewish, Irish, Italian, Cuban) together as a group before the conference was crucial. The staff's work during the conference day was an invaluable element of the experience, demonstrating the best of cultural pluralism in collaborative action.

The expectation of the staff was that most of the attending youth would be of the emotionally healthy variety, given that they were not drawn from the clinical population. However, that expectation was not met: Almost all of the nine group leaders later reported stories of addiction in the families of several of the youths.

One 12-year-old boy provided a detailed account of the warfare he experienced on a daily basis living in an alcoholic family. Although his description was graphic, his presentation was delivered with little emotion, highlighting the numbing effect of growing up in such an environment. His disclosure and that of others like him enabled the groups to learn more about the impact of addiction on the family, to discuss coping strategies, and to share resource information.

Many students talked about feeling unsafe in the schools, of the pervasiveness of drug and alcohol use, and of the tension between ethnic groups in school and on the streets of New Cassel. Most wondered if all of this talk would lead to any action, a sentiment shared by the adults.

Closing Group

Following a lively communal lunch hour featuring two 6-foot-long hero sandwiches, the day concluded with a large group meeting. The seating was transformed into two concentric circles. The first order of business was to hear from each of the small groups. Selected representatives reported on the major themes discussed. All attendees were respectful of the privacy of those who had chosen to reveal more intimate details during the small-group meetings.

Several of the groups chose an adult and a young person to report. One such combination was choreographed in a way that delighted the large group. After the adult reported, his younger partner "translated" in less-intellectual terms. The group was amused by this and laughed and applauded approvingly after each translation. This whole sequence highlighted the sense of intergenerational partnership that had been achieved, at least for the day.

Once the formal reports were completed there was open discussion. A Latino youth asked to address the group in Spanish. Despite the applause as he talked, it took almost 20 minutes for someone in the group, an educator, to ask the youth to translate. The group worker then asked the participants for a show of hands indicating how many did not understand what had been said in Spanish. With the majority of hands raised high, the worker asked why no one had asked for a translation sooner. This event led to a discussion of the rapidly changing face of the community and of the need to address the issues of cultural pluralism and intergroup conflict. This sequence emphasizes the importance of cultural awareness and sensitivity in group work.

Although the content issues of alcohol, tobacco, and other drug use were widely discussed during the closing segment, it was the kind of interactions described earlier and the challenge to think critically that demonstrated the preventive richness of the day.

Young and old alike had an opportunity to improve their social competency in a context that enabled them to experiment interactionally, across their reference groups, in a way that everyday experience did not afford. In an earlier action research project focused on the decaying physical and emotional environment we live in (Malekoff, 1990), the young people provided direct reassurance for the adults. They told them that it was okay to discuss scary and taboo issues with their children. As one 16-year-old girl declared:

> Parents (and other adults) have to try and make it known to their children, as early as they can, that it's okay to be afraid and unsure about things that you might be worried about; that it's all right to ask questions like, am I going to be all right?; are we going to be all right?; am I going to grow up?; am I going to live? (Malekoff, 1990, p. 65)

Beyond the preventive benefits of the intergroup conference itself was the unmistakable call for future action that echoed throughout the day.

Action

Although a few developments emerged as a result of the project during its early stages (an innovative drug education project in conjunction with the local high school, a support group of day-care providers concerned with drug abuse and its impact on young children, participation in the development of a local task force designed to address intergroup violence), some significant actions also grew out of the conference itself.

The conference was structured to move participants to the point of wanting to go further. For many of the adults, their formal roles enabled them to move to action naturally. For example, the bereavement counselor referred to earlier was called on by the school district to provide services for the school staff in the aftermath of the sixth grader's suicide. The edited videotape of the conference enabled agency staff to organize and lead various educational forums. However, the youth participants have a more ambiguous role in the community and often require support to move to action.

It was during the final group segment of the conference that several of the youths asked to return. Having anticipated this, agency staff took their names and followed up. Almost 1 year later, a stable core of 20 of these young people continued to meet in the same room in which they had initially met for the conference (there have been as many as 100 additional youngsters who have participated in events sponsored by this group). They call themselves the YOUTH OF CULTURE (Young, Original, Understanding, Truthful, Heritage, Open, Faithful, Caring, Useful, Loving, Trustworthy, Unique, Respectful, Educated) Drug-Free Club. They have chosen group colors and recite a drug-free pledge, which has become the opening and closing ritual of each meeting. Prevention activities, recreation, socialization, rap discussions, and community service represent some of the group activities. Two group workers work with the group, and other staff are available if necessary.

Conclusion

Early on, following several meetings in which they discussed the issues of violence, weapons in the schools, and racial tension in the community, the youths brought a friend to the meeting. After some global discussion about family problems, one of the members told the newcomer, "You can say anything here, you can tell them." With support from the others she proceeded to speak for the first time of a history of beatings by her Mom, whom she described as a cocaine user. This revelation opened the door for this young girl and her family to get the help they needed but were unable to get until that moment.

The group organized several drug- and alcohol-free parties/dances. They successfully organized 25 of their peers to participate in a multicultural march against violence following an interracial murder in the community (see Chapter 7). They have also organized an International Cultural Celebration. In its inaugural year more than 100 youths and adults attended this celebration of diversity (see Chapter 8). These are but a few examples of how this group has grown and touched the community. Whereas many of these examples represent some of the more formal developments, the individual applications and effects of this project, although less easily identifiable, are of equal or greater value.

Action research is an important bridge to an era of social work practice that has been down, but never quite out. A distinctive aspect of the ideas of the group work pioneers (Jane Addams, Mary Parker Follett, Grace Coyle, and others) was their shared concern for the development of a democratic society through "the role of groups and voluntary associations in a pluralistic society" (Shapiro, 1991, p. 9). Their vision included active participation, negotiated contributions, and mutual agreement among participants (Lewis, 1991) with a dual focus on social needs and individual growth (Garvin, 1991).

This case illustration describes an attempt to live up to the tradition of the settlement movement. Readers are encouraged to apply and adapt this model in their own unique way to awaken people, challenge them to think critically, and motivate them to work toward change.

Multiple-Family Group Work to Address Alcohol and Other Drug Abuse

As mentioned earlier, the setting for the second practice illustration is the same as the first. The services of the agency, the Tri-County Chemical Dependency Center for Youth (to be referred to as The Center), include an intensive after-school program comprised of a comprehensive blend of group, family, and individually oriented activities. The group program includes services for adults; children and adolescents; alcoholics and drug addicted people; nonaddicted substance abusers; and at-risk-non-substance-abusing significant other family members (youths and adults).

Some adolescents at The Center are seen as referred clients who are admitted to the program following a formal clinical evaluation. Others are seen in a variety of after-school programs that do not require a formal clinical evaluation. There are also special outreach, advocacy, and group services for Hispanic and Haitian immigrant youth and their families. Many adolescents are participants in both programs, as clients and as community members. Schorr (1989) points out that "most successful programs find that interventions cannot be routinized or applied uniformly. Staff members and program structures are fundamentally *flexible* and *see the child in the context of family and the family in the context of its surroundings*" (p. 257; emphasis in original).

Groups at The Center vary in composition, length, and purpose.

Content may include education, socialization, discussion, counseling, therapy, outings, arts and crafts, cultural awareness activities, and/or community service. Staff work as partners in teams. This enables program participants to become engaged with the agency as well as to an individual practitioner. Regularly scheduled team meetings are held for the purposes of case assignment and management, program development, supervision, skill development, and collegial support.

Family involvement is an important value at The Center. All incoming families with adolescents are assigned to an 8-week, multiple-family group program. This program is designed to help families with drug and alcohol problems to decrease isolation, learn from one another, and address the shame that children carry as a secret. The content includes a combination of alcohol and drug education, discussion, role play, and psychodrama. The first two meetings are structured to allow an opportunity for the adults and youth to meet for a brief time in separate groups to identify needs and make connections. The groups are coled by two or three social workers.

The Multiple-Family Group

The fifth session of one multiple-family group series began with a staff presentation of normal development in the latency and adolescent eras and its relationship to the family life cycle. Pychoeducation on "normal development" is of great value for the family whose members have grown accustomed to uncertainty and guessing at what normal is. In the group, this process serves to provide support, encourage dialogue, and reduce isolation. When the theme of "separation" was presented, one of the group members, a Hispanic mother, who understands and speaks English but prefers Spanish, addressed the bilingual worker in her native tongue, "If I may," she begins, "I want to respond to something that the other worker said about separation. In my country [Colombia, South America], it is different. The kids are expected to stay with their families until they marry. If they go to college they stay home. This discussion is a problem for us (*motioning to her husband, a practicing alcoholic*). It is upsetting that the children are encouraged to leave."

Once translated, a lively discussion ensued in this group of four families of various cultural origins (Colombian, African, Yugoslavian, and Italian). They exchanged their beliefs and feelings about separation, which varied from one culture to another. The worker's role was to promote cultural awareness and sensitivity by encouraging group members to share their views. "In rural agrarian societies—the closeness of family members and the individual's sense of being part of a larger whole have always been crucial to the community's survival," for example. In contrast, "In contemporary affluent American society, individualism, achievement, and mobility are generally regarded as the hallmarks of effectively reared offspring" (McConville, 1995, p. 21).

At one point, the Hispanic mother's 17-year-old son, Hector, who was referred to The Center following a single incident of binge drinking, spoke: "I didn't know this." Hector speaks in short, choppy sentences and is encouraged to elaborate. "Well, now that I know [what my mother thinks] I'll think about looking into colleges close to home, but I'm not staying home until I get married." Everyone laughed including Hector's parents. One of the group workers summed up, turning to Hector, "It sounds like you're willing to negotiate with your parents." He acknowledged her comment with a smile.

In this interchange the group is warming up to the meeting, testing the waters, and reestablishing trust. An emotionally charged issue surfaces. Differences along cultural and generational lines are drawn. Four different cultural groups (one bilingual), four sets of parents (and one grandparent), and four sets of adolescents, and no dire consequences.

All of the adolescents have abused alcohol and or have tried other drugs on at least one occasion. In all four families, the fathers, only one of whom is present, are alcoholic or drug addicted. As is often the case, the adolescents and their presenting problems provide the ticket to getting help. As the session proceeds, separation issues give way to issues of limits, boundaries, and private space. The adolescents and parents begin to draw battle lines as parents reveal their suspicions.

> The group discussion is now heated as the adolescents refer to their parents as "nuts," "stupid," "crazy," and "ridiculous." A 14-year-old girl, Lisa, who verbally assaulted her mother last week takes the offensive again. When one of the group workers reminds her of the rule of not attacking and allowing others to finish speaking, Lisa smiles and says, "OK, OK." The group worker then asks what a parent should do if she suspects that her child is using drugs? The parents discuss various strategies including under what circumstances they would search their children's rooms. Lisa's mother then reveals, somewhat defensively, "People don't know what they would do until it really affects them. I never thought I'd be going through my daughter's room but I had a feeling and it was right. It was a good thing I followed my instinct because now I can get help." Then for the first time in five meetings, the Hispanic mother spoke in English and directly to Lisa's mother. She exclaimed, "You did right! You did the right thing and I would too, to help my child." This is a moving moment, in which a mother who is struggling with an aggressive

14-year-old who abuses her in the group setting, is supported by others in the presence of her daughter.

At the same time she is receiving support, her daughter is encouraged to respect the norms of the group by not attacking and by waiting her turn to speak. This provides her with an opportunity to respond differently, to put a reflective pause between impulse and action. Lisa listens intently. Returning to Spanish, the Hispanic mother makes a passionate request of the worker, "Please tell her if she didn't love her daughter she wouldn't have done this. It is an act of caring, and her daughter is so aggressive . . . " Once translated, Lisa asks, "What's aggressive mean?" It is described as "hostile."

By this time the group is becoming very intense as the adolescents are beginning to bond in anger against the parents. Growing up with the ever present threat of violence (verbal and physical) contributes to a pervasive sense of fearfulness, hypervigilance, and despair. However, the group can become a place where differences can be safely expressed and conflicts need not lead to disastrous consequences.

As angry glances are exchanged across the generational dividing line, one of the group workers acknowledges the feelings and suggests an activity to promote empathy. Addressing Lisa, yet speaking to the group, she explains what a role reversal is and that "I find it helpful to try this when parents and children are in conflict." She then asks Lisa, providing an opportunity for her to move out of her rigid role and to empathize, to "put yourself in your mother's shoes. If you thought your child was in danger, that she might have weapons or drugs in her room, would you search it?" She becomes pensive and is clearly thinking deeply about this, as are the others judging from their facial expressions and body language. She finally responds, "Yes, I think I would." It is with this reflection, as the others soak in her response, that the group moves to an ending. Another group worker, reenforcing the structure, concludes with a brief restating of the rules regarding confidentiality and that there are to be no consequences for what is shared in the group. Lisa seems more relieved than offended by the labeling of her behavior as aggressive and hostile. A limit was being set that, paradoxically, she had been seeking all along. A sense of hope that things can change seemed to have been sparked in the group.

In this illustration, family members of all generations moved closer to the realization that conflicts can be resolved and differences respected in a thoughtful and increasingly mature manner.

CONCLUSION

In multiple-family groups that focus on concerns about alcohol and other drug abuse, attention to building trust over time and in each session is essential. Remember, for many of these families distrust has become the norm. In families where denial, secrecy and shame are familiar dynamics, processes of openly communicating feelings must be introduced with great care and sensitivity. One consequence of growing up in such an environment is that individuals have little or no practice with the skills of identifying and labeling feelings. Multiple-family groups can provide family members of all generations with an opportunity to enhance their competence by practicing these skills in a physically and emotionally safe environment.

CHAPTER 14

Loneliness, Social
Isolation, Scapegoating,
and Group Work
The Adolescent's Struggle to Fit In

The concluding chapter of Group Work with Adolescents is organized
around two practice illustrations, poetry, and an essay by a 16-year-old
refugee, each addressing variations on the themes of difference, loneliness,
and social isolation. Issues of chronic mental illness, scapegoating, and
immigration are provided to demonstrate the potential of the isolated
member and the group to reach out to one another despite differences and
to find acceptance and belonging.

LONELINESS, SOCIAL ISOLATION, AND GROUP WORK

Loneliness has been described as a longing and discomfort about one's sense
of being and one's apartness from places, states of life, or communion with
others (Garland, 1981). "In loneliness some compelling, essential aspect of
life is suddenly challenged, threatened, altered, denied" (Moustakas, 1951,
p. 21). The following propositions are offered to normalize the practitioner's understanding of loneliness (Garland, 1981).

- Loneliness is universal in human life.
- Its appearance varies from person to person.
- It appears and reappears in various forms throughout the life cycle
  and can produce growth.
- It occurs along with tendencies toward affiliation in all human groups.
- Group workers must exercise caution in hasty or excessive promo-
  tion of either side of this relational coin.

Three interrelated factors contributing to loneliness in adolescence are (Brennan, 1982):

- *Developmental changes*: that is, separation from parents, cognitive development, physical/sexual/emotional maturation, changing self-concept.
- *Social/structural factors*: that is, inadequate and marginal social roles, excessive expectations, unrealistic norms, social comparisons within adolescent culture, changing family structures, poor parent–child relations, limited opportunity to make use of their talents.
- *Personal traits*: that is, low self-esteem, powerlessness, apathy, aimlessness, poor social skills.

The impact and intensity of these factors is likely to be greater for the adolescent who is perceived as different—not non-conformist-acceptable-different, but strange-as-if-contagious-different (e.g., youths with emotional disorders, physical disabilities, medical problems, and/or other hard-for-others-to-accept differences). Social isolation may then follow as a result of hostile or fearful avoidance by others, or rejection of the overtures of others toward him/her.

If this process can be changed through the group experience, then there is "the hope, viewed by some as a distinct possibility, that once social withdrawal is reversed, important emotional changes will follow. The child may then escape from those circular behavioral patterns in which he/she is regularly the subject of a self-fulfilling prophecy of social alienation or the object of social attack" (Kolodny, 1992, p. 159). Perhaps such was the case for one such youngster, Matt, at least as he was remembered years later by a former fellow group member.

PRACTICE ILLUSTRATION 1:
DIFFERENCE, ACCEPTANCE, AND BELONGING[1]

> I don't think you can put him into a group
> with these other kids. He's crazy.
> —*A colleague*

Matt was different from the others. It wasn't as if each of them weren't unique, but he truly was different. He had a working understanding of the

---

[1]This practice illustration was originally published in Malekoff (1991c). Reprinted by permission of The Haworth Press, Inc.

stock market. His investments were modest but successful. He held three paper routes. None of his customers complained about missing their daily paper, although Matt did have some trouble keeping up with the collections. He liked to earn money and hoped to be wealthy one day. He had big dreams. Matt also laughed a lot. He often laughed for no apparent reason. Some years after the boys' group had disbanded, Tommy recalled the old days. He was completing a period of individual treatment, and in the final months he reminisced mostly about the old group. His memories and perceptions about getting to know Matt were especially poignant.

First Impression

Matt became a group member at age 15 after reportedly having had individual counseling and neuroleptic pharmacotherapy on and off since age 6. At first meeting, in a pregroup interview with his parents, Matt appeared as a moderately obese, almost electively mute, and extremely guarded adolescent, who maintained a steady rocking motion, punctuated by giggling, as he sat. Periodically his "far out" look was transformed into a fit of laughter as he arrived at some unknown destination. Inquiring about the source of hilarity didn't get very far, until it was suggested that he try to control himself or share what was so funny. The worker (the author) told him that if he were to join the group he would, in all likelihood, have to do one or the other. He finally opted for the latter and said, in detached staccato, "I'm thinking about having sex with animals." And his laughter grew. As Tommy remembered him: "He would startle you. Some the things he'd say were shocking—they'd jolt you. But it was funny too. But it might hurt him to laugh at him. For him, it's serious; for us it's funny. I guess that's not so nice the way it sounds. It's like someone tells you their mother died, and you start laughing."

After a few moments of deafening silence, the worker, frozen by the incongruity of the scene and trying to maintain his composure, glanced over to Matt's parents who sat expressionless, reminding him of the rural couple depicted in the painter Grant Wood's "American Gothic." Matt's mother then broke the ice by saying that he was like this much of the time at home (and reportedly in school), especially during the past year, spending time by himself in his room, laughing.

Common Ground

Beyond his lack of peer affiliation, the decision to try Matt in the group was based upon the worker's confidence in the other members' profound understanding of life at the margin, as well as their great capacity for accepting difference (a capacity that far outdistanced the worker's own at their age). As one group member put it, "It was a good thing for everyone in the group. It gave us a chance to learn how to deal with someone different than what is usually around us. He was different from most people we meet."

All but one of the boys had no steady peer relationship outside of those in highly structured, nonintimate settings. Each of them were described as "socially isolated" and all, to a greater or lesser degree, had experienced being scapegoated. Four of the boys were placed either in school settings outside of their home district or outside of the so called "mainstream" classes within their district. Two members had experienced a series of devastating early losses. Despite the tremendous obstacles facing these boys, including the poverty of meaningful peer relations, none of them could be considered "schizoid." All were interested in making friends and all clearly demonstrated the capacity to derive pleasure from peer interactions. What they did share in common was an uncanny sensitivity to empathize with the "underdog."

"It wasn't difficult having him in the group," said Tommy. "Everyone has problems. You had to contain him—no, help him to stop laughing. We had to help him, but we had to help each other too. Some people's problems are more noticeable. We had to help him to fit in better in the world."

The others reacted at first with astonishment, and then with anxious giggling, and a touch of curiosity at the strange creations produced by Matt's imagination. In time they were able to confront Matt's laughter and to demand that he make an effort to control himself. In the words of one member, "Did we help him? Not entirely, but a little bit. He did control himself a little bit better. Sometimes it seemed we were hard on him. Maybe we were just being firm. Maybe that is what he needed."

Each of the five boys then in the group made personal associations with what one of them referred to as Matt's "silliness," and they recalled their own immature beginnings in the group. By using their own personal frames of reference, they were able to reframe behavior that many would have labeled as "insane." Again, years later, Tommy put it aptly: "Everybody pretends, but he has a deeper pretending. Like, I'll make believe and I'll know I'm just joking around. He's playing also, but he's not joking around. He's doing it at a greater intensity."

The worker encouraged them to recall, and them proceeded to dramatize some of the idiosyncratic behavior that they described to bring it to life, and to cut through the staleness of time. As hilarious as this turned out to be, it also served to bring to the boys' awareness how far some of them had come (and still had to go), providing all with a renewed sense of hope. Since none of the boys had completely departed from his own "silly" beginnings, Matt's unusual behavior only served as a metaphor for the collective struggle of the group to achieve greater social competence. Matt was accepted on the same continuum rather than another plane, as was most often the case. One boy said, "Maybe he was like a radio, tuning in and tuning out, his plane and our plane, or he would be in both places at once. And sometimes he'd just be with us."

The People's Court

The group had been meeting for about a year when the oldest member, the indigenous leader, carried a folder into the meeting. He opened the folder, presented its contents (papers) and announced that he had a case to present for the "People's Court." Without hesitation he assigned the worker to be the judge, himself as the attorney for the defense and the others in a variety of roles (prosecuting attorney, court officer, defendant, plaintiff, witness). The others reluctantly agreed to cooperate with the drama. Their awkwardness was played out through giggling and horseplay, but they continued. The activity was introduced following many discussions of favorite television programs of which the "People's Court" was just one. The members had also been examining their behavior outside of the group after it had been discovered that two of the boys had been suspended from school for fighting.

For the next several weeks, the same boy brought in new "cases" to be heard. The initial resistance to continue this exercise was diminished as the sophistication of the activity grew. Creative possibilities emerged: (1) members assumed unfamiliar roles (e.g., eventually the judgeship was shared and assigned to the most ambivalent member, thus he had to become unequivocal and judicious; the least assertive group member took a turn as the prosecuting attorney, and so on); (2) In addition to addressing the facts of hypothetical cases, members readily assumed "third person" roles in which they were "cross-examined" about their "real selves." Experiences and feelings that seemed otherwise inaccessible emerged more readily in the "third person" context. Conflicts that occurred both in and out of the group setting were placed on the docket.

As did most local newsboys, Matt used a shopping cart to deliver his papers. Although he denied that he was referring to himself, he began to obsessively question the legality of the practice. Despite the others' reassurance that this wasn't "breaking the law," he persisted for weeks. Once instituted, the mock trial provided a new context for the discussion. An impartial jury consisting of all the group members was empaneled to reflect on and decide upon this case.

The result was a lively debate that concluded with a finding that the "defendant" was innocent of any crime. Distinctions were drawn between this and other related behavior. After the trial he never raised this issue again, but he did return to the "People's Court." As a young adult looking back, Tommy indicated that he had understood Matt's struggle with reality: "Life could be hard for him, kind of. But maybe not. It may be hard, but he may not feel it. I guess it is hard; he might need someone to depend on, a crutch. Certain people may not be very understanding. They may tease him or hurt him, maybe even physically. They're stupid. Maybe he won't need anyone, but he probably will. Everybody does."

After a while the group lost interest in the activity, especially as a weekly enterprise; however it became a valuable tool to return to as the group progressed. The mock trial provided the boys with an opportunity to experiment with values and to gain experience in critical thinking, problem solving and decision making. As one might expect, the activity was filled with humor which only served to bring the boys, including Matt, closer together as they learned to enjoy and appreciate one another.

R.S.V.P.

In addition to role playing activities, the group periodically organized and held parties at the center. The members took responsibility for the planning and preparation. After a time, and several parties and "trials" later, Matt came to one meeting awkwardly clutching several brightly colored envelopes. As he handed out these invitations for a party to celebrate his 16th birthday, the others fell silent. And then each of them in their own words said that they weren't sure if they could make it, for one reason or another. Matt seemed unfazed. He grunted something inaudibly and shrugged his shoulders. The worker simply suggested that they R.S.V.P., as requested on the cards.

Matt's mother later revealed that the scene at her home on the day of the party was one she hadn't experienced for at least the past 10 of Matt's 16 years. All of the boys showed up.

The birthday party was a turning point in the collateral work with Matt's parents, whose own loneliness emerged as they began to acknowledge their shattered dreams, which were covered over with years of denial. It also enabled the worker greater access to Matt's younger brother, who was confused about his big brother. He later said, "It was fun. It was nice. There was one thing bad. I ate so many potato chips, I couldn't eat the pizza. He was quiet. He knew we were there and acknowledged us. Matt was quiet. He knew we were there. But he wasn't there, kind of. We were telling jokes or playing Frisbee, and he was just there. He asked us if we wanted anything." The family's relationship to the center did not erase their loneliness, however it reduced their isolation, thus helping them to accept and move forward.

INTERMEZZO: POETRY[2]

Scapegoating in the Group

BABYBABYBABYSTICKYERHEADINGRAVY

YOU STINK	YOU FINK
CAN'T PLAY	YER GAY
TAKE THIS	ASS KISS
TAKE THAT	YER FAT
FOUR EYES	ALWAYS CRIES
WELL FED	FAT HEAD
BONY GEEK	GROSS FREAK
NO FUN	CAN'T RUN
OH NO	B.O.
EYES CROSSED	GET LOST
TALKS FUNNY	NO MONEY
RUNNY NOSE	UGLY CLOTHES
CREW CUT	LARD BUTT
ZIT FACE	DISGRACE
NOSE PICKER	ASS LICKER
NO GUTS	YOU PUTZ
GAP TOOTH	UNCOUTH
YOU BLOW	YOU SHMO

ICAN'TTAKEITANYMOREI'MGETTIN'OUTTAHERE

WHERE'D 'E GO?	WE DUNNO
GONE AWAY?	COULDN'T SAY
WANNA LOOK?	FOR THAT SCHNOOK?
HE'S OKAY	MAKE 'M STAY
MAY BE MAD	MAY BE SAD
CAN'T TELL	THAT'S SWELL
HE'S BACK	THAT A FACT?
BY THE DOOR	WANT MORE?
CUT THE SHIT	WHY QUIT?
HAD ENOUGH	KINDA ROUGH?
I'LL SAY	PLEASE STAY

OKAY

—A. Malekoff (1994c)

---

[2]From Malekoff (1994c). Reprinted in a slightly modified form by permission of Human Sciences Press.

SCAPEGOATING AND GROUP WORK
WITH ADOLESCENTS

> No single phenomenon occasions more distress to the outside
> observer than the act of scapegoating. . . . Attempts to deal
> with the scapegoating, whether as a single event or as a
> pattern, are likely to leave the worker feeling about as inept
> as he will ever feel as a practitioner. Try as he will, he may
> find it difficult to get beyond, "but that's not fair. Give the
> guy a chance."
> —*J. Garland and R. Kolodny (1973, p. 55)*

The scapegoat is a group member who becomes the target of verbal and/or physical assault by other members. There is the common belief that scapegoating is an expression of displacement or projection, whereas the attackers' negative feelings about themselves are attributed to a vulnerable target (Klein, 1972; Shulman, 1992). In the family group, the scapegoat (who may become known as an "identified patient") frequently assumes the functional role of maintaining equilibrium in the family, by becoming a lightning rod for all of their problems.

In a group it is rarely, if ever, the case that scapegoating is totally one-sided. Victim and victimizers bear mutual responsibility for the problem, and therefore must work in concert toward a substantive solution. Any unilateral attempts by the group worker to reactively "rescue" the scapegoat (e.g., by reprimanding, lecturing, or squashing the attackers) is likely to lead to an escalation of the very behavior one seeks to eliminate, further entrenching everyone involved in the process and their respective roles.

Among the vulnerabilities that may contribute to a group member becoming a scapegoat are: confused sexual identity, secondary pain, poorly organized or insufficient aggressive drive, and visible unorthodoxy (Garland & Kolodny, 1973).

- *Confused sexual identity.* Arousing fear in others of homosexual feelings or involvement (e.g., an effeminate boy might fall prey to that reviled epithet—faggot; or a girl who dresses, wears her hair, and/or carries herself in a certain style—dyke)
- *Secondary pain.* Attracting negative attention through ridicule (e.g., the pain associated with being put down becomes a price that the victim is willing to pay, an expense that he/she perceives to be greater than the cost of isolation)
- *Poorly organized or insufficient aggressive drive.* Often manifest through passivity or difficulty with assertive expression (e.g., the group

member who tries to innapropriately and/or ineffectively assert himself physically or verbally, such as the young group member who desperately tries to keep pace with the others' tales of bravado, by exaggerating physical/sexual exploits in such a transparent manner as to result in finding himself in a more loathed position than before—a vicious cycle)

- *Visible unorthodoxy.* Consisting of unusual appearance, style, or manner of expression that may be based in one's culture/religion (e.g., wearing religious clothing and/or artifacts), race (e.g., skin color, other physical/facial features), and physical/medical/pyschiatric status (e.g., disability, obesity); or with adolescents there is often the case of a group member trying too hard to fit into the youth "style-of-the-day" and then, as a result of trying too hard and without finesse, standing out like even more of a sore thumb

In a field study on little league baseball and young-adolescent culture, transcripts of tape-recorded accounts of young adolescents engaged in verbal combat are used to illustrate the "utility" of the victim who "unwittingly" enables his attackers to impress one another with their verbal skills (Fine, 1987). Surprisingly, there is no evidence of physical aggression suggested by this study. However, in his exploration into the professional avoidance of boyhood realities, Kolodny (1984) invokes Bradbury's fantasy "The Playground": "Who said childhood [is] the best time of life? When in reality it [is] the most terrible, the most merciless era, the barbaric time when there [are] no police to protect you, only parents preoccupied with themselves and their taller world" (Bradbury, 1967, p. 153).

Whether enacted through verbal or physical hostility, or a combination of both, Wineman (1959) views scapegoating as "a life event to be clinically exploited." He advocates for the practitioner calling the entire group's attention to the interaction. Some of the approaches that have been recommended to address scapegoating in the group are: diverting the members through activity and conversation; structuring the group in such a way as to limit the free moments available for attack; reframing the scapegoating to suggest to the group that they have been unable to meet the challenge of helping the scapegoat to change his/her behavior; and experimenting through role playing to give different members a chance to experience being victimized, presumably to develop empathy with the scapegoat, for example. Removal of the scapegoat should be considered only as a last resort (Garland & Kolodny, 1973).

Shulman (1967) contends that the practitioner is likely to feel protective of the individual who is subject to hostile attack in the group. This may explain why the term scapegoat (implying a one-sided interaction from group to member) "is often used to describe what is really a two-way interaction" (p. 39). It is when the worker intervenes, in response to his/her own emotional response, to protect the attacked group member from the others, that this may be classified as a "preemptive" intervention. An alternative approach, is one in which the worker mediates between the individual and the group, in order to overcome the obstacles in the way of them reaching out to one another. Various other analyses and approaches to addressing scapegoating in the group have been presented by Gadlin (1991), Gemmill (1989), Soo (1983), Scheidlinger (1982), and Eagle and Newton (1981).

One approach, illustrated below, is humanizing the scapegoat, an interactional process of gently confronting, probing, and clarifying, to provide group members with the opportunity to transform their perceptions of a fellow member from detested "object-hood" to valued "person-hood."

PRACTICE ILLUSTRATION 2:
HUMANIZING THE SCAPEGOAT[3]

The Group and the Scapegoat

> The entire world is his jury. By the age of twelve he has
> experienced more crises than Lord Jim. . . . [He is] the subject
> of savagery, scorn, and satire—who belongs to that great
> group that goes under several identifiable genera, namely,
> pansies, woosies, dinks, wimps, nerds, losers, screamers,
> pineapples, schlemiels, lunchmeat, turkeys, simps, geeks
> and dipshits.
> —*A. Theroux (1974)*

The following group consisted of six boys, mixed racially and ethnically, and all roughly 12 years of age. They were all referred to the community outreach center for problems ranging from social isolation and depression to violent acting-out behavior. The six boys had been together for almost 8 months at the time of the meeting to be discussed.

The youngest member of the group, Mark, had become the scapegoat. Physically on the soft and chunky side, Mark had been extremely resistant to joining the group. His reticence in the group, manifested

---

[3]This practice illustration was first published in Malekoff (1994b) and is reprinted in a slightly modified form by permission of Human Sciences Press.

by his shyness and obvious desire not to be there, caused him to stand out.

"Hey, Paco, how come you never talk?" If ever there was a reason for what had been referred to as "confessional constipation" (i.e., clamming up) this question brought it to life.

The other guys didn't know much about Mark, and certainly had not a hint that a year earlier he had exited a summer youth travel program early, following a period of severe depression. As he much later told the others, "I felt like I wanted to die, I just didn't fit in." The information that they did have was derived from what they could infer, from their observations; "Hey, Paco, why are you all dressed up, preppy-like?" Mark explained that he hosted a television program in school called, "Good Morning Young America." Another boy in the group asked him, in an incredulous tone, "You're a television anchor?"

When he did talk, Mark, whose nickname in the group had become "Paco," would use multisyllabic words, and occasionally affect what appeared to be an exaggerated French accent. Apparently he had a strong identification with a deceased grandparent from France. He told the group that he learned of her death when, "The *gendarme de ville* cabled us." This, and his interest in acting/drama explained the accent, which he described as, "the European way."

Well, poor Mark had done just about everything short of painting a bulls-eye across his chest. He was too quiet, too intellectual, too soft, too fat, and too weird for the other guys to take. The scapegoating consisted mainly of verbal insults, taunting, menacing, and an occasional chair pulled out from under. All prior attempts to put an end to it (e.g., moral sanction, protection, diversion) had failed to bring about any sustained change. Ironically, at least to the worker (the author) at the time, the group had the solution.

The Turning Point: Humanizing the Scapegoat

The following illustrates the group's work leading to Mark's metamorphosis from scapegoat to one of the guys.

Mark came in late to the meeting, again. Whenever he arrives the others greet him in unison with the familiar refrain: "Paco!" He smiles sheepishly, turns red, and finds his usual seat nearest to the door. Following the greeting there is a pause. The silence is broken by the most out-of- control member, who addresses Mark, "Hey, Paco, why are you so fat?" While this query seems to be delivered, believe it or not, in a more conciliatory tone than the content suggests, laughter follows. The worker has an immediate urge to protect him, to squash the others. But he resists the urge by recognizing that such an intervention will plunge Mark into even more intense disfavor with the others.

On this particular occasion, in a rush to fill the silence just after the final giggles, the worker, anticipating another questionable question, addressed the group, "Do you really want to know, as you say, 'why he's so fat' or was that just another put down?" After a moment a couple of them actually answered, "Yeah," meaning why he's so fat. All eyes were then on Mark, who said, "I don't know." One of the others, sitting directly across from Mark and who as a child was abused, abandoned, and bounced from one foster home to another, responded, "It's because he's depressed." Then another whose parents' relationship was in turmoil and who was struggling to fit in at school added, "It's social." He then proceeded to ask Mark why he had no friends, a conclusion he must have inferred since Mark never shared this information. Mark replied that where he lives there is little access to other kids.

At this point, it occurred to the worker that the boys didn't really know anything about Mark, aside from the defensive and vulnerable impression he had projected, or what they had projected of themselves onto him. Sensing that the others might be willing to listen, he asked Mark to describe where he lives, not just the location but the physical setting. As the worker led him from his neighborhood to his home, to his personal space, Mark went on to describe a cramped studio apartment located in an urban high rise that his mother could barely afford, a consequence of trying to make it as a single mother. He revealed having no room of his own, only a semi-private space walled off by a makeshift room divider that separated him and his younger brother from his mother.

As he proceeded with greater prodding from the worker, the boy who asked him, "Why are you so fat?" told the group, "I used to have it like that when my parents first divorced. I mean I had no space. I felt violated." Mark nodded in agreement, amidst the group's increasingly somber mood. The worker, sensing an opportunity, then asked the group, "Do you see Mark any differently now?" One boy replied, "I didn't realize how hard his life is." Another added, "I thought he was rich because of the way he talked and dressed, like a preppie. We don't want to make fun of you anymore." Realizing that this pledge would be virtually impossible to keep and not wanting to set them up for failure, the worker addressed Mark, "Suppose they do tease you?" Mark thoughtfully responded, "It won't be the same as before," obviously sensing that something had changed. He then added, "If they tease me again it will be different than before. You know, I'm the one who usually helps everyone else, I'm like everyone's psychiatrist. This is the first time anyone has tried to help me."

This group meeting was a rare one, in the sense that focused and sustained verbal interaction had temporarily replaced the non-verbal action so characteristic of young-adolescent groups. Often there is a shifting rhythm that occurs throughout the life of an adolescent group. Vertigo-inducing chaos and confusion alternate with brief interludes of clarity, catharsis, and integration. Neither one is of greater value than the other, although it is the rare moment that practitioners seem to cherish, to value the most. It is easy to be seduced by such moments, seduced into believing that "this moment will last forever" (or should), particulary when the quality of verbal interaction is highest. Such thinking leads to unrealistic expectations and inevitable disappointment when the group fails to perform "up to standard" the next time. Any group worker who believes that his/her only real job, as one boy in the group suggested (see below), is to get the members to talk about their problems like little adults, is sorely mistaken.

At the meeting's end the worker thanked the members for revealing parts of themselves that he hadn't experienced before. And he thanked them for being good listeners. To this, one of them proclaimed, "You're probably glad because it's like you did your job good—we talked about our problems." While the group usually darts out at meeting's end, they lingered for a while as the meeting winded down. As they passed through the door on their way out, one of them put his arm around Mark's shoulder and said, "C'mon, Paco."

The experience carried over. The others could finally *see* Mark.

FROM VIETNAM TO THE U.S. CONGRESS: A REFUGEE SPEAKS OUT

In the preceding chapter on alcohol and other drug abuse, the integrated use of group work and action research was detailed. The same approach was used in another project that investigated how adolescents view the future, with hope or despair (Malekoff, 1990). Some of the questions posed by the project's participants during an intergenerational group meeting included:

- If adolescents perceive an uncertain future, how might that affect the quality of their commitments?
- If adolescents feel hopeless about the future, are they more likely to be impulsive and self-centered in attitude and lifestyle?
- If you cannot see the future as getting better, and you see yourself as helpless to turn things around and make a difference, is it likely that you will stop coping today?

The 6-hour-long meeting was structured in an integrated large- and small-group format that was designed to build trust, raise consciousness, maximize interaction, and motivate change among the 100 participants (see Chapter 13). To the surprise of the adults involved in the meeting, the young people were very tuned in to issues such as the proliferation of nuclear arms, the decaying environment, and the impact of war on recently arriving immigrants. Their message to the adults was not one of hopelessness or helplessness. In fact it was the youth who provided reassurance for the adult participants. They told them that it was okay to discuss "scary" issues with their children.

The adults responded by stating that the group meeting enabled them to "practice" discussing issues, with a variety of youngsters, that they were too uncomfortable or frightened to discuss with their own children. It was their hope that they could borrow the experience and transfer it to their families.

One of the project participants was especially quiet and reserved. Hao was a 16-year-old Vietnamese refugee who came to the United States on July 11, 1980. In an automobile ride to a follow-up meeting, he revealed to me that he was committed to the project, but he wasn't sure how to contribute. Hao said that he couldn't talk that easily in a group, and explained how isolated he had been since arriving in the United States. He hadn't been the target of hostility as Mark, in the scapegoating example, had been. And he didn't draw attention to himself through any unusual mannerisms as Matt, in the earlier illustration, did. Instead, Hao seemed to have become invisible. What everyone eventually learned was that his subdued demeanor didn't mean that he had nothing to offer. He just needed another way to be heard. In group work, it is through the use of program (see Chapter 8) that some group members, like this special young man, can discover new ways to find and amplify their voice.

In this project, the evolving program allowed for alternative means of expression. One of those was through an essay contest entitled, "The Future: How I Can Make a Difference." Several area libraries agreed to sponsor the contest. Over 600 local youth contributed their writings about the state of the family, nuclear arms, the environment, and treatment of the eldery, for example. Over 200 people attended the celebration to honor the participants and to listen to and read their words.

The young Vietnamese immigrant's essay was an elegant tribute to the stabilizing tradition in which Hao had been raised and a reflection of the conflicting cultural values that he faced as an immigrant, new to the United States. The essay captured the spirit of mutuality across the generations, the spirit that the intergenerational group meetings had aimed to stimulate. He appeared to move everyone who heard and read his essay, enabling him to find his special place in the group. The essay later appeared in the U.S. Congressional Record, just 5 years after his perilous journey here.

Essay: Respect for the Elderly—Vietnamese Style

When I first came to the United States, I was shocked by what I heard about how old people are being treated in this country. I heard that an old man had been dead in his house for a week before his children knew what had happened. Old people are being put in care centers away from their homes. To me, care centers are not homes; care centers are places where old people are away from their grandchildren and other loved ones, and they feel rejected by their children. This was not how I used to see old people being treated in my country.

I remember when I was in Vietnam every new year, the first person my father took us to visit was my dear old grandmother, who was living with my uncle. When all our relatives had arrived, my uncles and aunts, with my parents, each carried a cup of warm tea and walked toward my grandmother. They wished her a long life and good health. Then all her grandchildren, from the eldest to the youngest stood in line; each of us walked toward my grandmother and wished her a happy new year, and we would say things that lightened her heart. In reply, she wished us a brilliant future and a great career. This was what I used to see and remember. I used to think that being old was so rewarding, and how happy I would be to grow old.

My father had set a fine example for all his children. He had shown that old people like my grandmother need comfort, not loneliness. I will take care of my parents as they had once taken good care of theirs. It won't be a special thing to do, it will be a normal thing to do.

I want you to take a look at the world around you; it was made especially for you by the contributions of your elders. I want you to feel your heart: the blood that is pumping in your heart is as pure as your parents. When you were born, a stranger to the world, you were not able to take care of yourself. Who took care of you? Now, your parents are old, and unable to support themselves, it's your chance to take good care of them. It's not a matter of tradition, it's a matter of right. Is it right to take care of your own flesh and blood? The answer should naturally be yes.

You know, you are the one that will influence the next generation. I want you to set a fine example, to all your children. show them that you care for your parents emotionally and financially, show them you respect them. There may have been some rough times between your parents and you, but when you have finally grown, you should give and forgive.

I know I can do for my family alone, but if all in America set a fine example for their families, there will be no more bitter tears of loneliness. The problem of how to treat old people will be solved, and there will be a difference in our future.

For every action, there is a reaction. How you treat your parents will be how your children will treat you, and what your parents receive from you will be what you will receive from your children. (Hoang, 1985)

CONCLUSION

The preceding three illustrations, and many more of those provided throughout the pages of this book, demonstrate the capacity of young people, known too often for their deficiencies, to touch one another and reach beyond themselves by summoning forth their unique strengths to create times and spaces never to be forgotten.

References

Acosta, E., and Yamamoto, J. (1984). The Utility of Group Work Practice for Hispanic Americans. *Social Work with Groups, 7*(3), 63–73.

Addams, J. (1912). *The Spirit of Youth and the City Streets.* New York: Macmillan.

Addams, J. (1961). Child Labor and Pauperism. Proceedings, Annual Meeting, National Conference of Charities and Corrections (pp. 114–121). In R. E. Pumphrey and M. W. Pumphrey (Eds.), *The Heritage of American Social Work* (pp. 278–283). New York: Columbia University Press. (Original work published 1903)

Aichorn, A. (1925). *Wayward Youth.* New York: Meridian.

Alan Guttmacher Institute. (1994). *Sex and America's Teenagers.* New York: Author.

Allen, L. (1990). Working with Bereaved Teenagers. In J. Morgan (Ed.), *The Dying and Bereaved Teenager* (pp. 39–41). Philadelphia: Charles Press.

Allport, G. (1958). *The Nature of Prejudice.* New York: Doubleday Anchor.

American Psychiatric Association. (1994). *Diagnostic and Statistical Manual of Mental Disorders* (4th ed.). Washington, DC: Author.

Anderson, A. (1992). High Risk Sexual Behavior in the General Population: Results from a National Survey, 1988–90. *Sexually Transmitted Diseases, 19,* 320–325.

Anderson, A. (1993). *Identifying the Strengths of Gay Male Youth: Self-Esteem, Locus of Control, and Perceived Social Support.* Doctoral dissertation, University of Pennsylvania, Philadelphia.

Anderson, J. (1984). *Counseling through Group Process.* New York: Springer.

Anderson, J. (1990). Group Work with Families: A Multicultural Perspective. *Social Work with Groups, 13*(4), 85–101.

Anthony, E., Koupernik, C., and Chiland, C. (Eds.). (1978). *The Child and His Family: Vol. 4. Vulnerable Children.* New York: Wiley.

Aponte, H. (1994). *Bread and Spirit: Therapy with the New Poor; Diversity of Race, Culture and Values.* New York: Norton.

Aristotle. (1927). *Selections* (W. D. Ross, Ed.). New York: Scribner's.

Ascherman, L. (1993). The Impact of Unstructured Games of Fantasy and Role Playing on an Inpatient Unit for Adolescents. *International Journal of Group Psychotherapy, 43*(3), 335–344.

Bachman, J., Wallace, J., Jr., Kurth, C., Johnston, L., and O'Malley, P. (1991). *Drug Use among Black, White, Hispanic, Native American and Asian American High School Seniors (1976–1989): Prevalence, Trends and Correlates.* Ann Arbor: Institute for Social Research, University of Michigan.

Balgopal, P., and Vassil, T. (1983). *Groups in Social Work: An Ecological Perspective.* New York: Macmillan.

Bargal, D. (1992). Conflict Management Workshops for Arab Palestinian and Jewish Youth: A Framework for Planning, Intervention and Evaluation. *Social Work with Groups, 15*(1), 51–68.

Bargal, D., and Bar, H. (1994). The Encounter of Social Selves: Intergroup Workshops for Arab and Jewish Youth. *Social Work with Groups, 17*(3), 39–59.

Barth, R., Claycomb, M., and Loomis, A. (1988). Services to Adolescent Fathers. *Health and Social Work, 13*(4), 277–287.

Barth, R., and Schinke, S. (1984). Enhancing the Social Supports of Teenage Mothers. *Social Casework, 65*(9), 523–531.

Bell, P. (1990, June). *Is Drug Abuse Color Blind?* Keynote address presented at a conference sponsored by the Regent Hospital, New York.

Bell, P. (1991). The Impact of Substance Abuse on the Black Community. *Fair Oaks Hospital Psychiatry Letter, 8*(2), 1–6.

Benne, K., and Sheats, P. (1948). Functional Roles of Group Members. *Journal of Social Issues, 4,* 41–49.

Berkovitz, I. (1987). Aggression, Adolescence and Schools. In S. Feinstein (Ed.), *Adolescent Psychiatry: Developmental and Clinical Studies* (Vol. 14, pp. 483–498). Chicago: University of Chicago Press.

Berman-Rossi, T. (Ed.). (1994). *Social Work: The Collected Writings of William Schwartz.* Itasca, IL: Peacock.

Bernard, B. (1991). *Fostering Resiliency in Kids: Protective Factors in the Family, School and Community.* Portland, OR: Northwest Regional Training Laboratories.

Bernstein, S. (1973). Conflict and Group Work. In S. Bernstein (Ed.), *Explorations in Group Work* (pp. 72–106). Boston: Milford House.

Bilides, D. (1990). Race, Color, Ethnicity and Class: Issues of Biculturalism in School-Based Adolescent Counseling Groups. In K. Chau (Ed.), Ethnicity and Biculturalism: Emerging Perspectives of Social Group Work [Special Issue]. *Social Work with Groups, 13*(4), 43–58.

Bilides, D. (1992). Reaching Inner-City Children: A Group Work Program Model for a Public Middle School. *Social Work with Groups, 15*(2/3), 129–144.

Bilken, D. (1983). *Community Organizing: Theory and Practice.* Englewood Cliffs, NJ: Prentice-Hall.

Birnbaum, M., and Auerbach, C. (1994). Group Work in Graduate Social Work Education: The Price of Neglect. *Journal of Social Work Education, 30*(3), 325–335.

Black, C. (1970). Children of Alcoholics. *Alcohol Health and Research World, 1*(1), 23–27.

Bloch, H. (1995). *Adolescent Development, Psychopathology, and Treatment.* Madison, CT: International Universities Press.

Blos, P. (1979). *The Adolescent Passage: Developmental Issues.* New York: International Universities Press.

Boyd, N. (1971). Social Group Work: A Definition with Methodological Note. In P. Simon (Ed.), *Play and Game Theory in Group Work: A Collection of Papers by Neva Leona Boyd* (p. 149). Chicago: Jane Addams Graduate School of Social Work at the University of Illinois at Chicago Circle.

Bradbury, R. (1967). The Playground. In *Fahrenheit 451* (p. 153). New York: Simon and Schuster.

Brandeis University, Institute for Health Policy. (1993). *Substance Abuse: The Nation's Number One Health Problem; Key Indicators for Policy.* Princeton, NJ: Robert Wood Johnson Foundation.

Brandler, S., and Roman, C. (1991). *Group Work: Skills and Strategies for Effective Interventions.* Binghamton, NY: Haworth.

Brandler, S., and Roman, C. (1995). Uncovering Latent Content in Groups. In R. Kurland and R. Salmon (Eds.), *Group Work Practice in a Troubled Society* (pp. 19–32). New York: Haworth.

Brennan, T. (1982). Loneliness at Adolescence. In L. Peplau and D. Perlman (Eds.), *Loneliness: A Sourcebook of Current Theory, Research and Therapy* (pp. 269–290). New York: Wiley.

Breton, M. (1990). Learning From Social Work Traditions. *Social Work with Groups, 13*(3), 21–34.

Breton, M. (1991). Reflections on Social Action Practice in France. *Social Work with Groups, 14*(3–4), 91–107.

Briar, S. (1967). *The Current Crisis in Social Casework, Social Work Practice* (pp. 19–33). New York: Columbia University Press.

Brown, A., and Mistry, T. (1994). Group Work with "Mixed Membership" Groups: Issues of Race and Gender. *Social Work with Groups, 17*(3), 5–22.

Brown, J. (1984). Group Work with Low-Income Black Youths. In L. Davis (Ed.), Ethnicity in Social Group Work Practice [Special Issue]. *Social Work with Groups, 7*(3), 111–124.

Brown, M. (1993). Successful Components of Community and School Prevention Programs. *National Prevention Evaluation Research Collection, 1*(1), 3–5.

Caetano, R. (1986). *Report of the Secretary's Task Force on Black and Minority Health: Chemical Dependency and Diabetes, VII.* Washington, DC: U.S. Government Printing Office.

Carnegie Council on Adolescent Development. (1992). *A Matter of Time: Risk, Opportunity and the Non-School Hours.* New York: Carnegie Corporation of New York.

Carnegie Council on Adolescent Development. (1995). *Great Transitions: Preparing Adolescents for a New Century.* New York: Carnegie Corporation of New York.

Carrera, M. (1996). *Lessons for Lifeguards: Working with Teens When the Topic Is Hope.* New York: Donkey Press.

Castaneda, C. (1974). *A Separate Reality.* New York: Pocket Books.

Catalano, R., Morrison, D., Wells, E., Gillmore, M., Iritani, B., and Hawkins, D. (1992). Ethnic Differences in Family Factors Related to Early Drug Initiation. *Journal of Studies on Alcohol, 55*(3), 208–217.

Centers for Disease Control and Prevention. (1996). *HIV/AIDS Surveillance Report, 8*(1), 12.

Cerda, R., Nemiroff, H., and Richmond, A. (1991). Therapeutic Group Approaches in an Inpatient Facility for Children and Adolescents: A 15-Year Perspective. *Child and Adolescent Group Psychotherapy* [Special Issue], 15(2), 71–80.

Chamberlain, E. (1987). Needs and Rights: Strategies for Development. *Social Development Issues, 11,* 56–66.

Chan, L. (1990). Application of Single-Session Groups in Working with Vietnamese Refugees in Hong Kong. *Social Work with Groups, 13*(4), 103–120.

Chau, K. (1990). Facilitating Bicultural Development and Intercultural Skills in Ethnically Heterogeneous Groups. *Social Work with Groups, 13*(4), 1–6.

Chesler, M. (1991). Participatory Action Research with Self Help Groups: An Alternative Paradigm for Inquiry and Action. In T. Borkman (Ed.), Self Help Groups [Special Issue]. *American Journal of Community Psychology, 19*(5).

Chess, S., and Hassibi, M. (1978). *Principles and Practice of Child Psychiatry.* New York: Plenum.

Children's Defense Fund. (1983). *Child Watch 1983: Looking Out for America's Children.* Washington, DC: Author.

Chu, J., and Sue, S. (1984). Asian/Pacific-Americans and Group Practice. *Social Work with Groups, 7*(3), 24–36.

Cicarelli, V. (1980). A Comparison of College Women's Feelings Towards Their Siblings and Parents. *Journal of Marriage and the Family, 42*(1), 111–117.

Costantino, G., Malgady, R., and Rogler, L. (1988). Folk Hero Modeling Therapy for Puerto Rican Adolescents. In Mental Health Research and Service Issues for Minority Youth [Special Issue]. *Journal of Adolescence, 11*(2), 155–165.

Coyle, G. (1930). *Social Process in Organized Groups.* New York: Richard R. Smith.

Coyle, G. (1937). *Studies in Group Behavior.* New York: Harper.

Coyle, G. (1947). *Group Experience and Democratic Values.* New York: Woman's Press

Coyle, G. (1948). *Group Work with American Youth: A Guide to the Practice of Leadership.* New York: Harper.

Coyle, G. (1955). Group Work as a Method in Recreation. In H. B. Trecker (Ed.), *Groupwork: Foundations and Frontiers.* New York: Whiteside and William Morrow. (Original work published 1947)

Dalrymple, J., and Burke, B. (1995). *Anti-Oppressive Practice: Social Care and the Law.* Buckingham, England: Open University Press.

Davis, L. (1984). Ethnicity in Social Group Work Practice [Special Issue]. *Social Work with Groups, 7*(3).

Deckman, J., and Downs, D. (1982). A Group Treatment Approach for Adolescent Children of Alcoholic Parents. *Social Work with Groups, 5*(1), 73–77.

De La Rosa, M., and Adrados, J. (1993). *Drug Abuse among Minority Youth; Advances in Research and Methodology* (NIDA Research Monograph 130). Washington, DC: U.S. Department of Health and Human Services.

Delgado, M., and Humm-Delgado, D. (1984). Hispanics and Group Work: A Review of the Literature. *Social Work with Groups, 7*(3), 85–96.

Dempsey, C. (1994). Health and Social Issues of Gay, Lesbian and Bisexual Adolescents. *Families in Society, 75*(3), 160–167.

Dewey, J. (1910). *How We Think.* Boston: Heath.

Dewey, J. (1916). *Democracy and Education.* New York: Macmillan.

Dewey, J. (1938). *Experience and Education.* New York: Macmillan.

Doherty, M. (1995). *Alcohol, Other Drugs, Gangs and Violence Prevention* (pp. 18–22). Pipeline, WA: Center for Substance Abuse Prevention.

Donovan, R., Kurzman, P., and Rotman, C. (1993). Improving the Lives of Home Care Workers: A Partnership of Social Work and Labor. *Social Work, 38*(5), 579–585.

Dore, M., and Dumois, A. (1990). Cultural Differences in the Meaning of Adolescent Pregnancy. *Families in Society, 71*(2), 93–101.

Dryfoos, J. (1990). *Adolescents at Risk: Prevalence and Prevention.* New York: Oxford University Press.

Dryfoos, J. (1993). Lessons from Evaluation of Prevention Programs. *National Prevention Evaluation Research Collection, 1*(1), 2–4.

Dryfoos, J. (1994). *Full Service Schools: A Revolution in Health and Social Services for Children, Youth and Families.* San Francisco: Jossey-Bass.

Duffy, T. (1994). The Check-In and Other Go-Rounds in Group Work. *Social Work with Groups, 17*(3/4), 163–175.

Dulit, E. (1972). Adolescent Thinking à la Piaget: The Formal Stage. *Journal of Youth and Adolescence, 1*(4), 281–301.

Durkheim, E. (1947). *The Division of Labor in Society.* Glencoe, IL: Free Press.

Eagle, J., and Newton, P. (1981). Scapegoating in Small Groups: An Organizational Approach. *Human Relations, 34*(4), 283–301.

Edwards, E., and Edwards, M. (1984). Group Work Practice with American Indians. *Social Work with Groups, 7*(3), 7–21.

Efron, D. (1987). Videotaping Groups for Children of Substance Abusers: A Strategy for Emotionally Disturbed Acting Out Children. *Alcoholism Treatment Quarterly, 4*(2), 71–85.

Elkind, D. (1974). *Children and Adolescents: Interpretive Essays on Jean Piaget.* New York: Oxford University Press.

Emshoff, J. (1989). A Preventive Intervention with Children of Alcoholics. *Prevention in Human Services, 17*(1), 225–253.

Erikson, E. (1968). *Identity, Youth, and Crisis.* New York: W. W. Norton.

Ethnicity and Mental Health Associates. (1992). *Cultural Diversity and Social Services* (pp. 8–13). Bronxville, NY: Author.

Fatout, M. (1992). *Models for Change in Social Group Work.* New York: Aldine de Gruyter.

Felner, R., Silverman, M., and Adix, R. (1991). Prevention of Substance Abuse and Related Disorders in Childhood and Adolescence: A Developmental Based, Comprehensive Ecological Approach. *Family and Community Health, 14*(3), 12–22.

Fine, G. (1987). *With the Boys: Little League Baseball and Preadolescent Culture.* Chicago: University of Chicago Press.

Fischer, E. (1973). Ritual as Communication. In J. D. Shaughnessy (Ed.), *The Roots of Ritual* (pp. 161–185). Grand Rapids, MI: W. B. Eardmans.

Fischer, J. (1973a). Is Casework Effective? A Review. *Social Work, 18*(January), 5–20.

Fischer, J. (1973b). Has Mighty Casework Struck Out? *Social Work, 18*(January), 107–110.

Follett, M. (1940). Constructive Conflict. In H. Metcaf and L. Urwick (Eds.), *Dynamic Administration: The Collected Works of Mary Parker Follett.* New York: Harper. (Original work published 1926)

Frank, A. (1995). *The Diary of a Young Girl* (O. Frank and M. Pressler, Eds.). New York: Doubleday. (Original work published 1947)

Freire, P. (1982). *Pedagogy of the Oppressed.* New York: Continuum.

Fresco, R., and Peracchio, A. (1990, September 25). A World Apart: Segregation on Long Island. Racism: A Bedrock of Segregation. *Newsday,* pp. 7, 32–38.

Freud, A. (1985). *The Writings of Anna Freud,* Vol. II: *The Ego and the Mechanisms of Defense.* New York: International Universities Press.

Friedman, A., and Utada, A. (1992). Effects of Two Group Interaction Models on Substance Using Adjudicated Adolescent Males. *Journal of Community Psychology* [Special Issue: Programs for Change, Office of Substance Abuse Prevention], 106–117.

Frost, R. (1971). The Road Not Taken. In E. C. Lathem (Ed.), *The Poetry of Robert Frost.* New York: Henry Holt.

Fuller, J. (1977). Duo Therapy. *Journal of Child Psychiatry, 16*(3), 469–477.

Gadlin, W. (1991). On Scapegoating: Biblical-Classical Sources, Group Psychotherapy, and World Affairs. In S. Tuttman (Ed.), *Psychoanalytic Group Theory and Therapy* (pp. 27–44). Madison, CT: International Universities Press.

Garfat, T. (1985). *Reflections on the Words of Dr. Fritz Redl.* Unpublished paper presented at the First International Child and Youth Care Conference. Vancouver, British Columbia, Canada.

Garland, J. (1981). Loneliness in the Group: An Element of Treatment. *Social Work with Groups, 4*(3/4), 95–110.

Garland, J., Jones, H., and Kolodny, R. (1973). A Model For Stages of Development in Social Work Groups. In S. Bernstein (Ed.), *Explorations in Group Work* (pp. 17–71). Boston: Milford House.

Garland, J., and Kolodny, R. (1973). Characteristics and Resolution of Scapegoating. In S. Bernstein (Ed.), *Further Explorations in Group Work* (pp. 55–74). Boston: Milford House.

Garland, J., and Kolodny, R. (1981). *The Treatment of Children Through Social Group Work: A Developmental Approach* [uncorrected advance proof]. Boston: Charles River.

Garmezy, N., and Rutter, M. (1983). *Stress, Coping and Development in Children.* New York: McGraw-Hill.

Garmezy, N. (1991). Resiliency and Vulnerability to Adverse Developmental Outcomes Associated With Poverty. *American Behavioral Scientist, 34*(4), 416–430.

Garvin, C. (1997). *Contemporary Group Work* (3rd ed.). Boston: Allyn and Bacon.

Garvin, C. (1991). Barriers to Effective Social Action by Groups. *Social Work with Groups, 14*(3–4), 65–76.

Geismar, L. (1972). Thirteen Evaluative Studies. In E. J. Muller and J. R. Dumpson (Eds.), *Evaluation of Social Intervention* (pp. 15–38). San Francisco: Jossey-Bass.

Gemmil, G. (1989). The Dynamics of Scapegoating in Small Groups. *Small Group Behavior, 20*(4), 406–418.

Gibbs, J., and Moskowitz-Sweet, G. (1991). Clinical and Cultural Issues in the Treatment of Biracial and Bicultural Adolescents. *Families in Society, 72*(10), 579–592.

Gitterman, A. (1971). Group Work in the Public Schools. In W. Schwartz and S. Zalba (Eds.), *The Practice of Group Work* (pp. 45–72). New York: Columbia University Press.

Gitterman, A. (1986). The Reciprocal Model: A Change in the Paradigm. In A. Gitterman and L. Shulman (Eds.), *The Legacy of William Schwartz: Group Practice as Shared Interaction* (pp. 29–38). New York: Haworth.

Glasgow, G., and Gouse Sheese, J. (1995). Themes of Rejection and Abandonment in Group Work with Caribbean Adolescents. *Social Work with Groups, 17*(4), 3–27.

Glassman, U., and Kates, L. (1990). *Group Work: A Humanistic Approach.* Newbury Park, CA: Sage.

Golding, W. (1959). *Lord of the Flies.* New York: G. P. Putnam's Sons.

Goldstein, H. (1990). Strength or Pathology: Ethical and Rhetorical Contrasts in Approaches to Practice. *Families in Society, 71*(5), 267–275.

Goodman, P. (1960). *Growing up Absurd.* New York: Random House.

Gonzales, R. (1967). *I Am Joaquin: An Epic Poem.* New York: Bantam.

Government Subcommittee of the New Cassel Task Force. (1986). *The New Cassel Survey Project.* Nassau County, NY: Nassau County Department of Drug and Alcohol Addiction and the Nassau County Youth Board.

Gozzi, R. (1995). The Generation X and Boomer Metaphors. *ETC: A Review of General Semantics, 52*(3), 331–335.

Greir, W., and Cobbs, P. (1968). *Black Rage.* New York: Bantam.

Gross, J., and McCane, M. (1992). An Evaluation of a Psychoeducational and Substance Abuse Risk Reduction Intervention for Children of Substance Abusers. *Journal of Community Psychology* [OSAP Special Issue], 75–87.

Hamburg, D. (1993). *Children and Youth—An Action Agenda.* New York: National Center for Children in Poverty, Columbia University School of Public Health.

Hamburg, D. (1986). *Preparing for Life: The Critical Transition of Adolescence. Presidential Essay.* New York: Carnegie Corporation of New York.

Hanley-Hackenbruck, P. (1989). Psychotherapy and the "Coming Out" Process. *Journal of Gay and Lesbian Psychotherapy, 1*(1), 21–39.

Hansen, W. (1992). School Based Substance Abuse Prevention: A Review of the State of the Art in Curriculum, 1980–1990. *Health and Education Research: Theory and Practice, 7*(3), 403–430.

Hartford, M. (1971). *Groups in Social Work.* New York: Columbia University Press.

Hawkins, J. D. (1995). Controlling Crime Before It Happens: Risk Focused Prevention. *National Institute of Justice Journal,* pp. 10–18.

Hawkins, J., Catalano, R., Jr., and Associates. (1992). *Communities That Care: Action for Drug Abuse Prevention.* San Francisco: Jossey-Bass.

Hawkins, J., Catalano, R., Jr., and Miller, J. (1992). Risk and Protective Factors for Alcohol and Other Drug Problems in Adolescence and Early Adulthood: Implications for Substance Abuse Prevention. *Psychological Bulletin, 112*(1), 64–105.

Healy, A., Keesee, P., and Smith, B. (1985). *Early Services for Children with Special Needs: Transactions for Family Support.* Ames: University of Iowa.

Henry, S. (1992). *Group Skills in Social Work: A Four-Dimensional Approach.* Pacific Grove, CA: Brooks/Cole.

Ho, M. (1984). Social Group Work with Asian/Pacific-Americans. *Social Work with Groups, 7*(3), 49–62.

Hoang, H. (1985). Respect for the Elderly—Vietnamese Style. *U.S. Congressional Record, 131*(99): E3451.

Hoffer, E. (1971). *First Things, Last Things.* New York: Harper and Row.

Holinger, P., Offer, D., Barter, J., and Bell, C. (1994). *Suicide and Homicide among Adolescents.* New York: Guilford Press.

Holzhauer, E. (1993). The Hidden Minority: Lesbian and Gay Students in Our Schools. *School Social Work Journal, 18*(1), 9–16.

Horowitz, N. (1978). Adolescent Mourning Reactions to Infant and Fetal Loss. *Social Casework, 59*(9), 551–559.

Hosang, M. (1991, November). *Groupwork with Children of Substance Abusers: Beyond the Basics.* Paper presented at the 13th Annual Symposium of the Association for the Advancement of Social Work with Groups.

Hunter, J., and Schaechter, R. (1987). Stresses on Lesbian and Gay Adolescents in Schools. *Social Work in Education, 9*(3), 180–190.

Hurdle, D. (1991). The Ethnic Group Experience. In K. Chan (Ed.), Ethnicity and Biculturalism: Emerging Perspectives of Social Group Work [Special Issue]. *Social Work with Groups, 13*(4), 59–69.

Hurley, D. (1984). Resistance and Work in Adolescent Groups. *Social Work with Groups, 7*(4), 71–82.

Irizarry, C., and Appel, Y. (1994). In Double Jeopardy: Preadolescents in the Inner City. In A. Gitterman and L. Shulman (Eds.), *Mutual Aid Groups, Vulnerable Populations, and the Life Cycle* (2nd ed., pp. 119–149). New York: Columbia University Press.

Jacobsen, E. (1988). Lesbian and Gay Adolescents: A Social Work Approach. *The Social Worker/Le Travailleur Social, 56*(2), 65–67.

Kahn, S. (1982). *Organizing.* New York: McGraw-Hill.

Kantor, G., Candill, B., and Ungerleider, S. (1992). Project Impact: Teaching the Teachers to Intervene in Student Substance Abuse Problems. *Journal of Alcohol and Drug Education, 38*(1), 11–29.

Katz, P., and Longden, S. (1983). The Jam Session: A Study of Spontaneous Group Process. *Social Work with Groups, 6*(1), 37–52.

Kavanagh, A. (1973). The Role of Ritual in Personal Development. In J. D. Shaughnessy (Ed.), *The Root of Ritual* (pp. 145–161). Grand Rapids, MI: W. B. Eerdmans.

Kirby, D. (1984). *Sexuality Education: An Evaluation of Programs and Their Effects.* Santa Cruz, CA: Network Publications.

Kirby, D., Short, L., Collins, J., Rugg, D., Kolbe, L., Howard, M., Miller, B., Sonenstein, F., and Zabin, L. (1994). School Based Programs to Reduce Sexual Risk Behaviors: A Review of Effectiveness. *Public Health Reports, 109*(3), 339–360.

Klein, A. (1972). *Effective Group Work: An Introduction to Principle and Method.* New York: Association Press.

Knight, S., Vail-Smith, K., and Barnes, A. (1992). Children of Alcoholics in the Classroom: A Survey of Teacher Perceptions and Training Needs. *Journal of School Health, 62*(8), 367–371.

Kolodny, R. (1976). *Peer-Oriented Group Work for the Physically Handicapped Child.* Boston: Charles River Books

Kolodny, R. (1984). Get'cha After School: The Professional Avoidance of Boyhood Realities. *Social Work with Groups, 7*(4), 21–38.

Kolodny, R. (1992). Retrospective on Reaching Out: Boston's Late Department of Neighborhood Clubs. *Social Work with Groups, 15*(2/3), 157–170.

Kolodny, R., and Garland, J. (Eds.). (1984). Group Work with Children and Adolescents [Special Issue]. *Social Work with Groups, 7*(4).

Konopka, G. (1949). *Therapeutic Group Work with Children.* Minneapolis: University of Minnesota Press.

Konopka, G. (1988). *Courage and Love.* Edina, MN: Burgess.

Kurland, R. (1978). Planning—The Neglected Component of Group Development. *Social Work with Groups, 1*(2), 173–178.

Kurland, R. (1982). *Group Formation: A Guide to the Development of Successful Groups.* Albany, NY: Continuing Education Program, School of Social Welfare, State University of New York at Albany and United Neighborhood Centers of America.

Kurland, R. (1996). *Class Notes on "Beginnings, Middles, and Endings."* Unpublished manuscript.

Kurland, R., and Malekoff, A. (1993a). Editorial. *Social Work with Groups, 16*(3), 1–4.

Kurland, R., and Malekoff, A. (1993b). Editorial. *Social Work with Groups, 16*(4), 1–4.

Kurland, R., and Malekoff, A. (1996). Editorial. *Social Work with Groups, 18*(2/3), 1–3.

Kurland, R., and Salmon, R. (1992). Group Work vs. Casework in a Group: Principles and Implications for Teaching and Practice. *Social Work with Groups, 15*(4), 3–14.

Lee, E. (1988). Cultural Factors in Working with Southeast Asian Refugee Adolescents. *Journal of Adolescence, 11*(2), 167–179.

Lee, P., Juan, G., and Hom, A. (1984). Group Work Practice with Asian Clients: A Sociocultural Approach. *Social Work with Groups, 7*(3), 37–48.

Levine, B. (1979). *Group Psychotherapy, Practice and Development* (pp. 21–25). Englewood Cliffs, NJ: Prentice-Hall.

Levine, I. M. (1982). Ethnicitiy and Familiy Therapy: An Overview. In M. McGoldrick, J. K. Pearce, and J. Giordano (Eds.), *Ethnicity and Family Therapy.* New York: Guilford Press.

Levine, M. (1991). Group Work: Antidote to Alienation During a Time of Family Transition. In A. Malekoff (Ed.), Group Work with Suburbia's Children:

Difference, Acceptance and Belonging [Special Issue]. *Social Work with Groups, 14*(1), 29–42.

Levinson, H. (1973). Use and Misuse of Groups. *Social Work, 18,* 66–73.

Lewis, E. (1991). Social Change and Citizen Action: A Philosophical Exploration for Modern Social Group Work. *Social Work with Groups, 14*(3–4), 23–34.

Lewis, E. (1992). Regaining Promise: Feminist Perspectives for Social Group Work Practice. *Social Work with Groups, 15*(2/3), 271–284.

Lewis, E., and Ford, B. (1990). The Network Utilization Project: Incorporating Traditional Strengths of African-American Families into Group Work Practice. *Social Work with Groups, 13*(4), 7–22.

Lifton, R. (1995). Trials and Transformation: A Conversation with Robert J. Lifton (Interviewer: M. B. Snell). *Utne Reader, 70,* 62–70.

Lopez, J. (1991). Group Work as a Protective Factor for Immigrant Youth. In A. Malekoff (Ed.), Group Work With Suburbia's Children: Difference, Acceptance and Belongings [Special Issue]. *Social Work with Groups, 14*(1), 29–42.

MacLennan, B., and Dies, K. (1992). *Group Counseling and Psychotherapy with Adolescents.* New York: Columbia University Press.

Maier, H. (1991). What's Old—Is New: Fritz Redl's Teaching Reaches Into the Present. In W. C. Morse (Ed.), *Crisis Intervention in Residential Treatment* (pp. 15–30). New York: Haworth.

Maier, H. (1994, October 29). *Social Groupwork and Developmental Groupcare in Retrospect and the Prospects for Both.* Paper presented at the Annual Meeting of the Association for the Advancement of Social Work with Groups, Hartford, CT.

Malekoff, A. (1984). Socializing Pre-adolescents into the Group Culture. *Social Work with Groups, 7*(4), 7–19.

Malekoff, A. (1987). The Pre-adolescent Prerogative: Creative Blends of Discussion and Activity in Group Treatment. *Social Work with Groups, 10*(4), 61–81.

Malekoff, A. (1990). Hope or Despair: Suburbia's Children Look into the Future. *Social Work with Groups, 13*(3), 51–70.

Malekoff, A. (1991a). *Group Work with Suburbia's Children: Difference, Acceptance and Belonging.* New York: Haworth.

Malekoff, A. (1991b). "What's Goin' on in There": Alliance Formation with Parents Whose Children Are in Group Treatment. *Social Work with Groups, 14*(1), 75–85.

Malekoff, A. (1991c). Difference, Acceptance and Belonging: A Reverie. *Social Work with Groups, 14*(1), 105–112.

Malekoff, A. (1991d). Diary of a Boy's Group: January 16, 1991. *Families in Society, 72,* 4.

Malekoff, A. (1993). Group Work with Children and Adolescents (Poetry). *Journal of Child and Adolescent Group Therapy, 3,* 4.

Malekoff, A. (1994a). Action Research: An Approach to Preventing Substance Abuse and Promoting Social Competency. *Health and Social Work, 19*(1), 46–53.

Malekoff, A. (1994b). Moments and Madness: Humanizing the Scapegoat in the Group. *Journal of Child and Adolescent Group Therapy, 4*(3), 169–176.

Malekoff, A. (1994c). Scapegoating in the Group (Poetry). *Journal of Child and Adolescent Group Therapy, 4*(3), 169–170.

Malekoff, A. (1994d). What is Going on in There (Question and Response). *Social Work with Groups, 17*(1/2),

Malekoff, A. (1994e). A Guideline for Group Work with Adolescents, *Social Work with Groups, 17*(1/2), 5–19.

Malekoff, A. (1994f). John Gone (Poetry). *Social Work with Groups Newsletter, 9*(3), 20.

Malekoff, A. (1994g). New Member: Act One (a true story) (Poetry). *Social Work with Groups Newsletter, 9*(3), 14.

Malekoff, A. (1994h). Beware of Mangled Care: DSM R US (Poetry). *Social Work with Groups Newsletter, 19*(2, July), 15.

Malekoff, A. (1995). "They've Started Dropping Bombs:" A Boy's Group Confronts War. *Narratives: Reflections on Helping in the Human Services, 1*(3), 27–32.

Malekoff, A. (1997a). Group Work in the Prevention of Adolescent Alcohol and Other Drug Abuse. In P. Ephross and G. Greif (Eds.), *Group with Vulnerable Populations*. New York: Oxford University Press.

Malekoff, A. (1997b). Structural Social Work to Address Bureaucratic Barriers to Effective Service Delivery for Children, Youth and Their Families. In R. Middleman and G. Goldberg Wood (Eds.), *A Case Book on the Structural Approach to Direct Practice in Social Work*. Manuscript submitted for publication.

Malekoff, A., Johnson, H., and Klappersack, B. (1991). Parent-Professional Collaboration on Behalf of Children With Learning Disabilities. *Families in Society, 72*(7), 416–424.

Malekoff, A., and Kolodny, R. (1991). Memories and Memory Building: Reflections on Group Work With the Lonely Child. *Social Work with Groups, 14*(1), 87–103.

Malekoff, A., Quaglia, S., and Levine. M. (1987). An Attempt to Create a New "Old Neighborhood": From Suburban Isolation to Mutual Caring. *Social Work with Groups, 10*(3), 55–68.

Martin, A., and Hetrick, E. (1988). The Stigmatization of the Gay and Lesbian Adolescent. *Journal of Homosexuality, 15*(1/2), 163–183.

McConville, M. (1995). *Adolescence: Psychotherapy and the Emergent Self.* San Francisco: Jossey-Bass.

McKnight, J. (1987). Regenerating Community. *Social Policy, Winter,* 54–58.

McLuhan, M., and Fiore, Q. (1967). *The Medium is the Massage: An Inventory of Effects.* New York: Bantam.

Mead, M. (1973). Ritual and Social Crisis. In J. D. Shaughnessy (Ed.), *The Roots of Ritual* (pp. 87–103). Grand Rapids, MI: W. B. Eerdmans.

Meeks, J. (1986). *The Fragile Alliance: An Orientation to the Outpatient Psychotherapy of the Adolescent.* Melbourne, FL: Krieger.

Meyer, H., Borgatta, E., and Jones, W. (1965). *Girls at Vocational High: An Experiment in Social Work Intervention.* New York: Russell Sage Foundation.

Middleman, R. (1968). *The Non-verbal Method in Working with Groups.* New York: Association Press.

Middleman, R. (1981). The Use of Program: Review and Update. In S. L. Abels and P. Abels (Eds.), *Social Work with Groups Proceedings, 1979 (pp. 187–205)*. Louisville, KY: Committee for the Advancement of Social Work with Groups.

Middleman, R. (1983). Activities and Action in Group Work [Special Issue]. *Social Work with Groups, 6,* 1.

Middleman, R. (1985, March 22). *Integrating the Arts and Activities in Clinical Group Work Practice.* Paper presented at the Center for Group Work Studies, Barry University School of Social Work, Miami Shores, FL.

Middleman, R. (1990, March 8). *The Doings of Groups: Doing as Life Learning.* Paper presented at the Toronto Region Group Workers Network Chapter, Association for the Advancement of Social Work with Groups, Toronto, Ontario.

Middleman, R. R., and Wood, G. G. (1990a). *Skills for Direct Practice in Social Work.* New York: Columbia University Press.

Middleman, R., and Wood, G. G. (1990b). From Social Group Work to Social Work with Groups. *Social Work with Groups, 13*(3), 3–20.

Millan, F., and Chan, J. (1991). Group Therapy with Inner City Hispanic Acting-Out Adolescent Males: Some Theoretical Observations. *Group, 15*(2), 109–115.

Moore-Kirkland, J., and Irey, K. (1981, July). A Reappraisal of Confidentiality. *Social Work,* pp. 319–322.

Morgan, J. D. (Ed.). (1990). *The Dying and the Bereaved Teenager.* Philadelphia: Charles Press.

Morrow, D. (1993). Social Work with Gay and Lesbian Adolescents. *Social Work, 38*(6), 655–660.

Moustakas, C. (1951). *Loneliness.* Englewood Cliffs, NJ: Prentice-Hall.

Moyse-Steinberg, D. (1990). A Model for Adolescent Pregnancy through the Use of Small Groups. *Social Work with Groups, 13*(2), 57–68.

Mullender, A. (1990). The Ebony Project–Bicultural Group Work with Transracial Foster Parents. *Social Work with Groups, 13*(4), 23–41.

Munoz, V. (1995). *"Where Something Catches": Work, Love, and Identity in Youth.* Albany, NY: State University of New York Press.

Neikrug, S. (1985). Community Organization and Housing Policy in Israel. *Journal of Jewish Communal Service, 61,* 342–352.

Newstetter, W. (1935). What Is Social Group Work? In *Proceedings of the National Conference of Social Work* (pp. 291–299). Chicago: The University of Chicago Press.

Newton, M. (1995). *Adolescence: Guiding Youth through the Perilous Ordeal.* New York: Norton.

Northen, H. (1988). *Social Work with Groups.* New York: Columbia University Press.

North Shore Child and Family Guidance Center. (1995). *ART (Advocacy, Research, Treatment Data) Form.* Roslyn Heights, NY: Author.

Offer, D., Marohn, R., and Ostrov, E. (1975). Violence among Hospitalized Delinquents. *Archives of General Psychiatry, 32,* 1180–1186.

The Oxford Dictionary of Quotations (3rd ed.). (1979). New York: Oxford University Press.

Papell, C. (1983). Group Work in the Profession of Social Work: Identity in Context. In N. Lang and C. Marshall (Eds.), *Patterns in the Mosaic* (pp. 1193–1209). Toronto: Committee for the Advancement of Social Work with Groups.

Papell, C., and Rothman, B. (1980). Relating the Mainstream Model of Social Work with Groups to Group Psychotherapy and the Structural Group Approach. *Social Work with Groups, 3*(2), 5–23.

Peck, H. (1983, April). *An Integrated Large and Small Group Approach Dealing with Denial of Nuclear Danger.* Paper presented at the 60th Annual Meeting of the American Orthopsychiatric Association, Boston.

Pedersen, P. (1988). *A Handbook for Developing Multicultural Awareness.* Alexandria, VA: American Association for Counseling and Development.

Philips, M., and Markowitz, M. (1989). *The Mutual Aid Model of Group Services: Experiences of New York Archdiocese Drug Abuse Prevention Program.* New York: Fordham University Graduate School of Social Service.

Piaget, J. (1950). *The Psychology of Intelligence.* London: Routledge and Kegan Paul.

Pierce, W., and Singleton, S. (1995). Improvisation as a Concept for Understanding and Treating Violent Behavior Among African American Youth. *Families in Society, 76*(7), 444–450.

Pinderhughes, E. (1989). *Understanding Race, Ethnicity and Power: The Key to Efficiency in Clinical Practice.* New York: Free Press.

Portner, J. (1994). Teenage Birthrates Decline for First Time Since '86. New Federal Study Reports. *Education Week, 14*(9), 9.

Pozatek, E. (1994). The Problem of Certainty: Clinical Social Work in the Postmodern Era. *Social Work, 39*(4), 396–404.

Price, R. (1992). *Clockers.* Boston: Houghton Mifflin.

Prothrow-Stith, D. (1995, March 29). *Conference Proceedings, Keynote Address, Violence: A Community Issue, Creating Safe Environments for Children and Families.* Uniondale, NY: North Shore Child and Family Guidance Center.

Quadrel, M., Fischoff, B., and Davis, W. (1993). Adolescent (In)vulnerability. *American Psychologist, 48*(2), 102–116.

Rachman, A., and Raubolt, R. (1984). The Pioneers of Adolescent Group Psychotherapy. *International Journal of Group Psychotherapy, 34*(3), 387–413.

Redl, F. (1951). The Art of Group Composition. In S. Schulze (Ed.), *Creative Group Living in a Children's Institution* (pp. 79–96). New York: Association Press.

Redl, F., and Wineman, D. (1951). *Children Who Hate.* New York: Macmillan.

Redl, F., and Wineman, D. (1952). *Controls from Within: Techniques for the Treatment of the Aggressive Child.* New York: Macmillan.

Rittner, B., and Nakanishi, M. (1993). Challenging Stereotypes and Cultural Biases through Small Group Process. *Social Work with Groups, 16*(4), 5–23.

Roberts, E. (1983). Teens, Sexuality and Sex: Our Mixed Messages. *Television and Children, 6*, 9–12.

Roberts, R., and Northen, H. (1976). *Theories of Social Work with Groups.* New York: Columbia University Press.

Roller, B. (1989). Having Fun in Group. *Small Group Behavior, 20*(1), 97–100.

Rose, S. R. (1972). *Treating Children in Groups.* San Francisco: Jossey-Bass.

Rose, S. D. (1977). *Group Therapy: A Behavioral Approach*. Englewood Cliffs, NJ: Prentice-Hall.

Rose, S. D., and Edelson, J. (1987). *Working with Children and Adolescents in Groups*. San Francisco: Jossey-Bass.

Rose, S. R. (1989). Members Leaving Groups: Theoretical and Practical Considerations. *Small Group Behavior, 20*(4), 524–535.

Rosenberg, P. (1980). Communication about Sex and Birth Control between Mothers and Their Adolescent Children. *Population Environment, 3*(1), 35–50.

Rubin, H., and Rubin, I. (1986). *Community Organizing and Development*. Columbus, OH: Charles E. Merrill.

Rutter, M. (1979). Protective Factors in Children's Responses to Stress and Disadvantage. In M. W. Kent and J. E. Rolf (Eds.), *Primary Prevention of Psychopathology: Social Competence in Children* (Vol. 3). Hanover, NH: University Press of New England.

Rutter, M. (1984, March). Resilient Children. *Psychology Today*, pp. 57–65.

Saleeby, D. (1994). Culture, Theory, and Narrative: The Intersection of Meanings in Practice. *Social Work, 39*(4), 351–361.

Sameroff, A. (1988). *The Concept of the Environtype: Integrating Risk and Protective Factors in Early Development*. Keynote Address for North Shore Child and Family Guidance Center Conferences, June 8, Garden City, NY.

Sancier, B. (1984). Working with Gay and Lesbian Clients. *Practice Digest, 7*(1) [entire issue].

Sarri, R., and Galinski, M. (1974). A Conceptual Framework for Group Development. In P. Glasser, R. Sarri, and R. Vinter (Eds.), *Individual Change through Small Groups* (pp. 71–88). New York: Free Press.

Sarri, R., and Sarri, C. (1992a). Organizational and Community Change through Participatory Action Research. *Administration in Social Work, 16*(3/4), 99–122.

Sarri, R., and Sarri, C. (1992b). Participatory Action Research in Two Communities in Bolivia and in the United States. *International Social Work, 35*(2), 267–280.

Scales, P. (1996, Winter). Nonsensical Beliefs That Get in the Way of Helping Youth. *FL Educator*.

Schave, D., and Schave, B. (1989). *Early Adolescence and the Search for Self: A Developmental Perspective*. New York: Praeger.

Scheidlinger, S. (1982). On Scapegoating in Group Psychotherapy. *International Journal of Group Psychotherapy, 32*, 131–143.

Schinke, S., Orlandi, M., and Cole, K. (1992). Boys and Girls in Public Housing Developments: Prevention Services for Youth at Risk. *Journal of Community Psychology* [OASP Special Issue], 118–128.

Schorr, L. (1989). *Within Our Reach: Breaking the Cycle of Disadvantage*. New York: Doubleday.

Schrag, P., and Divoky, D. (1975). *The Myth of the Hyperactive Child*. New York: Pantheon Books.

Schwartz, W. (1961). *The Social Worker in the Group*. New Perspectives on Services to Groups: Theory, Organization and Practice. New York: National Association of Social Workers.

Schwartz, W. (1971). On the Use of Groups in Social Work Practice. In W. Schwartz and S. Zalba (Eds.), *The Practice of Group Work*. New York: Columbia University Press.

Schwartz, W. (1976). Between Client and System: The Mediating Function. In R. Roberts and H. Northen (Eds.), *Theories of Social Work with Groups*. New York: Columbia University Press.

Schwartz, W. (1986). The Group Work Tradition and Social Work Practice. In A. Gitterman and L. Shulman (Eds.), The Legacy of William Schwartz: Group Practice as Shared Interaction [Special Issue]. *Social Work with Groups, 8*(4).

Schwartz, W. (1994a). Between Client and System: The Mediating Function. In T. Berman-Rossi (Ed.), *Social Work: The Collected Writings of William Schwartz* (pp. 324–351). Itasca, IL: F. E. Peacock.

Schwartz, W. (1994b). Social Work with Groups: The Search for a Method (1968–1972). In T. Berman-Rossi (Ed.), *Social Work: The Collected Writings of William Schwartz* (pp. 1–194). Itasca, IL: F. E. Peacock.

Setterberg, S. (1991). Inpatient Child and Adolescent Therapy Groups: Boundary Maintenance and Group Function. In Child and Adolescent Group Psychotherapy [Special Issue]. *Group, 15*(2), 89–94.

Shapiro, B. (1991). Social Action, the Group and Society. *Social Work with Groups, 14*(3–4), 7–21.

Sherif, M., and Sherif, C. (1953). *Groups in Harmony and Tension*. New York: Harper.

Shields, S. (1985/86). Busted and Branded: Group Work with Substance Abusing Adolescents in Schools. In A. Gitterman and L. Shulman (Eds.), The Legacy of William Schwartz: Group Practice as Shared Interaction [Special Issue]. *Social Work with Groups, 8*(4), 61–82.

Shulman, L. (1967). Scapegoats, Group Workers and Pre-emptive Intervention. *Social Work, 12*(2), 37–43.

Shulman, L. (1985/86). The Dynamics of Mutual Aid. In A. Gitterman and L. Shulman (Eds.), The Legacy of William Schwartz: Group Practice as Shared Interaction [Special Issue]. *Social Work with Groups, 8*(4).

Shulman, L. (1992). *The Skills of Helping: Individuals, Families, and Groups* (3rd ed.). Itasca, IL: F. E. Peacock.

Simonetti, C., Simonetti, V., Arruda, S., and Rogow, D. (1996). Listening to Boys: A Talk with Ecos Staff. In S. Zeidenstein and K. Moore (Eds.), *Learning about Sexuality: A Practical Beginning* (pp. 324–332). New York: Population Council International Women's Health Coalition.

Slavson, S. R. (1937). *Creative Group Education*. New York: Association Press.

Slavson, S. R. (1939). *Character Education in a Democracy*. New York: Association Press.

Slimmon, L. (1975). Affective Education as Both a Prevention and a Treatment Modality. In I. Senay (Ed.), *Developments in the Field of Drug Abuse* (pp. 710–717). Cambridge, MA: Schenkman.

Smith, B. (1973). Values Clarification in Drug Education: A Comparative Study. *Journal of Drug Education, 3*, 369–376.

Smith, T. (1985). Group Work with Adolescent Drug Abusers. *Social Work with Groups, 8*(1), 55–64.

Smothers, R. (1986, August 1). For L. I. Blacks—Prosperity Is a Relative Term. *New York Times,* pp. B1–B2.

Somers, M. (1976). Problem Solving in Small Groups. In R. Roberts and H. Northen (Eds.), *Theories of Social Work with Groups* (pp. 331–367). New York: Columbia University Press.

Soo, E. (1983). The Management of Scapegoating in Children's Group Psychotherapy. In M. Aronson and J. Wolberg (Eds.), *Group and Family Therapy 1983: An Overview* (pp. 115–124). New York: Brunner/Mazel.

Soriano, F. (1993). Cultural Sensitivity and Gang Intervention. In A. Goldstein and C. Huff (Eds.), *The Gang Intervention Handbook* (pp. 441–461). Champaign, IL: Research Press.

Soriano, F., and De La Rosa, M. (1990). Cocaine Use and Criminal Activities Among Hispanic Juvenile Delinquents in Florida. In R. Glick and J. Moore (Eds.), *Drugs in Hispanic Communities.* New Brunswick, NJ: Rutgers University Press.

Sorin, G. (1990). *The Nurturing Neighborhood: The Brownsville Boys Club and the Jewish Community in Urban America, 1940–1990.* New York: New York University Press.

Spergel, I., and Curry G. (1990). *Survey of Youth Gang Problems and Programs in 45 Cities and 6 Sites (National Youth Gang Suppression and Intervention Program).* Washington, DC: U.S. Department of Justice, Office of Juvenile Justice and Delinquency Prevention.

Spergel, I., Curry G., Chance, R., Kane, C., Ross, R., Lexander, A., Simmons, E., and Oh, S. (1990). *Youth Gangs: Problem and Response: Stage 1 Assessment.* Washington, DC: U.S. Department of Justice, Office of Juvenile Justice and Delinquency Prevention.

Spiegel, J. (1965). Some Cultural Aspects of Transference and Countertransference. In M. Zald (Ed.), *Social Welfare Institutions: A Sociological Reader* (pp. 575–593). New York: Wiley.

Staub-Bernasconi, S. (1991). Social Action, Empowerment and Social Work–An Integrative Theoretical Framework for Social Work and Social Work with Groups. *Social Work with Groups, 14*(3–4), 35–51.

Steinberg, L. (1986). *When Teenagers Work: The Psychological and Social Costs of Adolescent Employment.* New York: Basic Books.

Strasburger, V. (1995). *Adolescents and the Media: Medical and Psychological Impact.* Thousand Oaks, CA: Sage.

Straus, M. B. (1994). *Violence in the Lives of Adolescents.* New York: Norton.

Sue D., and Sue, D. (1991). The Culturally Skilled Counselor. In *Counseling the Culturally Different* (pp. 159–179). New York: Wiley.

Sullivan, H. S. (1953). *The Interpersonal Theory of Psychiatry.* New York: Norton.

Tarasoff v. Board of Regents of the University of California, 33 Cal. Rptr. 14 (1976).

Theroux, A. (1975, October). The Sissy. *Esquire Magazine,* p. 199.

Tomkins, C. (1968). *Eric Hoffer: An American Odyssey.* New York: E. P. Dutton and Co.

Toseland, R., and Rivas, R. (1995). *An Introduction to Group Work Practice.* Boston: Allyn and Bacon.

Treadway, D. (1989). *Before It's Too Late: Working with Substance Abuse in the Family.* New York: Norton,

Trecker, H. (1973). *Social Group Work—Principles and Practices.* New York: Whiteside.

Trieschman, A., Whittaker, J., and Brendtro, L. (1969). *The Other 23 Hours.* Chicago: Aldine.

Troiden, R. (1988). Homosexual Identity Development. *Journal of Adolescent Health Care, 9,* 105–113.

Tropp, E. (1976). A Developmental Theory. In R. Roberts and H. Northen (Eds.), *Theories of Social Work with Groups* (pp. 198–237). New York: Columbia University Press.

Tsui, A., and Sammons, M. (1988). Group Intervention with Adolescent Vietnamese Refugees. *Journal for Specialists in Group Work, 13*(2), 90–95.

Vega, W., Zimmerman, R., Warheit, G., Apospori, E., and Gil, A. (1993). Risk Factors for Early Adolescent Drug Use in Four Ethnic and Racial Groups. *American Journal of Public Health, 83*(2), 185–189.

Vinter, R. (1974). Program Activities: An Analysis of Their Effects on Participant Behavior. In P. Glasser, R. Sarri, and R. Vinter (Eds.), *Individual Change Through Small Groups* (pp. 233–246). New York: Free Press.

Vinter, R., and Galinsky, M. (1985). Extra-Group Relations and Approaches. In M. Sundel, P. Glasser, R. Sarri, and R. Vinter (Eds.), *Individual Change through Small Groups* (pp. 266–276). New York: Free Press.

Vorrath, H., and Brendtro, L. (1974). *Positive Peer Culture.* Chicago: Aldine.

Wagner, D. (1991). Reviving the Action Research Model: Combining Case and Cause With Dislocated Workers. *Social Work, 36,* 477–482.

Wallace, B. (1993). Cross Cultural Counseling with the Chemically Dependent: Preparing for Service Delivery Within a Culture of Violence. *Journal of Psychoactive Drugs, 25*(1), 9–20.

Walthrust, N. (1992). *Program Description for Youth of Culture Drug Free Club* (an edited and revised program concept derived from the 100% Drug Free Club, with permission from Dr. L. F. Brisbane). Roslyn Heights, NY: North Shore Child and Family Guidance Center.

Watterson, S. (1995, July 30). Calvin and Hobbes. *Newsday.*

Watzlawick, P. (1978). *The Language of Change: Elements of Therapeutic Communication.* New York: Basic Books.

Wegscheider, S. (1981). *Another Chance: Hope and Health for the Alcoholic Family.* Palo Alto, CA: Science and Behavior Books.

Werner, E. (1986). Resilient Offspring of Alcoholics: A Longitudinal Study From Birth to Age 18. *Journal of Studies on Alcohol, 44*(1), 34–44.

Werner, E. (1989). High-Risk Children in Young Adulthood: A Longitudinal Study From Birth to 32 Years. *American Journal of Orthopsychiatry, 59,* 72–81.

Werner, E. (1990). Protective Factors and Individual Resilience. In S. Meisels and J. Shonkoff (Eds.), *Handbook of Early Childhood Intervention.* New York: Cambridge University Press.

Werner, E., and Smith, R. (1992). *Overcoming the Odds: High-Risk Children from Birth to Adulthood.* Ithaca, NY: Cornell University Press.

Wilson, H. (1991). The Black Experience in Suburbia: Prospects and Possibilities for Group Work Intervention. In A. Malekoff (Ed.), Group Work with Suburbia's Children: Difference, Acceptance and Belonging [Special Issue]. *Social Work with Groups, 14*(1), 29–42.

Wilson, H., and Ryland, G. (1949). *Social Group Work Practice.* Boston: Houghton Mifflin.

Wineman, D. (1959). The Life Space Interview. *Social Work, IV*(1), 10.

Wodarski, L., and Wodarski, J. (1995). *Adolescent Sexuality: A Comprehensive Peer/Parent Curriculum.* Springfield, IL: Charles C. Thomas.

Wood, G., and Middleman, R. (1995, October). *Constructivism, Power, and Social Work With Groups.* Keynote Address at the Annual Symposium of the Association for the Advancement of Social Work With Groups, San Diego, CA.

Wood, K. M. (1978). Casework Effectiveness: A New Look at the Research Evidence. *Social Work, 23*(November), 437–458.

Wujcik, E. (1985). *Teenage Mutant Ninja Turtles and Other Strangeness.* Sharon, CT: Palladium Books.

Yalom, I. (1975). *The Theory and Practice of Group Psychotherapy.* New York: Basic Books.

Yalom, I. (1985). *The Theory and Practice of Group Psychotherapy* (3rd ed.). New York: Basic Books.

Yoshikawa, E. (1981). *Musashi.* New York: Harper & Row.

Zelnik, M., and Shah, F. (1983). First Intercourse Among Americans. *Family Planning Perspectives, 15*(2), 64–70.

Zuckerman, B. (1995, March 29). *Conference Proceedings: Keynote Address, Violence: A Community Issue, Creating Safe Environments for Children and Families.* Uniondale, NY: North Shore Child and Family Guidance Center.

Index

Date Due

MY 1 05			
SE 6 05			
AG 23 '07			